Start Your Own

CLEANING SERVICE

Additional titles in *Entrepreneur's **Startup Series***

Start Your Own

Bar and Tavern

Bed & Breakfast

Business on eBay

Business Support Service

Car Wash

Child-Care Service

Clothing Store

Coin-Operated Laundry

Consulting

Crafts Business

e-Business

e-Learning Business

Event Planning Business

Executive Recruiting Service

Freight Brokerage Business

Gift Basket Service

Growing and Selling Herbs and Herbal
  Products

Home Inspection Service

Import/Export Business

Information Consultant Business

Law Practice

Lawn Care Business

Mail Order Business

Medical Claims Billing Service

Personal Concierge Service

Personal Training Business

Pet-Sitting Business

Restaurant and Five Other Food Businesses

Self-Publishing Business

Seminar Production Business

Specialty Travel & Tour Business

Staffing Service

Successful Retail Business

Vending Business

Wedding Consultant Business

Wholesale Distribution Business

Entrepreneur MAGAZINE'S

startup

3RD EDITION

Start Your Own

CLEANING SERVICE

*Maid Service ◆ Janitorial Service
Carpet and Upholstery Service
and More*

Entrepreneur Press and Jacquelyn Lynn

EP
Entrepreneur
Press

Jere L. Calmes, Publisher
Managing Editor: Marla Markman
Cover Design: Beth Hansen-Winter
Production and Composition: Eliot House Productions

This publication is designed to provide accurate and authoritative information in regard to the subject matter covered. It is sold with the understanding that the publisher is not engaged in rendering legal, accounting or other professional services. If legal advice or other expert assistance is required, the services of a competent professional person should be sought.

Library of Congress Cataloging-in-Publication Data

Lynn, Jacquelyn.
    Start your own cleaning business/by Entrepreneur Press and Jacquelyn Lynn.—3rd ed.
      p. cm.
    Rev. ed. of: Start your own cleaning service. 2nd ed. c2006.
    Includes index.
    ISBN-13: 978-1-59918-332-9 (alk. paper)
    ISBN-10: 1-59918-332-3
    1. Building cleaning industry—Management. 2. House cleaning—Management.
3. New business enterprises—Management. I. Lynn, Jacquelyn. Start your own cleaning service. II. Entrepreneur Press. III. Title.
    HD9999.B882L96 2010
    648'.50681—dc22   2010008655

Printed in Canada

14 13 12 11 10   10 9 8 7 6 5 4 3 2 1

Contents

▲

Chapter 4

Janitorial Service 39

Chapter 5

Carpet and Upholstery Cleaning Services 59

▲

Preface

Have you ever stopped to think about how much time you spend cleaning things? Your house, your car, your clothes—the list goes on and on. And how often have you wished there were some magic way to get your cleaning chores done so you could move on to the activities you really enjoy?

That mind-set is behind one of the most lucrative and recession-resistant industries in America: cleaning. Certainly you look at cleaning in a less-than-enchanted light as you're toiling through your own kitchen and bathrooms on a Saturday when you'd rather be going to the movies. But mopping, vacuuming, and polishing all take on quite a different connotation when they're the foundation for a business that can provide you with a secure financial future. That business is a cleaning service, and the industry is rich with a variety of markets ranging from residential to industrial, from basic to high-tech.

Regardless of the industry niche you choose, one of the appealing aspects of a cleaning service is the opportunity for repeat business—when things get cleaned, they usually get dirty and have to be re-cleaned. It's a wonderful, inevitable cycle that means regular revenue for a cleaning business.

You may already know what type of cleaning business you want to start, or you may still be exploring your options. This book will give you the information and tools you need to start a residential cleaning service, a commercial janitorial service, and a carpet cleaning business. It will also introduce you to a variety of specialty cleaning services that will work as independent operations or adjuncts to another cleaning business.

This guide is structured to take you step-by-step, starting with your decision to start a cleaning service through running a successful, profitable operation. It begins with an introduction to the industry, a look at how successful operators got their starts, and some basic business planning elements. Next, it looks at specific types of cleaning services, including a residential cleaning service, janitorial service, carpet and upholstery cleaning service, and other specialty cleaning businesses. Then it discusses various startup and operational issues, such as your legal structure, insurance, location, vehicles, personnel, purchasing, equipment, and financial management.

It's a good idea to read every chapter in this book, whether you think it applies to the particular business you want to start or not. For example, even if you're planning to start a residential cleaning service, you may pick up some good ideas from the chapters on janitorial and carpet cleaning services. And when you read about other cleaning businesses, you may decide to offer similar services.

Because the best information about business comes from people who are already in the trenches, we interviewed successful cleaning service business owners who were happy to share their stories. Their experience spans all types of cleaning service operations, and several of them are examples themselves of how to blend more than one type of operation into a successful business. Throughout the book, you'll read about what works—and doesn't—for these folks, and how you can use their techniques in your own business.

You'll also learn what the cleaning service business is really like. The hours can be flexible, but they're usually long. The profit margins are good, but only if you're paying attention to detail. The market is tremendous, but you'll have a substantial amount of competition, which means you need a plan to set yourself apart.

Like anything else, there's no quick path to success. The cleaning service business takes hard work, dedication, and commitment. It's not glamorous; in fact, one of the biggest challenges you'll face is the industry's menial image. But by investing your time, energy, and resources, you can be the one who is truly cleaning up, both literally and figuratively.

An Introduction to Cleaning Services

No matter what it is, if it can get dirty, chances are someone will be willing to pay you to clean it. And that's why few industries can claim the variety and depth of opportunities that professional cleaning can.

The cleaning industry has two primary market groups: consumer and commercial. The consumer arena consists primarily of residential cleaning services (traditionally known as maid services), along with carpet cleaners, window cleaners, and a variety of other cleaning services required on a less frequent basis. The commercial arena is dominated by janitorial services, which typically provide a wider range of services than residential services, along with other cleaning companies, such as carpet and window cleaners, that target businesses rather than individual consumers. While it's recommended that you decide on a niche and concentrate on building a business that will serve your chosen market, it's entirely realistic to expect to be able to serve multiple markets successfully.

With all this opportunity, what does the competition look like? Glance through your telephone directory or do a local internet search—the number of cleaning services may make you think the market is already flooded and there's no room for you. That's not true.

First, anyone can list in the Yellow Pages just by having a business telephone line. A mere listing doesn't mean the company is offering quality service to the market you're targeting. Anyone can get on the internet by setting up a website. And while a website is an important part of being in business today, simply having a website doesn't mean you have a competitive business.

Second, the demand for cleaning services is tremendous. Plenty of residential cleaning companies have waiting lists for clients because they simply can't serve the entire market. Many carpet cleaners and other types of specialized cleaning services aren't full-time operations and therefore don't offer serious competition. And a significant number of janitorial services are mom-and-pop operations run by people who want just enough work to earn a living.

Third, cleaning service customers want quality, and many operators are unable to deliver that. Ask anyone who has ever hired a company to clean something in their home or office if they've had any bad experiences, and chances are you'll hear some nightmarish stories of poor-quality work, damage to property, and even theft.

If you offer quality service, operate with integrity, and charge reasonable prices, you'll be a success in a cleaning service business.

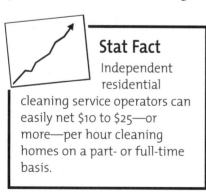

Stat Fact
Independent residential cleaning service operators can easily net $10 to $25—or more—per hour cleaning homes on a part- or full-time basis.

The Driving Forces

Shifting demographics and changing lifestyles are driving the surge in residential cleaning businesses. Busy consumers don't have the time or inclination to clean for themselves; they want to spend their limited leisure hours doing things they enjoy, so they're looking for personal support in the form of housecleaning services, lawn maintenance, errand-running services, and more. They want someone else to handle these tasks, and they want them done well.

The service providers in these areas that will thrive will be the ones with an emphasis on quality and personal service. "Every one of my customers is different and special, and I treat them that way," says Wanda Guzman, owner of Guzman Commercial Cleaning in Orlando.

Stat Fact
There are an estimated 4.2 million building cleaning workers in the United States, according to the Bureau of Labor Statistics, and more than 7 percent of them are self-employed.

Guzman began her business as a residential cleaning service and expanded to commercial accounts. "It's a relationship—I take care of them, and they are loyal to me."

On the commercial side, the dual trends of outsourcing and niche businesses are behind the growing number of janitorial and specialty cleaning services. Businesses need to have their offices and plants cleaned, but it doesn't always make sense for

Polishing the Industry's Image

The cleaning services industry provides a critical service to both individuals and commercial enterprises. It requires hard work, professionalism, and an awareness of evolving technologies and information. Yet it suffers from an image problem. What's the solution?

The first step to improving the industry's image is developing a higher level of self-esteem in the participants. The positive results of properly done commercial cleaning include providing a safe, healthy indoor environment for workers and helping people avoid symptoms and illnesses caused by unhealthy environments. Every person on your staff needs to understand the value of the work they do.

Another critical element in industry image is appearance. Cleaners who are well-groomed and wear neat, professional-looking uniforms elevate not only their own personal self-esteem but the image of their company and the entire industry.

Finally, it's important that everyone in the organization, from the front-line cleaning staff to senior management, work to continuously increase their knowledge and enhance their skills. This means comprehensive training at both basic and advanced levels, using a variety of learning techniques.

them to employ their own cleaning staffs. Nor does it make sense for them to own the equipment and expertise necessary for jobs such as carpet shampooing, which are done infrequently.

"We're not just a cleaning company," says Mike Blair, owner of AAA Prestige Carpet Care in St. George, Utah. "It's not just about pushing a wand or running a machine. It's not just kicking the dirt out. It's a matter of taking good care of people."

This is good news for an entrepreneur who is more interested in building a solid, profitable business than in conquering new horizons.

Before you leap into the cleaning business, it's important to look at it with 20/20 vision. Though technology certainly impacts cleaning services, this isn't a high-tech business. Nor is there any glitz to it. And there will be times when you'll have as much trouble as comedian Rodney Dangerfield had getting respect.

The upside is that you can build a profitable business that will generate revenue quickly. Most cleaning service businesses can be operated on either a part- or full-time basis, either from home or from a commercial location. That flexibility gives this industry a strong appeal to a wide range of people with a variety of goals.

Another positive aspect of the industry is that within each category of cleaning businesses are market niches and operating styles that vary tremendously. Michael W. Ray, owner of Pro Building Services Inc. in Salt Lake City, says, "We offer a wide range of services to a very limited clientele. We have refined our customer base to a group that we feel we can best serve in a way that will allow us to maintain those customers permanently."

This means you can build a company that suits your individual style and talents. If you like doing the work yourself, you can stay small and do so. If your skills are more administrative and supervisory in nature, you can build and manage teams to do the work. For people who like working outside, the opportunities in service areas such as window cleaning and pressure washing are abundant. Residential cleaning services offer fairly predictable hours; disaster restoration and cleanup can mean calls at all hours of the day or night.

Stat Fact
The number of building cleaning workers is expected to grow 14 percent between 2006 and 2016, which is faster than the average for all occupations, according to the Bureau of Labor Statistics.

Few industries offer this tremendous range of choices and opportunities, and the need for general and niche cleaning is expected to increase in the future. To help you find your place in this thriving field, let's take a look at the day-to-day operations of some typical cleaning businesses.

Startup
and Operations

Ask school-age youngsters what they want

to do when they grow up and chances are slim they'll say they

want to be in the cleaning business. But when you talk to the

owners of successful cleaning businesses, they're full of enthu-

siasm about their chosen profession.

Most took a roundabout path to owning and running their businesses. For example, prior to starting her residential cleaning service in Orlando, Fenna Owens worked in the service department of a transportation company, and before that, she owned an automotive business that specialized in replacing

Smart Tip

Never ask to use a customer's phone or bathroom unless it's an emergency.

brakes. In her personal life, she had used the same cleaning person for eight years and was pleased with her work. But when her cleaning person relocated and Owens had to hire someone else to do the job, she realized how challenging it was to find a quality service.

"I was paying somebody every week to clean my house, and if I put my finger on the mantel, I found dust," she recalls. "I was also not really happy with my job. I had enjoyed working for myself [with the brake business]. So I started telling my friends that I was going to start a cleaning business, and some of them said to come to their house."

Another residential cleaning service operator we talked to had been a preschool teacher and gymnastics instructor. She started her cleaning business when her marriage ended and she needed more money than she was making. Still another admits she had no job skills, and cleaning was all she knew how to do—so after working for an established company for a while, she left and started her own business.

Michael Ray started his janitorial service, Pro Building Services Inc. in Salt Lake City, to support himself and his family while he was working on a college degree in public relations. He had been a custodian for another company, where he was encouraged to start his own business by one of the vendor's sales representatives. So, with an investment of less than $400, he took the seats out of his Volkswagen Beetle, loaded it up with equipment and supplies (including an old buffer his father-in-law gave him), and went looking for clients. His first customer was a small independent grocery store, and he did all the work himself. After he graduated from college, he decided he didn't want to work in the public relations field; he wanted to continue operating the company he already owned. Today, his janitorial service employs more than 100 people.

Mike Blair was teaching at a college and doing some consulting work when he met someone with a carpet cleaning business for sale. He bought the business and realized he enjoyed being an entrepreneur. When he decided to move his family to St. George, Utah, there was no question that he would start another carpet cleaning company. He decided to buy new equipment for the new operation, and his startup capital consisted of $25,000, which he borrowed using the equity in his home.

Today's cleaning industry attracts people from all walks of life with a wide range of skills and experience and an even wider range of available capital. It's truly a something-for-everyone business.

What Are the Qualifications?

The necessary qualifications depend, of course, on the type of cleaning service you decide to start. But for any type of service business, you need the determination to make the business work, a willingness to please the customer, and the dedication to provide a thorough cleaning job.

Many residential cleaning business operators are perfectionists. A significant number of them were prompted to start their own companies after unpleasant and unfortunate experiences with other services, taking an "I-can-do-it-better,-so-I-may-as-well-make-money-at-it" attitude.

Another critical requirement for the owner and the employees of any type of cleaning service is honesty. "Clients must have total trust in the people who come to clean their homes," says Owens. This is important, whether they're cleaning bathrooms every week, carpets twice a year, or dusting and vacuuming an office at night.

A residential cleaning service is probably the simplest business in terms of necessary cleaning skills. Janitorial services, carpet cleaning businesses, and other niche

---

Privacy Act

Regardless of the type of cleaning business you start, chances are you'll have the opportunity to learn very personal things about your customers.

"I am not there to read anything; I am there to clean the house," says Orlando residential cleaning service owner Fenna Owens. "If anyone leaves delicate papers out, or anything else laying around, they don't have to worry about it, because I'm not going to stand still and read it. It's not mine, and it's none of my business."

If you accidentally find out sensitive information, never repeat it. "Don't ever talk about your customers to other customers, especially if they know each other," says Owens. "It's nobody's business what they have in their house."

Wanda Guzman, who operates a combined residential and commercial cleaning service also in Orlando, agrees. "When you're cleaning, you're in the most private part of someone's home. People have to feel safe that you're going to keep their confidence," she says. "Sometimes in offices people will leave important papers and files out. When that happens, my policy is don't look, don't touch."

cleaning operations often require the use of special equipment and/or cleaning solutions for which you must be trained.

Beyond actually being able to do the work, a cleaning service operator needs some basic business skills. You need to understand the administrative requirements of running a company, you should be able to manage your time efficiently, and you must be able to build relationships with your employees and your customers.

None of the requirements of being a cleaning business owner are highly complex, nor do they require anything more than average intelligence. Many successful cleaning businesses were started on a shoestring, with just a few dollars' worth of supplies and plenty of energy and enthusiasm. Of course, if you have capital available, your options are greater.

Predictable? Yes and No

The level of predictability in the cleaning business depends on your particular operation and clientele. With a residential or janitorial service, most of your business will be long-term contracts, where you're cleaning the same home or business on a regular basis. You'll likely do some one-time jobs, or occasionally do extra things for existing customers, but the bulk of your business will be on a routine schedule.

Carpet cleaners have plenty of repeat customers, but not at the same level of predictability as residential and janitorial services. The frequency of service is significantly less, since most consumers have their carpets cleaned one to three times a year, and businesses typically only slightly more often. Also, when the economy contracts, many customers will opt to extend the time between carpet cleanings.

For most types of cleaning service businesses, the best business is repeat business—in fact, for many, it's the only business. Repeat customers will make up 75 to 90 percent of your accounts. This is the bread-and-butter of the industry, since one-time-only cleanings bring you one-time-only income. It's up to you to turn these one-time jobs into repeat customers.

If you do a one-time cleaning as a residential or janitorial service, follow up with a telephone call one or two days after your visit to find out how the customer liked your service. Then tell the customer about your regular

> **Smart Tip** *Tip...*
>
> Let your employees know you expect them to be polite and friendly, but they should avoid getting into long conversations with customers. They're there to work, not to talk—and if they're going to stay on schedule, they don't have time for a lot of chitchat.

On With the Show

Regardless of what part of the cleaning industry you're in, trade shows and conventions are an excellent source of information. Exhibitors are eager to show off their latest products and show you how these items can enhance your business. For many homebased business owners, these shows may be your only opportunity to meet face-to-face with a sizable number of prospective suppliers and customers in a short time.

Check with industry trade and professional associations, as well as your suppliers, for information about upcoming shows. Ask for a list of exhibitors in advance so you can decide ahead of time which companies you want to contact. Keep an open mind while at the show, because you may find an unexpected sales or productivity tool. And if necessary, be willing to travel to attend the right show; it could be one of the best investments of time and money you make for your business.

You can choose from large, national shows sponsored by associations (for a list of associations, see this book's Appendix) to smaller, regional shows that are often sponsored by manufacturers. Mike Blair, owner of AAA Prestige Carpet Care in St. George, Utah, recommends both types of trade shows to get a true picture of what's going on in the industry and what all your resources are.

---

cleaning programs. Be friendly and gracious even if the customer says no. They may call you when they need a one-time job again, or they may change their minds about regular service at some future point.

If you do carpet cleaning or another type of cleaning that typically isn't done frequently, set up a system to remind customers when their next service should be performed, whether it's annually, semiannually, or quarterly. They may not think to call you, but if you call them, they'll most likely schedule a cleaning.

Some cleaning service businesses are strongly seasonal; others are not. Janitorial services are probably the most stable in terms of volume, unless they have customers in seasonal businesses. Residential services tend to enjoy a fairly consistent volume year-round, with perhaps some extra one-time-only cleanings around the winter holidays and some additional spring cleaning requests when the weather begins to warm up. Carpet cleaning services are typically busier in the spring and summer, with volume dropping in the fall and becoming very light in the winter. The seasonality of other types of cleaning services depends on what's being cleaned and the climate of the region in which clients are located.

Franchise or Independent Operation?

It's an advantage that franchises will work closely with you as you start your business and take it to the point where it's running smoothly and profitably, especially in the beginning. But you may find that once you become established and are financially secure, a franchise agreement is a decided disadvantage.

A franchise is the way to go for people who want to own their own business but would rather choose an opportunity that has proved successful for many others rather than gamble on developing their own system. Also, most franchises provide a degree of marketing support—particularly in the area of national advertising and name recognition—that's difficult for individuals to match.

In the long run, you'll likely invest far less money operating as an independent service than as part of a franchise. Also, as an independent, you're not tied to any pre-established

> **Tip...**
>
> ### Smart Tip
> One of the most common cleaning mistakes is to apply a cleaning compound and then start scrubbing or rinsing before the compound has a chance to loosen the dirt or grease. Whenever you apply a cleaning compound, follow the manufacturer's instructions, which will usually tell you to wait 30 seconds or longer before you wipe or scrub.

formulas for concept, name, services offered, etc. That's both an advantage and a drawback. The advantage is that you can do things your way. The drawback is that you have no guidelines to follow. Everything you do, from defining your market to cleaning a bathtub, is a result of trial and error. As an independent owner, you must research every aspect of the business, both before and during your business's lifetime, so you'll start right and adapt to market changes. It's very important to thoroughly investigate any franchise offering before you invest.

Buying an Existing Business

An alternative to starting your own cleaning service business is to take over an existing operation. This may seem like an attractive and simple shortcut to skip over the work involved in building a business from ground zero, but you should approach this option with caution.

You'll find cleaning businesses for sale advertised in trade publications, local newspapers, and through business brokers. The businesses can often be purchased lock, stock, and barrel, including equipment, office supplies, existing accounts—and reputation. Be sure you're getting the quality you're paying for in all aspects.

Of course, there are drawbacks to buying a business. Though the actual dollar amounts depend on the size and type of business, it often takes more cash to buy an existing business than to start one yourself. When you buy a company's assets, you usually get stuck with at least some of the liabilities, as well. And it's highly unlikely that you'll find an existing business that's precisely the company you would have built on your own. Even so, you might find the business you want is currently owned by someone else.

Why do people sell businesses—especially profitable ones? There are a variety of reasons. Many entrepreneurs are happiest during

Above and Beyond

Regardless of the type of cleaning business you start, you'll probably have the opportunity to do more for your customers than simply clean. Residential cleaning operators regularly alert their clients to potential problems, such as frayed electrical cords and leaky faucets. Commercial cleaners can provide similar observations. In fact, in early 2005 in Montreal, Quebec, a sharp-eyed janitor did more than point out a problem—he saved the life of a 4-year-old boy.

While taking out the garbage at a restaurant, the janitor spotted a car in the normally empty parking lot. He decided to check it out, and when he did, he realized the car was running and saw a plastic tube going from the exhaust pipe into the trunk. The janitor called 911, and when police arrived, they found the boy and his 28-year-old father in the car. The father was in the midst of a bitter divorce and custody battle with the child's mother and was trying to kill himself and his son. Because the janitor was paying attention and took action, both the boy and his father were saved, and the father was charged with attempted murder.

Jani-King International Inc., a commercial cleaning franchisor, now trains its franchisees to assess potential building and workplace security threats and report them to authorities. "Our crews clean the same buildings night after night. We see the normal activity. We want our employees to understand how to spot suspicious activity and then how to report it," says Jerry Crawford, the company's president.

the startup and early growth stages of a company; once the business is running smoothly, they get bored and begin looking for something new. Other business owners may grow tired of the responsibility, or be facing health or other personal issues that motivate them to sell their companies. They may be ready to retire and want to turn their hard work into cash for their golden years. In fact, some of the most successful entrepreneurs go into business with a solid plan for how they're going to get out of the business when the time comes.

It's also possible that the business is for sale because it has problems—and while that may not stop you from buying it, you should know all the details before you make a final decision. The following steps will help you:

- *Find out why the business is for sale.* Don't accept what the current owner says at face value; do some research to make an independent confirmation.
- *Examine the business's financial records for the previous three years and for the current year-to-date.* Compare tax records with the owner's claims of revenue and profits.
- *Spend a few days observing the cleaning operation.* Monitor several work crews on the job.
- *Speak with current customers.* Are they satisfied with the service? Are they willing to give a new owner a chance? Ask for their input, both positive and negative, and ask what you can do to improve the operation. Remember, even though sales volume and cash flow may be a primary reason for buying an existing business, customers are under no obligation to stay with you when you take over.
- *Consider hiring someone skilled in business acquisitions.* He or she can assist you in negotiating the sale price and terms of the deal.
- *Remember you can walk away from the deal at any point in the negotiation process—* before a contract is signed.

> **Beware!**
> Always use caution when cleaning around computer equipment and electronics, whether you're in a home or an office, especially when you're using chemicals. Never unplug electrical cords, and be careful not to get any liquids on the devices.

Sometimes an owner who is selling a business will stay on after the sale for a time to help the new owner learn the ropes. Depending on the size and complexity of the business and your familiarity with the industry, you may want to negotiate this as part of your purchase contract.

Regardless of whether you start from scratch, buy an existing business, or purchase a franchise, you need a plan. In Chapter 7, we'll talk about how to put that all-important plan together.

Residential Cleaning Service

Housecleaning: It's one of those necessary evils that most people dislike intensely. Even people who don't mind doing housework often find their time budgets stretched thin. The solution? Hire someone to do it. And that "someone" is usually a cleaning service.

Although providing residential cleaning services isn't exactly glamorous, the low startup costs and high sales potential make it attractive to many entrepreneurs. You probably have enough in the way of supplies and equipment in your own home right now to start a residential cleaning service. Another attraction of this business is the hours. A 40-hour workweek is virtually unheard of in the entrepreneurial world, but it's quite realistic with a residential cleaning service. Many operators work Monday through Friday, 8 A.M. to 5 P.M., doing the housecleaning during the day while their clients are at work. And they get to take holidays off because their clients don't want them around on those days.

A residential cleaning service is a great homebased business that you can run by yourself or with employees. As your business grows, you may choose to rent a small office with some storage space, but many successful operators never need to take that step.

Today's typical residential cleaning service has several cleaners on staff, and the owner participates minimally in the cleaning duties, if at all. Owners generally take care of scheduling, handling customer relations issues, ordering supplies, answering the telephone, payroll, and billing, while the cleaners do the actual cleaning. Certainly, there are owners who also clean, but as your business grows, you'll find your time is better spent running the business.

Who Are Your Customers?

Having a maid or housekeeper used to be a symbol of wealth. Only the rich could afford to hire someone to come into their homes to clean. Middle-class women who stayed home while their husbands worked were expected to do their own cleaning. But times have changed. Residential cleaning services no longer cater only to the wealthy. Both middle- and upper-income consumers recognize the value of cleaning services and can afford to hire them.

The primary benefit a residential cleaning service provides is time savings. What would take some customers a whole day, or even an entire weekend, can be handled by a professional cleaner or team of cleaners in just a few hours.

Some customers have the service do all their cleaning; others do light cleaning themselves and depend on their service for heavier, more thorough tasks such as scrubbing floors and toilets, removing cobwebs, and handling other tasks that don't need to be done frequently.

One of the primary reasons behind the tremendous growth in the residential cleaning industry is that more women have joined the work force over the past 40 to 50 years. In families where both the husband and wife work, neither spouse wants to spend their limited leisure time on housework, which makes them great candidates for a cleaning service. Families with both spouses working and whose incomes are $60,000 and up are strong candidates for a cleaning service; households with incomes topping $100,000 are even more likely to hire a service to do their cleaning. Even very wealthy families with high six- or seven-figure incomes who have full-time domestic help will often hire outside professional cleaners to assist their employees.

Of course, two-income families aren't your only prospective customers. You'll also work for affluent families in which the wives aren't employed but prefer to spend their time doing things other than housecleaning, as well as singles who don't have the time or inclination to do their own cleaning, and senior citizens who no longer have the physical stamina to clean their homes.

While some businesses have limited customer bases, residential cleaning services have literally millions of potential customers who either rent or own their homes and live in single-family residences, apartments, and condominiums.

Tracking Time

Some cleaning service owners pay employees by the hour, including travel time; others pay only for cleaning time. In either case, you'll need a way—typically a time sheet—for your employees to record hours worked.

At the top of your time sheets, include a place for the employee's name, employee identification number, and pay period. At the bottom, have a place for the employee and the supervisor to sign and date the form. Set up the middle so your employees can legibly record the time they left the office, the location of each job, the time they arrived, the time they completed each job, travel time, and when they returned to the office at the end of the day. Breaks and lunch periods should also be logged on the time sheet. Use daily time sheets that are turned in at the end of each day rather than weekly logs.

You can use the information you collect on time sheets for more than only payroll. You'll be able to evaluate your scheduling by reviewing the amount of time your crews spend driving. You'll be able to track productivity and address minor problem areas with training before they become major. The information on time sheets also lets you evaluate how accurately you've done your estimates, which means you can determine your profitability before you prepare your monthly financial statements. For a sample employee time sheet, turn to page 34.

Beyond Individual Homes

In addition to occupied homes, you may find a lucrative market cleaning rental homes and apartments between tenants, and in cleaning new homes after the construction crews are finished and before the buyers move in.

Cleaning rental units between tenants requires that you shampoo carpets; scrub floors; clean windows, bathroom, and kitchen fixtures; clean inside and outside of appliances; and wipe down interiors of all cabinets and shelving. Some property managers will also want you to include painting the interior walls as part of your service. You may want to outsource the painting and carpet cleaning.

Builders often have their new homes cleaned when construction is complete. You'll dust; wipe down sinks, tubs and countertops; clean any installation debris from cabinets; wash windows; vacuum; and do other cleaning tasks necessary to get the house ready for occupancy.

One of the biggest appeals of vacant property is that you don't have to navigate around furnishings, and you can usually work fairly quickly. Of course, cleaning rental property that has been abused by the previous tenant can be a particularly unpleasant experience; just wear gloves and, if necessary, a mask, and charge a fair price for the work.

Another opportunity with builders is to clean model homes. Though the homes aren't actually lived in, they sustain a tremendous amount of traffic, and it's critical that they be maintained in sparkling condition, so attention to detail is especially important. Even though they're furnished, model homes don't have the volume of belongings and clutter that occupied dwellings do, and you can generally clean them faster.

Multi-unit residential complexes—either apartments or condos—also need to have their common areas cleaned, such as the laundry rooms, clubhouses, and offices. While this may seem more like a job for a janitorial service, you can present a strong case for using your service if you regularly have crews on the property cleaning the units themselves.

While each of these markets represents a serious business opportunity, it's important to keep in mind that they're very different from cleaning occupied homes. Some people enjoy this kind of work, and others don't. You'll typically have more of a personal relationship with your customers when you do residential cleaning rather than construction or rental home cleaning, so decide if this is important to you as you plan your business.

> ## ! Beware!
>
> Start small. The demand for good cleaning services far outweighs the availability in the marketplace, and you may be tempted to hire too many employees and try to serve too large an area when you first start. A better approach is to limit your geographic market to reduce travel time and expenses when you're starting out.

Who Are Your Competitors?

Your primary competition will come from other residential cleaning services, both franchises and independents. When you compete with a franchise, you compete with a name that's usually supported by a strong marketing machine. This may seem intimidating, but if you distinguish yourself with superior service and special touches, you'll succeed.

A large competitor won't necessarily compete more intensely than a smaller one. Generally it's the quality of service, rather than the size of the operation, that determines customer satisfaction and leads to referrals.

If your market includes apartment complexes, you may be competing against the cleaning staff of the complex, or against janitorial services that also target this market.

Of course, you're always going to be competing against your own customers. After all, you provide a service that most of your customers could do for themselves. This is important to remember when you're developing your sales strategy. Though your customers may not want to, the reality is that most of them could do for themselves what they're paying you to do for them. Because of this, you need to remind them of the opportunity cost of your service—that is, help them see how much your service is worth to them.

For example, say your customer earns $20 per hour at her job. If she were to clean her own home, it would take her five hours. But if she were working for those five hours, she would have earned $100. As a professional, you can clean her home in less time and for less money—say, in three hours for $75. Now it's up to the customer to determine the opportunity cost of using your service. This is your chance to point out how valuable and limited her time is, and how you can enrich her life by freeing her up to concentrate on her career or participate in leisure activities.

> **Tip...**
>
> ## Smart Tip
>
> Many customers view their relationships with housecleaners as personal, so they look for a cleaning service that's stable and has been around for a while. Your marketing materials and personal sales efforts should reflect your commitment to the business and longevity in the community.

Equipment

The basic equipment necessary to start a residential cleaning service is the same equipment you use to clean your own home—and chances are, you already own just about everything you need. The essential list includes a vacuum cleaner, mop, broom, dustpan, all-purpose cleaner, glass cleaner, and rags. Even if you have to buy everything new, about $350 to $450 should cover the cost for a one- or two-person operation. Many solo cleaning service operators use their customers' equipment and supplies, so you could probably get started for far less than that.

The only major piece of equipment you'll need is a vehicle. Just about any economical car—including the one you already own—will be adequate. You need one vehicle per crew, or you might allow your cleaners to use their own cars. You may also want your employees to wear uniforms, which allows them to be easily identified and add a degree of professionalism to your operation.

Beyond the items you'll use for cleaning, you'll need some office equipment and furnishings so you can conduct your administrative tasks, and store equipment and supplies.

> ## Smart Tip
>
> Tip...
>
> Soft-bristle paint brushes are great for dusting louvered doors, vents, and similar surfaces. Soft toothbrushes can get the dust out of furniture that has intricate detail carved in the wood.

Initial Equipment and Supply Checklist

- ❏ Abrasive tile cleanser
- ❏ All-purpose cleaner
- ❏ Brooms
- ❏ Buckets
- ❏ Upright vacuums
- ❏ Canister vacuums
- ❏ City maps
- ❏ Company vehicle
- ❏ Cotton mops
- ❏ Degreaser
- ❏ Dishwashing soap
- ❏ Dust cloths
- ❏ Dust mops
- ❏ Dustpans
- ❏ Extension cords
- ❏ Furniture oil

- ❏ Furniture polish
- ❏ Hand brushes
- ❏ Nonabrasive tile cleanser
- ❏ Paper facemasks
- ❏ Rags
- ❏ Rubber gloves
- ❏ Security system
- ❏ Signage
- ❏ Sponge mops
- ❏ Sponges
- ❏ Spray bottles
- ❏ Stepladders
- ❏ Upright vacuums
- ❏ Window/glass cleaner
- ❏ Wood floor cleaner

The first item you buy will most likely be an industrial vacuum cleaner. Residential vacuum cleaners may do the job, but they're designed for occasional use, not for heavy use on a daily basis. Industrial vacuum cleaners are available in both upright and canister models, and you should buy at least one of each. They generally start between $200 and $300 and up, but they last longer than less expensive units. To prevent vacuums from marking furniture if they bump up against it, place a protective pad around the machine.

You'll need a complete set of equipment and supplies for each of your cleaning crews. Each team should have a cotton mop, sponge mop, dust mop, stepladder, extension cord for each vacuum, and plenty of rags and cleaning cloths. Each team should have one of the following items per person: hand brush, spray bottle of each cleaning solution you use, and a pair of rubber gloves. Two buckets are required for each person conducting wet work—one to hold the cleaning solution, and one to use to wring out your sponge or mop.

It's also a good idea for each crew to have more than one vacuum as a backup, since you can't stop cleaning just because the vacuum cleaner breaks.

Many one-person operations opt to use their customers' supplies and equipment. They charge for labor only, and use the products and tools their customers prefer. One of Fenna Owens' Orlando customers says, "When Fenna told me I needed a new vacuum cleaner, I just asked her what she wanted and bought that."

Supplies

Take a stroll down the cleaning products aisle of your local supermarket, and you may be overwhelmed by the number and variety of products. Many of these items claim to be designed for specialized cleaning tasks. In reality, you need only a handful of cleaning supplies to make a house sparkle—and those supplies don't need to come in fancy packaging, either. Basically, you'll need window cleaner, degreaser, all-purpose cleaner, furniture polish, tile cleanser, wood floor cleaner, paper facemasks, and dust cloths. The more homes you clean in a given day, the more supplies you'll use.

You may find that you need to use additional cleaning chemicals for specific cleaning jobs your customers request. For example, if you service a number of homes with marble, you may want to clean the marble as part of your basic service, and you'll need a special cleaner to do it properly without damaging the surface.

If you offer additional specialty services, such as silverware or brass polishing, you'll need to purchase cleaning solutions for these jobs, as well. If you're unsure about which chemical you need to clean a particular item, ask your customer if they have a preference, or ask a knowledgeable colleague. If they can't help, your local library should have plenty of books on how to clean a variety of different—and even unusual—items. You can also find plenty of help on the internet. For additional advice, you can contact companies that manufacture cleaning products.

For an idea of how much you'll spend on cleaning supplies, see the chart below.

Standard Operations

Before you can set up an operational plan, you need to decide if you'll clean multi-unit dwellings, single-family residences, or a mixture of both. Single-family residences are considered best when you're starting out. They offer more rooms and more square footage. This results in higher revenue than apartments and condominium units, which are typically smaller. As you and your staff gain experience and your efficiency improves, you'll find multi-unit dwellings will become profitable.

What Will You Clean?

Your service will clean the same rooms you usually clean in your own home. A basic cleaning typically includes dusting, vacuuming, cleaning fixtures, mopping floors, wiping counters, and making beds. For an extra charge, some residential cleaning services wash windows, clean carpets, buff floors, wash walls, clean basements, and clean patios and balconies. You may want to establish a list of what you will and won't do, or you may choose to be more flexible. Many cleaning operators use a checklist,

Monthly Supply Costs

The amount you spend on cleaning supplies will vary depending on the size of your operation; the ranges below cover a small, homebased operation up to a very large, commercially based cleaning service.

Abrasive tile cleanser	$25–$300	Nonabrasive tile cleanser	$18–$195
All-purpose cleaner	$38–$510	Paper facemasks	$15–$50
Degreaser	$8–$90	Rags	$25–$75
Dishwashing soap	$10–$75	Sponges	$40–$425
Dust cloths	$25–$145	Window/glass cleaner	$20–$125
Furniture oil	$9–$65	Wood floor cleaner	$15–$70
Furniture polish	$20–$225		

Beware!
Feather dusters are great cleaning tools, but they can also be dangerous. If you're not careful with them, they can knock over and damage delicate figurines. Or, as they begin to wear down, the tips of the feathers can scratch wood surfaces. Use feather dusters with caution.

but Owens says she does "anything that the person who owns the house doesn't like to do."

Most residential cleaning services have a list of tasks that are part of their basic services, plus a list of tasks that they will do for an extra fee. Sometimes your customers will ask you to do things that aren't on either of these lists, such as carpet cleaning, stripping and buffing floors, and exterior window washing.

You can, of course, simply decline some jobs, explaining that you don't offer these services. Or you can subcontract them to reliable companies. If you're going to do this, remember to choose your subcontractors with care, because how well they perform will reflect on you. Or you may choose to rent the necessary equipment and handle the job yourself. If you're asked to do a particular job frequently enough, you may consider purchasing the appropriate equipment and adding it to your list of available extras.

How Will You Clean?

Either an individual or a team can clean a home. Although it naturally takes longer for an individual to do the job, some customers would rather have only one person clean for them. This way, they deal with the same person every time, building a strong, more personal relationship with the cleaner.

Team cleaning allows your firm to operate more efficiently. Customers who are concerned about how much time your cleaners will be in their homes will appreciate the speed of a team. Teams typically consist of two or three people. One approach is to assign each team member certain rooms to clean. Another approach for a two-member team is for one to take care of all the dry work (vacuuming, dusting, making beds, taking out the trash), while the other handles the wet work (mopping, wiping counters, scrubbing bathrooms, and washing dishes). As a way to break the monotony, team members can alternate duties at each home or on a daily or weekly basis.

Encouraging good chemistry between team members is essential. Keep teams together as much as possible; switching crew

Tip...

Smart Tip
Plastic spray bottles work better than aerosol cans because they allow you to spray chemicals more directly; aerosol cans tend to waste cleansers because they release particles into the air as well as on the surface you're cleaning. Also, spray bottles are refillable, and aerosol cans aren't.

On Duty

To clean efficiently, conduct the same cleaning services at each customer's home. As part of their basic service, most residential cleaning services offer the following:

- Dust entire home, including furniture and blinds
- Vacuum entire home, including carpeting and furniture
- Scrub bathtubs and showers
- Clean toilets
- Scrub sinks and faucets
- Clean kitchen and bathroom countertops
- Clean outside of appliances
- Wipe down inside of microwave oven
- Wipe down outside of kitchen cupboards
- Make beds
- Polish furniture
- Collect and dispose of trash
- Clean mirrors
- Wipe television screens

In addition to these basic tasks, you may offer additional services for an extra charge. Those services may include:

- Change bed and bath linens
- Clean inside of refrigerator
- Defrost freezer
- Clean oven and underneath stovetop
- Wash walls
- Clean out fireplace
- Strip, wax, and buff floors
- Oil woodwork
- Clean carpets
- Wash windows
- Wipe windowsills, baseboards, doors, and door frames

members from one team to another tends to destabilize all the teams. Make changes within teams only when a crew member is promoted to supervisor, when a member requests a transfer, or when a personality conflict arises.

If a crew member isn't getting along with his or her teammates and team morale and productivity seem to be affected because of it, transfer the crew member to another team. But do such a transfer only once. If that person doesn't get along with the new teammates, it's probably time to let him or her go.

You may want to designate one member of the team as the team leader or supervisor. Usually, that person has the most experience with your company and knows all your policies and procedures. If you have a large enough staff, you may want a supervisor to oversee several teams. Typically, supervisors assign duties to team members, hold customers' keys, and drive team members to each home. The best approach is to promote from within after someone has demonstrated that they're responsible and trustworthy and will represent the company in a positive manner.

Scheduling

It's important to schedule your work in a way that keeps travel time between jobs to a minimum. For example, if you have two or more customers in an apartment or condominium complex, clean them on the same day. The same advice applies to single-family homes; schedule clients who are close together or in the same neighborhood on the same day. You can schedule the home closest to your office (or wherever the cleaners are starting from) first, and proceed in order to the home furthest away, or vice versa. Always account for both cleaning time and travel time when you establish your work schedules.

Owens says when she first started her Florida business, her clients were spread all over the greater Orlando area. It didn't take her long to realize she was spending almost as much time traveling between jobs as she was cleaning. So she restructured her schedule based on her clients' geographic locations and is now far more productive.

The ideal travel time is no more than 15 to 20 minutes between each client. Volume is the name of the game in this business. The more time you spend cleaning and the less time you spend traveling, the more you'll earn.

A two-person cleaning team can usually clean an apartment in about an hour. The same team may take between one and two hours to clean a moderately sized house. This team could reasonably be expected to clean seven individual apartments in the same complex in one day, or as many as four or five houses, if travel time isn't excessive.

What Does a Typical Day Include?

The day should begin with each crew checking its equipment to make sure team members have everything they need and that there's enough of each cleaning solution

▲

Bright Idea

If your employees drive their own cars to jobs, invest in magnetic signs that they can place on their vehicles to promote your company. The signs can be easily removed when employees aren't working and they cost far less than painting a car.

to last the entire day. They should gather whatever paperwork they need and then head to their first job.

Each crew should fill out a checklist of routine cleaning duties on each job, which is then placed in the customer's file (see page 35 for a sample checklist). The checklist includes a space for the date of the service and the initials of the individual who performs each duty. This serves as a reminder to the cleaners so they don't accidentally forget to do something, and it gives you a way to follow up with the appropriate person if the customer complains about the quality of the work.

Your cleaners should clean according to a system. Most people cleaning their homes waste time retracing their steps because they don't use a systematic plan. They miss things, forget what they've cleaned, and keep running back to the kitchen for sponges or sprays. Certainly allow your crews some flexibility in how they operate, but be sure they're cleaning in the most efficient, logical way. Clockwise from the top of the house is a good method to use.

At the end of the day, crews should turn in their paperwork, replenish their supplies, and advise their supervisor of anything that occurred during the day that might need attention.

From That First Phone Call

When a prospective customer calls, be friendly and knowledgeable about all the services you offer. Be prepared to explain your pricing policy, the services included in a basic cleaning, and when you expect payment. Keep customer information forms close to your telephone so you can write down the information as you get it. The form will also serve as a guide for you so you're sure to ask for all the necessary information.

You may give your estimates over the phone or in person (see Chapter 9 for an explanation of how to set your prices). Estimating over the phone saves you the time of traveling and walking through the prospect's home. On the other hand, when you can't see the home, you don't

Smart Tip

Tip...

You may want to charge extra for the first cleaning, especially if the home hasn't been professionally cleaned in a long time. You can justify an additional fee because you'll likely spend more time on your initial visit.

know its true condition—your crew may get there and find that it's extremely dirty and has a lot of items lying around that need to be moved and cleaned.

Whether you make your quote over the phone or in person, you need to know how many square feet the home is, what tasks the customer wants done, how many bedrooms there are and how many beds each has, the number of bathrooms, the number of people who reside in the home, the number of children, the number and type of pets, whether there's an alarm system, and where your staff can obtain a key if the owner won't be home when the crew arrives. You'll need to know if there are any expensive items in the house, such as figurines and artwork. If there are a lot of

Pay Day

Many residential cleaning services expect payment either before or at the time of cleaning. This isn't unusual, and most customers are used to this type of arrangement and won't object to it. Some services are more flexible and will arrange other payment terms.

If your policy is payment in advance or at the time of cleaning, decide what you will do if your crew arrives at the home and the customer hasn't left a check. You may want to clean the home anyway and leave a reminder notice for the customer to mail a check. Or you may not clean that day. Sometimes this is a judgment call you'll make based on the customer, how long they've been with you, and how confident you are of payment.

If you decide to not clean a home because the customer failed to pay, you also need to have a policy on paying your cleaners. Some services simply tell their employees to move on to the next job, and they're only paid for what they actually do. If they don't get a full day's work in, they only receive a partial day's wages.

Orlando cleaning service operator Wanda Guzman says dealing with the payment issue is one reason she likes being small enough to know her customers. "If someone forgets to leave a check, I don't worry about it," she says. "My longtime customers do that once in a while, and they always remember the next time. If it's a relatively new customer, I might leave a note or call them." Most of Guzman's established customers pay by the month, even though she cleans every week for them. Patti Page, owner of Page's Personal Cleaning in Cincinnati, has a website set up where customers can pay online; many customers prefer the convenience of not having to write a check.

If customers are consistently late with payment or fail to pay on a regular basis, you may want to drop them.

knickknacks, this can affect your price, because moving and dusting them takes time.

Although walk-through estimates take more time, they give you a chance to meet the customer, calculate more accurately how long it will take you to clean the home, and present your company in a favorable light. During the walk-through, look for evidence of pets and children, as well as noting breakable items and small items, such as collectibles and figurines. Ask if there's anything that shouldn't be touched or needs any sort of special handling. If the customer has pets, ask that they be kept in cages, a closed room, or outside in a locked area so they won't interfere with your staff's work and safety. Make a note of the animal's name so your cleaners can use it if the animal should become disagreeable or disappear. Ask about the pet's favorite hangouts so you can pay special attention to cleaning those areas. You should also show the customer evidence of bonding, liability, and workers' compensation insurance.

> ## Bright Idea
>
> Provide your customers with a list of the cleaning products you'll be using in their homes and ask them to let you know if they have any allergies to chemicals or if there are any products they would prefer you not use.

At the end of your walk-through, calculate your estimate and give the price to the customer. If the customer agrees to the fee, complete a customer agreement form that you both sign and both keep a copy of, and put the customer on your cleaning schedule. Obtain a key to the customer's home, and, if there's an alarm system, get the code and special instructions your crew will need to avoid setting off the alarm.

Keep in mind that the first time you clean a customer's home will usually take longer than your subsequent visits. The home might need a thorough cleaning before you can shift to regularly scheduled maintenance cleaning, and you may want to send extra crew members in for that first visit.

Maintaining Customer Records

Keep a file on each prospective customer that includes their name, address, size of home, services inquired about, the quote you gave, and the results of your sales contact. If they didn't hire you, you should find out why. If you're consistently losing jobs because your prices are high, you may want to think about restructuring your pricing or operation to make yourself more competitive. If the problem was that you couldn't meet the prospect's schedule—for example, if they want you to clean on a day that you don't have any crews in the area—make a note and follow up in a few months to see if their needs have changed.

Once someone agrees to use your service, set up a customer file. Even if it is only a one-time visit, you may be able to turn that visit into a regular contract with proper follow-up.

Your customer file should include a customer information sheet (see sample on page 36) that includes:

- Customer's name
- Spouse's name
- Address
- Home and work telephone numbers
- Contact person, in case the customer is unavailable
- Number of bedrooms
- Number of bathrooms
- Total square footage of home
- Type of residence (apartment, condo, townhouse, house)
- Number and ages of children
- Number and type of pets
- If pets are kept indoors or outdoors
- If the home has an alarm system

Additional information you want to gather is up to you. You may also want to note on your customer information sheet the cost estimate and service description you provided.

When customers agree to use your service, it's a good idea to have them sign agreements that clearly state how often your cleaners will visit, how much each visit will cost, which cleaning services you'll provide during each visit, when payment is due, and your cancellation policy. A signed contract will prevent future misunderstandings. Keep it in the customer's file.

> **Bright Idea**
> Be willing to make your sales calls and do your estimates in the evenings and on weekends. Although most of the work involved in running a residential cleaning service is done during normal business hours, you may need to make your initial visits to customers' homes at times convenient to them so they don't have to take time off work.

You should also file the completed checklists that cover all the duties the cleaners need to perform with each cleaning in the customer's file. If the customer complains that the bed wasn't made or the kitchen floor wasn't cleaned properly, you can refer to the checklist to see who was responsible for the particular task. If there's ever any damage to a customer's property, you'll want to complete a damage report (see sample on page 37) and maintain it in the customer's file.

Additional documents that you'll keep in a customer's file include cleaning schedules, billing sheets, and any correspondence or special notes you may make about the customer.

Pitfalls

As with any business, there are certain pitfalls that go along with running a cleaning service. No matter what you do, some customers will never be satisfied. These customers typically want absolutely everything cleaned but also want the lowest price.

To handle problem customers, start by recognizing and addressing their concerns. While you shouldn't admit to a mistake until you're sure you're at fault, always recognize the validity of the customer's feelings. Say something like "I can certainly understand why this is an important issue for you. I need to get a little more information before I can take the appropriate action."

Ask them what aspects of the service they're dissatisfied with and what needs to be improved. If the problem is with the quality of service, discuss the situation with the employees responsible for cleaning that customer's home. Take the time to visit the customer's home before and after your crew cleans.

> **Tip...**
>
> **Smart Tip**
> Always discuss customer concerns and complaints with the employees responsible for the work. If the concern is valid, address the issue by training the employees. If it's not, go back to the customer and clear up the communication problem.

If, after doing this, the customer still feels they aren't receiving their money's worth, but your crew members are doing their jobs properly, explain what your basic services cover and give your customer the option of paying a higher price for additional service. If they're not willing to pay more but are still demanding more, it may be better to drop the customer rather than dealing with complaints after every cleaning.

Another pitfall facing cleaning service owners is that some customers may take a haughty attitude with the cleaners, which can have an impact on your employees' morale. While it's a fact that cleaning homes isn't the most prestigious or financially rewarding line of work, that's no reason for your customers to treat your employees poorly. Cleaning is an honest and necessary job, and your employees deserve to be treated with respect. If you become aware that a customer isn't treating your cleaners with respect, have a tactful conversation with the customer, pointing out that your employees come from good backgrounds, are trustworthy and well trained, and are providing a valuable service that your customer probably doesn't want to do without. This is usually sufficient to correct the situation, but if the customer continues to adopt an attitude that distresses your employees, you may want to consider dropping the account.

In several parts of the country, many cleaning service employees are recent immigrants who may have a difficult time assimilating and communicating. Consider working with local community resources that offer an English as a Second Language class so these employees can learn to communicate better with other employees and customers. Keep in mind that they won't adjust to American culture and to using English overnight. Give them time, and work with them. But if they don't seem to be making sufficient effort or progress, and their work—and consequently your business—suffers as a result, you may not be able to afford to keep them on.

One of the challenges of owning a residential cleaning service is scheduling around holidays. Most of your customers will prefer that their cleaning be done when they're not home, and they certainly won't want you around during their holiday parties. So if a client's regular cleaning day is Monday, you need a plan for how you're going to

Security Is the Key

The majority of your customers won't be home when you or your employees clean their homes, so you need to arrange for access to the premises. Some residential cleaning services require the customer to provide a key to the house or the code to a keyless entry system.

Others are more flexible. Because some customers are reluctant to hand over their keys, some cleaning service operators are willing to pick up a key from a neighbor, from the mailbox, or from some outside hiding place. This isn't a great idea, because an absent-minded customer can disrupt your work schedule by forgetting to leave the key in the agreed-on spot. Or the neighbor who has the key may not be home when your crew arrives. And, leaving a key outside is a security risk for your customer. The easiest, most efficient policy is to have a key or some other form of assured access to the residence.

For both your own and your customers' protection, create a security system for the keys. Tag each key with a code that doesn't identify your customer or their address. The corresponding identification information for the code should be kept in a location separate from the keys, ideally in a password-protected computer file or in a locked safe. Keep the keys in another safe or locked key box. To increase your customers' peace of mind, explain your key security system to them.

If a key is lost or stolen while in your possession, notify the customer immediately and offer to pay the cost of rekeying the locks.

handle all the holidays that fall on Mondays, such as Presidents' Day, Memorial Day, and Labor Day. If the regular cleaning day is Thursday, know how you'll handle Thanksgiving. Be sensitive to ethnic and religious holidays that you may not celebrate but your clients do—and consider how you'll handle things if the situation is reversed and you're observing holidays

> **Smart Tip**
> Test every surface before using a new cleaning solution. Be sure the solution won't remove color or mar the finish.

your clients don't. Check the calendar at the beginning of the year to see what day other major holidays fall on and put together a plan for how you're going to handle every holiday and vacation.

Some of your weekly customers won't mind if you just skip them once. Others will prefer that you reschedule for the day before or after the holiday. It's a juggling act that can test every bit of your managerial talent, so plan for holidays well in advance by discussing the schedule with your customers and employees.

In addition to regular cleaning, you may want to offer your customers special services—such as a spring cleaning—once or twice a year, where you do such extras as cleaning the inside of cabinets, help with closet cleaning and organizing, and even help with cleaning out the garage, attic, or basement. Your customers may be comfortable telling you what they want and leaving you to do the job, or they may want to work with you to direct the sorting and organizing. In the latter case, they may prefer to schedule these projects on weekends, which means overtime for you and your crew.

Oops!

Accidents happen, so from time to time, damage to a customer's property may occur. Most customers are reasonable when these things happen, especially if you immediately accept your responsibility to repair or replace the item. If the damage is minor, you'll probably want to just absorb the cost of the repair; if it's major, you'll file a claim with your insurance company.

You should have a procedure in place to deal with damage incidents. Begin with a report form that the responsible employee should fill out and turn in to his or her supervisor, or to you. The form should include the employee's name, the date of the incident, the customer, the item involved, the value of the item, a full description of how the damage or breakage occurred, and what follow-up actions took place (see the Damage Report form on page 37).

For minor damage, you may just leave your customer a note explaining what happened and outlining what you intend to do to rectify the situation. For a more serious incident, call the customer immediately to discuss the best way to handle it.

Cleaning for a Reason

Deborah Sardone, president and CEO of Buckets & Bows Maid Service Inc. in Lewisville, Texas, has been touched by both clients and employees who have experienced the devastating impact of cancer. In 2006, she formed the Cleaning for a Reason Foundation to provide free professional housecleaning services for women who are undergoing cancer treatment. In dealing with a cancer diagnosis, the patient and caregivers tend to focus primarily on medical issues; basic lifestyle matters are often overlooked. Yet a clean environment, while always important, is especially valuable to cancer patients, and many of them don't have the financial resources to pay for professional cleaning. Hundreds of cleaning services across the country partner with the foundation to clean the homes of women who are struggling with the debilitating effects of cancer and chemotherapy—doing it at no charge as a way of helping others and giving back to their communities.

To learn more about the foundation and how your cleaning service can participate, visit cleaningforareason.org.

Always offer to arrange for the repair yourself; never suggest that your customer do it and just tell you how much it cost. Remember, the primary benefit of using a cleaning service is saving time, and your customers will probably not be happy about having to spend their time replacing or repairing a broken item. Of course, if they offer to do it, it's OK to agree.

In addition to making the customer happy, you'll also want to find out if the damage was a genuine accident or if the employee was careless. You may want to implement a policy in which all or part of the cost (up to the amount of your insurance deductible, of course) of replacing or repairing damaged items is deducted from the responsible person's pay; this reduces your expenses and keeps employees on their toes.

Whether or not you file a claim with your insurance company depends, of course, on the amount of the claim and the type of coverage you have.

Make it clear to your employees that all incidents of damage, no matter how minor they may appear, must be reported, and that failing to do so could result in disciplinary action up to and including termination.

Employee Time Sheet

Name: _____

Social Security number: _____

Date: _____

Time left office: _____

Customer (Include address and phone number)	Time Arrived	Time Completed

Time returned to office: _____

Employee signature: _____ Date: _____

Supervisor signature: _____ Date: _____

Checklist of Routine Cleaning Duties

Duty	Date	Initials
Restrooms		
Empty trash		
Dust light fixtures		
Dust counters		
Wipe mirrors		
Clean sink		
Wipe countertops		
Wipe cabinets		
Clean tub/shower/toilet		
Bedrooms and/or Living Room, Study, etc.		
Empty trash		
Make beds		
Dust furniture		
Dust miniblinds		
Vacuum drapes		
Vacuum floor and under bed		
Kitchen		
Dust tops of cabinets		
Wipe tops and front of appliances		
Wipe cabinets		
Clean sink		
Clean countertops		
Sweep floors		
Mop floors		
General Cleaning		
Empty trash		
Clean windows		
Wipe windowsills		
Remove cobwebs		
Clean light switches		
Wipe walls		
Wipe door handles and frames		
Wipe telephones		
Dust miniblinds		
Dust furniture		
Polish furniture		
Clean mirrors		
Sweep floors		

Customer Information Sheet

Name: _____ Spouse's name: _____

Address: _____

Home phone: _____ Work phone: _____

Number to call in case of emergency: _____

Type of facility: House ❏ Apartment/Condo ❏ Townhouse ❏

Square footage: _____

Number of bedrooms: _____

Number of bathrooms: _____

Number of children: _____ Ages: _____

Number of pets: _____ Types: _____ Indoors/Outdoors

Does home have security system? _____ Code: _____

Date received customer's key: _____

Additional comments: _____

_____

_____

_____

_____

_____

_____

_____

_____

_____

_____

_____

_____

_____

_____

Damage Report

Date:

Customer name:

Address:

Home phone: Work phone:

Staff person responsible:

Item(s) description:

Replacement value of item(s):

Please describe the incident that caused the damage:

Can item be repaired?

Was customer notified?

By whom?

Date and time:

Please describe follow-up procedure (i.e., item repaired or replaced):

Cost:

Was insurance company notified?

Date of notification:

4

Janitorial Service

Look around. Just about any place where you see a commercial facility, you're looking at a cleaning opportunity. While residential cleaning services typically only clean residences, janitorial services clean businesses—offices, hospitals, restaurants, and schools, to name a few. And what a janitorial service lacks in glamour it makes up for in potential profits.

The demand for janitorial services is strong and will likely continue to be. It just makes sense that as long as there are commercial buildings, there will always be a need for someone to clean them. Even during recessions, janitorial businesses do well.

While it typically takes more than a residential cleaning service, the startup costs for a janitorial business are still relatively low. It's possible to get started working from a homebased office with just a vehicle and a minimal amount of equipment.

But while residential services are pretty much "normal business hours" operations, janitorial services are almost the opposite. You'll find some customers who want you to clean during the day, but most will prefer that you clean after their staff has finished their work and gone home.

With few exceptions, janitorial jobs are going to be substantially larger than residential cleaning ones—even if you start with very small customers. "If you took someone who was used to cleaning homes and put them in a large office building, they would hesitate and think they couldn't do that huge space," says Michael W. Ray, owner of Pro Building Services Inc., a janitorial service in Salt Lake City. The key is to not be intimidated; just break the work down into tasks that can be done in a logical, reasonable order.

Who Are Your Customers?

Though not all businesses will hire an outside janitorial service company, their facilities all need to be cleaned. Not only must they meet health code requirements, but they also want to make a favorable impression on their customers. Offices and office buildings are the primary customers of most janitorial services, but you can also do well cleaning restaurants, schools (including colleges and universities), hospitals, medical offices, museums, retail stores, warehouses, and manufacturing facilities.

Many janitorial companies begin by cleaning small offices. The work involves dusting, vacuuming, removing trash, and cleaning restrooms and lunchrooms. When you're ready, you can expand your services to include cleaning windows, buffing floors, and shampooing carpets.

After you get some experience with small offices, you can move up to larger facilities and other types of businesses.

What and how you clean depends on the customer and their type of business. For example, when you clean medical facilities, you'll be

> **Bright Idea**
> Consider backpack-style vacuum cleaners. Michael Ray says his Salt Lake City employees can vacuum three to five times the amount of space in the same time with a backpack vacuum as they can with a standard upright. Good backpack vacuum cleaners run about $250 to $450 and higher.

cleaning the general office, public areas, and the examination rooms. You need to be aware of blood-borne pathogens, which are microorganisms that are present in human blood and can cause disease in humans, such as hepatitis B virus (HBV) and HIV. Take preventive measures to protect yourself and your employees. When handling any waste that may have been contaminated with blood, always wear latex gloves to reduce the risk of coming in contact with blood-borne pathogens.

You might consider targeting the food-service industry. A growing number of restaurateurs are choosing to hire janitorial services rather than have their own employees clean their facilities. You'll need to go in after the restaurant closes, and clean the waiting area, dining rooms, restrooms, and sometimes the kitchen. You'll vacuum, mop, and clean all glass and light fixtures. If you're responsible for the kitchen, you'll need to clean the grill, other cooking surfaces, and appliances.

Who Are Your Competitors?

Because janitorial services don't require a lot of cash or experience to start, this is a relatively simple business to enter. For the same reason, it's also a competitive one. But if you clean well and provide exceptional customer service, you'll succeed.

Of course, you'll be competing against other janitorial services that range from independent, mom-and-pop operations to large corporations. To compete effectively, it helps to understand how these companies are structured and run. In fact, you'll probably see a description of the company you want to build here.

Often, people will start a janitorial service with every intention of staying small, just to provide a way for couples and families to work together as they service accounts and earn a living. Sometimes the couples are middle-aged, or retired from their first careers. They may have only a few accounts, do the cleaning themselves, and don't need any employees. By working from home and using general cleaning equipment rather than the industrial-quality variety, they keep their overhead low. However, these companies are often so small they can't afford to buy insurance, which means they aren't protected if something happens to their equipment or vehicle, or if they cause—or are injured in—an on-the-job accident. A janitorial service that's adequately insured and bonded has a competitive edge over one that isn't.

Large commercial cleaning companies and franchised operations generally have a name recognition you may find intimidating. They're probably well insured and have top-of-the-line equipment and a sophisticated marketing plan. The real question is, How good is their service? One of the industry's biggest problems is employee turnover, and the more employees a company has, the harder it is to monitor their performance and ensure that the work is being performed satisfactorily. To compete with a large operation, emphasize in your marketing materials that you provide top-quality, personal service, and that your employees are carefully supervised.

Suck It Up

The issue of indoor air quality makes choosing the right vacuum cleaner increasingly important for janitorial services. It's not enough to make the carpet look good; you must consider what the vacuum actually traps and what it allows to escape in the way of particles. Here are some points to consider when shopping for a vacuum cleaner:

○ *Efficient filters*. Filters play a critical role in preventing dust and soil particles from being redistributed into the air. Your best choices are HEPA or HEPA-type filters and machines that feature air-filtering processes that trap and hold dust, soil, allergens, and breathable particles.

○ *Aggressive pile lifting and grooming*. This opens the carpet to allow for more efficient removal of dry soil, dust, and debris. If the vacuum cleaner does this, you can eliminate the need to lift the pile as a separate step, which reduces labor costs.

○ *Strong, consistent airflow*. A powerful airstream will draw more dry soil out of carpet and carry it through the machine into the vacuum bag.

○ *Airtight collector*. Whatever container collects the soil should hold the soil and not release it back out into the air to settle on the building's contents and be inhaled by building occupants.

Salt Lake City's Michael Ray says that when he takes over a building and begins vacuuming with quality equipment, there's a noticeable drop in the dust level within the first 30 days.

You'll also be competing against in-house cleaning staffs. If a company you contact already has in-house custodians, don't discount that company as a potential account. Stress your quality of service and point out that using your company is more cost-effective than maintaining an in-house staff. Many companies today are outsourcing as much as they can, and your sales efforts should put you in an ideal position to win the account if and when the company decides to restructure how they handle cleaning.

Equipment

Though it's not ideal, it's possible to start a janitorial service with as little as a mop, bucket, broom, vacuum cleaner, rags, and some all-purpose cleaner. As you grow, you'll be able to purchase other equipment, such as a floor buffer, a carpet cleaning machine, and better-quality vacuums.

To avoid spending your limited capital on equipment you won't use very often, especially in the beginning, consider renting machines as you need them. Another option is to subcontract jobs requiring special equipment to companies that focus on that type of work, such as carpet cleaning and window washing.

For most janitorial jobs, you'll need a mop, mop bucket and wringer, push broom, baseboard brush, straw broom, pail, scrub brush, squeegee, 6-foot ladder, upright vacuum cleaner, three-prong adapter (to be sure you have power for your electrical equipment), hand scrubbing pads, dustpan, spray bottles, extension ladder, heavy-duty extension cords in either 50- or 75-foot lengths, wax applicator, wheeled trash can, and floor scraper/putty knife.

Floor Cleaning Equipment

In addition to regular vacuuming, janitorial services are often expected to clean floors, which means you may need your own special equipment. To make the best decision on a carpet cleaner, see the equipment section in Chapter 5.

Initial Equipment and Supply Checklist

❏ All-purpose cleaning powders	❏ Hand scrubbing pads
❏ All-purpose cleaning solutions	❏ Ladder
❏ Brooms	❏ Metal storage cabinet
❏ Brushes	❏ Mop bucket and wringer
❏ Buffing machine pads	❏ Mops
❏ Carpet cleaning machine	❏ Pumice sticks
❏ Cleaning carts	❏ Security system
❏ Company vehicle(s)	❏ Signage
❏ Dust cloths	❏ Soap
❏ Dustpans	❏ Sponges/pails
❏ Extension cords	❏ Spray bottles
❏ Extension ladder	❏ Squeegees
❏ Feather dusters	❏ Three-pronged adapters
❏ Floor cleaning machine	❏ Upright vacuum
❏ Floor scraper/putty knife	❏ Wax applicators
❏ Floor signs	❏ Wet/dry vacuum
❏ Glass cleaner	❏ Wheeled trash cans

▲

You may also want to buy a floor buffer to wax and shine vinyl and tile floors. This machine also strips wax build-up before applying another coat of wax. A basic buffer operates at a speed of 175 to 1,500 RPM. A burnisher is a kind of floor buffer but operates at 1,000 RPM and higher. A new, low-speed floor buffer costs $400 to $1,200, and a burnisher costs $900 to $2,000. If your accounts have a lot of floor space that needs to be shined, a burnisher might be worth the investment. But if you only have a few accounts with uncarpeted floors, a basic buffer will be sufficient.

Chemicals

Most of the cleaning products you'll use aren't dangerous, but you still need to be concerned with issues such as chemical composition, proper storage and use, and environmental friendliness.

"We try to use products that are as safe as possible and yet still effective for the job we need them to do," says Ray. "The strongest chemicals we have are spotters for carpet. Strippers for floor wax are also pretty strong, and so are toilet bowl acids." Some tasks require more powerful compounds than others, and it's important that every worker using dangerous products understand how to use them properly and with as little risk of harm to themselves, the materials being cleaned, and the environment as possible.

Follow the manufacturer's instructions for storage and use. Be sure to provide your employees with proper safety equipment, such as eyeglasses or goggles to shield against chemical splashes, and gloves to protect their hands when they're doing wet work.

Standard Operations

If you like a steady, dependable routine, don't start a janitorial service. Owners in this business can never predict when their days will start or what hours they'll work.

Typically, though, you'll probably start about 9 A.M. Your first order of business will likely be answering customer complaints and questions regarding work your employees did the night before. Clients might complain that carpets weren't properly vacuumed, windows weren't cleaned, restrooms weren't scrubbed, or paper towel dispensers weren't filled. If the complaint is minor and can wait, have the crew

> **Smart Tip** *Tip...*
>
> Keep a good backup file of temps you can call on short notice either to substitute for a sick or vacationing employee or as a permanent replacement if necessary.

supervisor or other designated employee in charge of that account take care of the problem on the next visit. If the problem warrants immediate attention, visit the account personally the day you receive the complaint and correct the problem.

The next order of business will be to make customer service calls. Just because customers aren't complaining doesn't mean they're totally satisfied. You should be calling your customers regularly—ideally at least once a week—to make sure they're happy and that there are no areas where you could improve your service.

With your existing customers properly attended to, it's time to get out of the office and call on potential accounts. As your business grows, you may eventually hire a full-time salesperson to handle this aspect of your business, but in the beginning, you'll need to make sales calls yourself.

The cleaning work typically begins in the late afternoon or early evening. Depending on the size of your operation and the number of people on your staff, you may or may not be involved in the actual cleaning work, but it's still a good idea for you to be visible when crews begin their shifts.

Night and Day

Though most janitorial work is performed at night after employees have gone home for the day, there will be times when you'll need to supply workers during the day. A large office building may want you to have a custodian around during the day to maintain the restrooms and clean up unexpected spills. You may want to charge a slightly higher labor rate for this person than you do for your night workers, and be sure you choose someone who not only cleans well but also has good people skills.

Restaurants that cater to lunch and dinner crowds may prefer that you clean in the morning, rather than after closing. Customers that operate 24 hours a day will probably want you to clean during their slowest periods, which will vary depending on the type of business. Never assume the hours your customers want you to work; always ask to be sure.

That's a Lot of Elbow Grease

Square feet cleaned per hour by one FTE, based on interior building area with medium obstructions:

Type of Building	Average	Low	High
School (K-12)	3,047	2,737	3,358
College/university	2,924	2,510	3,338
Industrial plant or warehouse	3,212	2,468	3,957
Hospital	2,473	1,715	3,230
Nursing home	1,192	896	1,488
Private office building	3,127	2,304	3,949
Government facility	3,494	2,630	4,359
Other	2,783	2,060	3,505

Source: Cleaning & Maintenance Management *magazine*

The typical janitorial service that cleans offices begins cleaning after the office employees have left for the day. If the office closes at 5 P.M., you may be able to begin cleaning as early as 6 P.M. But most clients don't want you to begin cleaning until after all the employees have left the building, and if they tend to work late, you may not be able to enter the building until 9 P.M. or later. Some clients will want you to clean daily, others every other day, and still others may only need you to come once a week.

Typically, your employees will be divided into crews of two to six, including a supervisor. The team's supervisor should be someone who knows the job and cleans well, has been with the company a while (usually, but not always, longer than others on the team), and can represent your company well. Supervisors or crew chiefs generally earn one to two dollars more per hour than other team members.

Setting up teams not only speeds the cleaning process but improves efficiency, boosts morale, and promotes honesty. Teams are essential when cleaning large accounts because there's so much work to do, and one person can't handle it alone.

Teams should remain intact from job to job. Moving crew members from team to team is destabilizing. If a team is effective and all the

> **Tip...**
>
> **Smart Tip**
> When you're cleaning, keep moving forward. Plan your work so everything gets done on the first pass through any given space.

workers get along well, keep them productive by not switching them around unless you really need to.

In general, team members share the responsibility of cleaning a facility with the supervisor. Divide them into two groups: one doing wet work and the other doing dry work.

Wet work consists of scrubbing or mopping floors and counters, washing walls, cleaning sinks and toilets, and other tasks that involve water. Dry work is virtually everything else, from dusting to vacuuming to polishing floors. If specific team members prefer doing a certain type of work or are better at some tasks than others, accommodate them as much as possible. They'll be happier, and boosting morale means boosting your bottom line.

Team members should also assist in maintaining equipment, which includes helping the supervisor clean the equipment at the end of each day (or, more likely, night). This is a chore that can be rotated among crew members. Be sure they understand that they're responsible for immediately reporting to the supervisor any problems

Bright Idea

If a prospective customer is considering changing to your company from another service, find out why. If you know exactly what they weren't satisfied with, you can pay more attention to those concerns.

A Little Help

When a customer asks you to handle a chore that's not part of your normal service, you can do one of three things. One, you can explain that you don't do that and risk damaging your relationship with the customer by forcing him to find another resource. Two, you can agree to do it, then scramble for the necessary equipment and skills to handle the job, and hope you're pricing it reasonably. Or three, you can hire an independent contractor who specializes in that type of work.

Subcontracting special janitorial jobs can save you money on payroll and keep your equipment investment down. For example, you might want to subcontract your carpet cleaning work to a carpet cleaning company, or window washing to a window washer. Other services janitorial customers might occasionally need include ceiling cleaning, sandblasting, and pressure washing.

You would typically use an independent contractor for jobs that only a few of your clients request and that don't need to be performed often.

they have with equipment, either when they're using it or cleaning it, or any other type of on-the-job problems.

In addition to your daily routine, you'll need to plan and carry out a number of weekly and monthly procedures. It's a good idea to maintain a quarterly master plan so you don't forget anything and you properly schedule your time and your staffing.

Like any other business owner, you have to maintain your records and take care of administrative tasks. If you can't find the time during the week, you'll have to devote a few hours on weekends—but whatever you do, you must keep your financial records, including payroll and taxes, current and accurate. To make good operating decisions, you must know where your business is headed at all times. If you neglect these nuts-and-bolts tasks, your entire operation will suffer, no matter how high your sales are.

Laundry

Unless you plan to operate a small, part-time janitorial service, you'll need your own laundry facility. "We use fresh laundry every day," says Ray. That includes rags, towels and mop heads. He maintains an industrial-capacity washer and dryer in his office.

If you're small, your washer and dryer at home may be able to handle your laundry load, or you might choose to use a commercial coin-operated laundry. What's important is that you accurately estimate your laundry needs and are able to meet them. Remember, using dirty equipment won't produce the quality results you've promised and your customers demand.

Maintaining Customer Records

Keep a file on each customer. It should include a schedule of the cleaning duties you perform for them. For example:

- *Daily.* Empty trash, clean restrooms, and restock paper products.
- *Every other day.* Clean windows, vacuum, and dust desks.
- *Weekly.* Mop floors.
- *Monthly.* Dust plastic plants and clean light fixtures.
- *Quarterly.* Clean carpets and dust corners and tops of shelves.

Consider writing dates next to each of these duties so you know just when a certain task needs to be done and when it's actually performed. You may even want to give a copy of this schedule to your customers so they know just what you do and when you do it.

Task Times

Time it takes one FTE to complete cleaning tasks, based on 1,000 square feet of unobstructed floor:

	Average	Low	High
Wet mopping	20.6 minutes	18.9	22.3
Vacuuming	18.2 minutes	16.7	19.8
Dust mopping	12.2 minutes	10.8	13.7

Source: Cleaning & Maintenance Management magazine

Bidding

When you sell your janitorial services, for the most part, you'll be dealing with experienced businesspeople who prefer to work with professional suppliers. You'll probably be asked to submit a written bid outlining the services you'll perform and the prices you'll charge.

Use the "Estimate Form" on page 57 to determine what services the customer wants performed and to calculate how much to charge for the job. After you've come up with an estimate, present it formally to the customer in the form of a proposal (see page 58).

Most businesspeople are reasonable and understand that you get what you pay for. Certainly they want to get the lowest price possible—just as you do on the goods and services you have to buy for your own company. But they realize that the lowest price isn't always the best deal if it means sacrificing quality.

"They will try to get the lowest price they can for the service they want," Ray says. "When they find they can no longer get the services they need, we see them willing to pay more." The level of service required usually depends on the type of facility.

"The people who really care a lot about their buildings are people who have important and demanding clientele in them, or a company that has a top executive who operates from that building who says cleaning is important to him," Ray says. Branch offices may be more focused on price than service, although they're

Beware!

Until you've developed some skill at estimating charges, be careful about committing yourself to long-term contracts. If you accidentally bid too low, you don't want to have to do the job for a year or more at a loss.

usually willing to pay extra to have the place polished before a visit from a headquarters big shot.

Although much of the bidding process seems to be centered on pricing, be sure to emphasize the quality of your service and the value you provide. However, you must deliver what you promise, so never promise more than you can deliver.

Recognize your abilities—and your limitations. When you bid on a job, be sure you can handle it. Ask about the customer's special needs, and pay attention to details. Courtesy, genuine interest in meeting the customer's needs, and fair pricing will set you apart from the competition and help you build a reputation as a responsible operator.

> **Tip...**
>
> **Smart Tip**
>
> Even though you may not want to be in the disaster restoration business, your crew may be the first ones on the scene in the event of a broken water pipe or other problem. Be flexible, and do what you can to help your customers when they need you, even if it's beyond your normal service package.

Visit your prospective customers' sites and don't give an estimate until after you've seen the condition of the facility and have discussed with the client which services you'll provide. Never just "guesstimate" over the phone; you could lose the opportunity to make a serious bid if your figure is too high, or the customer may question your integrity if your phone quote is significantly lower than the final bid you make after you find out what the job really entails.

Ray says his normal approach is to work with property managers to establish the customers' preferred procedures before putting together a proposal. Usually they'll have put together a set of cleaning specifications, but you may need to ask how they want particular tasks handled, such as cleaning an office that has a lot of knickknacks, or what your responsibility is if people leave papers out on their desks at night (obviously, this happens often). You may want to establish a schedule for certain chores, such as rotating things that don't need to be done every night to balance the overall workload.

Estimating a Job

The first step in preparing an estimate is to identify the variables that will affect the time it takes to perform the required cleaning work (use the "Estimate Form" on page 57). Those variables may include:

- Size, in square feet, of the area to be cleaned
- Layout of the facility
- Number of employees

Main Floor

Let's get down to the nitty-gritty. Follow these instructions for floor cleaning, and your customers will sing your praises.

Stripping Old Wax and Dirt

1. Clear the floor of all obstacles, such as chairs, wastebaskets, and other movable items.
2. Sweep, dry-dust, or vacuum the floor completely.
3. Remove any heavy spot, dirt, or gum with a putty knife.
4. Mix the wax stripper and hot water according to the manufacturer's recommendations.
5. Apply the solution to the floor with a mop, and let it stand for a few minutes.
6. Scrub the floor with a scrub brush, steel wool pad, or nylon pad, depending on how much dirt and/or wax you have to remove.
7. Mop up the dirty solution.
8. Rinse the mop well and pick up any remaining solution with clean water.
9. Let the floor dry thoroughly.

Helpful Hints

○ Remove dirt in corners and along baseboards.
○ Wipe up any splashes on the walls, furniture, and baseboards.
○ Never allow water to stand on a tile floor; tile that stays wet too long may start to lift.
○ Don't attempt to scrub more than 100 square feet at once.

Waxing the Floor

1. Make sure the floor is clean.
2. Apply an even coat of wax or finish with a strong mop or wax applicator.
3. Wax evenly.
4. Let the wax dry for about 20 minutes. Apply a second coat if necessary.
5. Buff the floor if you use natural carnuba wax.

Helpful Hints

○ If you use a polymer finish, make sure to remove all old wax, resin finishes, and soap scum from the floor. Polymers won't adhere properly to natural waxes.

Main Floor, continued

○ Don't apply wax with dirty applicators.

○ Don't use an oily sweeping compound on floors.

○ Don't let wax wear out in high-traffic spots. Touch up these spots from time to time.

○ Don't let polish build up along baseboards.

- Construction materials (carpeting, tile, glass, etc.)
- Location and position of furniture, equipment, appliances, etc.
- Number of offices, restrooms, and fixtures to clean
- Location of storage areas
- Areas requiring special attention
- Availability and location of electrical outlets
- Frequency of duties
- Hours during which cleaning can take place

Floors are always a major consideration. They may require as much as 60 percent of your time. If floors are carpeted, how often will they need shampooing? If they aren't carpeted, how often will they require scrubbing and refinishing? A fully carpeted office building will take one-half to one-third of the time to maintain than a completely tiled one will. A tiled floor is more costly to maintain because it requires more labor and more chemicals to keep it clean and polished. Another time-consuming task is cleaning glass surfaces. The more you have to clean, the longer it will take.

You also need to consider how crowded the area is. The more crowded it is, the longer it will take to clean. Scrubbing and polishing an empty ballroom floor will take much less time than cleaning an average office with the same floor space. Along with how much furniture is in the rooms, take a look at the amount of clutter. The greater the clutter on desktops, filing cabinets, window ledges, coffee tables, counters, bookcases, etc., the more time it will take to dust, because you must move these items to clean both the item itself and the surface it's on.

Smart Tip

Tip...

When putting together a bid, don't use the phrase "as needed" when describing task frequencies. Be specific about when various tasks are needed and what criteria are used to determine the need.

Confirm whether cleaning windows and window shades will be included in your contract. If so, calculate the dimensions of the windows and consider the accessibility from both sides. Window cleaning can be time-consuming; you may want to avoid this task or subcontract it to a specialist.

Once you've surveyed the premises, the next step is to map out specific jobs, deciding which tasks each worker or subcontractor will perform. Determine as best you can the time it will take to do the work, and don't forget the time needed to set up your equipment and supplies, and to put things away. If you plan to supervise or do part of the work yourself, be sure to include your time as part of the labor cost in your final estimate.

When you've figured out the number of hours required for your personnel to do their jobs according to the customer's specifications, you can calculate labor costs. If you're bidding on a job that calls for a monthly fee, figure the number of hours each worker will work in a month. If the job needs to be done five times a week, figure 21 workdays in a month. If it's to be done three times a week, figure 13 workdays in a month. Then multiply the wage rate for each worker by the number of hours you schedule for the job.

Next, calculate the cost of supplies. If you don't have actual cost records, estimate your supplies cost as a percentage of labor. Later, as you do more business and develop records, you can prepare estimates based on actual costs. This process is explained in detail in Chapter 9.

There are times when it will be to your advantage to offer premium or reduced pricing. When a customer wants immediate results and requests extended hours or more services, charging extra is reasonable and should be expected. (If the customer thinks you should provide these extra services for free, you need to consider whether this is a customer you really want to have.)

A long-term project with its accompanying long-term income or projects that may lead to lucrative follow-up business may warrant discounts. In such cases, you can consider a discount as an investment or even as part of your marketing costs.

Be sure you have a sound reason for any deviation from your normal pricing structure. If you arbitrarily decrease your rate, clients may believe you were overcharging them in the first place. When you give a discount, be sure your client understands that you have made a well-thought-out business decision and that you expect a return on your decision.

Be Prepared to Answer Questions

Purchasers of janitorial services are usually professional buyers who are accustomed to negotiating commercial product and service contracts. You'll impress them if you're prepared to provide the following information about your company:

- *How long you've been in business.* When you're new, emphasize the preparation and planning that has gone into developing your operation. If you have experience working for another cleaning company, stress that as well.
- *Training program.* Explain how you and your employees are trained to deliver top-notch service. If you have specific certification areas, such as in blood-borne pathogens, be sure to point that out.
- *Insurance.* Provide proof of liability insurance, workers' compensation coverage, and bonding.
- *Customer support.* Describe your support program, including whom the customer can contact with questions or problems, and what hours you're available.
- *Billing.* Explain your billing policies and procedures. Most commercial clients prefer paying monthly.
- *Equipment and materials.* Describe the modern equipment and quality cleaning products you provide that help your customers maintain their company image.
- *Supplies.* Discuss your program of providing disposable supplies such as paper towels, toilet tissue and seat covers, hand soap, plastic trash liners, etc. Be sure your pricing in this area is competitive.

Beware!
Workers' perform-ance often deterio-rates after 6 to 12 months on the job. At this point, employees may either quit or need increased supervision.

- *Security.* Describe the measures you employ to assure your customers that you're responsible and can be trusted with keys and access to their premises after hours.
- *Attire and company identification.* Explain your uniform and employee identification program.
- *References.* Provide a client list and contact information so prospective customers can verify your service history and integrity.

Cash Flow Issue

Unlike many other types of cleaning businesses, janitorial services typically don't generate immediate cash flow. It will probably be at least 60 days or longer before you can write your first paycheck to yourself. You may get some one-time jobs like cleaning vacant homes, offices, or apartments for cash payment, but your most important source of income will be facilities you clean on a regular basis. You won't be paid for this work in cash. Some customers will pay on the 10th of the following month to earn a discount, while others will take the full 30 days to pay. You can expect to wait 45 to 50 days after signing your first big contract before receiving any money. This is why your startup capital needs to include enough funds to operate for at least the first quarter while you wait to start generating revenue.

If you start with insufficient cash on hand, you'll have a serious problem financing big accounts. You can't afford to bid on large jobs until you have the equivalent of at least two months' gross income from such a job in the bank so you can cover the labor costs for 60 days.

And unless you have an abundance of startup capital, you'll need to put every penny you possibly can back into your business to finance growth during your first critical year. You'll also work long hours, bidding during the day and supervising employees and even cleaning in the evening and on weekends.

Security

Because most janitorial cleaning crews work at night, you have some security concerns that other types of cleaning businesses don't. You must take the necessary steps to provide a safe environment for your employees and to protect your equipment.

If you transport equipment in your vehicle, always park in a well-lighted area, and keep the automobile doors locked at all times, except when you're loading and unloading equipment and supplies. Consider installing an alarm on your vehicle; it will provide an additional level of security and may also earn you a discount on your insurance.

Do you keep your equipment in your home or garage? You may want to invest in a security system to prevent theft or vandalism. If you rent a mini-storage facility to store equipment and supplies, you probably won't be permitted to use a security alarm for your unit. However, most storage facilities have a gate with restricted access for their customers. Keep a sturdy lock on the door of your unit. Also, confirm with your insurance agent that the contents are covered.

If you have a commercial office where you keep your equipment, investigate your area's crime history to determine the measures you need to take. Many commercial offices and storefronts have alarm systems already installed and included in the rental price. Most local police departments' crime prevention officers or community relations boards will provide you with information on the crime statistics in your area and prevention information.

Since your employees will often be arriving and/or leaving in the dark, be sure your parking facility is well-lighted, and establish a policy that employees must enter and leave the building in pairs.

Estimate Form

Date:

Estimator:

Referral source: Newspaper ad   Yellow Pages   Website   Other

Customer name:

Address:

Phone: Emergency number:

Service preferred: Daily   Weekly   Monthly   Other

Days/hours preferred:

Date services begin:

Location of keys:

Location of fuse boxes:

Customer preferences:

Carpets vacuumed:	Yes	No	Later (specify)
Windows cleaned:	Yes	No	Later (specify)
Walls washed:	Yes	No	Later (specify)
Floors stripped/waxed:	Yes	No	Later (specify)

Additional comments: Tasks/room(s)/frequency

Estimated time: Rate:

Total:

Proposal Form

Proposal submitted to: Date:

Address:

Job name and location:

Job phone:

We hereby submit specifications and estimates subject to all terms and conditions as set forth below.

We hereby propose to furnish material and labor in accordance with above specifications for the sum of $ _____ (_____ dollars).

Note:
This proposal may be withdrawn by us if not accepted within _____ days.

Authorized signature:

Accepted: The above prices, specifications, and conditions are satisfactory and are hereby accepted. You are authorized to do the work as specified. Payment will be made as outlined above.

Signature: _____ Date: _____

Signature: _____ Date: _____

5

Carpet and Upholstery Cleaning Services

Fifty years ago, most homes had hardwood floors and commercial establishments had tile floors. Today, you're likely to find wall-to-wall carpeting in every room of the house, often even in bathrooms and kitchens. Businesses do everything with carpet but line the walls—and a few (some would say misguided) decorators have even done that. The on-location

▲

carpet cleaning industry was born because removing wall-to-wall carpet to clean it is highly impractical.

It's important to recognize that there has been a shift among consumers to alternative floor coverings. About 63 percent of floors are covered with carpets; the remainder are such materials as laminates, ceramic tile, stone, and hardwood. Even so, there's still a clear opportunity for carpet cleaning services, especially those that are diversified and clean area rugs, upholstery, and those alternative floor coverings.

Most carpet cleaning services start as homebased businesses. As you grow, you may choose to move into a commercial location, but many highly profitable carpet cleaners never move out of their homes.

"This is a business that the average guy can really do without an enormous amount of education or expense," says Mike Blair, who owns AAA Prestige Carpet Care, a carpet and upholstery cleaning business in St. George, Utah. "It isn't for everybody. It's a physically and emotionally demanding business. You do it all when you're starting; you're the chief cook and bottle washer. But it's profitable enough."

Who Are Your Customers?

Every homeowner and business owner with installed carpeting and/or upholstered furniture is a prospective customer. Targeting a residential market will mean less in the way of startup costs and equipment since businesses typically require more than just having their carpets cleaned (you'll need more equipment to service them). However, because of the wide range of commercial businesses that use carpet and upholstery cleaning services, this is a lucrative market that is worth pursuing. Commercial operations that use carpet and upholstery cleaners include apartment buildings and condos, offices, schools, banks, restaurants, hotels, churches, bowling alleys, transportation terminals, and more.

Who Are Your Competitors?

Of course, you'll be competing against all the other carpet and upholstery cleaners in your area who target the same markets, but there are other sources of competition you need to be aware of.

Many commercial accounts prefer to contract with a janitorial service for their carpet cleaning and other miscellaneous cleaning jobs; it's easier for them to have a single source for these types of services. You need to convince these prospects that as a specialist, you'll do a better job. Or find out who their janitorial service is and work out a subcontracting deal with the service.

In the residential market, your primary competition (besides other carpet and upholstery cleaning services) will be the do-it-yourselfers. This includes people who rent carpet cleaning machines from local supermarkets, people who buy their own machines, and people who use spray-on-and-vacuum carpet cleaning products available in supermarkets and retail stores. One carpet cleaning service owner in Florida says that many of those spray-on products are the best sources of business he has, because they're often not used properly, don't generate the results people want, and may even leave carpets looking worse—which means he gets the call to do the job right.

Equipment

You have a wide range of choices when it comes to carpet cleaning and auxiliary equipment, and it could take you months to research them all. The following information should save you some time, but it's not a substitute for doing your homework and finding out what's on the market and how it works.

It's a good idea to avoid the older type of rotary-brush carpet cleaning machine. This is typically what's available for consumers to rent at retail stores. This type of machine is available in both consumer and commercial sizes, but even the large machines do an amateurish job—and therein lies the reason on-location carpet and upholstery cleaning businesses are booming. If homeowners and building superintendents were happy with poor results, they could hire any kid on the block to do their carpets and/or upholstery with a rented machine.

However, there's a demand for quality work—and if you provide it, you'll have a customer who will call you again and again. But you can't provide a better result than customers can achieve themselves if you don't use better equipment, and in most cases that means using commercial-grade machines.

Equipment manufacturers offer a wide range of styles and features with an equally wide range of prices and payment terms. Consider issues such as versatility—is the machine multi-functional (can it do more than just clean carpets?), and if so, what will you need in the way

> **Tip...**
>
> **Smart Tip**
> Keep your back in mind when shopping for equipment. Look for tools and designs that reduce the stress on your back so you can work longer hours and be less tired at the end of the day.

of accessories? What sort of warranty does the manufacturer provide? What about service contracts, training, and other support issues? Also, keep in mind that whether you choose truck-mounted or portable equipment, each of your service vehicles will need a carpet cleaning machine.

Initial Equipment and Supply Checklist

❑ Carpet cleaners
❑ Carpet cleaning machine (truck-mounted unit)
❑ Carrying case for accessories
❑ Emulsifiers
❑ Groomers
❑ Horsehair brushes (for upholstery)

❑ Miscellaneous
❑ Pile brushes
❑ Pre-spray and fabric protector
❑ Signage
❑ Spotting brushes
❑ Utility brushes
❑ Wall cleaning machine

Before you can decide what type and brand of equipment is most appropriate for your business, you need to determine which cleaning methods you want to offer. Let's look at your options.

Cleaning Methods

Each system has its own merits, and the industry itself is divided over which is the "best"—wet shampooing, steam cleaning (which uses hot water extraction), or chemical dry cleaning, often followed by application of a fabric protector such as Teflon. Blair uses a combination of steam and chemical dry cleaning methods, depending on the circumstances and needs of the customer.

Upholstery can be dry-cleaned or shampooed, depending on the fiber content, using the same equipment you use for carpet cleaning, with some additional attachments, which, among other things, help guard against over-wetting. Or you can opt to purchase machines specifically designed for upholstery and drapery cleaning. As you do with carpet, follow upholstery cleaning by treating the furniture with a fabric protector to prevent future stains.

For carpets, use a pile brush to remove loose soil and precondition the carpet pile. Then use a high-powered vacuum for further soil removal, followed by one of these three methods:

Smart Tip

Take advantage of all the services your equipment vendors offer. Equipment manufacturers want their customers to be satisfied, and most will work with you as you learn their equipment. They usually provide training in the form of classes and seminars, both when you first purchase the equipment and later, as you hire new people. They'll also help if you encounter problems.

1. *Wet shampooing.* At one time, the rotary scrubber was the most popular cleaning apparatus. But if it did a good job, your business opportunities would be seriously reduced because, as we have already mentioned, rotary scrubbers are commonly available to rent at retail stores. These machines apply detergent solutions to the carpet by rotating brushes that ostensibly work on the top carpet fibers to prevent wetting the bottom of the carpet. A wet pickup extractor is then used to remove excess moisture and soil. Critics claim the agitation by the brushes loosens the surface soil but then drives it deep into the pile backing, and the soil later works its way back to the surface. Also, despite the extraction process, it can take a wet-shampooed carpet up to five days to dry, which is a major inconvenience to consumers. Other cleaning methods have made wet shampooing outdated.

2. *Steam cleaning.* The term "steam cleaning" is a misnomer because the process doesn't use steam. Steam applied to a carpet could damage some materials because of the high temperatures involved, or it might cause shrinkage.

   What's often called "steam cleaning" is actually a hot water extraction process, which involves the application of a detergent by a spray-on method, employing water heated to approximately 150 degrees. The hot solution is forced into the pile through controlled jet streams and immediately removed by a powerful vacuum. The process is also known as "deep soil extraction."

   This method of steam extraction is commonly used on residential pile carpets. The criticism that shrinkage is a factor only becomes a problem if a nonprofessional overwets the carpet. Even so, the quality of the results depends on the skill of the technician.

   Critics claim that when cleaning a carpet with heavy traffic patterns laden with dirt, such as those in offices, the steam process is insufficient, so shampooing is recommended. They also claim that steam extraction is more of a "wet" steam method; the carpet pile becomes saturated, and the washed-down soil works its way back to resoil the surface. After a steam cleaning, it typically takes from two to four hours (and sometimes up to six hours) for carpet to dry. Blair believes this method provides the best overall results of all the carpet cleaning methods.

3. *Chemical dry cleaning.* The name may give the impression that no moisture is used in this method, but that's not the case. The carpet is sprayed with a carbonated

Beware!
The average carpet cleaner will burn out in five years, says St. George, Utah, carpet and upholstery cleaning entrepreneur Mike Blair. The most common reason is failing to hire appropriate support staff as it becomes necessary. Another reason is not buying the right kind of equipment.

▲

More than Carpet

Most carpet cleaning services do more than clean carpets. They also might offer:

- ○ Application of a fabric protector on carpet and upholstery
- ○ Carpet dyeing
- ○ Carpet restoration
- ○ Ceiling cleaning
- ○ Cleaning and restoration of other flooring materials, including tile, laminate, stone, and hardwood
- ○ Drapery cleaning
- ○ Flame-retardant treatment for drapes and upholstery
- ○ Odor control
- ○ Smoke damage cleanup and fire restoration
- ○ Spot and stain removal from upholstery
- ○ Upholstery cleaning
- ○ Wall cleaning
- ○ Water damage restoration

chemical that breaks down the soil, then buffed with a pad to pick up the dirt. Surface soil is removed, but if the vacuum is too weak, the sand and grit that grinds down the fibers remains, thus decreasing the life of the carpet. Critics of this method claim that while the carpet may appear cleaner, the dirt actually becomes smeared through the fibers, and most of it remains deep in the carpet. Many experts recommend that chemical dry cleaning be used only on an intermediate basis—in other words, between steam cleanings.

Chemicals

As wide as your selection for equipment is, your range of choices for solvents and cleaners is even greater. A good way to educate yourself in this area is to visit a local supplier where you can learn about the different types of chemicals available for cleaning carpets, draperies, upholstery, ceilings, walls, etc.

What you purchase depends on what you need to accomplish. There are spotters, liquid and powdered cleaners, sanitizers, stain-resistant coatings, concentrates, wrinkle removers (for drapery cleaning), deodorizers, anti-static protectors, and more.

With today's concern for the environment, many of these chemicals are supposedly nontoxic and/or biodegradable. The toxicity of chemicals and solvents can only be determined by visiting the supplier's warehouse and scrutinizing container labels. Many operators claim to use nontoxic chemicals, but the only way to be sure is to check with the Occupational Safety & Health Administration (OSHA). Most state laws require that every business or service possess a material safety data sheet (MSDS) that spells out the contents and level of toxicity (or nontoxicity) of each chemical agent used. Ask your supplier for copies of the MSDS for each product you're considering purchasing.

> **Bright Idea**
>
> Offer to clean the carpet at your place of worship at no charge for the opportunity to demonstrate the quality of your work. Be sure the arrangement includes displaying a flier or other information about your service in the building, and perhaps even an announcement in the newsletter.

Your chemicals and cleaning solutions will account for the majority of your inventory requirements, and you don't need to keep large quantities on hand. You can buy what you need to meet your customers' demands and avoid tying up your cash in excess inventory.

Larger carpet cleaning companies or those with multiple outlets or franchises typically keep a large inventory of cleaning supplies in storage at a central location. This allows them to take advantage of volume price breaks because their consumption rate justifies the investment in inventory and storage facilities. But this isn't the best strategy for a small startup operation.

In the beginning, buy your cleaning supplies in small amounts of about a gallon or so, and keep them in their original containers with the labels affixed. Depending on the type of equipment you have, you'll need different chemical compounds and solvents, such as special solvents for removing spots and stains. Your supplier can advise you on the types of solvents needed for removing specific kinds of stains.

Your initial supply, including the necessary brushes and applicators, should cost no more than a low of $500 to a high of $1,500.

Carpet Cleaning Basics

A great way to find out how to run your business in a way that will generate plenty of loyal, satisfied customers is to talk to people who have used carpet cleaning services.

Find out what they liked and didn't like, what made them happy and what caused dissatisfaction. Then use that information when formulating your operating procedures.

Some of the most common complaints:

- *Carpets taking too long to dry.* Customers don't mind waiting three or four hours for carpets to dry, but three or four days is too long.
- *Carpets not drying when promised.* Customers see this as a broken promise, and it makes them distrust you in the future. If you tell customers the carpets will be dry in a certain time, be sure they will.
- *Carpets still dirty after cleaning.* Inspect each job carefully to be sure you've gotten the carpets as clean as possible.

When the Damage Is Done

In addition to basic cleaning, many carpet cleaning services also do water damage restoration. Though the volume of this type of work is hard to predict, it can be lucrative and could help even out your workload during the year. And since you already have the ability to remove water from carpets, it's relatively easy to add this service to your business.

To offer water damage restoration, you must remove the water (which typically comes from a flood or a plumbing leak), dry the carpet with fans, and apply appropriate chemical compounds to sanitize and remove odors. St. George, Utah, carpet and upholstery cleaner Mike Blair recommends taking classes in the process before you begin marketing the service.

"Water damage restoration is a higher profit area that will sustain many carpet cleaners through the lean months of the winter and throughout the rest of the year," says Blair. "It's less competitive, meaning that it's a better-paid service, than a typical carpet cleaning business, which is very competitive."

Of course, there are reasons this service pays better than basic carpet cleaning. Water damage doesn't always happen during normal business hours, so you may be called out in the middle of the night to handle a job. The work can sometimes be dangerous; you'll risk exposure to molds, mildew, and potentially dangerous fungi. Also, combining water and electricity—which is necessary to get the work done—offers the potential for shocks.

Another profit center is in the rental of drying equipment, Blair says. Once you've done the primary water removal, you'll set up fans to blow the area dry, and you can charge for the use of that equipment.

- *Carpets not looking better after a professional cleaning.* Many do-it-yourselfers will hire a professional carpet cleaner expecting better results than they get from their own efforts. With your equipment and skill, you should be able to accomplish this.

- *Unprofessional service people.* Customers who are impressed with your sales presentation will be very distressed if your service technicians don't live up to your promises of professionalism and quality.

Stat Fact
In 2007 (the latest stats available), U.S. carpet manufacturers shipped 1.6 billion square yards of carpet (14.4 billion square feet), up from 97 million square yards in 1950, according to the Carpet and Rug Institute.

So what can you do to make sure your customers are satisfied and that they'll call you again and refer you to others?

- *Learn about carpet cleaning.* Cleaning a carpet isn't an exact science, and there's no one-size-fits-all formula that will work in every situation. Various materials require the use of different types of detergents, and different types of dirt and stains need different treatments. Your equipment manufacturer should provide you with guidelines that address just about every cleaning situation you'll encounter.

  Keep in mind that the companies that make carpet cleaning machines work closely with carpet manufacturers and will always be current on technological innovations, new carpeting materials, and improvements in the industry. They can keep you up-to-date on these matters. Most also offer training for you and your employees at either no charge or a nominal fee; your primary cost will be transportation to the training and lodging (if necessary), and it's well worth the investment.

- *Supervise your employees.* Don't just hire service technicians and turn them loose immediately to work on their own. Be sure they're trained and then accompany them on their jobs for at least the first few weeks (until you're certain they really know their jobs and can deal with both routine and unexpected situations). Then periodically drop in on a job in progress and follow up with your customers to be sure your service personnel are maintaining a high level of performance.

Smart Tip
Take your vacuum and solution hoses to the furthest point in the house; then work backward toward the entry. Don't pull hoses around corners; doing so could damage wallpaper and woodwork.

- *Estimate carefully.* This takes more time in the beginning, but it's critical that your estimates be accurate. When you overestimate, you'll lose jobs to your competition; when you underestimate, you'll either lose money on the job or you'll irritate customers when you present a bill for more than you said it would cost. (See Chapter 9 for an explanation of how to set your prices.)

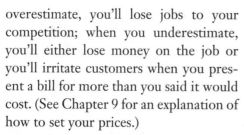

Smart Tip

Use caution signs where needed and warn customers that smooth surfaces may be slippery after cleaning.

- *Avoid high-pressure sales tactics.* Try to close the sale on the first call, but don't use high-pressure techniques. If your prospect hesitates and says he wants to shop around, don't immediately lower your price. Instead, call back in a day or two and ask if a decision has been made. You shouldn't have to pressure your customers or cut prices if your rates are competitive; you've made an accurate estimate and you did a good job of selling your superior service on your first contact. Consumers tend to be impressed by an honest salesperson who's easy to decline, rather than having someone shove the sale down their throat. In the end, even if you don't get a sale, you'll have a better reputation—and you may get the call the next time.

Carpet Cleaning Specifics

Specific aspects of your operation will be determined by which type of cleaning you decide to do, which chemicals suit that particular cleaning method, whether you want to charge for moving furniture, if you give estimates over the phone or in person, etc. However, you can still follow a basic planned procedure in conducting your operation, from the customer's initial call to collecting your final payment.

Handling the Initial Service Request

When a new customer calls for an estimate, their first question is likely to be about price. They'll also want plenty of other information, such as whether you'll move furniture, how long it will take for the carpet to dry, and if you can handle special situations, such as pet stains and odors. Give honest, complete answers and stress why your cleaning methods are superior. If the customer fails to ask questions most people ask, volunteer the information anyway.

Visiting the Customer's Home

If you can't avoid giving an estimate over the phone and the customer commits to the sale during the call, set an appointment for the work to be done. If you're going

Good News Travels Fast

Once you're up and running, the major portion of your business will come from referrals and repeat customers, so pleasing your clients with quality work and top-notch service is critical. St. George, Utah, carpet and upholstery cleaner Mike Blair says 85 percent of his business comes from existing customers and referrals. "We have worked hard to establish a reputation for reliability in the community with property managers, realtors, homeowners, commercial establishments, and insurance professionals so that they call us and refer us," he says.

Because so much of your carpet cleaning business will come from referrals, be sure you market to people who can refer customers to you. Blair says one of the most effective marketing techniques he has used is to work with retail carpet salespeople. He gives them a demonstration of his cleaning skill, either in their showrooms or in their homes. "When they see the quality of our work, they are comfortable referring us to their clientele," he says. "Most of the carpet suppliers in town refer cleaning to us, and we work hard to keep that relationship alive." He also maintains relationships with residential and commercial property management companies, which can both use his services in the properties they manage, as well as refer other customers to him.

out to do the estimate in person, set an appointment that's convenient for the customer with the understanding that if the estimate is acceptable, you'll be prepared to do the work at that time.

When you arrive at the home, calculate the square footage of the areas to be cleaned. Check for especially soiled areas that may need extra pre-spotting and/or conditioning. If you think certain areas will need extra work and, as a result, will cost more to clean, be honest about it upfront. Your customer will greatly appreciate knowing this before, rather than after, the bill is written up.

Writing the Invoice

On the invoice (or service order), list the specific tasks you'll perform, as well as each room and its dimensions. If you have to pre-spot and specially treat any areas, note this.

Smart Tip *Tip...*
Remind customers that you have to leave the door slightly open so they'll be sure to supervise small children or confine their pets.

Next to each task, list the price; then total the charges. Have the customer sign and date the invoice before you start to work.

Your invoice should also include the estimate date, job date, day of the week, what time the job is to be performed, a job number, and the customer's address and telephone numbers (home and work). Make this task easy on yourself: Use the "Service Order/Invoice Worksheet" on the next page.

Performing the Service

With the paperwork done, you're ready to begin the job. First, move whatever furniture you need to and have agreed to. Do any pre-treating and conditioning. Then shampoo the carpet following the equipment manufacturer's instructions.

After cleaning, carefully put the furniture back. Use foam blocks or some other shield to protect wood pieces from damp carpet. Tell the customer how long it will take for the carpet to dry; suggest that they keep fans and/or air conditioning units on to help speed the process. You may want to invest in a dryer as an additional service to your customers. Collect payment under the terms you agreed on when you made the estimate (cash, check, or credit card). Note the payment on the invoice and give the customer a copy. You may want to give the customer some advice on caring for their carpet, and tell them you'll be in touch in about six months to schedule their next cleaning.

> **Tip...**
>
> **Smart Tip**
> Place a furniture pad under your hoses when they're stretched across wood and tile floors to prevent scratches from the couplers.

Furniture Cleaning Specifics

A significant percentage of people who are having their carpets cleaned want their upholstered furniture cleaned at the same time. Most carpet cleaning systems include tools for cleaning upholstery, but it's important that you understand the intricacies involved before you provide this additional service.

Inspecting Furniture Before Giving an Estimate

You need to determine the overall condition of the furniture and the best cleaning method to use. Ask if the piece has ever been professionally cleaned and, if so, when and how. Also ask if the customer has ever done any spot cleaning, and have them show you the areas involved. Find out how old the piece is, what the material is made of, and if it has ever been reupholstered.

Service Order/Invoice Worksheet

Customer name: _____

Primary contact: _____

Address: _____

City: _____ State: _____ Zip: _____

Phone: (home) _____ (work) _____

Date of estimate: _____

Date of work performed: _____

                                   Date   Day   Time

Job number: _____

Areas to be cleaned:

Rooms: _____

Dimensions: _____

Square feet: _____

Total rooms: _____ Total square feet: _____

Work to be done: _____

_____

_____

_____

_____

_____

_____

_____

                                                      Total: _____

Customer signature: _____ Date: _____

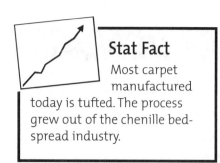

As you inspect the furniture, look for a recommended cleaning label; if it has one, follow those instructions. Note the overall condition of the fabric, check the back and arms for body oils and soil, check skirts and corners for shoe polish and scuff marks, check sides and back for dust or dirt filtration from exposure to air vents, examine heavily used areas for fabric fraying or thinness due to wear, look at both sides of cushions for stains or spots that may require special attention, unzip cushion covers and check the foam material inside for ink or marker that may have bled through. In homes with pets, look for pet oils, hair, and other stains. Confirm the sturdiness of all legs before moving the piece. Pretest to determine color-fastness and shrinkage risk.

Writing Your Estimate

Make notes on your invoice or work order of all problem areas, such as loose buttons, tears, holes, burns, shaky legs, and stains, and bring these imperfections to the customer's attention. Calculate your estimate, based on the cost of labor, supplies, overhead, and desired profit, and present it to the customer. See Chapter 9 for general price ranges of items you're likely to be cleaning. Before you begin, have the customer sign the work order, acknowledging that they're aware of the condition of the furniture.

Cleaning Furniture

Generally speaking, you should follow the furniture manufacturer's cleaning instructions, which are usually listed on a tag attached to the item. If there's no tag, use the procedures recommended by the equipment and chemical manufacturers.

Position the furniture toward the center of the room, away from walls and other furniture, and on pads to prevent overspray on floors, carpets, and other pieces. Most upholstered furniture can be wet-cleaned. In that case, begin by vacuuming to remove loose dirt and debris. Pre-spray and brush with a nylon brush to loosen embedded dirt; then clean. After cleaning, use a thick towel to wipe down furniture to remove residues and quicken the drying time. Wipe off any exposed wood. Arrange cushions on brown paper for drying, and be sure they're not touching each other.

If you're dry-cleaning furniture and drapes, be sure the area where you're cleaning is well-ventilated. Use the same procedure for positioning and preparing furniture; then follow the chemical manufacturer's cleaning recommendations.

Cleaning Drapes

As you do with furniture, reinspect drapes for spots or damage and bring those details to your customer's attention before you begin cleaning. Dust the surrounding areas; then vacuum drapes thoroughly, paying special attention to pleats or other areas where dust or dirt may have collected. Use a drapery board to prevent overspray on walls and windows. Take care to remove all solvent when finished; then towel the pleats to remove any remaining soil and help set and realign the pleats. Lined drapes may be cleaned on both sides; if you do this, adjust your price accordingly.

Other Cleaning Businesses

W e've discussed the most common
cleaning services, but there are many more niche cleaning
businesses you may want to consider, either as stand-alone
operations or as companion businesses to your primary cleaning company. This chapter is designed more as an introduction
to these specialty services rather than a comprehensive guide

to actually providing them. They all require varying levels of training, skill, and equipment, and you'll need to do additional research on the areas that interest you. On top of the information here, there are resources in the Appendix that can help you with more data.

Smart Tip

To tell which side of the window a streak is on, pull the squeegee down when you're cleaning the outside of the window and across when you're working on the inside. The direction of the streak will tell you which side it's on.

Window Cleaning

While some residential cleaning and janitorial services clean windows as part of their service, windows are a cleaning industry specialty. If you like working outside and you don't mind heights, window cleaning could be the perfect opportunity.

Some window cleaners charge by the pane (a piece of glass framed on all sides by wood or metal)—typically $2 to $7 each. Others charge by the job, using an hourly labor rate of $20 to $25 (and in some areas, up to $70 per hour) to calculate their fees.

Let It Shine

The basic equipment and supplies you need to get started in the window cleaning business include:

- ○ Bucket with handle
- ○ Cleaning agents
- ○ Extension ladder
- ○ Extension pole
- ○ Scrapers and spare blades
- ○ Soft, lint-free cloths (chamois)
- ○ Sponges
- ○ Squeegees
- ○ Tool belt or holster
- ○ Towels

If you're doing window cleaning as part of new construction cleanup, you'll need a vacuum cleaner to clean dirt and debris from the window tracks

Window cleaning is more than just removing dirt. Windows often have tape or glue on them, or they've been painted over completely to block out light. In the case of the latter, test-clean a small part of the window to see how difficult the job will be before you quote a price.

It's a good idea to start your window cleaning service by targeting one- and two-story office buildings, storefronts, and homes. As you become established and your skill level increases, you can expand to taller buildings. High-rise window cleaning requires an extra level of skill to ensure the health and safety of above-ground workers. You'll need a controlled descent system for access to exterior high-rise windows. There are a variety of excellent systems on the market; never purchase and use any system without thorough training by the manufacturer.

Disaster Cleaning and Restoration

Many carpet cleaning and janitorial service companies do disaster cleaning and restoration for their customers, but this is a specialty area in its own right. You'll need special knowledge in fire, water, and smoke damage cleaning and restoration that's beyond the scope of this book.

Once you're trained, you can work with insurance adjusters and other contractors to provide all or part of the services needed. The Association of Specialists in Cleaning and Restoration (see Appendix for contact information) offers training programs to help you develop the expertise necessary to provide this service.

Blind Cleaning

Mini-blinds aren't as trendy as they once were, but they are still common fixtures in homes and offices. Venetian blinds have enjoyed a resurgence in popularity, and many consumers are choosing interior shutters as window treatments. Along with vertical blinds and pleated shades, all these window coverings attract dust and need frequent cleaning—and the occasional pass with a feather duster isn't enough to keep them looking their best.

Without the proper equipment, cleaning blinds can be time-consuming and labor-intensive. Special blind-cleaning equipment (see this book's Appendix for equipment sources) can

Smart Tip

Tip...

After cleaning a window, seal it with protectants to prevent repeat staining and to make the next cleaning easier.

▲

Safety First

No matter what type of cleaning you're doing, always take proper safety precautions. For example, protect eyes from accidental splashes of harmful chemicals by wearing glasses or goggles. When working with acids, wear acid-resistant gloves. When working on construction sites or cleaning building exteriors, hard hats may be appropriate. The Occupational Safety & Health Administration (OSHA) can help you take the proper steps to create a safe working environment for yourself and your employees.

---

speed up the labor process and allow you to offer this service at an affordable price. You'll need to learn how to quickly and efficiently take down and rehang blinds, as well as operate your equipment.

As window coverings, blinds outnumber drapes 5-to-1, which means the need for blind cleaning is strong and likely to continue to grow.

Pressure Washing

Pressure washing can be added to an existing cleaning business or operated as an independent company for a modest initial investment. Some of the more common uses of pressure washing equipment include cleaning and maintenance of residential and commercial buildings, walkways, parking lots, heavy equipment and vehicles, truck and automobile fleets, trailers, engines, warehouse floors, machinery, kitchen areas, and sanitary areas.

Restroom Cleaning

Particularly in large public buildings, sports stadiums and arenas, and schools, there's a tremendous need for restroom cleaning, and companies that specialize in this work are busy and profitable. Businesses want to provide clean, pleasant, fresh-smelling restrooms for their employees and customers, and they're willing to hire specialists to get the results they need.

You'll clean and sanitize restrooms on a regular schedule and stock the facilities with soap and paper supplies as requested by your customers. You may work directly for the property owner or manager, or you may subcontract through a janitorial service.

Chimney Sweeping

Few things are more appealing to the senses than a crackling fire on a cold winter night. Even with central heat, many people still use their fireplaces. This means the chimneys need to be cleaned. The demand for chimney sweeping goes beyond residential fireplaces. The

Smart Tip

Tip...

When preparing your window-washing solution, add a few drops of cleaning solution to your bucket after you've filled it with water. Adding too much solution, or adding it before you fill the bucket, will create piles of suds, which inhibit quality work.

chimney sweep—or chimney service professional—aids in the prevention of fires, carbon monoxide intrusion, and other chimney-related hazards that can be caused by fireplaces; wood stoves; gas, oil, and coal heating systems; and the chimneys that serve them.

The basic task of a chimney sweep is to clean chimneys. That process includes removing the hazard of accumulated and highly combustible creosote produced by burning wood and wood products, eliminating the buildup of soot in coal- and oil-fired systems, and getting rid of bird and animal nests, leaves, and other debris that may create a hazard by blocking the flow of emissions from a home-heating appliance. Though the highest demand for chimney sweeps is in cold-climate regions, this is a service that's needed throughout the country. You should enjoy working outside and be comfortable with heights, because you'll spend a lot of time on roofs.

Beware!
New ladders include instructions for safe use. No matter how tempting it may be to take a shortcut, always follow the manufacturer's directions.

In addition to cleaning, chimney sweep services may also offer repairs and parts such as chimney caps that protect the chimney from water, leaves, debris, and animal intrusion. A chimney sweep's customer base is both residential and commercial. Training and certification are available through the Chimney Safety Institute of America (see the Appendix for contact information).

Ceiling and Wall Cleaning

Ceilings and walls trap odors, smoke, oils, cooking grease, films, nicotine, dust mites, and many more unsanitary pollutants. These contaminants can reduce light by

The Stain Game

Because window stains can have a variety of causes, they require different cleaning approaches. Here are some common problems window cleaners encounter; to tackle them, talk to your window cleaning chemical supplier and ask for the most appropriate product.

O *Everyday grime.* Windows are subject to exterior climatic conditions such as pollution, acid rain, and automobile exhaust. Inside, they can be abused by smoking, office equipment emissions, heating and air conditioning fumes, and fingerprints. To clean these films from transparent glass surfaces, you need a cleaning solution designed to reduce squeegee drag that will not bleed, dry, or streak and is strong enough to remove the dirt and grime.

O *Oxidation.* When metal is exposed to rain and humidity, it gradually deteriorates and causes a process called oxidation. When this occurs near a window, it can penetrate or cling to the glass and is often called etching, hazing, or screen burn. You'll see it most often on windows that are covered by metal screens or surrounded by metal frames.

O *Hard water stains.* When rainwater travels over concrete or precast surfaces, it can carry tiny particles from that surface onto the window. The dried rainwater leaves behind mineral deposits that are difficult to remove. Similar stains result from acid rain and irrigation systems.

O *Overspray.* This occurs in new buildings or when various types of exterior maintenance are done. Typically, windows are stained with paint, glue, tape, caulking, and waterproofing overspray. Cleaning overspray often requires a combination of chemicals and razor scraping.

as much as 60 percent, dull the appearance of a facility, and contribute to an unhealthy environment. Cleaning ceilings and walls is far more cost-effective than painting or replacing them. In fact, replacing a ceiling can cost up to 100 times more than cleaning it, and the replacement process is slow, messy, and extremely inconvenient. Besides being part of standard building maintenance, various ceiling and wall cleaning techniques may also be used in disaster restoration work.

To clean ceilings and walls, you must learn how to work with various porous, nonporous, and semiporous surfaces to remove pollutants without damaging the appearance or function of the surface. Most vendors of ceiling and wall cleaning equipment offer training courses in the proper use of their equipment and chemicals.

Post Death and Trauma Cleaning

Cleaning up after someone has died, whether the death was from natural causes, suicide, or homicide, requires an in-depth understanding of biohazards, a capacity to cope with being regularly confronted with trauma scenes, and a tremendous amount of compassion.

Post death and trauma cleaning services are usually called in after a homicide, suicide, unattended death, or a non-fatal trauma where property has been contaminated by blood or other bodily fluids and tissue. "It's gross. We deal with blood and body fluids, and maggots sometimes," says Benjamin Lichtenwalner, co-founder of Biotrauma Inc. in Gainesville, Georgia. Because of the potential health risks, it's critical that the job be done properly and thoroughly.

An estimated 32,000 suicides and 17,000 homicides occur in the United States each year, leaving behind traumatized survivors and contaminated homes and businesses. In most cases, your clients will be the family of the deceased and you'll be paid by an insurance company. You may also be called to clean up commercial facilities after an accident or crime that has contaminated a property.

To get started, you'll need to make a substantial investment in training, equipment, and supplies. OSHA requires that all workers performing this type of remediation receive the proper training and vaccinations, and be properly equipped with protective gear and cleanup tools. EPA regulations dictate the disposition of hazardous wastes, so you'll need the proper tools and procedures to be in compliance. In addition to cleaning, you may also want to offer repair or replacement of structural components, such as carpet, flooring, cabinets, doors, and walls.

Developing Your Plan

Some entrepreneurs would rather walk on hot coals than sit down and write a business plan. Other would-be business owners get so caught up in planning every detail that they never get their businesses off the ground. You need to find a happy medium between these extremes.

Begin your venture with a written business plan. Writing your plans down forces you to think them through and gives you a chance to examine them for consistency and thoroughness. Whether you've got years of cleaning service experience behind you or you're a novice in the industry, you need a plan for your business. This chapter will focus on a few issues particular to planning cleaning service businesses, but they are by no means all you need to consider when writing your plan.

If you're excited about your business, creating a business plan should be an exciting process. It will help you define and evaluate the overall feasibility of your concept, clarify your goals, and determine what you'll need for startup and long-term operations.

> **Bright Idea**
>
> Update your business plan every year. Choose an annual date when you sit down with your plan, compare how closely your actual operation and results mirrored your forecasts, and decide if your plans for the coming year need adjusting. You'll also need to make your financial forecasts for the coming year based on current and expected market conditions.

This is a living, breathing document that will provide you with a road map for your company. You'll use it as a guide, referring to it regularly as you work through the startup process and during the ongoing operation of your business. And if you're going to be seeking outside financing, either in the form of loans or investors, your business plan will be the tool that convinces funding sources of your venture's worth.

Putting together a business plan isn't a linear process, although the final product may look that way. As you work through it, you'll likely find yourself jumping from equipment requirements to cash flow forecasts to staffing, then back to cash flow, on to marketing, and back to equipment requirements. Take your time developing your plan; whether you want to start a part-time residential cleaning service or build a major janitorial service, you're making a serious commitment, and you shouldn't rush into it.

Business Plan Elements

Though the specific content of your business plan will be unique, there's a basic format that you should follow. This will ensure that you address all the issues you need to, as well as provide lenders and investors with a document organized in a familiar way. The basic elements are:

- *Front matter*. This includes your cover page, a table of contents, and a statement of purpose.

- *Business description.* Describe the specific cleaning service business you intend to start, and list the reasons you can make it successful. This section should also include your business philosophy, goals, industry analysis, operations, inventory, and startup timetable.

- *Marketing plan.* Include an overview of the market, a description of your potential customers, a discussion of the advantages and drawbacks of your location, an analysis of the competition, and how you plan to promote your specific business.

- *Company organization.* In this section, describe your management structure, your staffing needs and how you expect to meet them, the consultants and advisors who will be assisting you, your legal structure, and the licenses, permits, and other regulatory issues that will affect your operations.

- *Financial data.* This is where you show the source(s) of your startup capital and how you're going to use the money. Include information on real estate, fixtures, equipment, and insurance. You'll also include your financial statements: balance sheet, profit-and-loss statement, break-even analysis, personal financial statements, and personal federal income tax returns.

- *Financial projections.* Take your financial data and project it out to show what your business will do. Include projected income statements for three years, cash flow statements for three years, along with worst-case income and cash flow statements to show what you'll do if your plan doesn't work.

- *Summary.* Bring your plan together in this section. If you're trying to appeal to a funding source, use this section to reiterate the merits of your plan.

- *Appendices.* Use this for supporting documents, such as your facility design and layout, marketing studies, sample advertising, copies of leases, and licensing information.

To Market, To Market

Market research provides businesses with data that allows them to identify and reach particular market segments and to solve or avoid marketing problems. A thorough market survey forms the foundation of any successful business. It would be impossible to develop marketing strategies or an effective product line without market research.

The goal of market research is for you to identify your market, find out where it is, and develop a strategy to communicate with prospective customers in a way that will convince them to buy from you.

Market research will also give you information you need about your competitors. You need to find out what they're doing and how that meets—or doesn't meet—the needs of the market.

One of the most basic elements of effective marketing is differentiating yourself from the competition. One marketing consultant calls it "eliminating the competition." If you set yourself apart because no one else does exactly what you do, then you essentially have no competition. However, before you can differentiate yourself, you first need to understand who your prospective competitors are and why your prospective customers might patronize them.

> ## Smart Tip
>
> **Tip...**
>
> When you think your plan is complete, look at it with a fresh eye. Is it realistic? Does it take into account all the possible variables that could affect your operation? After you're satisfied, ask two or three professional associates you trust to evaluate your plan. Use their input to correct any problems before you invest time and money.

In the case of janitorial and carpet cleaning services, you'll be able to find many of your competitors listed in the Yellow Pages of your local telephone directory. For residential cleaning services, finding out who your competitors are will likely be more challenging since many small independent operators may not have business listings.

However, an increasing number of residential cleaning services of all sizes are creating websites, which you can visit to find out the type of services they offer. Or you can simply call them, posing as a prospective customer, and ask about what they do, how they operate, and how much they charge.

To find out how to differentiate yourself, consider doing a survey of your competitors' customers. If you're starting a cleaning service that has primarily businesses for customers, this won't be a difficult proposition. Identifying customers is pretty easy in this arena. Most office buildings use janitorial services of some sort; call them and ask for the building manager. For businesses, look them up in the phone book and ask if they use a janitorial service. If they say yes, go ahead with the survey.

However, if you own a residential cleaning service, surveying your competition's customers is likely to be quite a bit trickier. You could survey apartment building managers, of course. And you can ask people you know if they use a service.

After you've compiled a list of prospective survey respondents, call them and explain that you're not selling anything but rather are doing a marketing survey of consumers of the particular type of cleaning service you plan to offer. If the customer is a business, ask if the work is handled in-house or contracted with an outside company.

Ask what they like about the service they're using and what they wish that service did differently or better. You may even ask what it would take to persuade them to change companies. Take detailed notes, and use that information to formulate your service package and policies. Knowing what consumers want will help you create a business that's unique in your market. Once you've started your operation, you can sell to the people and companies you surveyed.

Are You on a Mission?

At any given moment, most cleaning service business owners have a clear understanding of the mission of their companies. They know what they are doing, how and where it's being done, and who their customers are. Problems can arise, however, when that mission isn't clearly articulated into a statement, written down, and communicated to others. A mission statement defines what an organization is and why it exists. Writing it down and communicating it to others creates a sense of commonality and a more coherent approach to what you're trying to do.

Even in a very small company, a written mission statement helps everyone involved see the big picture and keeps them focused on the true goals of the business. At a minimum your mission statement should define who your primary customers are, identify the products and services you offer, and describe the geographical location in which you operate. For example, a residential cleaning service's mission statement might read something like this: "To provide customers in single-family homes in the Cobb County area with high-quality, personalized residential cleaning done by a well-trained, trustworthy staff." A janitorial service's mission statement might read: "To serve commercial accounts in the Chicago area by delivering high-quality, professional cleaning services that keep our clients' facilities clean and attractive."

A mission statement should be short—usually just one sentence and certainly no more than two. A good idea is to cap it at 100 words. Anything longer than that isn't a mission statement and will probably confuse your employees. To help you get started on your statement, use the "Mission Statement Worksheet" on page 88.

Once you've articulated your message, communicate it as often as possible to everyone in the company, along with customers and suppliers. Post it on the wall, hold meetings to talk about it, and include a reminder of the statement in employee correspondence.

It's more important to adequately communicate the mission statement to employees than to customers. It's not uncommon for an organization to try to use a mission statement primarily

> **Bright Idea**
> Your business plan should include worst-case scenarios, both for your own benefit and for your funding sources. You'll benefit from thinking ahead about what you'll do if things don't go as you want them to. You'll also increase the comfort level of your lenders and investors by demonstrating your ability to deal with adverse and potentially negative situations.

▲

Mission Statement Worksheet

To develop an effective mission statement, answer these questions:

1. What products and/or services do we produce?_____
    _____
    _____
    _____

2. What geographical location do we operate in? _____
    _____
    _____
    _____

3. Why does my company exist? Whom do we serve? What is our purpose?____
    _____
    _____
    _____

4. What are our strengths, weaknesses, opportunities, and threats? _____
    _____
    _____
    _____
    _____

5. Considering the above, along with our expertise and resources, what business
    should we be in?_____
    _____
    _____
    _____

6. What is important to us? What do we stand for? _____
    _____
    _____
    _____
    _____

for promotion and secondarily to help employees identify what business they're in, but that doesn't work very well. The most effective mission statements are developed strictly for internal communication and discussion. Your mission statement doesn't have to be clever or catchy—just accurate.

Though your mission statement may never win an advertising or creativity award, it can still be an effective customer relations tool. One idea is to print your mission statement on a page, have every employee sign it, and provide every prospective and new customer with a copy. You can even include it on your brochures and invoices.

Finally, make sure your suppliers know what your mission statement is; it will help them serve you better if they understand what you're all about.

Smart Tip

Tip...

Know someone who might be interested in investing in your business? Don't ask them for money right away. Ask them to read your business plan and give you some input. At best, they'll like the plan and offer to invest before you ask; at worst, you'll get some valuable input and they'll let you know they don't want to invest before you have to risk rejection.

Structuring Your Business

There's a lot to do when you start a business. This chapter will address some of the general issues you need to work out as you create an operating infrastructure for your company.

You may be tempted to rush through some of these steps. Don't. Take your time and give yourself a chance to consider all the possible consequences of each decision you make. As anxious as you probably are to get out there and work, taking the time to put together a solid foundation in the beginning will make it easier for you to build and grow in the long run.

Naming Your Company

One of the most important marketing tools you'll ever have is your company's name. A well-chosen name can work hard for you; an ineffective name means you have to work harder at marketing your company.

Your company name should clearly identify what you do in a way that will appeal to your target market. It should be short, catchy, and memorable. It should also be easy to pronounce and spell—people who can't say your company name may use you, but they won't refer anyone else to you.

When Mike Blair formed his carpet and upholstery cleaning company in St. George, Utah, the entire family got involved in the process. "We brainstormed every possible name we could think of—from the kinky ones to the slinky ones," he recalls. "Finally, what came out of it all was the word 'prestige.' It said what we wanted to do. We wanted a quality company; we didn't want to do a cheapo clean; we wanted to be a first-class company offering what our customers wanted to have." The result was AAA Prestige Carpet Care.

Though naming your company is without a doubt a creative process, it helps to take a systematic approach. Once you've decided on a name, or perhaps two or three possibilities, take the following steps:

- *Check the name for effectiveness and functionality.* Does it quickly and easily convey what you do? Is it easy to say and spell? Is it memorable in a positive way? Ask several of your friends and associates to serve as a focus group to help you evaluate the name's impact.

- *Search for potential conflicts in your local market.* Find out if any other local or regional business serving your market area has a name so similar that yours might confuse the public.

Bright Idea

Once you've narrowed your name search to three or four choices, test market your ideas by asking a small group of people who fit the profile of your potential customers what they think of the names you're considering. Find out what kind of company the name makes them think of and if they'd feel comfortable hiring a cleaning service with that name. Finally, get them to explain the reasoning behind their answers.

- *Check for legal availability.* Exactly how you do this depends on the legal structure you choose. Typically, sole proprietorships and partnerships operating under a name other than that of the owner(s) are required by the county, city, or state to register their fictitious name. Even if it's not required, it's a good idea, because that means no one else can use that name. Registration procedures vary among the states, so check with your county office. Corporations usually operate under their corporate name. In either case, you need to check with the appropriate regulatory agency to be sure the name you chose is available.

- *Check for use on the internet.* If someone else is already using your name as an address on the internet, consider coming up with something else. Even if you have no intention of developing a website of your own, the use of your name by another company could be confusing to your customers.

- *Check to see if the name conflicts with any name listed on your state's trademark register.* Your state Department of Commerce can either help you or direct you to the correct agency. You should also check with the trademark register maintained by the U.S. Patent and Trademark Office (PTO), which is listed in this book's Appendix.

Once the name you've chosen passes these tests, you need to protect it by registering it with the appropriate state agency; again, your state Department of Commerce can help you. If you expect to be doing business on a national level—for example, if your long-term goal is to franchise your cleaning business—you should also register the name with the PTO.

Trademarks

Exactly what is a trademark? According to the PTO, "A trademark includes any word, name, symbol or device, or any combination, used, or intended to be used, in commerce to identify and distinguish the goods of one manufacturer or seller from goods manufactured or sold by others, and to indicate the source of the goods. In short, a trademark is a brand name."

Registering the name of your company as a trademark isn't essential, but it does offer some benefits. It gives notice to the public of your claim of ownership of the mark, a legal presumption of ownership nationwide, and the exclusive right to use the mark on or in connection with the goods or services set forth in the registration.

You can access information about applying for trademark protection and patents online or by contacting the PTO by phone. (See the Appendix for contact information.)

▲

Protect Your Mark

Once you've established a trademark, you must use it or risk losing it. Trademarks not actively used for two or more years may be considered abandoned, which means someone else can use the mark and you'll have no recourse.

You also need to control your mark. Don't allow others to use your mark without your consent or without restricting what product or service it represents. Think about how companies like McDonald's and The Walt Disney Co. aggressively pursue unauthorized use of their trademarks. They understand how much they have to lose if they fail to control their marks.

If you discover someone using your mark without your authorization, consult with an attorney to determine the most appropriate and effective action.

Legal Structure

One of the first decisions you'll need to make about your new cleaning service business is the legal structure of your company. This is an important decision, and it can affect your financial liability, the amount of taxes you pay, and the degree of ultimate control you have over the company, as well as your ability to raise money, attract investors and ultimately sell the business. However, legal structure shouldn't be confused with operating structure. Your legal structure is the ownership structure—who actually owns the company. The operating structure defines who makes management decisions and runs the company.

A sole proprietorship is owned by the proprietor, a partnership is owned by the partners, and a corporation is owned by the shareholders. Another business structure, the limited liability company (LLC), combines the tax advantages of a sole proprietorship with the liability protection of a corporation. The rules on LLCs vary by state; check with your state's department of corporations for the latest requirements.

Sole proprietorships and partnerships can be operated however the owners choose. In a corporation, the shareholders typically elect directors who, in turn, elect officers who then employ other people to run and work in the company. It's possible for a corporation to have only one shareholder and to function as a sole proprietorship. In any case, how you plan to operate the company shouldn't be a major factor in your choice of legal structures.

So what goes into choosing a legal structure? The first question to ask is who is actually making the decision on the legal structure. If you're starting the company by yourself, you don't need to take anyone else's preferences into consideration. If there are multiple people involved, you need to consider how you're going to relate to each other in the business. You also need to consider the issue of asset protection and limiting your liability in the event things don't go as you expect.

Something else to think about is your target customers and what their perceptions will be of your structure. There's a tendency to believe that the legal form of a business has some relationship to the sophistication of the owners, with the sole proprietor as the least and the corporation as the most sophisticated. If your primary customer group is going to be other businesses, it might enhance your image if you incorporate. Homeowners may be comfortable hiring a residential cleaning service that's a sole proprietorship, but property managers and business owners are probably going to be more comfortable dealing with a corporation.

Your image notwithstanding, the biggest advantage of forming a corporation is in the area of asset protection and making sure that the assets you don't want to put into the business won't be liable for business debt. However, to take advantage of the protection a corporation offers, you must respect the corporation's identity. That means maintaining the corporation as a separate entity; keeping your corporate and personal funds separate, even if you are the sole shareholder; and following your state's rules regarding holding annual meetings and other record-keeping requirements.

Is any one of these structures better than another? Not necessarily. We found cleaning service business owners operating as sole proprietors, partnerships, and corporations, and they made their choices based on what was best for their particular situation. Choose the form that's most appropriate for your particular needs.

Do you need an attorney to set it up? Again, no. There are plenty of good do-it-yourself books and kits on the market, and most of the state agencies that oversee corporations have guidelines. Still, it's a good idea to have a lawyer look over your documents before you file them to make sure they're complete and will allow you to function as you want.

Finally, your choice of legal structure isn't an irrevocable decision, although if you're going to make a switch, it's easier to go from the simpler forms to the more sophisticated ones than the other way around. The typical pattern is to start as a sole proprietor and then move up to a corporation as the business grows. But if you need the asset protection of a corporation from the beginning, start out that way.

Licenses and Permits

Most cities and counties require business operators to obtain various licenses and permits to comply with local regulations. In general, the licensing requirements for most cleaning service businesses are minimal. Even so, while you're still in the planning stages, it's a good idea to check with your local planning and zoning department or city/county business license department to find out what licenses and permits you'll need and what's involved in obtaining them. You may need some or all of the following:

- *Occupational license or permit.* This is typically required by the city (or county if you're not within an incorporated city) for just about every business operating within its jurisdiction. License fees are essentially a tax, and the rates vary widely, based on the location and type of business. As part of the application process, the licensing bureau will check to make sure there are no zoning restrictions prohibiting you from operating.

- *Fire department permit.* If you use flammable materials or if your business is located in a commercial facility and is considered open to the public, you may be required to have a permit from the local fire department.

> **Bright Idea**
>
> Make photocopies of all your required licenses and permits, and keep them in a safe, fireproof place—ideally away from your office. Or scan them and store the digital files in a safe, off-site location. If anything happens to your records, you'll still have proof that you're operating legally.

- *Sign permit.* Many cities and suburbs have sign ordinances that restrict the size, location, and sometimes the lighting and type of sign you can use in front of your business. Landlords may also impose their own restrictions. Most residential areas forbid signs altogether. To avoid costly mistakes, check regulations and secure the written approval of your landlord before you invest in and post a sign.

Tax Driver

You may need to collect and remit sales tax on all or part of what you charge your customers. To find out what's required by your state, contact your state's Department of Revenue. This is also the department that usually issues resellers' permits, which may allow you to avoid paying sales tax on some of the materials you use to provide your services.

Laws on sales tax vary by state, and in many states, the amount of tax can vary by county and even city. Check with your state or your accountant to make sure you're operating in compliance with the law.

- *State licenses.* Many states require persons engaged in certain occupations to hold licenses or occupational permits. Often, these people must pass state examinations before they can conduct business. States commonly require licensing for auto mechanics, plumbers, electricians, building contractors, collection agents, insurance agents, real estate brokers, repossessors, and personal service providers such as doctors, nurses, barbers, cosmetologists, etc. It's highly unlikely that you'll need a state license to operate your cleaning service business, but it's a good idea to check with your state's occupation licensing entity to be sure.

Be sure to check with city, state, and county government offices to make sure you've got all the permits you need.

Professional Services

As a business owner, you may be the boss, but you can't be expected to know everything. You'll occasionally need to turn to professionals for information and assistance. It's a good idea to establish a relationship with these professionals before you get into a crisis situation.

Even though you may know something about the issue in question, you probably don't have all the expertise you need. After all, you're an expert at cleaning—not taxes or legal issues. It's a lesson Michael Ray, owner of Pro Building Services Inc. in Salt Lake City, learned the hard way. "I thought I could do my accounting myself for a time and still succeed," he says. "But I didn't have the skills for it, and taking accounting classes in college didn't qualify me to understand what I needed to know."

To shop for a professional service provider, ask friends and associates for recommendations. You might also check with your local chamber of commerce or trade association for referrals. Find someone who understands your industry and specific business and appears eager to work with you. Check them out with the Better Business Bureau and the appropriate state licensing agency before committing yourself.

As a cleaning business owner, the professional service providers you're likely to need include:

- *Attorney.* You need a lawyer who understands and practices in the area of business law, who's honest, and who appreciates your patronage. In most parts of the United States, there's an abundance of lawyers willing to compete fiercely for the privilege of serving you. Interview several, and choose one you feel comfortable with.

Be sure to clarify the fee schedule ahead of time, and get your agreement in writing. Keep in mind that good commercial lawyers don't come cheap; if you want good advice, you must be willing to pay for it. Your attorney should review all contracts, leases, letters of intent, and other legal documents before you sign them. They can also help you with collecting bad debts and establishing personnel policies and procedures. Of course, if you're unsure of the legal ramifications of any situation, call your attorney immediately.

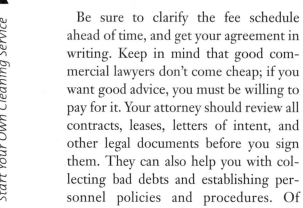

Smart Tip

When dealing with your banker, always remember that the bank is profiting from your business and that you're entitled to be treated with the same courtesy and respect with which you treat your own customers.

- *Accountant.* Among your outside advisors, your accountant is likely to have the greatest impact on the success or failure of your business. If you're forming a corporation, your accountant should counsel you on tax issues during startup. On an ongoing basis, your accountant can help you organize the statistical data concerning your business; assist in charting future actions based on past performance; and advise you on your overall financial strategies regarding purchasing, capital investment, and other matters related to your business goals. A good accountant will also serve as a tax advisor, making sure that you're not only in compliance with all applicable regulations, but also that you don't overpay any taxes.

- *Insurance agent.* A good independent insurance agent can assist you with all aspects of your business insurance, from general liability to employee benefits, and probably even handle your personal lines as well. Look for an agent who works with a wide range of insurers and understands your particular business. This agent should be willing to explain the details of various types of coverage, consult with you to determine the most appropriate coverage, help you understand the degree of risk you're taking, work with you to develop risk-reduction programs, and assist in expediting claims.

- *Banker.* You need a business bank account and a relationship with a banker. Don't just choose the bank you've always done your personal banking with; it may not be the best bank for your business. Interview several bankers before making a decision on where to place your business. Once your account is opened, maintain a relationship with the banker. Periodically sit down and review your accounts and the services you use to make sure you're getting the package most appropriate for your situation. Ask for advice if you have financial questions or are having problems. If you ever need a loan or a bank reference to provide to creditors, the relationship you've established will work in your favor.

- *Consultants.* The consulting industry is booming—and for good reason. Consultants can provide valuable, objective input on all aspects of your business. Consider hiring a business consultant to evaluate your business plan or a marketing consultant to assist you in that area. When you're ready to hire employees, a human resources consultant may help you avoid some costly mistakes. Consulting fees vary widely depending on the individual's experience, location, and field of expertise. If you can't afford to hire a consultant, consider contacting the business school at a nearby college or university and hiring an MBA student to help you.

- *Computer expert.* If you don't know much about computers, find someone to help you select a system and the appropriate software—someone who will be available to help you maintain, troubleshoot, and expand your system as you need it. If you're going to pursue internet sales, use a professional web designer to set up and maintain your site. Just as you wouldn't do an unprofessional cleaning job, you shouldn't put up an unprofessional web page. Ask other business owners in your community for recommendations and always check references before hiring.

Create Your Own Advisory Board

Not even the president of the United States is expected to know everything. That's why he surrounds himself with advisors—experts in particular areas who provide knowledge and information to help him make decisions. Savvy small-business owners use a similar strategy.

You can assemble a team of volunteer advisors to periodically meet with you to offer advice and direction. Because this isn't an official or legal entity, you have a great deal of latitude in how you set it up. Advisory boards can be structured to help both with the direct operation of your company as well as keeping you informed on various business, legal, and financial trends that may affect you.

Use these tips to set up your board:

- *Structure a board that meets your needs.* Generally, you'll want a legal advisor, an accountant, a marketing expert, a human resources person, and perhaps a financial advisor. You may also want successful entrepreneurs from other industries who understand the basics of business and can view your operation with a fresh eye.

> **Smart Tip** *Tip...*
>
> Choose professional advisors who want to take an active role in helping your business succeed. They should not only do what you ask but also take the initiative to offer suggestions about how you can increase sales and profits as well as operate more efficiently.

- *Ask the most successful people you can find, even if you don't know them well.* You'll be surprised at how willing people are to help another business succeed.

- *Be clear about what you're trying to do.* Let your prospective advisors know what your goals are and that you don't expect them to take on an active management role or to assume any liability for your company or for the advice they offer.

- *Don't worry about compensation.* Advisory board members are rarely compensated with more than lunch or dinner. Of course, if a member of your board provides a direct service—for example, if an attorney reviews a contract or an accountant prepares a financial statement—they should be paid at their normal rate because that's not part of their job as an advisory board member. However, even though you don't write them a check, keep in mind that your advisory board members will likely benefit from helping you in a variety of tangible and intangible ways. Being on your board will expose them to ideas and perspectives they may not otherwise have and will also expand their own networks.

- *Consider the group dynamics when holding meetings.* You may want to meet with all the members together or in small groups of one or two. It all depends on how they relate to each other and what you need to accomplish. Don't be afraid to vary your meeting structure or pattern as the circumstances require.

- *Ask for honesty, and don't be offended when you get it.* Your pride might be hurt when someone points out something you're doing wrong, but the awareness will be beneficial in the long run. Also, curb any impulse to be defensive and simply accept the input graciously.

- *Learn from failure as well as success.* Encourage board members to tell you about their mistakes so you can avoid repeating them.

- *Respect the contribution your board members make.* Let them know you appreciate how busy they are, and don't abuse or waste their time.

- *Make it fun.* You are, after all, asking these people to donate their time, so create a pleasant atmosphere.

- *Listen to every piece of advice.* Stop talking and listen. You don't have to follow every piece of advice, but you need to hear it.

- *Provide feedback to the board.* Good or bad, let the board know what you did and what the results were.

Insurance Issues

Insurance can be a tremendous challenge for cleaning service businesses. Many independent operators can't afford to purchase coverage, which puts them in a difficult Catch-22 situation if they're trying to get large accounts that require their suppliers to have certain levels of insurance. Of course, a very small company owned by one or two people who do all the work may not need insurance to cover employee theft and workers' compensation until they begin hiring employees. On the other hand, if you're doing something like high-rise exterior window cleaning, the building's owner will want to see proof that he's not going to be held liable if you're hurt on the job.

Having proper insurance is a good customer-relations move as well as a safety feature for your company. Having insurance shows your clients that you're a knowledgeable and serious business owner and that you're prepared to take responsibility for your employees' actions.

Issues of particular interest to cleaning services are liability coverage in case someone is injured as a result of your work or if something is damaged, and bonding to protect your customers if one of your employees steals something.

Your best strategy is to sit down with an insurance agent who understands the special needs of cleaning service businesses, discuss what's appropriate for your particular operation, and then make a final decision based on the benefits and costs of specific coverages.

> **Tip...**
>
> ## Smart Tip
>
> Sit down with your insurance agent every year and review your insurance needs; as your company grows, they are sure to change. Insurance companies are always developing new products to meet the needs of the growing small-business market, and it's possible one of these new policies is more appropriate for you.

Deliveries and Storage

When you're very new and small, it may be easier to run to your nearest supply house and pick up what you need in the way of chemicals and cleaning solutions. As you grow, it will be more efficient to have your suppliers deliver to you.

Whether the deliveries are being made by your supplier's truck or a commercial freight carrier, be sure to count and inspect every package before signing for the materials. Any shortages or external damage should be noted on the delivery receipt and claims filed promptly. If you find damage after the driver has left, notify the supplier and the carrier immediately.

▲

Store cleaning solutions and chemicals in a clean, dry space away from extreme temperatures. Follow the instructions on the product for any special storage requirements. Generally, metal shelves and metal cabinets are best for storing cleaning products.

Access to the storage area should be limited to supervisors and managers who are trained to use whatever inventory control methods you have in place. This is important both from a safety perspective and for the sake of accurate financial management.

Finally, as you use various products, be sure the empty containers are properly disposed of. As with use and storage, the manufacturers include instructions on the label if there are any special disposal requirements; be sure to follow their guidelines.

Cleaning service companies aren't likely to have much in the way of outgoing freight, but you'll probably use regular mail for functions such as marketing, invoicing, and other communications with customers and suppliers. For more information on mailing and shipping prices, check with the United States Postal Service.

> ### Bright Idea
>
> Never just sign a delivery receipt for packages. Even though you'll get to know your regular driver, always count the packages and do a quick visual inspection for signs of damage.

The Hidden Profit-Eater

Freight is a variable expense that can be hard to predict but has a definite—and often significant—impact on your bottom line. As you shop for and build relationships with suppliers, consider where they're located and how much it will cost for you to receive their goods.

Track your freight costs carefully, and be sure each charge is accurate. It's a good idea to periodically check to make sure the weight of the shipment matches the weight you were charged for. And if your supplier prepays the freight charges and adds it to your invoice, verify that the rates have been correctly calculated.

If you buy primarily from local suppliers and pick up the merchandise yourself, you still need to consider the cost of getting the materials from their location to yours. In this situation, your time and vehicle expenses need to be considered as freight costs when calculating your cost of supplies.

9

Money Matters

In the small-business world, there are two key sides to the issue of money: How much do you need to start and operate, and how much can you expect to take in? Doing this analysis is often extremely difficult for small-business owners who would rather be in the trenches getting the work done than bound to a desk dealing with tiresome numbers. A dirty floor or dusty armoire may have more appeal than a budget that needs planning, but the budget is critical, because if your business isn't profitable, you won't be around to do any cleaning.

Sources of Startup Funds

Most of the cleaning service operators we spoke with used personal savings to start their businesses and then reinvested their early profits to fund growth. If you need to purchase equipment, you should be able to find financing, especially if you can show that you've put some of your own cash into the business. Beyond traditional financing, you have a range of options when it comes to raising money. Some suggestions:

- *Your own resources.* Do a thorough inventory of your assets. People generally have more assets than they immediately realize. This could include savings accounts, equity in real estate, retirement accounts, vehicles, recreation equipment, collections, and other investments. You may opt to sell assets for cash or use them as collateral for a loan. Take a look, too, at your personal line of credit. Many a successful business has been started with credit cards.

- *Friends and family.* The next logical step after gathering your own resources is to approach friends and relatives who believe in you and want to help you succeed. Be cautious with these arrangements; no matter how close you are, present yourself professionally, put everything in writing, and be sure the individuals you approach can afford to take the risk of investing in your business. Never ask a friend or family member to invest or lend you money they can't afford to lose.

- *Partners.* Using the "strength in numbers" principle, look around for someone who may want to team up with you in your venture. You may choose someone who has financial resources and wants to work side-by-side with you in the business. Or you may find someone who has money to invest but no interest in doing the actual work. Be sure to create a written partnership agreement that clearly defines your respective responsibilities and obligations.

- *Government programs:* Take advantage of the abundance of local, state, and federal

> **Bright Idea**
>
> Looking for startup cash? Consider a garage sale. You may have plenty of "stuff" you're not using and won't miss that can be sold for the cash you need to get your cleaning business off the ground. Another option for turning your things into cash is to sell them on eBay (refer to Entrepreneur's *Start Your Own eBay Business*).

programs designed to support small businesses. Make your first stop the SBA, and then investigate other programs. Women, minorities, and veterans should check out niche financing possibilities designed to help these groups get into business. The business section of your local library is a good place to begin your research.

s# Setting Prices

Pricing can be tedious and time-consuming, especially if you don't have a knack for crunching numbers. Particularly in the beginning, don't rush through this process. If your quote is too low, you'll either rob yourself of some profit or be forced to lower the quality of your work to meet the price. If you estimate too high, you may lose the contract altogether, especially if you're in a competitive bidding situation. Remember, in many cleaning situations, you may be competing against the customer him- or herself; if your quote is high, he or she may think, "For that much money, I can do this myself."

Of course, you'll make mistakes in the beginning. For example, one residential cleaning service operator we spoke with started out quoting an hourly rate, but as she became more efficient and was able to clean faster, she realized it would be more profitable to charge by the job than by the hour. Charge for the value of your service, not the time you spend. Patti Page of Page's Personal Cleaning in Cincinnati offers this advice: "Make sure when you start your company that you charge what you would charge if you had employees. Some people make the mistake of undercharging when they start out just to get customers and then later on, when they grow and need to hire help, they aren't making enough money to pay that help. Also, if you are too cheap, customers will think you aren't experienced. So don't underprice your work."

During the initial days of your operation, you should go back and look at the actual costs of every job when it's completed to see how close your estimate was to reality. Learning how to accurately estimate labor and properly calculate overhead will let you set a competitive pricing schedule and still make the profit you require.

To arrive at a strong pricing structure for your particular operation, consider these three factors:

1. Labor and materials (or supplies)
2. Overhead
3. Profit

> **Smart Tip** *Tip...*
> Don't set prices low just to get business when you're starting out. Customers who use you based solely on price will leave you for the same reason. Be sure your prices are competitive, fair, and high enough for you to make a reasonable profit.

Bill Me

You'll set your prices for specific upholstery cleaning jobs based on the condition of the items you're cleaning, the labor and materials required, and the profit you want to make. The ranges below will give you an idea what to charge.

Cushions only	$10–$15 each
Dining room chairs	$9–$20
Draperies	$2.50–$8.00 per pleat
Foot stools and ottomans	$10–$25
Love seats	$40–$140
Occasional chairs	$20–$30
Recliners	$35–$50
Sofas (depending on size)	$60–$196
Stools and benches	$12–$20
Toss pillows	$5–$10 each

If odor control is necessary, add 25 percent

Labor and Materials

Until you establish records to use as a guide, you'll have to estimate the costs of labor and materials. Labor costs include wages and benefits you pay your employees. If you're even partly involved in executing a job, the cost of your labor, proportionate to your input, must be included in the total labor charge. Labor cost is usually expressed as an hourly rate.

Overhead

Overhead consists of all the non-labor, indirect expenses required to operate your business. Your overhead rate is usually calculated as a percentage of your labor and materials. If you have past operating expenses to guide you, figuring an overhead rate isn't difficult. Total your expenses for one year, excluding labor and materials. Divide this number by your total cost of labor and materials to determine your overhead rate. When you're starting out, you won't have past expenses to guide you, so use figures that are accepted industry averages. You can raise or lower the numbers later to suit the realities of your operation.

Let's Make a Deal

You may have some prospective customers who honestly believe your quote is too high, others who make it a habit to never accept the first price as the final one, and still others who simply enjoy haggling. Whether you choose to negotiate is entirely up to you. Orlando residential cleaning service owner Fenna Owens starts and sticks with what she believes is a fair price. "If they don't like it, that's their prerogative," she says. "I don't usually go lower than what I think it should be."

If you charge less than what you think the job is worth or less than it will take for you to make a reasonable profit, the quality of your work and, eventually, the overall success of your company will suffer. It's difficult to turn down work, especially when you're first getting started, but sometimes it's better to decline an account than to take it on at a loss.

One effective negotiating technique is to reduce your price only when you take something out of the service package. When a prospective customer says her price is too high, Wanda Guzman in Orlando goes through what her quote covers and suggests removing some of the services to bring the price down. Or you can ask what the customers are willing to pay and tell them how much you'll do for that price.

Profit

Profit is, of course, the difference between what it costs you to provide a service and what you actually charge the customer. Figure your net profit into your estimate by applying a markup percent to the combined costs of labor, materials, and overhead. The markup percent will be larger than the actual percentage of gross revenue you'll end up with for your net profit. For example, if you plan to net 38 percent before taxes out of your gross revenue, you'll need to apply a markup of about 61.3 percent to your labor and materials plus overhead to achieve that target. (To determine your markup percentage, refer to the "Calculating Markup" chart on page 115.)

Setting Residential Cleaning Service Prices

Most residential cleaning services don't have particularly high overhead costs. Figure that overhead runs from 10 percent to 40 percent of your labor and materials, depending on the size of your operation, whether you're homebased or commercial-based, and the number of employees you maintain on your payroll.

Here's an example:

Overhead expenses	$5,220
Estimate of labor-and-materials cost	$51,240
Overhead rate ($5,220 ÷ $51,240)	10%

To calculate the cost of a single cleaning, the example looks like this:

Labor-and-materials cost	$45.00
Overhead (10% of $45)	$4.50
Subtotal of operating expenses	$49.50

Most residential cleaning service operators expect to net 10 to 30 percent of their gross revenue. To continue our example with a target of netting 20 percent before taxes:

Subtotal of operating expenses	$49.50
Net profit (25% of $49.50)	$12.38
Total price quoted to the customer	$61.88

Note that the $12.38 net profit ends up as 20 percent of $61.88 (which is the "selling price").

Setting Janitorial Service Prices

Overhead for a janitorial service is somewhat higher than for a residential service, typically ranging from 20 to 50 percent of labor costs.

Labor-and-materials cost	$353
Overhead (38% of $353)	$134
Subtotal of operating expenses	$487

Supplies typically run about 5 percent of labor, although Salt Lake City's Michael Ray

Smart Tip

When your customers want you to provide consumable supplies, bill them for the actual amount they use. Some customers may try to get you to include those items in your basic fee, but the consumption rate can vary so significantly that you may find it impossible to make a fair estimate.

says his goal is to keep them between 3 and 4 percent. Use industry averages to help you calculate your estimates until you have a history and can use actual expenses.

Here's an example of a bid on a job that will take two hours of labor per day, five days a week, at $8 per hour, and using an overhead rate of 38 percent:

Subtotal of operating expenses	$487
Net profit (28% of $487)	$136
Total price quoted to the customer	$623

Bright Idea

Providing consumable items such as bathroom tissue, paper towels, hand soap, feminine hygiene products, and trash can liners can be profitable for you and save your clients money. If you take the volume pricing you receive from your suppliers and mark it up slightly, you'll still make money, and your customers will likely get lower prices than they could negotiate on their own.

Most janitorial service operators expect to earn a net profit of 10 to 28 percent of gross sales. In our example, we want to yield a 22 percent net profit before taxes.

Note that the $136 net profit ends up as 22 percent of $623 (which is the "selling price").

Setting Carpet Cleaning Prices

Most carpet cleaning services charge by the square foot. Mike Blair says prices can range from 15 to 45 cents per square foot, depending on the particular market, the total services provided, and the ability of the cleaning company to communicate its value. It may take experimenting with pricing in your market to determine the optimum price level that your customers will perceive as fair and yet will still allow you to make an adequate profit.

In the carpet cleaning industry, overhead typically costs from 47 to 54 percent of your labor-and-materials cost.

Let's say you cleaned 2,144,800 square feet of carpet in one year. Our example looks like this:

Overhead expenses	$61,080
Estimate of labor-and-materials cost	$128,688
Overhead rate ($61,080 ÷ $128,688)	47.5%

Using an overhead rate of 47.5 percent as just computed, we can take our example to the next step and calculate the cost to clean one square foot of carpet:

▲

Labor-and-materials cost	$0.06
Overhead (47.5% of $0.06)	$0.03
Subtotal of operating expenses	$0.09

The typical net profit for carpet cleaning businesses ranges from 38 to 49 percent of gross revenue. To calculate a net profit of 38 percent for our example, the numbers look like this:

Subtotal of operating expenses	$0.09
Net profit (66.7% of $0.09 or 40% of $0.15)	$0.06
Total price per square foot	$0.15
Price quoted to the customer for a 1,500-square-foot job ($0.15 x 1,500)	$225

If you compare the price of $0.15 above with the cost of labor and materials ($0.06) already estimated, you'll see that the quote is just a little more than double the labor charge. Some carpet cleaners use this ratio as a basis for determining price—they estimate their labor costs and then double that figure to arrive at their quotes.

Keeping Records

One of the key indicators of the overall health of your business is its financial status, and it's important that you monitor your financial progress closely. The only way you can do that is to keep good records. You may want to crunch your numbers manually. If not, there are a number of excellent computer accounting programs on the market. Ask your accountant for assistance getting your system set up. The key is to monitor your finances from the very beginning and keep your records current and accurate throughout the life of your company.

Keeping good records helps generate the financial statements that tell you exactly where you stand and what you need to do next. The key financial statements you need to understand and use regularly are:

- *Profit and loss statement* (also called the P&L or the income statement), which illustrates how much your company is making or losing over a designated period—monthly, quarterly, or annually—by subtracting expenses from revenue to arrive at a net result, which is either a profit or a loss
- *Balance sheet*, which is a table showing your assets, liabilities, and capital at a specific point. A balance sheet is typically generated monthly, quarterly, or annually when the books are closed.

Something's Afoot

The factor that has the biggest impact on the square foot rate for carpet cleaning is whether the property is empty or furnished. The next most important factor is the degree of soil and general condition of the carpet.

"How we distinguish the price has to do with the number of square feet and the number of furnishings we have to negotiate or don't have to negotiate," explains Mike Blair, owner of AAA Prestige Carpet Care in St. George, Utah. "If the property is empty, it's less in almost every application." The condition of the carpet, type of soil, and traffic patterns can also affect the time it takes—and therefore the cost—to clean.

You'll also want to consider the type of fiber in the carpet. "There are some unique fabrics that have to be considered," Blair says. For example, cleaning a valuable Oriental rug will cost more than the typical low-end carpet used in apartment complexes because of the expertise required.

- *Cash flow statement*, which summarizes the operating, investing, and financing activities of your business as they relate to the inflow and outflow of cash. As with the profit and loss statement, a cash flow statement is prepared to reflect a specific accounting period, such as monthly, quarterly, or annually.

Successful cleaning service operators review these reports regularly, at least monthly, so they always know where they stand and can quickly move to correct minor difficulties before they become major financial problems.

Billing

! Beware!

Mail thieves operate even in the nicest of neighborhoods. If you receive checks in the mail, rent a post office box so you know they'll be secure.

If you're extending credit to your customers—and it's likely you will if you have corporate accounts or if you are in the janitorial business—you need to establish and follow sound billing procedures.

Coordinate your billing system with your customers' payable procedures. Candidly ask what you can do to ensure prompt payment; that may include confirming the correct billing address and finding out what documentation may be required to help the customer determine the validity of the invoice. Keep in mind that many large companies pay certain types of invoices on certain days of the month; find out if your customers do that, and schedule your invoices to arrive in time for the next payment cycle.

Most computer bookkeeping software programs include basic invoices. If you design your own invoices and statements, be sure they're clear and easy to understand. Detail each item and indicate the amount due in bold with the words "Please pay" in front of the total. A confusing invoice may be set aside for clarification, and your payment will be delayed.

Your invoice should also clearly indicate the

Beware!

If you offer an early-payment discount, be prepared for some customers to deduct the discount but still take 30 days or longer to pay. Some business owners say this is a good reason not to offer such discounts because if you try to collect them when they've been incorrectly taken, you risk damaging your relationship with your customer. It's a judgment call only you can make.

terms under which you've extended credit. Terms include the date the invoice is due, any discount for early payment and additional charges for late payment. For example, terms of "net 30" means the entire amount is due in 30 days; terms of "2–10, net 30" means that the customer can take a 2 percent discount if the invoice is paid in 10 days, but the full amount is due if the invoice is paid in 30 days.

It's also a good idea to specifically state the date the invoice becomes past due to avoid any possible misunderstanding. If you're going to charge a penalty for late payment, be sure your invoice states that it's a late payment or rebilling fee, not a finance charge.

The Taxman Cometh

Businesses are required to pay a wide range of taxes, and there are no exceptions for cleaning service business owners. Keep good records so you can offset your local, state, and federal income taxes with the expenses of operating your company. If you have employees, you'll be responsible for payroll taxes. If you operate as a corporation, you'll have to pay payroll taxes for yourself; as a sole proprietor, you'll pay a self-employment tax. Then there are property taxes; taxes on your equipment and inventory; fees and taxes to maintain your corporate status; your business license fee (which is really a tax); and other lesser-known taxes. Take the time to review all your tax liabilities with your accountant.

Finally, use your invoices as a marketing tool. Mention any upcoming specials, new services, or other information that may encourage your customers to use more of your services. Add a flier or brochure to the envelope—even though the invoice is going to an existing customer, you never know where your brochures will end up.

Establishing Credit Policies

When you extend credit to someone, you're essentially providing them with an interest-free loan. You wouldn't expect someone to lend you money without getting information from you about where you live and work, and your potential ability to repay. It makes sense that you would want to get this information from someone you're lending money to. Reputable companies won't object to providing you with credit information.

Extending credit involves some risk, but it's an essential part of operating successfully, especially if your customer base is primarily other businesses.

Typically, you'll only extend credit to commercial accounts, although some residential cleaning services will extend credit to individuals. But most residential customers will likely pay with cash, check, or a credit card at the time you provide the service. You need to decide how much risk you're willing to take by setting limits on how much credit you'll allow each account.

Your credit policy should include a clear collection strategy. Don't ignore overdue bills; the older a bill gets, the less likely it will ever be paid. Be prepared to take action on past due accounts as soon as they become past due.

Red Flags

Just because a customer passed your first credit check with flying colors, don't neglect to re-evaluate their credit status—in fact, you should do it on a regular basis.

Tell customers when you initially grant their credit applications that you have a policy of periodically reviewing accounts so that when you do it, it's not a surprise. Things can change quickly in the business world, and a company that's on sound financial footing this year may be wobbly next year.

An annual reevaluation of all customers on open accounts is a good idea—but if you start to see trouble in the interim, don't wait to take action. Another time to reevaluate customers' credit is when they request an increase in their credit lines.

Some key trouble signs are a slowdown in payment and difficulty getting answers to your payment inquiries. A sharp increase in complaints could be a red flag; they may be preparing to decline payment based on unsatisfactory service. Also, pay attention to what your customers are doing. A major change in their customer base or product line is something you may want to monitor.

Take the same approach to a credit review that you do to a new credit application. Most of the time, you can use what you have on file to conduct the check, but if you're concerned for any reason, you may want to ask the customer for updated information.

Most customers will understand routine credit reviews and accept them as a sound business practice. A customer who objects may well have something to hide—and that's something you need to know.

Tip...

Smart Tip

Once you've established your policies on extending credit, be sure to apply them consistently. Failure to do so will confuse your customers, make them wonder about your professionalism, and leave you open to charges of discrimination.

Accepting Credit and Debit Cards

Whether your target market is business accounts or individual consumers, it will help if you're able to accept credit and debit cards. Though most businesses prefer to be billed directly for cleaning services, some smaller businesses may want to charge the amount to their company credit card—if for no other reason than to rack up frequent flier miles. And while many consumers will write a check or even pay in cash, a significant number would prefer to use their credit cards—and may even buy more of your services than if they had to pay cash.

Today, it's much easier to get merchant status than it has been in the past because merchant status providers are competing aggressively for your business.

To get a credit card merchant account, start with your own bank. Also check with professional associations that offer merchant status as a member benefit. Shop around; this is a competitive industry, and it's worth taking the time to get the best deal.

Patti Page of Page's Personal Cleaning in Cincinnati says the easiest and least expensive way to accept credit cards is by using PayPal, an online payment service that allows your clients to pay with their credit cards, but you don't have to get merchant status. The primary drawback is that your clients have to be willing to go online to make their payments. A benefit is that the money is transferred to your account immediately.

Calculating Markup

Unless you're a mathematics whiz, you may find calculating markup confusing. The following table shows you the percentage you need to mark up your operating costs to reach the desired net profit. Here's how it works: Choose the desired net profit from the left-hand column, then use the markup percent from the corresponding column on the right. For example, if you want a net profit of 4.8 percent, you need to use a markup of 5.01 percent.

Net Profit Percent	Markup Percent	Net Profit Percent Cont'd.	Markup Percent Cont'd.	Net Profit Percent Cont'd.	Markup Percent Cont'd.
4.8	5.01	22.5	29.0	41.0	70.0
5.0	5.3	23.0	29.9	42.0	72.4
6.0	6.4	23.1	30.0	42.8	75.0
7.0	7.5	24.0	31.6	44.4	80.0
8.0	8.7	25.0	33.3	46.1	85.0
9.0	10.0	26.0	35.0	47.5	90.0
10.0	11.1	27.0	37.0	50.0	100
10.7	12.0	27.3	37.5	52.4	110
11.0	12.4	28.0	39.0	54.5	120
11.1	12.5	28.5	40.0	56.5	130
12.0	13.6	29.0	40.9	58.3	140
12.5	14.3	30.0	42.9	60.0	150
13.0	15.0	32.0	47.1	61.5	160
14.0	16.3	33.3	50.0	63.0	170
15.0	17.7	34.0	51.5	64.2	180
16.0	19.1	35.0	53.9	65.5	190
16.7	20.0	35.5	55.0	66.7	200
17.0	20.5	36.0	56.3	69.2	225
18.0	22.0	37.0	58.8	71.4	250
18.5	22.7	37.5	60.0	73.3	275
19.0	23.5	38.0	61.3	75.0	300
20.0	25.0	39.0	64.0	76.4	325
21.0	26.6	39.5	65.5	77.8	350
22.0	28.2	40.0	66.7	78.9	375

Setting Up Your Business

Homebased businesses are common these days, and cleaning services are excellent candidates for this type of setup. After all, your customers will likely never come to your facility since all your work is done on their premises. But that's not the only issue influencing your decision to operate from a homebased office or a commercial location.

Many municipalities have ordinances that limit the nature and volume of commercial activities that can occur in residential areas. Some outright prohibit the establishment of homebased businesses. Others may allow such enterprises but place restrictions regarding issues such as signage, traffic, employees, commercially marked vehicles, and noise. Before you apply for your business license, find out what ordinances govern homebased businesses; you may need to adjust your plan so you comply. If you live in a neighborhood with a homeowners association, you may be subject to additional restrictions; find out what those are before you get too far along in your planning.

Beyond the specific regulations, it's reasonable and fair to operate your business in a manner that won't negatively affect the neighborhood. Be a good citizen, and don't give your neighbors any reason to complain.

Where in your house should your office be? Of course, it's your house—and your decision. When choosing where to set up, first do an analysis of your expected needs and your available space; then try to blend the two. Most cleaning services will need space for two primary functions: administration and storage for equipment and supplies.

It's ideal to locate your business separate from your living area (a spare bedroom is perfect). If that's not possible, you may need to apply some creativity to arranging work areas so they are effective and at the same time don't overtake your personal space. Take the same basic approach to furnishing and equipping your office: Figure out what you need and what you can afford, then begin shopping and setting up.

The Homebased Tax Advantage

Because expenses related to running your business are generally tax-deductible and the IRS has relaxed the rules on what is an allowable home-office deduction, the tax advantage of being homebased is more attractive than ever. The IRS says a home office "will be considered a principal place of business if you perform administrative or management activities there and there is no other fixed location of that trade or business where you conduct substantial administrative or management activities of that trade or business." In other words, even though your actual work will be performed outside your home, your home office will be deductible.

What can you deduct? You can deduct directly related expenses, which are costs that benefit only the business part of your home, as well as a portion of indirect expenses, which are the costs involved in keeping up and running your entire home. For example, your office furniture and equipment are fully deductible and directly related expenses. In the area of indirect expenses, you may deduct a portion of your household utilities and services (electric, gas, water, sewage, trash collection, etc.) based on the percentage of space you use for business purposes. Other examples of indirect expenses include real estate taxes, deductible mortgage interest, casualty losses, rent, insurance, repairs, security systems, and depreciation.

Although you may be concerned that taking the home office deduction will trigger an IRS audit, if your deductions are legitimate and you've kept good records, that shouldn't be an issue. Keep your records for at least three years from the date the return was filed or two years from the date the tax was paid, whichever is later.

The Commercial Option

Smart Tip *Tip...*

If you're planning to be homebased and live in an area with extreme temperatures, consider storing your cleaning supplies and chemicals inside your home in a metal storage cabinet so they're protected from excessive heat and cold. In any case, be sure the temperature of the storage area stays within the range recommended by the manufacturers of the products you keep on hand.

Many industry veterans believe that to achieve authentic business growth, you must get out of the home and into a commercial facility. Certainly, doing so will help you create a successful and professional image, but before you begin shopping for an office, think carefully about what you'll need.

Your office should be large enough to have a small reception area, work space for yourself and your administrative staff, and a storage area for equipment and supplies. You may also want to have space for a laundry and possibly even a small work area where you can handle minor equipment repairs. Depending on the size of your staff, consider allowing for a small break area, perhaps with lockers for members of your cleaning crews, so they have a place to sit and store personal items when they're in the office at the beginning and end of their shifts.

Regardless of the type of cleaning business you have, remember that chances are slim that your customers will ever come to your office. So look for a facility that meets your operational needs and is in a reasonably safe location, but don't pay for a prestigious address—it's just not worth it.

Vehicles

Because your work is done at your customers' sites, vehicles are important to your business. In fact, your vehicles are essentially your company on wheels. They need to be carefully chosen and well-maintained to adequately serve and represent you.

Smart Tip

Tip...

If your equipment needs to be mounted in your vehicle (as a number of carpet cleaning machines do), choose your equipment before you buy a truck to be sure the truck can adequately accommodate the weight and design of the machinery.

For a residential cleaning service, an economy car or station wagon should suffice. You need enough room to store equipment and supplies and to transport your cleaning teams, but you typically won't be hauling around pieces of equipment large enough to require a van or small truck.

You can either provide vehicles or have employees use their own. If you provide the vehicles, you can paint your company's name, logo, and telephone number on them. This advertises your business all over town—and especially in the neighborhoods where you're cleaning, since the car will be parked outside your customers' homes while your crews are inside working.

If your employees use their own cars—which is particularly common with residential cleaning services—ask for evidence that they have sufficient insurance to cover them in the event of an accident. Also, confirm with your insurance agent that your own liability policy protects you under those circumstances.

The type of vehicles you'll need for a janitorial service depends on the size and type of equipment you use as well as the size and number of your crews. An economy car or station wagon could work if you're doing relatively light cleaning in smaller offices, but for most janitorial businesses, you're more likely to need a truck or van. A van is preferable over a pickup truck since it allows you to lock your equipment inside, protecting it from theft and the elements. Also, a van painted with your company name, logo, and telephone number will help promote your business.

For carpet cleaning services, you'll need a truck or van, either new or used, for each service person and his or her equipment. A good used truck costs about $10,000 to $12,000, while a new one will run from $19,000 up. You can reduce your startup costs by leasing a truck rather than buying one. There may be other financial and tax benefits to leasing; you need to do an analysis of your situation to make the best decision.

Because your vehicles represent your business, they need to be free of dents and always kept clean, inside and out. This is, after all, a cleaning service—you don't want your customers wondering how good a job you'll do for them if you can't keep your own vehicles clean.

Dollar Stretcher

Take the time to check tire pressures on company vehicles daily. Properly inflated tires are the easiest way to keep your fuel expenses as low as possible.

Build a Fleet

When your business grows to the point that you require several vehicles, you can turn to a fleet lessor or dealer program. These programs, designed to help you set up a fleet of commercial vehicles, are run by manufacturers, dealers, leasing companies, and fleet management firms. In the past, only companies with very large fleets could expect special consideration or price breaks on their vehicles. In recent years, vehicle sellers and lessors have recognized the potential market represented by small businesses and have developed fleet programs for companies with as few as three vehicles. It's worth your time to research these programs; you could save lots of money.

Check Out the Drivers

When your employees (or independent contractors) are on the job, you'll likely be liable if an accident occurs while they're driving—whether they're in their own vehicles or yours. Of course, the monetary issues can be handled by insurance—and your insurance agent can help you determine the best types and amounts of coverage to buy—but you'll also want to take steps to prevent problems.

Begin by setting a policy on driver qualifications and history. Be sure anyone driving on company business holds a valid driver's license. Then you need to decide what is and isn't acceptable in the way of violations. A typical policy may be that three or more serious violations (such as reckless driving, speeding 15 miles or more over the speed limit, leaving the scene of an accident, or racing) over a period of two or three years would be cause to reject a prospective job candidate. A drunk driving conviction alone may be reason enough not to hire an applicant who has to drive on the job. You should also look at the individual's accident history. Whatever your policy, apply it consistently to avoid any charge of discrimination.

Drive Safely

Driving a van can be hazardous because the driver sits so close to the front of the vehicle. Also, vans and other marked business vehicles are often the target of scam artists looking to cause a wreck and then file a fraudulent insurance claim. Caution anyone who drives for you on company business—whether in your vehicle or their own—to follow all traffic laws and to leave plenty of space between themselves and the vehicle ahead of them.

When you check references on new employees, ask about their overall dependability and reliability, then find out if they drove a company vehicle in their previous jobs and if they had any driving-related problems.

You may want to require a commercial driver's license. This is more important if the employee will be driving trucks rather than cars. The various classes of commercial licenses vary by state, but they typically require a greater degree of knowledge and experience than a basic operator's license.

Your insurance company may help you develop a policy and screen potential drivers. It's to their benefit, so find out if they'll help you confirm that your employees hold valid licenses and that they have good driving records.

Consider doing an annual review of driving records of all employees who drive on company business. If you see a potential problem, such as a pattern of tickets, you can address it with discipline, training, or even removing the person from their driving position before a situation of serious liability occurs.

Smart Tip

Use a street address on your business cards and brochures, even if you operate from home. A street address makes you appear stable and reliable. If your customers mail payments and you wish them to go to a post office box for security reasons, indicate on your invoices that payments should be mailed to a different address. But using a post office box as your primary address makes you look like a temporary, fly-by-night operation, and people might not trust you with cleaning their homes and offices.

Office, Suite Office

You may want to consider setting up your office in an executive suite, where you have access to a range of administrative and support services—such as fax and photocopy machines, and a receptionist—without having to purchase them, and then rent space at a mini-warehouse to store equipment and supplies. The drawback to this, of course, is that you'll have to travel between the two sites.

Human Resources

Although you may eventually be able to operate as an absentee owner, most cleaning service business owners prefer to actively run their businesses. When you're starting out, you'll be wearing a variety of hats, from cleaning technician to salesperson to manager and more. It's not easy, but it will pay off.

You may choose to keep your business small so you can do all the work yourself. This lets you avoid many of the headaches that come with growth and hiring employees. But this isn't a very realistic approach. Operating a cleaning service business is hard enough without complicating it by refusing to recruit employees.

One of the biggest challenges you'll share with businesses in all industries is the demand for qualified workers and rising labor costs. The problem is not so much finding people who can do the work but finding people who want to do the work and who will do it well for wages you can afford to pay.

The first step in a comprehensive human resources program is to decide exactly what you want an employee to do. The job description doesn't have to be as formal as one you might expect from a large corporation, but it needs to clearly outline the person's duties and responsibilities. It should also list any special skills or other required credentials, such as a valid driver's license and clean driving record for someone who's going to be driving a company vehicle.

Next, you need to establish a pay scale. You can do some research on your own to find out what the pay rates are in your area. You'll want to establish a minimum and maximum rate for each position; you'll pay more, even at the start, for better-qualified and more experienced workers.

You'll also need a job application form. You can get a basic form at most office supply stores or you can create your own. In any case, have your attorney review the form you'll be using for compliance with the most current employment laws.

Every prospective employee should fill out an application—even if it's someone you know, and even if they have submitted a detailed resume. A resume isn't a signed, sworn statement acknowledging that you can fire them if they lie; the application is. The application will also help you verify their resumes; compare the two and make sure the information is consistent.

Now you're ready to start looking for candidates.

What Makes a Good Cleaning Service Employee?

What kinds of people make good employees for cleaning service businesses? It depends on what you want them to do. But in general, your ideal employee will enjoy their work and have a great attitude. Certainly they must do a good job, but even if they leave the home or office sparkling, you'll lose business if they're rude to customers. If a cleaner has a poor attitude, chances are they don't truly enjoy the work. And if they don't enjoy the work, it will eventually become evident in the quality of their performance. Look for people who will be enthusiastic about their work and who enjoy cleaning.

Of course, some applicants who love cleaning their own homes may find the reality of cleaning as a job not quite as pleasant. You'll find people who say they love to clean and want to do it for a living, but they don't completely realize that as a job, it's hard work and physically tiring. If you sense a prospective employee feels that they are "above" cleaning for a living, probe further during the interviewing process.

If they really feel this way, they may come to work for you because they need a job and the money, but they probably won't stick around very long. Turnover is expensive; it's best to take the time to hire the right people in the first place.

For his St. George, Utah, carpet cleaning business, Mike Blair looks for employees who are personable and have good communication skills. "I call this a white-collar cleaning company—and we do wear white collars—because we require our people to be sharp and reasonably well-educated," he says. "They deal with such a wide variety of situations, and they need to know how to communicate, to ease people's minds, and to develop relationships in addition to simply cleaning."

Look In the Right Places

Picture the ideal candidate in your mind. Is this person likely to be unemployed and reading the classified ads? It's possible, but you'll probably improve your chances for a successful hire if you're more creative in your searching techniques than simply writing a "help wanted" ad.

Stat Fact

Most job openings for building cleaning workers result from the need to replace workers who leave these jobs because they provide low pay and few benefits, limited opportunities for training or advancement, and often only part-time or temporary work.

Sources for prospective employees include suppliers, customers (use caution here; you don't want to lose a client because you stole an employee), and professional associations. Put the word out among your social contacts as well—you never know who might know the perfect person for your company.

College students make good employees, especially for janitorial services that are often looking for night workers. Students who attend

People Who Need People

Do you need employees to start your cleaning business? Consider these startup staffing suggestions:

For a Residential Cleaning Service

Your initial staffing needs will depend on how much capital you have, how large a business you want to have, and the volume of customers you can reasonably expect to service. Many independent residential cleaning services start with just the owner. Others will start with the owner and an appropriate number of cleaners. If you handle the administrative chores, chances are you won't need to hire office help right away.

For a Janitorial Service

You may be able to start with no employees—or just one or two part-timers. If you have the capital available and the business lined up, you may need to hire more. You may also want to consider an administrative person to handle the records and answer the phone during the day; after all, if you're working all night, you need to schedule some time to sleep. As your business grows, consider a marketing/salesperson, a customer service manager, and crew supervisors as well as additional cleaning personnel.

For a Carpet Cleaning Service

Depending on the strength of your pre-opening campaign and your startup budget, hire at least one service person and possibly two as you're getting started, along with an employee experienced in clerical work who can book appointments and handle administrative chores. Though most residential jobs can likely be handled by one person, you may want to consider staffing each truck with two people: a senior technician and a helper. The helper can assist with the prep work for each job (unloading equipment, moving light furniture, etc.), mix chemicals, empty buckets, clean up afterward, etc. This will make each job go faster, which is more efficient and cost-effective and also generates a greater degree of customer satisfaction.

classes during the day are often available to work for you at night. And if you find them in their freshman and sophomore years, you'll have employees with the potential of working for you for the next three or four years. Residential cleaning services often find that mothers represent a strong pool of candidates, especially those looking to work part time while school is in session.

Consider using a temporary help or employment agency to help you find qualified employees. Many small businesses shy away from agencies because they feel they can't afford the fee—but if the agency handles the advertising, initial screening, and background checks, the fee may be worth paying.

Use caution if you decide to hire friends and relatives—many personal relationships are not strong enough to survive an employee–employer situation. Small-business owners in all industries tell of nightmarish experiences when a friend or relative refused to accept direction or abused a personal relationship in the course of business.

The key to success as an employer is making it clear from the start that you're the one in charge. You don't need to act like a dictator, of course. Be diplomatic, but set the ground rules in advance, and stick to them.

Evaluating Applicants

When you actually begin the hiring process, don't be surprised if you're as nervous at the prospect of interviewing potential employees as they are about being interviewed. They may need a job, but the future of your company is at stake.

It's a good idea to prepare your interview questions in advance. Develop open-ended questions that encourage candidates to talk. In addition to knowing what they've done, you want to find out how they did it. Ask each candidate the same set of questions, and take notes as they respond so you can make an accurate assessment and comparison later.

When the interview is over, let the candidate know what to expect. Is it going to take you several weeks to interview other candidates, check references, and make a decision? Will you want the top candidates to return for a second interview? Will you call the candidate, or should they call you? This is not only a good business practice, but it's also just simple common courtesy.

Always check former employers and personal references. Though many companies are restrictive as to what information they'll verify, you may be surprised at what you can find out. At least confirm that the applicant told the truth about dates and positions held. Personal references are likely to give you some additional insight into the general character and personality of the candidate; this will help you decide if they'll fit into your operation.

Be sure to document every step of the interview and reference-checking process. Even small companies are finding themselves targets of employment discrimination suits; good records are your best defense if it happens to you.

Be particular about whom you hire, even if you're in an area where competition for workers is fierce. A good rule to follow is to only hire people you would trust in your own home—that way, you'll know you can trust them in your customers' homes and

Do You Need a Break?

No matter how much you enjoy your work, you need an occasional break from it. This is a particular challenge for solo operators, but it's critical. You need to be away from your operation occasionally, not only for vacations, but for business reasons, such as attending conferences and trade shows. Also, you need a plan in place in case of illness, accidents, or other emergencies.

If you take a long weekend or just one or two days off, with proper planning, your customers won't even know you were gone. For longer periods away, you have two choices: Ask someone you trust to run the business in your absence, or just close temporarily.

With a staff as your backup, taking a vacation is easier—just be sure your people are well trained and committed to maintaining your service levels when you aren't there.

offices. Remember, good employees are the key to happy customers, and happy customers are loyal.

Take Care of Your Employees

Keep in mind that the only thing you have to sell is service, and the only way for your service to be delivered is through your employees. Treat them with respect and let them know you recognize and appreciate their contributions to the company. Pay competitive wages, give increases and bonuses regularly, and always be fair.

Orlando cleaning service operator Wanda Guzman says she worked for an independent cleaning company for a few years before starting her own business. She received no benefits; the company's owner routinely criticized her in front of clients; if a client canceled a cleaning appointment at the last minute, she didn't get paid; and when she left, it had been more than a year and a half since she had received a raise. Now that she's on her own, she makes more money even after factoring in administrative costs. And when she hires people

Bright Idea
Post the duties of all positions clearly so new people can quickly see what they're supposed to do each day, and also have a clear picture as to how their positions interact with others.

to help her, she treats them with the respect she wanted from her former boss, who did absolutely nothing to earn her loyalty.

A smart strategy is to pay your cleaners slightly more than the going rate in your area. You'll get the best workers, and your turnover will be lower.

Mike Blair pays his carpet cleaning technicians on commission. "We pay them a specific percentage based on their experience and ability," he says. "I think it gives the technician incentive to know that the job is his complete operation. He's responsible for satisfying the customer and making sure the job is done right, all the way to the finish." He says other carpet cleaning companies vary in their compensation plans from the straight commission he pays, to a base salary plus commission, to an hourly rate with no commission.

Now That They're Hired

The hiring process is only the beginning of the challenge of having employees. In an ideal world, employees could be hired already knowing everything they need to know. But this isn't an ideal world, and if you want the job done right, you have to teach your people how to do it.

It's likely that the majority of applicants for entry-level cleaning jobs will need training. This isn't necessarily a disadvantage; in fact, you may prefer to handle this yourself since hiring individuals without professional cleaning experience lets you train them to clean your way. Also, training—especially when it's ongoing—is a great tool for building loyalty. When you show your employees that you're willing to invest in them, it helps build a bond that has a positive impact on your service and turnover rates.

Many small businesses conduct their "training" by throwing someone into the job, but that's not fair to the employee, and it's certainly not good for your business. And if you think you can't afford to spend time on training, think again—can you afford *not* to adequately train your employees? Do you really want them interacting with your customers or cleaning homes and offices when you haven't told them how you want things done?

Why Do We Clean?

The reality is that there isn't a lot of prestige associated with working in the cleaning industry, and yet the work itself is extremely important. Teach your employees why doing their jobs well is essential. It's not just to make homes and commercial facilities look nice; it's for public health and a healthy environment, and to protect the building and its contents. The benefits of proper cleaning include:

○ Security, comfort, and productivity in the workplace are increased.
○ Property value is maintained, and the rate of depreciation is reduced.
○ Quality of life is enhanced.
○ Occupants enjoy an elevated sense of well-being and are comfortable reusing space and materials.
○ Waste and hazards are managed, and sanitation is assured.

The amount of training you'll need to do depends largely on the type of cleaning service you have, the equipment your employees use, and what you expect them to do.

Take a positive approach to training. Show your cleaners how to do the job; then, as they begin doing the cleaning themselves, give lots of positive reinforcement for what they're doing well. Rather than harping on the things they're doing wrong, simply show them again how to do those tasks properly.

Blair expects to have to train his carpet cleaning technicians because, he says, finding experienced technicians is rare. "People would be surprised at the level of learning that's required to become a seasoned technician," he says. He sends his new and existing technicians to training programs offered by equipment manufacturers and professional organizations. "It's important to pay the price and get the training," he says.

New technicians begin working with Blair himself or another experienced technician until they know the business well enough to be sent out on their own. Training can take several months, and their first solo job is more likely to be an empty rental than an occupied home or office.

Training Techniques

Whether done in a formal classroom setting or on the job, effective training begins with a clear goal and a plan for reaching it. Training will fall into one of three major categories:

1. orientation, which includes explaining company policies and procedures;

2. job skills, which focuses on how to do specific tasks; and

3. ongoing development, which enhances basic job skills and grooms employees for future challenges and opportunities.

These tips will help you maximize your training efforts:

- *Find out how people learn best.* Delivering training is not a one-size-fits-all proposition. People absorb and process information differently, and your training method needs to be compatible with their individual preferences. Some people can read a manual, others prefer a verbal explanation, and still others need to see a demonstration. In a group training situation, your best strategy is to use a combination of methods; when you're working one-on-one, tailor your delivery to fit the needs of the person you're training.

   With some employees, figuring out how they learn best can be a simple matter of asking them. Others may not be able to tell you because they don't understand it themselves; in those cases, experiment with various training styles and see what works best for the specific employee.

- *Use simulation and role-playing to train, practice, and reinforce.* One of the most effective training techniques is simulation, which involves showing an employee how to do something and then allowing them to practice it in a safe, controlled environment. If the task includes interpersonal skills, let the employee role play with a co-worker to practice what they should say and do in various situations.

- *Be a strong role model.* Don't expect more from your employees than you're willing to do. You're a good role model when you do things the way they should be done all the time. Don't take shortcuts you don't want your employees to take or behave in any way that you don't want them to behave. On the other hand, don't assume that simply doing things the right way is enough to teach others how to do things. Role modeling is not a substitute for training. It reinforces training. If you only role model but never train, employees aren't likely to get the message.

> **Smart Tip**
> *Tip...*
>
> Training employees—even part-time, temporary help—to your way of doing things is important. These people represent your company, and they need to know how to maintain the image and standards you've worked hard to establish.

- *Look for training opportunities.* Once you get beyond basic orientation and job skills training, you need to constantly be on the lookout for opportunities to enhance the skills and performance levels of your people.

- *Make it real.* Whenever possible, use real-life situations to train—but avoid letting customers know they've become a training experience for employees.

- *Anticipate questions.* Don't assume that employees know what to ask. In a new situation, people often don't understand enough to formulate questions. Anticipate their questions and answer them in advance.

- *Ask for feedback.* Finally, encourage employees to let you know how you're doing as a trainer. Just as you evaluate their performance, convince them that it's OK to tell you the truth, ask them what they thought of the training and your techniques, and use that information to improve your own skills.

Uniforms

Some cleaning services require their employees to wear uniforms on the job. Uniforms allow customers to identify your workers easily; they also give your operation a professional appearance and advertise your business. Uniforms generally consist of a shirt with your company's name and logo, and comfortable pants that allow employees to bend and stoop easily. You may opt to provide shirts and let your employees wear their own jeans or trousers.

Residential cleaning and janitorial service workers can also benefit from wearing smocks. Smocks with pockets allow your cleaners to carry all their supplies with them—sponges, dust cloths, and spray bottles are always within reach. Not only do smocks save time because cleaners don't have to run around for supplies, but they also keep employees' hands free for cleaning, which means they work more efficiently. Smocks can also protect and prolong the life of a uniform.

Franchises usually sell their franchisees uniforms at discounted prices. A local screen-printing shop can print your company's name and logo on T-shirts for employees to wear as part of their uniforms. You can also check out local uniform shops to see what's available.

If you're going to require your employees to wear uniforms, you should provide at least two or three sets initially and then consider paying a small uniform allowance for maintenance and replacement of garments. How many uniform sets and the amount of the allowance will depend on the cost, durability, and style of the uniform you choose.

Employee Benefits

The wages you pay may be only part of your employees' total compensation. While many very small companies don't offer a formal benefits program, many business owners have recognized that benefits—particularly in the area of insurance—are

Bright Idea

As a benefit, let your employees use the company's equipment to clean their own homes. The wear on the equipment is negligible, and your employees will appreciate not having to rent or buy these cleaning tools.

important in attracting and retaining quality employees.

Typical benefits packages include group insurance (your employees may pay all or a portion of their premiums), paid holidays, and vacations. You can build employee loyalty by offering additional benefits that may be somewhat unusual—and they don't have to cost much. For example, if you're in or near a retail location, talk to other store owners in your shopping center to see if they're interested in providing your employees with discounts. You'll provide your own employees with a benefit and generate some new customers for your business neighbors.

Beyond tangible benefits, look for ways to provide positive working conditions. Uniforms are one way to create a positive environment. Be sure the equipment and tools you ask your employees to use are in good working condition; substandard supplies can reduce their productivity and their morale. Consider a comfortable break room with adequate lockers and vending machines. You may even want to provide the coffee at no charge. Show your appreciation for jobs well done by paying for lunch (even though "lunch" comes in the middle of the night for third-shift workers); a few pizzas or sandwiches are an inexpensive investment that will pay you back many times over in loyalty and productivity. Insist that everyone in your company, from the most junior part-time cleaner up to and including yourself, be treated and treat others with respect and courtesy at all times—there's just no excuse for operating any other way.

Bright Idea

Find out what your employees want in the way of benefits before you spend time and money developing a package. Do a brief survey; ask for their ideas, and ask them what they think of your ideas. If they want something you can't afford, don't reject it immediately; figure out what you can afford, and explain the situation to your employees.

Child Labor Laws

Though teenagers don't make up a significant portion of the cleaning service industry's labor force, it's important that you understand the child labor laws that apply to your operation. Many entrepreneurial cleaning businesses are family-owned, and these owners often employ their kids during summer vacation or for extended

133

periods. The Fair Labor Standards Act has provisions designed to protect the education opportunities of youths and prohibit their employment in jobs and under conditions detrimental to their health and well-being.

The minimum age for most nonfarm work is 16; however, 14- and 15-year-olds may be employed outside of school hours in certain occupations under certain conditions. At any age, youths may work for their parents in their solely owned nonfarm businesses (except in mining, manufacturing, or in any other occupation declared hazardous by the Secretary of Labor); this means your minor children can work in your cleaning service business if you're the sole owner, and as long as you're not violating other age-related laws.

The basic age-related guidelines of the Fair Labor Standards Act are:

- Youths 18 years or older may perform any job for unlimited hours.
- Youths age 16 and 17 may perform any job not declared hazardous by the Secretary of Labor for unlimited hours.
- Youths age 14 and 15 may work outside school hours in various nonmanufacturing, nonmining, nonhazardous jobs under the following conditions: no more than three hours on a school day, 18 hours in a school week, eight hours on a nonschool day, or 40 hours in a nonschool week. In addition, they may not begin work before 7 A.M. nor work after 7 P.M., except from June 1 through Labor Day, when evening work hours are extended to 9 P.M.
- Youths aged 14 and 15 who are enrolled in an approved Work Experience and Career Exploration Program may be employed for up to 23 hours during school weeks and three hours on school days, including during school hours.

> **Bright Idea**
>
> Give your employees subscriptions to industry trade magazines and newsletters, and encourage them to use and share the information they learn from those publications. The cost is nominal, and the result is that you'll increase their value to the company as well as their sense of self-esteem.

> **Smart Tip**
>
> *Tip...*
>
> From the day they're hired, tell employees what they need to do to get a raise without having to ask for it. Then follow up by increasing their pay rates when they've earned it.

Department of Labor regulations require employers to keep records of the dates of birth of employees under age 19, their daily starting and quitting times, daily and weekly hours of work, and their occupations. Protect yourself from unintentional violations of the child labor provisions by keeping on file an employment or age certificate for each youth employed to show that they're the minimum age for the job.

Keep in mind that, in addition to the federal statutes, most states also have child labor laws. Check with your own state Labor Department to see what state regulations apply to your business. When both the federal law and the state law apply, the law setting the higher standards must be observed.

What Should You Pay?

The Fair Labor Standards Act also establishes minimum wage, overtime pay, and record-keeping standards. The act permits the employment of certain individuals at wage rates below the statutory minimum wage, but they must be working under certificates issued by the Department of Labor. Those individuals include student learners (vocational education students), full-time students in retail or service establishments, and individuals whose earning or productive capacity is impaired by a physical or mental disability, including those related to age or injury. Because laws change, check with your state labor board and/or the U.S. Department of Labor Wage and Hour Division for the current minimum wage amounts.

There's much more involved in setting your wage scales than understanding what the law requires. You must also consider issues such as the skills you require; whether you pay by the hour, by the job, or on a commission basis; whether you offer benefits; whether the people working for you are employees or independent contractors; what the going rates in your area are; and a variety of other factors.

The following are reasonable ranges (you must still study your local market and consider the other factors when setting pay rates). Don't be reluctant to go over these ranges if it's appropriate in your market. If you're in New York City, Chicago, or Los Angeles, for example, you would most likely pay more. The going hourly rate for a residential cleaner is $8 to $12 per hour. For a janitor, it's $8.50 to $12.50 per hour. For a carpet cleaner, hourly wages are approximately $10 to $15 per hour. Keep in mind that the carpet cleaning figure could be less if the worker is also on commission.

Beware!

Employees are sometimes driven to steal because they feel that they're being underpaid or that the business owner is making excessive profits on workers' efforts, so the employee feels "entitled" to steal. Help prevent this attitude by paying fair wages and treating your employees with respect.

Employee Theft

Business owners often work hard to protect their operations from external thieves, without realizing that employees and on-site contract workers actually pose a greater chance of theft. Employee theft can have a serious impact on your bottom line as well as on the morale of other employees who may be aware of what's going on.

As a cleaning service owner, part of the service you offer is trustworthiness, so it's critical that you screen all applicants to reduce the risk that any of your employees will steal either from you or from one of your customers.

Of course, pre-employment screening is just the first step. You should also set policies designed to reduce the opportunity to steal. For example, don't allow employees to take personal items such as purses, bags, or backpacks with them onto the customer's premises. These items can be used to hide stolen items. It's also possible that personal items can get left behind at the customer's site, and retrieving them can be inconvenient for both you and your customer. Prevent either possibility by requiring that all personal belongings be kept locked in the company vehicle or stored in your office in an assigned locker.

Be sure workers are adequately supervised. This not only prevents theft but also assures a quality result. Finally, let there be no misunderstanding about the consequences for stealing, which should be immediate termination.

When You Suspect a Problem

When you become aware of actual or suspected employee theft, you need to act quickly—but carefully—to resolve the situation.

"Treat the complaint as valid until it is established otherwise, and treat the accused as innocent until proven guilty," says Michael P. O'Brien, a labor and employment attorney with Jones, Waldo, Holbrook & McDonough in Salt Lake City. "Also, treat the matter confidentially to the greatest extent possible." In today's litigious world, protecting the privacy of a suspect is essential; failing to do so can leave you vulnerable if that individual decides to sue later on—regardless of whether the person was actually guilty.

The first step is to conduct a thorough investigation, including a review of all relevant documents, such as personnel files, time sheets, performance evaluations of involved persons, inventory and delivery records, and any applicable financial records. If the premises where the theft occurred have a security system that includes video surveillance, you'll want to review the tapes. You may also want to interview witnesses and others who may have knowledge of the situation. Of course, you should also interview the accused—without making an accusation. When conducting interviews, be clear that the issue under investigation isn't to be discussed with unconcerned parties. "If a witness can't be trusted, think carefully about involving that person [in the investigation] in order to avoid possible defamation problems," says O'Brien.

Regardless of how much you trust a particular witness, avoid disclosing information unnecessarily, and don't ask questions that indicate the direction of your inquiry. Document every step of the investigation, and maintain those records in a secure place separate from your personnel records. Don't make details of an investigation part of an employee's personnel file unless and until the results are in and misconduct has been proved.

If your investigation confirms misconduct of any sort, take immediate and appropriate disciplinary action that's consistent with your general policies. "The worst thing you can do is nothing," O'Brien says. "You need to take some sort of disciplinary action against the individual you've concluded has done an inappropriate act." Certainly you'll want to consider the severity, frequency, and pervasiveness of the conduct—for example, occasionally eating candy from the dishes on the desks of your customers' employees is certainly less severe than taking cash or valuable items out of their desks—but whatever remedy you apply must end the offensive behavior. Keep in mind that whatever you do may wind up in court, so maintain good records and be sure you can always justify your actions.

You must also decide whether to involve law enforcement. Weigh the potential for negative publicity against the potential good, which could include restitution and the fact that the perpetrator may receive some much-needed rehabilitation.

12

Purchasing

When it comes to business purchasing, even the smartest consumer is playing a new game. The rules are different and the stakes significantly higher. But correctly done, purchasing—or procurement—will increase your net income.

Choosing Suppliers

Whether you're buying a major piece of equipment or a bottle of cleaning solution, you should evaluate each vendor on quality, service, and price. Look at the product itself, as well as the supplementary services and support the company provides.

Verify the company's claims before making a purchase commitment. Ask for references, and do a credit check on the vendor just as you would on a new customer. A credit check will tell you how well the supplier pays its own suppliers. This is important because it could ultimately affect you. If your vendor isn't paying his own vendors, he may have trouble getting materials, and that may delay delivery of your order. Or he may simply go out of business without any advance notice, leaving you in the lurch. Also

> ## Bright Idea
>
> Get input from employees when making purchasing decisions on supplies and equipment. The people who are using these items every day know what works and what doesn't, what's efficient and what isn't.

Make a List and Check It Twice

Tracking inventory for a cleaning service business isn't complicated, but it's important. Unlike a retail store, you don't have a wide variety of items to keep up with, but you do need to be sure you have what you need when you need it.

Janitorial services with large buildings as clients usually store products and supplies on site, which means you'll have to track inventory located in multiple sites.

Mike Blair, owner of AAA Prestige Carpet Care in St. George, Utah, says he keeps most of his carpet cleaning supplies on his trucks. "We have shelves on each truck, and we keep a wide variety of chemicals that we utilize in a large variety of situations. It's just a matter of assessing at least once a week what is on the trucks, or having the technicians tell you what they need. I keep [two layers of each item] on the shelf, and when one comes off, I go ahead and order it. We do have a backup inventory, probably another truck's worth, that we keep on the shelves in the storage area. But we don't have to keep a lot of inventory because we can have anything here in two days."

Set up an inventory control and replacement system early and stick with it.

confirm the company's general reputation and financial stability by calling the Better Business Bureau, any appropriate licensing agencies, trade associations, and D&B.

A major component of the purchasing process is the supplier's representative, or salesperson. The knowledge and sophistication levels of individual salespeople often depend on the product or industry; however, they can be a tremendous source of education and information. Make it a rule to treat all salespeople with courtesy and respect.

Besides telling you what they have, salespeople should ask questions. A good salesperson will find out what your needs are and how his company can satisfy them. Just as in the consumer sales arena, commercial salespeople use both high- and low-pressure tactics. Consider studying sales techniques so you can recognize and respond to the methods being used with you.

Buying Supplies

To be sure you don't run out of supplies, you must purchase wisely and in a timely manner. This means establishing and maintaining an effective inventory control system so you'll know when to purchase, what—and what not—to purchase, and how much to purchase. Keep in mind that the caliber of service you provide can be affected by the quality of supplies you use, so choose your products and sources with care.

You probably won't have to use more than a few suppliers to obtain all the supplies you need. Sometimes the suppliers will contact you through their sales reps, but more often, particularly in the beginning, you'll need to locate them. You'll find suppliers of janitorial products in the Yellow Pages of your local telephone directory. They also advertise in trade journals and buyers' directories and exhibit at trade shows and conventions. You'll have two basic types of sources: manufacturers and distributors.

You can buy directly from manufacturers through their own salespeople or independent representatives who handle the product lines of several different companies. These sources usually offer the lowest prices but are also likely to have sizable minimum purchase requirements. Also, they may add on the cost of freight, so be sure to get the total price of getting the products to your door before making a buying decision.

You may choose to buy from a distributor, also known as a wholesaler, broker, or jobber. These operators use quantity discounts to buy

Dollar Stretcher

It's more cost effective to purchase supplies in bulk rather than in small quantities. You'll also save money by buying larger containers rather than smaller ones.

Sign on the Dotted Line

Contracts are a way to make sure both vendor and customer are clear on the details of the sale. This isn't "just a formality" that can be brushed aside. Read all agreements and support documents carefully, and consider having them reviewed by an attorney. Make sure everything that's important to you is in writing. Remember, if it's not part of the contract, it's not part of the deal—no matter what the salesperson says. And if it's in the contract, it's probably enforceable—even if the salesperson says that never happens.

Any contract the vendor writes is naturally going to favor the vendor, but you don't have to agree to all the standard boilerplate terms. In addition, you can demand the inclusion of details that are appropriate to your specific situation. Consider these points when you're negotiating contracts:

○ *Make standard provisions apply to both parties.* If, for example, the contract exempts the vendor from specific liabilities, request that the language be revised to exempt you, too.

○ *Use precise language.* It's difficult to enforce vague language, so be specific. A clause that states the vendor isn't responsible for failures due to "causes beyond the vendor's control" leaves a lot of room for interpretation; more precise language forces a greater level of accountability.

○ *Include a "vendor default" provision.* The vendor's contract probably describes the circumstances under which you would be considered to be in default; include the same protection for yourself.

○ *Be wary of vendor representatives who have to get any contract changes approved by "corporate" or some other higher authority.* This is a negotiating technique that generally works against the customer. Insist that the vendor make available personnel with the authority to negotiate.

from various manufacturers, and then warehouse the goods for sale to janitorial services. Although their prices will be higher than if you bought directly from the manufacturer, they can supply you with smaller quantities, which lets you avoid tying up your cash in excess inventory. Typically, they'll be closer to you than the manufacturer, which means quicker delivery time and a lower freight charge. Many manufacturers will only sell to distributors, so if you contact them, they will refer you to a distributor who can work with you.

Dealing with Suppliers

Reliable suppliers are an asset to your business. They can bail you out when you make an ordering mistake or when your clients make difficult demands on you. But they'll do so only as long as your business is profitable to them. Suppliers are in business to make money. If you argue over every invoice, ask them to shave prices on everything they sell you, or fail to pay your bills promptly, don't be surprised when their salespeople stop calling on you or refuse to help you when you're in a bind.

Of course, you want the best deal you can get on a consistent basis from your suppliers—this is good business. Keep in mind that no worthwhile business arrangement can continue for long unless something of value is rendered and received by all involved. The best approach is to treat your suppliers the way you would like each of your customers to treat you.

Suppliers Are Also Creditors

Most business advice focuses on dealing with your customers, but you're also going to become a customer for your suppliers. That means you'll have to pay for what you buy.

Find out in advance what your suppliers' credit policies are. Most will accept credit cards but will not put you on an open account until they've had a chance to run a check on you. They may ask you to provide a financial statement; if they do, don't even think of inflating your numbers to cover a lack of references. This is a felony, and it's easily detected by most credit managers.

If you do open an account with a supplier, be sure you understand the terms and preserve your credit standing by paying on time. Typically, you'll have 30 days to pay, but many companies offer a discount if you pay early.

Negotiating a Deal

Negotiating doesn't mean that there has to be a winner and a loser. The adversarial relationship that has existed in the past between supplier and customer isn't the best strategy. The most profitable approach is to partner with your suppliers, develop the relationship over time, and work out your differences for a mutual benefit.

The ideal sequence of events in the purchasing process is to determine that the vendor has the product you need, the quality is satisfactory, and the availability in terms of quantity and delivery date meets your requirements. Only then do you begin negotiating price.

Dollar Stretcher

Ask suppliers if payment terms can be a part of your price negotiation. For example, can you get a discount for paying cash in advance?

Price can be approached from several angles. Consider the cost of the item itself, the quantity discounts, add-ons such as freight and insurance, and the payment terms. To determine the true value of a quantity discount, calculate how long you can expect to have the material or merchandise on hand and what your cost of carrying that inventory is. Payment terms are another important consideration. Some vendors offer substantial discounts for early payment; others will extend what amounts to an interest-free, short-term loan by offering lengthier payment terms.

Of course, price isn't the only negotiable point. Every element of the sale is open for negotiation. At all stages of the process, leave room for some give and take. For example, if you're asking for a lower price or more liberal payment terms, can you agree to a more relaxed delivery schedule?

Young and growing businesses are often at a disadvantage in the negotiating process because their initial volume is small or they don't know what their sales will be. Be honest with vendors. Ask them to take a chance on working with you while you're small, in exchange for future potential. Set a time in the future to analyze how you've done and, if necessary, to renegotiate your terms.

Dollar Stretcher

Purchase used towels in bulk from linen services. Cleaning services will have a variety of uses for towels and other linens that are stained or torn and can no longer be used by the linen services' customers.

The key to successful purchasing is becoming partners with your vendors. Choose them carefully and then nurture your relationships for a mutually rewarding alliance.

Equipment

As you're getting started, you may be focused on buying cleaning equipment—but take your blinders off. You'll also need to stock your office with the equipment and supplies necessary to run your business.

Basic Office Equipment

Many entrepreneurs find a trip to the local office supply store more exciting than any mall. It's easy to get carried away when you're surrounded with an abundance of clever gadgets, all designed to make your working life easier and more fun. But if, like most new business owners, you're starting on a budget, discipline yourself to buy only what you need. Consider these primary basic items:

- *Computer and printer.* A computer can help you manage complex bookkeeping and inventory control tasks, calculate estimates, coordinate work loads, maintain customer records, and produce marketing materials. It's a valuable management and marketing tool, and an essential for growing a strong and profitable business, especially in today's technology–dependent world. Printer technology is advancing rapidly; an office supply dealer can help you decide what type of printer(s) you'll need based on what you expect your output to be.

- *Software.* Think of software as your computer's brains, the instructions that tell your computer how to accomplish the functions you need. There are many programs on the market to handle your accounting, inventory, customer information management, and other administrative tasks. Software can be a significant investment, so do a careful analysis of your needs and then study the market and examine a variety of products before making a final decision.

- *Modem.* Modems are necessary to access the internet and online services, and have become a standard component of computers. High–speed internet access is essential for an efficient business operation. Your choices will typically include a high–speed telephone line, cable service, or satellite, although not all these options will be available in every area. The type of modem you'll need depends on how you'll be accessing the internet, and prices can vary depending on the service you need. Shop around for the best service and price package.

Beware!
Although multi-function devices—such as a copier/printer/fax machine or a fax/telephone/answering machine—may cost less initially and need less space in your office than stand–alone items, if the equipment fails, you'll lose all these functions simultaneously. Also, consider the machine's efficiency rating and cost to operate; compare that with stand–alone items before making a purchase. Tough decision? Pick the machine that best suits the needs of your business.

Beware of extremely low prices, as–is deals, and closeouts when it comes to purchasing computer equipment. Deals like these often hide problems you wouldn't want, even for free.

- *Photocopier.* The photocopier is a fixture of the modern office and can be useful to even the smallest cleaning service business. You can get a basic, low–end, no–frills personal copier for $100 to $500 in just about any office supply store. More elaborate models increase proportionately in price. If you anticipate a heavy volume (rare for a cleaning service), consider leasing.

- *Fax machine.* Fax capability has become another must in modern offices, and with the rapidly dropping prices for faxes, it's also becoming more affordable. You can either add a fax card to your computer, use an online fax service, or buy a multifunction printer with fax capability, or a stand–alone machine. If you use your computer, it must be on to send or receive faxes, and the transmission may interrupt other work. Most residential cleaning operations will have limited fax needs; commercial cleaners will likely have a higher demand for fax service. Expect to pay about $100 for a single–function plain–paper fax to $175 to $750 for a multifunction device (fax/copier/printer/scanner).

- *Postage scale.* Unless all your mail is identical, a postage scale is a valuable investment. An accurate scale takes the guesswork out of postage and will quickly pay for itself. It's a good idea to weigh every piece of mail to eliminate the risk of items being returned for insufficient postage or overpaying when you're unsure of the weight. Light mailers—one to 12 articles per day—will be adequately served by inexpensive mechanical postal scales, which typically range from $10 to $25. If you're averaging 12 to 24 items per day, consider a digital scale, which is somewhat more expensive—generally from $50 to $200—but significantly more accurate than a mechanical unit. If you send more than 24 items per day or use priority or expedited services frequently, invest in an electronic computing scale, which weighs the item and calculates the rate via the carrier of your choice, making it easy for you to compare. Programmable electronic scales range from $80 to $250.

- *Postage meter.* Postage meters allow you to pay for postage in advance and print the exact amount on the mailing piece

> **Bright Idea**
>
> Postage stamps come in an array of sizes, designs, and themes, and can add elements of color, whimsy, and even thoughtfulness to mail. Stamps look more personal; metered mail looks more corporate. Consider using metered mail for invoices, statements, and other official business, and stamps for thank–you notes and similar marketing correspondence that could use a personal touch.

when it's used. Many postage meters can print in increments of one–tenth of a cent, which can add up to big savings for bulk mail users. Meters also provide a "big company" professional image, are more convenient than stamps, and can save you money in a number of ways. Postage meters are leased, not sold, with rates starting at about $20 per month, or you can get a meter/electronic scale combo for $30 to $120 per month. They require a license, which is available from

> ### Bright Idea
> Be sure to include your area code with your phone number on all your printed materials (stationery, brochures, signs, etc.). As more areas convert to ten–digit dialing, more consumers will see a seven–digit number as incomplete.

your local post office. Only four manufacturers are licensed by the U.S. Postal Service to manufacture and lease postage meters; your local post office can provide you with contact information. An alternative to a postage meter that will allow you to avoid buying stamps is to print your postage online. Visit the U.S. Postal Service website at usps.gov or check out private companies, such as stamps.com, for more information.

- *Paper shredder.* A response to both a growing concern for privacy and the need to recycle and conserve space in landfills, shredders are increasingly common in both homes and offices. They allow you to destroy incoming unsolicited direct mail, as well as sensitive internal documents before they're discarded. Shredded paper can be compacted more tightly than paper tossed in a wastebasket, so conserves landfill space. Light–duty shredders start at about $25, and heavier–capacity shredders run $150 to $500.

- *Credit– and debit–card processing equipment.* This could range from a simple imprint machine to an online terminal. Consult with several merchant status providers to determine the most appropriate and cost–effective equipment for your business.

Telecommunications

The ability to communicate quickly with your customers and suppliers is essential to any business. Also, being able to reach your employees when they're out on jobs is important. Advancing technology gives you a wide range of telecommunications options. Most telephone companies have created departments dedicated to small and homebased businesses; contact your local service provider and ask to speak with someone who can review your needs and help you put together a service and equipment package that will work for you. Specific elements to keep in mind include the following.

Telephone

Whether you're homebased or in a commercial location, a single line should be adequate during the startup period. As you grow and your call volume increases, you'll add more lines.

Your telephone can be a tremendous productivity tool, and most of the models on the market today are rich in features you'll find useful. Such features include automatic redial, which redials the last number called at regular intervals until the call is completed; programmable memory for storing frequently called numbers; and speakerphones for hands–free use. You may also want call forwarding, which allows you to forward calls to another number when you're not at your desk, and call waiting, which signals you that another call is coming in while you're on the phone. These services are typically available through your telephone company included in your monthly charge or for a fee.

If you're going to be spending a lot of time on the phone, perhaps doing marketing or handling customer service, consider a headset for comfort and efficiency. A cordless phone lets you move around freely while talking. You may find that this wide variety of products will help you in your business; however, these units vary in price and quality, so research them before making a purchase.

Stock Me Up

In addition to equipment, you'll need an assortment of office supplies. Those items include:

- ❏ Correction fluid or tape (to correct typewritten or hand-written documents)
- ❏ Desktop document trays
- ❏ Letter opener
- ❏ Paper and other supplies for your fax machine
- ❏ Paper clips
- ❏ Pens, pencils, and holders
- ❏ Plain paper for your copier and printer
- ❏ Scissors
- ❏ Scratch pads
- ❏ Staplers, staples, and staple removers
- ❏ "Sticky" notes in an assortment of sizes
- ❏ Tape and dispensers
- ❏ Trash cans

Answering Machine/Voice Mail

Because your business phone should never go unanswered, you need some sort of reliable answering device to take calls when you can't do it yourself. Whether you buy an answering machine (expect to pay $40 to $150 for a model that's suitable for a business) or use the voice–mail service provided through your telephone company depends on your personal preferences, work style, and needs.

Cell Phone

Once considered a luxury, cell phones are almost as common as land lines and have even replaced land lines for many users. You may want a cell phone that you use exclusively for business so that your staff can reach you at any time. Most have features similar to your office phone—such as caller ID, call waiting, and voice mail—and equipment and service packages are reasonably priced.

Bargain Basement

When you begin shopping for equipment for your cleaning service, keep in mind that you can buy secondhand equipment for a fraction of its retail cost. Businesses that have failed, merged, or outgrown their existing equipment are often good sources for used office equipment. Janitorial and residential cleaning companies can be sources of used cleaning equipment, and carpet cleaning businesses may be selling their used carpet cleaning equipment.

Judicious shopping can turn up some excellent bargains. Check the classified section of your daily paper and the weekly business journal for furniture and equipment bargains. Also check the "Business Opportunities" or "Businesses for Sale" categories—businesses that are being liquidated or sold may have excess furniture or equipment for sale at substantial savings. Check eBay and other online auctions, as well as online classified sites such as Craigslist, for new, used, and reconditioned equipment.

Another good source for used equipment is new equipment suppliers. They frequently have trade–ins or repossessions for 50 percent off. Often, these items have been refurbished and even include a warranty.

Toll–Free Number

Most cleaning services are local operations. But if you're planning to build a large operation, or if you're in a niche business and targeting a customer base outside your local calling area, you'll want to provide a toll–free number. This way, customers can reach you without having to make a long–distance call. Most long–distance service providers offer toll–free numbers, and they have a wide range of service and price packages. If you have a regional business, you may also find a toll–free number useful. Shop around to find the best deal for you.

E–Mail

E–mail is a standard element in any company's communication package. It allows for fast, efficient, 24–hour communication. If you have e–mail, check your messages regularly and reply to them promptly. E–mail costs range from free to $20 per month.

Dollar Stretcher

When a postage increase is coming up, stock up on "forever" stamps, which can be purchased at the current rate and are good for mailing one–ounce first–class mail anytime in the future, regardless of price changes.

Marketing

If you've built the proverbial better mousetrap, will the world really beat a path to your door? Only if they know about your business. Of course, you must provide quality service, but you must also create a marketing machine to help drive your sales. Check out *Start Your Own Business* (Entrepreneur Press), which explains how to create a basic marketing plan, but

▲

there are issues and ideas specific to the cleaning service business that you need to know as you develop your plan.

Researching and Defining Your Market

Though the total market for cleaning services is tremendous, you must decide on the particular niche you'll target. If you want to do residential cleaning, do you want to clean private homes, condos and apartments, or empty rental units? If you're starting a janitorial business, will you focus on offices, retail operations, or manufacturing facilities? And will you target small, medium, or large customers? As a carpet cleaner, will you clean residential or commercial facilities—or both? And what services other than shampooing carpets will you provide?

Once you've decided on a market niche, you must look at the geographic area you want to serve. If you're starting a maid service, as we discussed in Chapter 3, you want to be able to schedule cleanings in a way that minimizes your travel time, so you need to restrict your service area to a particular part of town. The same applies to carpet cleaners. Janitorial crews that must move from building to building have a similar concern.

Talk of the Town

A prospective customer begins forming an opinion of your operation from the moment your phone is—or isn't—answered. Handling incoming calls should be an important part of your marketing strategy. Regardless of the size of your company and whether you answer incoming calls yourself or have a receptionist, consider these suggestions:

○ Answer all calls promptly; a good goal is by the second ring.
○ Speak clearly and distinctly so there is no doubt as to what company the caller has reached.
○ Give the name of the company, the individual's name, and then offer to help. For example: "Good morning, ABC Cleaning. This is Julie. How may I help you?"
○ Always get permission before placing a call on hold.
○ Use a warm, friendly tone; smile at callers even though they can't see you.

After you've identified what you want to do and where you'd like to do it, research the demographics of the area to be sure it contains a sufficient number of potential customers. If it does, you're ready to move ahead. If it doesn't, you'll need to reconsider how you've defined your niche or the geographic area.

Your market research doesn't have to be extremely sophisticated. Many small maid service owners simply talk to their friends. Carpet and upholstery cleaning service owner Mike Blair began by talking with people he knew in the St. George, Utah, community. When they indicated there was room for another quality cleaner, he checked the Yellow Pages to identify how many companies he would be competing with, did some basic demographic analysis, and got to work.

> **Smart Tip** Tip...
>
> Once you're established, be sure to use your longevity as a marketing tool. Because many cleaning service businesses require a minimal investment and are easy to start, the attrition rate is high. Customers prefer to do business with companies they believe will be around in the future, so after you've been in business a few years, trumpet that fact in your marketing efforts.

Part of your market analysis includes your costs to serve that market. A densely populated market allows you to serve a greater number of customers because your travel time is minimal, but it also means you'll be consuming more supplies. This needs to be planned for as well as factored into your rates.

You can build a successful cleaning business based on referrals, but you need those first customers to get started. Where are they? Indianapolis–based Bane–Clene Corp. suggests you start by contacting the following groups:

- Friends and relatives
- Neighbors
- Former co–workers and employers
- Social groups and clubs, including card clubs, bowling teams, athletic leagues, lodges, fraternities, alumni groups, and neighborhood associations
- Church or religious acquaintances

Communicating with Your Market

Communicating with your market to encourage people to become customers is known as marketing. Marketing isn't an exact science, and what works for one company may not work for another. Even so, the best approach is to look at what other successful companies are doing and adapt their techniques to your operation. Give each marketing effort a reasonable chance to work, but if you aren't getting an adequate return on your investment, try something else.

Most of your marketing efforts will cost money, which is why you need to be able to measure the results of the campaigns. You don't want to keep spending money on an advertising program that isn't working, and when you find something that's successful, you'll probably want to do more of it. If you use coupons, you can code them. When new customers call, ask how they heard about you. If it was from an ad, find out which one. If it was a referral, get the name of the person who recommended you.

Networking is one of the most difficult marketing efforts to measure. It won't be exact, but you should keep track of how much time you spend on various networking efforts and how much business you credit to those contacts so you can be sure your time is well spent.

> **Smart Tip** *Tip...*
>
> Ask every new customer how they found out about you. Make a note of where they heard about you and what kind of business they represent. This will tell you how well your various marketing efforts are working. You can then decide to increase certain programs and eliminate those that either aren't working or are attracting a type of business you don't want.

Carpet and upholstery cleaner Blair says he invests 5 to 8 percent of his gross profit in marketing. "We do coupons, radio ads, and some television and print media," he says. "Then we call our customers back after the job is done and let them know we're grateful for their business and make sure the work was done to their liking. If we can't reach them by phone, we send a personal note."

Wherever you place it, your marketing message should contain these basic elements:

- What you do
- The benefit the customer will receive when they buy your service
- Who you are
- How to reach you

Here is what some successful cleaning business owners do to market their companies:

- *Make customer service a marketing tool.* There is probably no business where customer service works better as a marketing tool than in the cleaning business. You'll have a lot of opportunity to interact with your customers; take advantage of each contact to demonstrate your superior service.
- *Make people want to talk about you in a positive way.* Word–of–mouth is absolutely the best advertising—and it's free. If you do a great job, your customers will tell their friends and associates. (Of course, they'll also tell their friends and associates if you do a bad job!) Especially if you're small and want to stay that way, word–of–mouth may be your primary method of advertising.

Dead as a Doorknob

Many cleaning services that target residential customers use doorknob hangers to let neighbors know they've done a job in the area. While this may generate some new business for you, it's an approach that could backfire.

When the service subsidiary of Indianapolis–based Bane–Clene Corp. conducted a survey on the issue, they found that the majority of consumers don't wish to be used as referrals unless they decide to do the referring themselves. Another objection to doorknob hangers is that if the resident is out of town, your sales piece becomes an alert to burglars that no one is at home.

Bane–Clene advises limiting your use of doorknob hangers to serving as a notice of your visit and instructions for rescheduling if the customer isn't at home at the time of your appointment.

Orlando maid service owner Fenna Owens says, "I've never advertised because other people refer me."

- *Reward referrals.* An existing customer who refers a new customer should at the very least be thanked, and at the most receive some sort of compensation or reward. An important point to keep in mind about referrals is that people rarely make a referral because you're going to give them something. They make referrals because they like what you do, they believe you'll do a good job for the other person, and when you do, you make them look like stars because they were smart enough to know you. But a referral reward of some sort is a way to emphasize to your existing customers how important referrals are to you.

- *Make yourself visible.* One of the simplest ways to build business and set yourself apart from the competition is to just get out there and be visible. Knock on doors, hand out brochures, go to networking events—do whatever it takes to make sure people know about your company and understand what you do.

Bright Idea

If you operate a residential cleaning business, offer gift certificates so your services can be purchased as a gift. People will give one–time–only cleanings to friends and relatives for special occasions, before holidays, or to help out during a crisis. This will not only generate extra revenue for you, but the recipients of the gift may become customers.

- *Get professional help.* Your marketing materials project the image of your company—and if you want to be perceived as a professional operation, your marketing materials need to look professional. Just because you have a computer and a laser printer doesn't mean you can turn out quality ads and brochures.

> ## Bright Idea
>
> Human nature mandates that people will go to greater lengths to avoid pain than they will to seek pleasure. As you develop your marketing plan, focus on communicating the message that you can help your customers avoid the pain of doing the cleaning themselves.

If you can't afford to hire an ad agency, look for less expensive alternatives. Blair suggests checking with the marketing department at your local college or university. Students will often take on your business as a project at no cost (or a nominal fee for materials) and help you develop a marketing plan and professionally designed collateral material.

Another thing you may want to consider is joining a lead–exchange club to kick start your referrals. Most of these clubs are groups of local business owners, professionals, and salespeople who want to build their customer base. Typically, they restrict membership to one person in a given industry, so you won't have any competitors in the group. They meet regularly—weekly, biweekly, or monthly—and each member is expected to bring at least one lead to the meeting. The lead can be for any other member or for the group at large. Members of these groups usually become each other's customers as well.

To find a lead–exchange group, check the business calendar section of your local paper; many post notices of their meetings and will have a number you can call for more information. Check out several before deciding which one to join; make sure the group you choose is dynamic and will generate some good leads for you.

Do You Need a Website?

In the internet age, every business should have an online presence, even if it's only a basic website. If you're starting a janitorial or other cleaning service that targets business customers, a website is important because it helps establish you as a legitimate, credible company. If you're planning to be a small, one- or two–person operation targeting residential clients, you can probably get by without a site. Of course, if you're going to accept online payments through a service such as PayPal, a website is essential.

A website will allow prospective customers to learn more about you before they call. You can include the services you offer, the geographical area you serve, and contact information, and have a form that will let visitors ask questions or request a quote. Your site should be professionally designed, user–friendly, and always up–to–date.

The Elements of Image

One of your most important marketing tools is the image you project. Jim Cavanaugh, founder of Jani–King International, a commercial cleaning franchise in Dallas, says image is made up of several components, including:

- *The way you and your crew look.* Are your workers clean and neat, wearing attractive uniforms or at least nice jeans or slacks?

- *Your printed materials.* Are your invoices and statements typed neatly or computerized? Do the documents you produce display professionalism, or do you damage your image by using handwritten bills and scrap paper for notes?

- *Equipment.* Is your equipment clean and in good repair, or dirty, with loose wheels, taped cords, and in general disrepair?

- *Integrity.* Do you operate and behave in such a way that building managers and owners are comfortable trusting you and your employees with unsupervised access to their facilities?

- *Insurance.* Having adequate business insurance, including liability, workers' compensation, and bonding your employees, builds your credibility and image.

- *Your vehicles.* Are your company vehicles clean, running properly, and neatly marked with your company name and logo? A dirty, dented truck that belches smoke won't impress your clients.

You can create a positive image for your company by getting involved in a community service program. In 1996, Ann Arbor, Michigan–based Molly Maid, a residential cleaning franchise, established its Ms. Molly Foundation, which holds an annual "Making a Difference" drive to assist victims of domestic violence. The foundation was established to provide financial and in–kind support to safe houses and shelters, as well as promote education on issues related to domestic violence, including the dynamics involved, safety tips, and escape planning.

Each year in October, Domestic Violence Awareness Month, Molly Maid's home service professionals place a small card in the home of each customer explaining the mission of the Ms. Molly Foundation. This offers the customer an opportunity to participate by donating needed items to shelters. The program lets Molly Maid's home service workers, many of whom are unable to make sizable cash donations, contribute meaningfully to a cause that's important to them. It also boosts the company's image with its current customers as well as within the community at large.

You may not be in a position to form your own nonprofit foundation, but you can easily do small–scale activities, such as sponsoring teams in fund–raising walks, making a contribution to a charity as a referral reward, or donating a few hours of your cleaning services to a worthy cause.

Trade Shows

Trade shows can be a tremendous source of education and information about the cleaning industry, and they can also be a great way to market. Blair attended a number of trade shows, especially when he was new to the business. "They were very beneficial, and I highly recommend trade shows as a way to shop," he says. But when you're at a show, don't just shop.

In addition to attending trade shows to find equipment and supplies and learn more about running your business, consider exhibiting at trade shows to market your services. Local trade shows can provide a tremendous amount of exposure at a very affordable cost.

There are two types of shows—consumer (which focus on home, garden, and other consumer themes) and business–to–business (where exhibitors market their products and services to other companies). Which will work best for you depends on the type of cleaning business you have and the market you're targeting.

"When you go to a show, you're tapping into an audience that is typically outside your network," says Allen Konopacki, a trade show consultant with Incomm Research Center in Chicago. "The other important thing is that the individuals who are going to shows are usually driven by a need. In fact, 76 percent of the people who go to a show are looking to make some kind of a decision on a purchase in the near future."

To find out about shows in your area, call your local chamber of commerce or convention center and ask for a calendar. You can also check out *Trade Show Week Show Directory*, which should be available in your public library, or do an internet search.

When you have identified potential shows, contact the sponsor for details. Find out who will attend—show sponsors should be able to estimate the total attendance and give you demographics so you can tell if the attendees fit your target market profile.

Trade Secrets

Trade shows and conventions are valuable business tools, whether you're attending to shop and learn or exhibiting to get more business. For more information on how to get more out of trade shows, and to find show schedules, visit these trade show websites: Incomm Research Center, tradeshowresearch.com; Trade Show Central, tscentral.com; Trade Show News Network, tsnn.com; and Tradeshow Week Online, tradeshowweek.com.

Also ask if it's appropriate to make sales from your booth so you can plan your display and bring sufficient inventory.

Give as much thought to the setup of your booth as you would to an in–store display. Your exhibit doesn't need to be elaborate or expensive, but it does need to be professional and inviting. Avoid trying to cram so much into your booth that it looks cluttered.

Your signage should focus first on the problems you solve for clients and then list your company name. If you have a maid service, one of the major benefits you pro-

> **Spend Saturdays doing what you want.**
> **We'll clean your house**
> **so you don't have to.**
> **ABC Maid Service**

vide to customers is giving them some free time. So your sign might read:

Although the show sponsors will probably provide one, don't put a table across the front of your exhibit space; that creates a visual and psychological barrier and will discourage visitors from coming in.

Don't leave your booth unattended during exhibit hours. First, it's a security risk— at a busy show, it would be easy for someone to walk off with valuable equipment. More important, you could miss a tremendous sales opportunity. Even if you're a one–person operation, find someone who can work the show with you so that you can take breaks during the day.

Consider some sort of giveaway items such as pens, mugs, or notepads imprinted with your company name. But, says Konopacki, don't display these items openly; that will only crowd your booth with "trade show tourists." Instead, store them discreetly out of sight and present them individually as appropriate. You should also have a stock of brochures, business cards, and perhaps discount coupons.

To collect lead information for later follow–up, consider giving away a reasonable amount of your services. If you have a maid service, you could give away a certificate worth three hours of cleaning time. A carpet cleaner could give away cleaning three rooms of carpet, or one room and two pieces of upholstered furniture. Hold a drawing that people must register for, and make the registration form a lead qualification tool. For example, if it's a business–to–business show, the registration form should ask their name, company name, whether an outside janitorial service is used, who in the company should be contacted to learn more about what you have to offer, and, of course, complete address and telephone information. At a consumer show, find out if they live in apartments, condos, or single–family homes, if they own or rent, and get addresses. Depending on the size and duration of the show, consider giving away more than one service package so you can hold drawings several times during the course of the show.

When the show is over, immediately send a follow–up letter to all the qualified leads you collected, thanking them for visiting your booth and reminding them of the services you offer. Don't assume that they'll keep the information they picked up at the show; chances are, it will be lost in the pile of material from other exhibitors.

Trade Show Tips

A carnival–like atmosphere permeates many trade shows. You want all involved to enjoy themselves, but remember this is a business occasion. Your booth is your store/office for the duration of the show, and it should be a place where you're proud to meet with customers. Establishing dress and conduct rules for your booth staff will make your trade show experience much more rewarding.

- *No smoking, drinking, eating, or gum–chewing by booth staffers.* Too many people are offended by cigarette smoke, and most exhibit halls restrict smoking to designated areas. While most shows provide refreshments, bringing food and beverages into the booth creates an unattractive mess. Who wants to talk to a sales rep whose mouth is full?

- *Dress appropriately.* Just because the show is taking place in a resort doesn't mean you should wear shorts. Standard business attire and comfortable shoes are the best bet.

- *Staff the booth properly.* Two people for every ten feet of space is a good rule of thumb. The key is to make sure your booth isn't overcrowded with your own people or understaffed so visitors can't get the assistance they need.

- *Take regular breaks.* Trade shows can be exhausting. Plan to allow everyone a few minutes away from the booth at scheduled intervals. Also allow time for personnel to see the entire show as early as possible; they'll gain a feel for the competition and pick up ideas for your next show.

- *Remain standing.* Talk to each other only when necessary. Potential visitors may be reluctant to approach your booth if it appears that your salespeople are just relaxing and having a great time chatting among themselves.

> **Tip...**
>
> ## Smart Tip
> When you hand someone your business card, always give them two—one for them to keep and one for them to pass on to someone else.

15

Tales from the Trenches

By now, you should know how to get started and you have a good idea of what to do—and not to do—in your own cleaning service business. But nothing teaches as well as the voice of experience. So we asked established cleaning service business operators to tell us what has contributed to their success and what they think causes some companies to fail. Here are their stories.

Never Stop Learning

The cleaning industry may not be the most glamorous or complex, but established business owners say there's always something to learn. Technology advances affect the equipment you use, safety issues affect the chemicals you clean with, and there will always be ways you can enhance your organizational and managerial skills.

Read industry publications, go to meetings and conventions, participate in trade organizations, and encourage your suppliers to keep you up to date.

Tap All Your Resources

A wide range of associations serves various aspects of the professional cleaning industry. These groups can help you with operational, marketing, and management issues. Many state and government agencies also offer support and information for small businesses. Salt Lake City janitorial service owner Michael Ray says using professional associations and seeking help from the government are great ways to maximize your resources.

Clean It Like It's Your Own

Regardless of what you're cleaning and whether you're doing traditional housecleaning or janitorial work, or providing a specialty cleaning service, clean like you're cleaning your own home or office. Residential cleaning service owner Fenna Owens in Orlando has a waiting list of people who want to hire her because, she says, "I do what I would like to have done at my house."

Develop Systems

Systems provide a structure that allows you to work consistently and efficiently, and also let you create a company that will continue to run whether you're there or not. Ray has created systems for every function: cleaning, laundry, supervision, reporting, customer service, accounting, and management.

Be Careful!

Though time is your most valuable commodity, don't rush so much that you get careless. Owens once accidentally vacuumed up some computer wires; fortunately, the replacement part only cost $70 (it could have been substantially more). More important, the customer wasn't happy.

Customers will usually understand that accidents happen, but you're better off if you don't have to fall back on that. Also, the cost to repair or replace something—in out–of–pocket cash, time lost, and damaged customer relations—is usually far more than the time you might save by working carelessly.

Don't Undersell Yourself

When you're starting out, you may be tempted to try to undercut the competition's prices. A better strategy is to simply outperform them by providing quality work.

"When I first started, if somebody was charging $50, I would do it for $40," Owens says. Now she quotes strictly on the amount of work involved. "If you're good, people will pay you—and they'll see within one week whether you're good or not."

Take Care of Your Employees

Your employees are critical to your success; after all, it's the quality of their performance that determines whether your customers are satisfied. Look for ways to make them want to do their best. Train them well, don't micromanage, and treat them with respect. Provide bonuses and incentives for top performance, and consider offering perks such as letting your employees use company equipment in their own homes.

Prepare for the Worst

No matter how knowledgeable or skilled you are, you'll always have problems, and you need to be prepared to deal with them. "There is never a day when you would say everything is perfect," Ray says. "Today, I'm not asking *if* there are problems in my company, I'm asking *where* they are. I can go to any building and find some problems. It's a humbling thing, because there is always something around the corner that needs to be addressed."

Watch Your Chemical Combos

Be careful not to mix cleaning solutions except as suggested by the manufacturer; you could inadvertently create a dangerous compound. Owens learned that the hard way when she followed a customer's request to use a particular chemical combination—which created fumes that caused Owens and her customer to flee the house, gasping for air.

Find a Niche

Don't try to be all things to all people; pick the market you can best serve, and focus on that. For example, Ray's janitorial service market consists of office buildings, manufacturing plants, and corporate headquarters that are more than 100,000 square feet. Because a supervisor is assigned to each work site, Ray's company can't provide quality work at a profitable price level to smaller facilities. "Excel in what you're doing and build consistency in the services you provide," he says. When you try to serve too many markets, you won't be successful in any of them.

Develop Your Computer Skills

You need to be as skilled with your computer as you are with a mop or buffer. The cleaning business may not be particularly high tech, but you don't have time to do estimates, billing, payroll, inventory control, and other record–keeping by hand.

Ray recommends using a spreadsheet program to calculate the workload for janitorial jobs. "You owe it to yourself to get familiar with a spreadsheet program," he says. "You can use it for so many things."

Track Labor Costs

The biggest single expense you have is labor, and you must stay on top of it. "If you are not watching your labor costs every day, it will get away from you like a two–year–old left alone in the kitchen," says Ray. "Work fills the time allowed for its completion. Watch your labor every day. Make sure it's within your budget. We have a daily over and under report, which is one of our most effective tools." The report makes it easy to spot trends before they become major issues.

If labor is on the increase, figure out where the problem is. Is the customer asking for extra services you aren't charging for? Did you underestimate the time it would take to do the work? If you're under on your labor estimates, make sure your employees are providing the quality you've promised.

Invest in Customer Service

The quality of your cleaning is important, but it's not everything. Building strong relationships with your clients requires a serious commitment to customer service. Don't assume that just because the work looks satisfactory to you that it is to your customers—or that there's nothing else they want or need.

Ray has a full–time customer service manager. "His full–time job is to go out to our buildings and talk to the customers, inspect their facilities, make sure they're happy, make sure they know we're interested, that we care, that we want to know how things are going," he says. "Most companies have somebody in management who doubles as that and goes out to talk to customers when there's a problem. But we have somebody who's proactive. He does a written report on every building, and the customer gets a copy of that report. They see what we see as problems and our plans for improvement."

Keep Your Eye on the Economy

As long as things get dirty, there will be a need for professionals to clean them. But economic changes can mean changes in your market. Residential cleaning services, for example, are often seen as luxuries, and an economic downturn could affect your customers' willingness and ability to pay to have their homes cleaned. When business profits shrink, companies look for ways to cut expenses, which means they may examine their cleaning budgets for services that can be reduced or eliminated.

Also consider how the world economy can impact your profitability. If oil prices skyrocket, you'll have to spend more to operate your vehicles, and your general utility costs will probably increase. When the cost of lumber goes up, so does the cost of bathroom tissue, paper towels, and other disposable paper products you provide to your customers. You may be able to pass along some of those costs, but don't let that be your only strategy for dealing with such occurrences.

Don't depend on a thriving economy to keep your business profitable. Have plans in place so you can shift your market focus if necessary. You may want to target a different group of customers or adjust your service offerings and pricing. Don't invest a great deal of time on this issue too far in advance, but be prepared to deal with it if it becomes necessary.

Don't Take Every Job

If you can't make money on a job, or if the work is undesirable for any reason, turn it down. It's better to focus your time and energy on profitable work you enjoy.

Appendix
Cleaning Services Resources

They say you can never be too rich or too thin. While these could be argued, we believe you can never have too many resources. Therefore, we present for your consideration a wealth of sources for you to check into, check out, and harness for your own personal information blitz. These sources are tidbits, ideas to get you started on your research.

They are by no means the only sources out there, and they shouldn't be taken as the Ultimate Answer. We have done our research, but businesses tend to move, change, fold, and expand. As we have repeatedly stressed, do your homework. Get out there and start investigating.

Associations

Association of Residential Cleaning Services International
7870 Olentangy River Rd., #300
Columbus, OH 43235
(614) 547–0887
arcsi.org

▲

Building Service Contractors Association International
401 N. Michigan Ave., 22nd Fl.
Chicago, IL 60611
(800) 368–3414, (312) 321–5167
bscai.org

Carpet and Rug Institute
P.O. Box 2048
Dalton, GA 30722–2048
(706) 278–3176
carpet–rug.org

Carpet Cleaners Institute of the Northwest
Association Management Inc.
P.O. Box 6906
Tacoma, WA 98417
(877) 692–2469, (253) 265–3042
ccinw.org

Chimney Safety Institute of America
2155 Commercial Dr.
Plainfield, IN 46168
(317) 837–5362
csia.org

Cleaning Equipment Trade Association
P.O. Box 1710
Indian Trail, NC 28079
(800) 441–0111, (704) 635–7362
ceta.org

Cleaning Management Institute
cminstitute.net

Institute of Inspection, Cleaning and Restoration Certification
2515 E. Mill Plain Bl.
Vancouver, WA 98661
(360) 693–5675
iicrc.org

International Janitorial Cleaning Services Association
2011 Oak
Wyandotte, MI 48192
(888) 626–6611
ijcsa.com

International Window Cleaning Association
400 Admiral Bl.
Kansas City, MO 64102
(800) 875–4922, (816) 471–4922
iwca.org

ISSA: The Worldwide Cleaning Industry Association
7373 N. Lincoln Ave.
Lincolnwood, IL 60712–1799
(800) 225–4772, (847) 982–0800
issa.com

Professional Carpet & Upholstery Cleaners Association
P.O. Box 21412
Denver, CO 80221
(877) 447–2822
pcuca.org

Society of Cleaning and Restoration Technicians
234 Cedric St.
Leesburg, GA 31763
(800) 949–4728, (229) 883–1202
scrt.org

Consultants and Other Experts

David Cohen
President, Expense Reduction Group Inc.
945 Clint Moore Rd.
Boca Raton, FL 33487
(561) 852–1099
expensereductiongroupinc.com

Allen Konopacki
Trade Show Consultant
Incomm Research Center
5574 N. Northwest Hwy.
Chicago, IL 60630
(312) 642–9377
tradeshowresearch.com

Credit Card Services

American Express Merchant Services
(888) 829–7302
americanexpress.com

Discover Card Merchant Services
(800) 347–6673
discovercard.com

Master Card
(914) 249–4843
mastercard.com

PayPal
paypal.com

VISA
(800) VISA–311, ext. 96
visa.com

Equipment and Supply Sources

Bane–Clene Corp.
Carpet and floor cleaning equipment supplies, training, and services
3940 N. Keystone Ave.
Indianapolis, IN 46205
(800) 428–9512
baneclene.com

DirtyBlinds.com
Blind cleaners and light lens cleaners
11256 Broadway
Alden, NY 14004
(800) 976–6427, (716) 685–9203
dirtyblinds.com

Industrial Supply
Safety equipment, cleaning equipment, and supplies
1635 S. 300 West
Salt Lake City, UT 84115

(801) 484–8644
indsupply.com

International Ceiling and Wall Cleaning Inc.
Ceiling and wall cleaning products and equipment
1555 Sunshine Dr.
Clearwater, FL 33765
(800) 628–4422
icwc.com

J. Racenstein & Co. Inc.
Window cleaning tools and equipment
74 Henry St.
Secaucus, NJ 07094
(800) 221–3748
jracenstein.com

Powr–Flite
Commercial floor care equipment
3101 Wichita Ct.
Fort Worth, TX 76140–1710
(800) 880–2913, (817) 551–0700
powr–flite.com

Pro–Team
Backpack vacuums
(866) 888–2168
pro–team.com

Royce Rolls Ringer Co.
Carts, buckets, and wringers
(800) 253–9638
roycerolls.net

Franchise and Business Opportunities

Coverall Cleaning Concepts
Coverall North America Inc.
Commercial cleaning
(800) 537–3371
coverall.com

Jani–King International
Commercial cleaning
16885 Dallas Pkwy.
Addison, TX 75001
(800) 526–5464, (972) 991–0900
janiking.com

MaidPro Corp.
180 Canal St.
Boston, MA 02114
(617) 742–8080
maidpro.com

The Maids International
4820 Dodge St.
Omaha, NE 68132
(800) 843–6243
maids.com

Molly Maid
3948 Ranchero Dr.
Ann Arbor, MI 48108
(800) 665–5962
mollymaid.com

ServiceMaster Co.
Residential and commercial cleaning, other service franchises
860 Ridge Lake Bl.
Memphis, TN 38120
(901) 597–1400
svm.com

Swisher Hygiene Co.
Restroom hygiene
4725 Piedmont Row Dr., #400
Charlotte, NC 28210
(877) 7SWISHER
swisheronline.com

Internet and Government Resources

CleanLink
Information resource for sanitary supply distributors, building service contractors, and in–house cleaning professionals
cleanlink.com

CleanOutlook
Web and logo design
cleanoutlook.com

Occupational Safety & Health Administration
osha.gov

Salary.com
On–demand data and software related to employee compensation
salary.com

U.S. Department of Labor
dol.gov

U.S. Patent and Trademark Office
uspto.gov

Magazines and Publications

Cleanfax
Carpet care and disaster restoration
National Trade Publications Inc.
13 Century Hill Dr.
Latham, NY 12110–2197
(518) 783–1281
cleanfax.com

Cleaning & Maintenance Management *magazine*
National Trade Publications Inc.
13 Century Hill Dr.
Latham, NY 12110–2197
(518) 783–1281
cmmonline.com

Cleaning Business *magazine*
cleaningbusiness.com

Construction Cleanup: A Guide to an Exciting & Profitable Cleaning Specialty
Don Aslett
Marsh Creek Press
(888) 748–3535

Don Aslett's Stainbuster's Bible: The Complete Guide to Spot Removal
Don Aslett
Plume
(888) 748–3535

Entrepreneur's Almanac: Fundamentals, Facts and Figures You Need to Run and Grow Your Business
Jacquelyn Lynn
Entrepreneur Press
entrepreneurpress.com

Green Cleaning for Dummies
Stephen Ashkin and David Holly
greencleaningfordummies.com

How to Clean Windows Like the Pros
John Baxter
International Window Cleaning Association
iwca.org

How to Upgrade and Motivate Your Cleaning Crews
Don Aslett
Marsh Creek Press
(888) 748–3535

In Search of the Five–Cent Nickel: More than 399 Ways to Get Ahead in Any Economy
Don Abbott and Jacquelyn Lynn
Liza Jayne Publishing
lizajaynepublishing.com

Successful Cleaning Services

AAA Prestige Carpet Care
Mike Blair

St. George, UT
(435) 652–3736

Biotrauma Inc.
Ryan Sawyer and Benjamin Lichtenwalner
999 Chestnut St.
Gainesville, GA 30501
(770) 262–7206
biotrauma.com

Page's Personal Cleaning
Patti Page
Cincinnati, OH
pagespersonalcleaning.net

Pro Building Services Inc.
Michael W. Ray, CBSE
2698 S. Redwood Rd., Ste. J
Salt Lake City, UT 84119
(801) 887–0840

Glossary

Attached cushion: a cushioning material, such as foam, rubber, urethane, etc., adhered to the backing fabric side of a carpet to provide additional dimensional stability, thickness, and padding.

Backing: materials (fabrics or yarns) comprising the back of the carpet as opposed to the carpet pile, or face.

Biological hazard (biohazard): an organism or substance derived from an organism that poses a threat to human health; can include substances harmful to animals.

Bleeding: transfer of fiber dyes from carpet or other fabrics by a liquid, usually water, with subsequent redepositing on other fibers.

Blend: a mixture of two or more fibers or yarns.

Carpet cushion: a term used to describe any kind of material placed under carpet to provide softness and adequate support when it is walked on.

CBSE: Certified Building Service Executive, a designation awarded by the Building Service Contractors Association International.

Degreaser: a cleaner designed to remove oils and greases.

Disinfectants/disinfecting: killing microorganisms (bacteria, viruses, fungi) with a chemical agent; many disinfectants are safe and commonly available, some are toxic and damaging to surfaces.

Dry cleaning: a cleaning process that uses chemicals rather than water; dry cleaning isn't necessarily done without moisture.

Dry compound cleaner: carpet cleaning preparation consisting of absorbent granules impregnated with dry cleaning fluids, detergents, and other cleaners; dry powder is sprinkled on the carpet, worked into the pile with a brush, left to absorb soil for a short time, then removed with the absorbed soil by vacuuming.

Environmental Protection Agency (EPA): U.S. government agency responsible for setting and administering air and water standards.

Fastness: retention of color by carpet or other materials.

Occupational Safety & Health Administration (OSHA): U.S. government agency that oversees laws requiring employers to provide employees with a workplace free of hazardous conditions.

Resellers' permits: state Department of Revenue–issued permits that allow you to purchase items you intend to resell without paying sales tax; you're responsible for collecting and remitting sales tax on those items when they're sold.

Rug: carpet cut into room or area dimensions and loose–laid.

Soil retardant: chemical used to help textile fibers resist soiling.

Solvent: any liquid capable of dissolving other liquids or solids; in cleaning, it generally means one of the volatile petroleum or plant distillates used to dissolve oily and greasy soils.

Spot–clean: cleaning a small portion of an object—typically carpet, furniture, or walls—rather than the entire item.

Stripping: process of removing numerous applications of floor finishes (or wax) from hard–surface flooring.

Wet–clean: a cleaning process using water and detergents or soaps.

Index

TOURMALINE

TOURMALINE

A NOVEL

JOANNA SCOTT

Little, Brown and Company
Boston   New York   London

First Edition

The characters and events in this book are fictitious. Any similarity to real persons, living or dead, is coincidental and not intended by the author.

ISBN 0-316-77618-1
LCCN 2002102895

10   9   8   7   6   5   4   3   2   1

Q-MART

Text design by Meryl Sussman Levavi/Digitext
Printed in the United States of America

For Maureen Howard

and Mark Probst

October 1, 1999

WATER LAPS AGAINST THE QUAY OF PORTOFERRAIO. HUNgry dogs blink in the sunlight. A grocer stacks oranges. A carabiniere checks the time on his wristwatch. A girl chases a cat into a courtyard. Men argue in the shade of an archway. A woman rubs a rag over a shop window. Heels click on stone. Bottles rattle in the back of a flatbed truck. A boy writes graffiti on the wall above the steps leading to the Liceo Raffaello. German tourists hesitate before filing into a bar. An old woman, puzzled to find herself still alive at the end of the century, sits on a bench in Piazza Repubblica, her eyes closed, her lips moving in a silent prayer to San Niccolò.

I have seen the faded frescoes of San Niccolò in the church in San Piero. I drove to this little enclave yesterday in search of a grotto that is supposed to be full of tourmaline. After wandering through the hills without finding the grotto, I returned to San Piero to explore the village and the deserted ruins of the Appiano fortress. The emptiness felt so complete that the shadow of a man on the granite wall startled me — my own shadow, squat in the light of late morning.

Inside the church, Niccolò has watched the world with knowing eyes for six hundred years. Bloodied Niccolò, who knows everything about everyone and will never be surprised.

When the earth's ancient fire cooled and shrank toward the core, it left behind a hard, uneven shelf of land along the west coast of the peninsula of Italy that was extraordinarily rich with minerals — with hematite, magnetite, pyrite, quartz, agate, and tourmaline running in pure veins through the deep folds of metamorphic rock. Millions of years later, the fire inside the earth flared, tremors vibrated in the glaciers, and the Tuscan Archipelago broke away from the continent. Vents opened in mountain peaks. Basaltic lava flowed over the land. Rain cooled the lava into rock, storm winds wore the rock smooth, rivers cut channels, dust turned to soil, soil softened to fertile mud along the deltas. New forests grew, diverse species of plants and animals evolved. A unique species of poisonous snake made its home on Montecristo. Each island had its own kind of beetle. At one time, small brown bears lived in the caves of Elba, a prehistoric species of rhinoceros roamed the fields, and lynx hunted the newborn foals of wild horses.

Like all bodies of land, the island of Elba would continue to change. Everything on Elba would change, except the minerals. Deep inside the ground the minerals of Elba would remain what they were, pure, intact, untouched by measurable time.

At Pomonte, follow the road to the right of the church beyond the last of the village houses. Continue up the rise. At the fork, cross the little cement bridge and climb the granite steps to the mule track. Follow the track through the vineyards, keeping the stream to your left. Continue past the last vines and into the woods. Cross through a chestnut grove, go forward about a hundred meters, wade through the stream, cross a valley, and continue into another wood of white poplar and oak.

Eventually you will come to an old sheepfold and shepherd's cottage at the top of Grottaccia hill. If you look carefully at the dome of the cottage, you will see that no mortar was used. The skillful builders constructed the dome simply by putting one stone on top of another.

Four thousand years ago, a woman stood in the grotto of San Giuseppe and poured oil from a vase into a bowl. She crumbled dried rosemary into the oil and pounded it to make a paste. She rubbed the paste on the forehead of her sleeping child to take away his fever.

Three thousand years ago, two Greeks, who happened to be brothers, tended a smelting fire. When the burning wood suddenly popped and sparked, the brothers lurched back with a gasp. The fire burned on. The ore melted. The brothers laughed at their cowardice. They decided to name the island Aethalia after the sparking fires. They knew these fires would burn for centuries.

Twenty-five hundred years ago, an Etruscan patriarch stood on the steps of the acropolis on Volterraio and admired the island's beauty. He decided then and there to deliver an edict moving the smelting furnaces to the mainland territory of Populonia.

Two thousand years ago, a Roman mapmaker wandered the island, recording the contours of land, the presence of rivers and streams, the size of villages. The most prosperous villages belonged to the Ilvates — settlers who had come from Liguria — so the mapmaker decided to name the island Ilva.

The name of Elba, replacing Ilva, first appears in Gregory the Great's *Dialogues,* written in the second half of the sixth century A.D.

Hair tangled by the salty seabreeze. Sparkle of quartz dust. Pigskin ball sailing through the air. Clamor of American soldiers in pursuit. Confusion, laughter, protest, happiness, youth.

Still the men in the shade of the archway are arguing, still the old woman sitting on the bench in Piazza Repubblica in Portoferraio is mouthing a silent prayer. The boy who was writing on the wall has left. French tourists stand outside a bar, trying to decide whether or not to go in.

Follow the path from Marciana toward the San Cerbone monastery. At the little lay-by area beyond the woods, take the steep narrow track through the shade of tree-heath. Climb over the broad granite slabs and across the screes to the ridge, where the paths for Poggio and Sant'Ilario meet. Keep following the track up the eastern slope of Monte Capanne, through the scrub of lavender and genista, proceed in a steep climb for about half an hour to the summit. If the day is clear, you will be able to see the coast of Tuscany in one direction, the mountains of Corsica in the other.

Five hundred years ago, a mother hid with her three children in the family's dank lightless cantina in Marina di Campo. The father had locked the door from the outside and left to fight with his neighbors against Khayr ad-Dīn, the pirate known as Barbarossa. The mother sang to her children, and then the children took turns telling stories. They had only a loaf of bread between them and nothing to drink but wine. When the father unlocked the door three days later, his family tumbled out, dissolute, overcome with hilarity.

Four hundred and fifty years ago, twelve young men and women were dragged from their homes in the township of Fabricia onto a boat bound for Tunisia, where they would serve as slaves for the rest of their lives.

Two hundred years ago, the young British painter John Robert Cozens, son of the painter Alexander Cozens, looked out through a window of the chiesetta di Madonna di Monserrato and tried to mix colors on his pallet to match the color of the hills above Porto Azzurro. He decided the best he could hope for was honorable failure.

Follow the road to the right of the Fortezza pisana for about a hundred meters. Turn left onto the mule track that continues into the woods. Continue past the bronze statue of the angel to the paved road that is flanked by the fourteen Stations of the Cross. Follow this through the woods and up the rocky slope to the shrine of Madonna del Monte.

According to the legend, shepherds discovered an image of the Virgin painted on a chunk of granite. They carried the rock to their valley, but the next morning when they woke the rock had been returned to the exact place where they'd first found it on Monte Giove. The shepherds took this as a sign that they should erect a church at the site.

It was here that Napoleon stayed for two weeks during his exile in 1814.

The sun. The wind. Fragrance of rosemary and rock roses, lavender and beer. Sound of pebbles sloshing in the lazy waves. American soldiers breaking from a huddle. Run, jump, twist, crash, fall, get up again, and hike. Yessirree, we could get used to this place! Touchdown!

After the short reign of Napoleon, the island reverted to the Grand Duchy of Tuscany and, in 1860, to the Kingdom of Italy. During the Risorgimento, the mines of Elba were expanded to meet Italy's growing demand for iron. During the First World War, more than two hundred young Elban men were killed fighting on the mainland. After the war, labor unrest escalated on the island. In 1920, miners occupied the administrative offices of the Alti Forni of Portoferraio, demanding an improvement in working conditions and a reduction in prices for food and dry goods. An agreement was reached after a two-month standoff.

The Cinema Moderno opened in Portoferraio in 1924. The Festa dell'Uva was initiated. Mussolini visited the island on several occasions between 1928 and 1936.

The Second World War arrived on Elba in September 1943. On the sixteenth of the month, beginning at 11:30 A.M., seven German bombers buzzed across the sky above Portoferraio. By 4:00 in the afternoon, more than one hundred civilians were dead, and the people of Elba had surrendered.

Nine months later, the Allies attacked in an invasion called "Operation Brassard," planned by General De Lattre de Tassigny. A group of "commandos d'Afrique" led the way early in the morning on the seventeenth of June, followed by French marines. During the night between the seventeenth and eighteenth, Portoferraio was bombed sixteen times. The fighting was swift and severe. The Ninth French Colonial Division lost hundreds of men but managed to take twelve hundred German soldiers prisoner.

What had begun as an apparently minor Allied operation reawakened and reinforced German fears of Allied landings behind the Germans' western flank. The Germans retreated into the

Appenines. The Allies instated a military government on Elba. And in July an obscure American Division arrived to oversee the distribution of supplies.

The Americans, with their chocolate and cigarettes, Spam and rice. The American boys turning war into a holiday. The Americans wanting to do nothing but strip down to their shorts and play football on the beach at Le Ghiaie. Bare toes curling over hot gravel. Shining faces and salt-bleached hair.

The men are arguing about the war. I know because I started the argument. I'd fallen into conversation with one of the men, stopping to ask for directions and then going on to ask more probing questions in hopes of learning something about the history of the island. I asked him if he remembered the American soldiers who came to Elba in the summer of 1944. He said he'd been serving in the Italian navy in Puglia at the time, but he'd heard about the Americans and their games. We were joined by his friend. The two men got to talking about the occupation of the Germans and the invasion of the Allies. The men disagreed about the value of the Liberation. Other men joined us. They talked rapidly, but I could make out the gist of the argument. Some believed the Allies had saved the island; others thought they'd come close to destroying it. One man ripped up a receipt he'd carried from the grocer and threw the pieces on the ground. *Eccola.* That is what the man would have his friends do with the past.

They seemed to forget me, and I withdrew without a word. I walked from the archway into the piazza and saw the old woman sitting on the bench. I was about to go up and ask her for directions when I noticed that her eyes were closed and her lips moving in silent prayer.

I spent the morning wandering the island. Walking back through the piazza later, I saw the same old woman on the bench and the men still arguing in the archway. I saw an English couple coming out of a bar, balancing cones topped with towers of gelati. I read the graffiti on the wall above the stairs leading to Liceo Raffaello: "Michela è un sogno."

I returned to my hotel room and opened the window. The hotel is adjacent to the vineyard of La Chiusa, and I can smell the ripe grapes. I hear doves cooing in the palms, a rooster crowing up in the hills, motorcycles buzzing and trucks rattling along the main road.

On the table in front of me I've set out the faded deed I found among my father's papers last month when I was helping my mother get ready for a yard sale. The deed names my father as owner of five hectares of Elban land. I flatten the worn creases with my thumb. Though there are many signatures and a stamp on the last page, the claim is worthless, local officials have already informed me. Why, then, don't I just turn around and go home?

The woman I lived with for seven years called two weeks ago to tell me that she is getting married. When I invited her to come to Elba with me, she laughed, her tone one of easy fellowship, as if she'd just chucked me on the shoulder.

This is my first visit back to the island since the mid-1950s, and though I've only been here for three days I'm already looking forward to returning again soon. I consider myself lucky to have the liberty and resources to travel. My brothers agree among themselves that I'm indulging in nostalgia and remind me that there are better ways to spend my money.

Our father had been to Elba himself during the war and stayed long enough to play football on the beach and swim in the tepid sea. Based on his firsthand experience, he could assure us that the sun always shines on Elba, wildflowers bloom year round, Elbans will give away the jackets off their backs, and pirates know it is a good place to bury stolen treasure.

Where on earth is Elba? we wanted to know. It is an island not far from the coast of Italy, our father said. Napoleon once reigned in exile there.

Where is Italy? we asked while we watched our parents pack for the journey. Who is Napoleon? What is exile?

Forty-three years later, I am like a blind man feeling my way through a house that has appeared repeatedly in my dreams. I recognize everything, though nothing is familiar. Much has changed, of course. When I came here with my family, Elba was still dependent on its mining industry. Now it is an active tourist resort. It is just after the high season, and the island seems tranquil to me, but it is overrun in summer, people say. I have been warned to stay away from the main centers of Portoferraio and Porto Azzurro during July and August. Hotel reservations should be made far in advance, expect traffic jams, don't bother with the crowded beaches at Bagnaia and Procchio and Marciana Marina, forget about getting into the Villa Demidoff or hiking to the top of Volterraio or riding the Monte Capanne cable car. Better yet, avoid Elba altogether and go to Corsica.

The soft breeze of the scirocco. The rustle of palm fronds. Piping of a nightingale. Two girls riding bareback on the same brown horse. The granite cap of Monte Capanne shining like snow in the distance. Dust rising behind a jeep as it climbs a cart road to Buraccio and disappears beneath the holm oaks. Mouflons grazing on the grassy slope of Monte Calamita.

The war might be continuing elsewhere, but it is over on Elba, and the American soldiers are leaving. Mementos are traded. The Americans give the Elbans matchbooks and dollar bills. The Elbans give the Americans quartz crystals and polished hematite. My father comes away with a small chunk of a dusky mineral tinged at the center with blue, identified for him later as tourmaline, which he will carry back to New York and sell to a jeweler for twenty-five dollars, telling himself as he walks away from the shop that he'd just made the best deal of his life.

The Casparia

A BOUQUET OF RED BALLOONS BROKE FREE FROM A VENDOR on the pier and fell upward through the haze as the ship's whistle blew its deafening farewell. Our cat yowled in her cage. From the deck below someone threw a cap into the water. We noticed one old woman dressed in black linen blotting tears with the remnants of a tissue, but the other passengers cheered and waved at the dispersing crowd.

It was all so splendid that we never stopped to miss what we were leaving behind. We were heading out to sea on a ship so huge it dwarfed the tankers in the harbor. We watched the city's skyline shrink to nothing. Our father looked more pleased with himself than ever, and we shared with him the sense that we were at the start of an adventure far grander than anything we would have allowed ourselves to imagine.

While our parents lingered at the rail, we explored the maze of upper decks and corridors. Everywhere we went, there were doors we weren't supposed to open and pranks easy to devise. We snuck into the kennel and fed a puffed, nervous poodle a handful of the saltines our mother had given us to forestall seasickness. Through straws we'd found in a deserted saloon we blew paper peas at passengers dozing in deck chairs. We let Meena the cat roam free in our cabin, though after Nat pushed her from the upper berth, she took refuge in the shower, where she deposited four neat little turds for the steward to discover when he came to deliver fresh towels.

We were traveling first class, an extravagance paid for with borrowed money. To our father, luxury was a deserved reward. To our mother, luxury was an awkwardness, and the wealth of her fellow passengers seemed an amusing secret which she could only fail to guess, while surely they would see right through her to the truth of our prohibitive debts. We were living a sham life onboard the *Casparia,* and Claire told herself that she'd participate in the ruse only because it was temporary.

From the bow we watched the hull split through colliding waves. From the leeward deck we saw sun pillars shining on the horizon. From the promenade at the stern we watched seagulls soar, dip toward the wake, and then wheel around in what we presumed was defeat and head back toward land. We felt sorry for them. We wished we could have collared the birds and pulled them along on leashes.

I picture my parents that first evening sitting in oversized chairs in the ship's grand dining room, Murray veiled by the smoke of his cigarette, Claire holding herself stiffly, elbows pressed against her sides, fingers clutching the edge of the table as the passengers traded introductions. Beside her was a man named Walter Fugle, a retired banker with a round belly curving neatly inside his three-piece suit, a round, bald head, and a round face tipped with a shaggy white goatee. Teresa Fugle, a seventy-year-old woman with hair tinted an odd, rusty red, sat opposite, with Murray on her right. At the end was the fifth passenger at the table, a young engineer from Ohio, whose name Claire would go on to forget.

My brothers and I had been fed earlier. Thanks to the indulgent Italian stewards, we were free to roam around the dining room in search of fun. Or my brothers roamed while I toddled after, losing them, finding them, and losing them again.

Claire says she doesn't remember how the conversation began. Probably with idle chat about the menu followed by an exchange of information concerning work and home. At some point Murray wanted to talk about the glorious island of Elba. "Able was I . . ." Walter Fugle joked. Murray shot back defensively, "Go ahead and laugh, but I tell you, life there will cost you next to nothing." Mrs. Fugle asked if Elba was close to Capri. The Fugles had been to Capri. They'd thought it lovely, though inconvenient. But Mrs. Fugle was wondering about the weather for tomorrow. Her husband wanted to talk about storms. Claire recalls that it was the engineer who turned the conversation to the subject of great ships lost at sea.

Walter Fugle said he'd had a gardener long ago who had been a crew member on the *Carpathia,* the ship that had made the forced draft run to rescue the *Titanic*'s survivors. The engineer explained that if the *Titanic* had hit the iceberg head-on, the bulkheads would have saved it. Mr. Fugle and the engineer moved into a more heated discussion about the disaster, while the others at the table listened. The engineer mentioned the *Normandie,* which had caught fire and capsized in the Hudson in 1942. Mr. Fugle spoke of seeing the burned-out hull of the *Morro Castle* off the Jersey coast. Murray, to prove his own knowledge, reminded them that the *Lusitania* was sunk with just one torpedo.

The engineer asked if anyone at the table had ever heard of the *Eastland.* Walter Fugle had a vague memory of it. No one else knew anything about the ship. The engineer offered to tell the story — a story my mother can still recount almost word for word.

The *Eastland* was an excursion steamer taking two thousand passengers from Chicago across Lake Michigan — this was in the summer of 1915 — and she was being loaded at her pier on the Chicago River between LaSalle and Clark Streets when a deckhand noticed she had a list. The passengers were told to move to the other side. The ship resumed an almost even keel, and more passengers were allowed to board. Then a woman screamed and slipped on the tilting deck. That's when people on land noticed that the ship was listing again, and they watched in horror as the great ship slowly rolled and capsized. Hundreds of people, mostly women and children, lost their lives, the engineer said, adding that a salvage diver went insane after investigating the submerged parts of the steamer.

The group sat silently as a waiter cleared their plates. Teresa Fugle asked to see the dessert tray before choosing her main course. Walter Fugle suggested a game of rummy after dinner. Claire wondered aloud how many people were onboard the *Casparia.*

"Nearly two thousand," the engineer said.

"Are there enough lifeboats onboard for two thousand passengers?" Claire asked.

The engineer said yes indeed there were enough lifeboats onboard, and he reminded Claire that people were more likely to die in their own bedrooms at home than on a ship. "The most dangerous thing you can do ..." The engineer paused to sip his water. "The most dangerous thing you can do in your life is to get out of bed in the morning."

"All the more reason ..." Murray began. But Claire's attention had shifted. She started to rise from her chair and called to Nat, who had been skipping between the tables and right then slammed into a steward's elastic belly. The steward stepped back, his full tray wobbled, the china clattered, the crystal chimed. Conversations stopped abruptly as everyone turned to watch. But the steward, an experienced seaman, nimbly steadied the tray and marched

into the galley without a word. When the doors swung closed behind him, the room exploded in applause.

"What happened?" Nat asked, running up to the table.

"You're famous," Murray said.

"You're stupid," Patrick said.

"What did I do?"

"Nothing at all, son," Walter Fugle said. Nat took a few hop-
skips and climbed onto Claire's lap; but Mama's lap belonged to
me, and I began to cry because Mama was my mama, no one else's
mama, and Nat was a big fat —

"You have charming boys," said Mrs. Fugle. Her husband
squawked with laughter and Mrs. Fugle tilted her head and smiled
at Claire, her expression conveying something close to pity for the
poor woman who dared to pose as a first-class passenger.

Later, Claire imagined meeting Teresa Fugle's ridicule with a
cold stare. At the time she'd been flustered and could do no better
than join Walter Fugle in weak laughter, but afterward she wished
she'd been icy and dignified. A woman should always have an extra supply of dignity on hand, especially a woman in our mother's
position, lacking as she believed she was in *background*. She felt as
if she'd come to an elegant party dressed in a cheap gingham sun-
dress — a charming dress, and she was the mother of charming
children.

In our cabin Nat and I fell asleep before Claire had finished
reading us a story. While Harry and Patrick whispered in the top
bunk, Claire cleaned her face with cold cream and lazily brushed
her hair. She turned out the overhead light and shed her dress —
not a gingham dress, not cheap, just an inappropriate light polka-
dot rayon that would have been more suitable for a secretary heading off to work. She slid naked between the cool sheets.

Murray had stayed in the saloon to play cards with the Fugles.
One more round, he'd said, though Claire expected he'd play for
another hour or two. She wanted to be awake when he returned.

Once she was certain all of us were asleep, she turned on her bed-side lamp to read. She started the novel her sister had given her that morning — Hawthorne's *The Marble Faun.* "Four individuals, in whose fortunes we should be glad to interest the reader . . ." She read and reread the first page, pondering the images: the swooning marble Gladiator and the Lycian Apollo, women hanging out their wash in the sun, the Alban Mountains, the great sweep of the Col-liseum. She let her mind wander and found herself picturing white sheets billowing on a clothesline strung over a street.

"Side by side with the massiveness of the Roman Past, all mat-ters that we handle or dream of nowadays look evanescent and vi-sionary alike." Claire read on. She was half asleep when Murray lay down beside her, still fully dressed in his suit, the smell of ciga-rettes overpowering the lingering fragrance of Claire's own per-fume, signaling to her that he'd been among friends and had enjoyed himself. She liked the smell of his cigarettes. She liked the way his body on top of the bedspread tightened the covers around her. She yawned so he'd know she was still awake. He floated his hand lazily along her shoulder.

"I wish we didn't have Teresa Fugle at our table," she whispered.

"I could tell she'd gotten your goat. He, on the other hand —"

"He seems decent."

"He's a cheat. Took me for five dollars."

"You placed bets?"

"It was his idea."

He stroked her lips and dipped his fingertips into her mouth. She tasted brandy, salt, tobacco. He withdrew his hand, traced the curve of her chin. She tried to forget that Murray had lost at cards. She asked herself how much she was prepared to lose and for a moment felt only a surge of dejection, until she remembered the sum: five dollars. Maybe she didn't mind if Murray lost a little money at cards now and then. He may not have had much win-ner's luck, but he didn't play often.

She rolled over and locked her mouth against his and began

unbuttoning his shirt. He peeled her free of the sheet, followed with his open hand the rise of her hip, moved in a smooth familiar spiral around her thigh.

Later that night Patrick was woken by the wind shushing against the thick glass of the porthole. He put on his glasses, which he'd left hanging on the headboard of his bunk, and peered into the night. A creamy brown halo surrounded the moon. The mist had thickened; stars were visible only as occasional glitter behind the haze. And as though in reflection, whitecaps sparked across the water and then disappeared, folded back into the darkness. Patrick says he remembers this like it was yesterday.

Harry says he remembers playing miniature golf and Ping-Pong. Nat says he remembers our parents tossing him between them in the pool. He remembers his shrieks echoing off the metal roof. Patrick remembers the sink in our cabin overflowing because Harry forgot to turn off the water. Harry insists that it was Nat who left the water running.

The voyage from New York to Genoa took a week. But somehow we became convinced that while the ship was surging forward, the ocean was flowing backward and we were going nowhere. We didn't mind. If we'd been offered the choice, we would have stayed on the *Casparia* forever, and forever looked forward to reaching Elba.

After breakfast we'd go to the rec room. After lunch we'd go to the pool. After the pool our parents would take us to the nursery, and our father would play cards with the Fugles while our mother claimed a deck chair for herself and read until someone came by and engaged her in conversation.

Usually it was the engineer from Ohio who would pull up a chair. He was eager to talk, and when he learned that our mother had never before taken an ocean voyage, he was eager to tell her what he knew. It turned out he knew a lot. He explained the tug of the Gulf Stream and the constituents of salt. He explained how bromine could be extracted from the sea and used to make ethyl gasoline. Magnesium hydroxide could be filtered and used directly as milk of magnesia. Uranium could be extracted, and silver, and even gold. According to the engineer, a troy ounce of gold is found in every eight million tons of sea water.

Whenever the engineer sat down in the chair beside her, our mother would close her book and listen politely, because that's what she'd have done with anyone. He seemed trustworthy. And he was more interesting than she'd expected him to be. She found herself intrigued by his mix of information and disclosure, and she looked forward to their conversations.

He said he planned to go first to Florence and spend a week there seeing the sights. Then on to Venice for another week, and then to Turin, where he would serve for three months as a site planner — a *field dog,* he was called — for an expanding textiles mill. He'd return to the States by December and spend Christmas with his brother's family in Ashville.

He mentioned his ex-wife only once, when he spoke about selling his house in Cincinnati the previous spring. He didn't mention any children, and Claire didn't ask. He complained about his insomnia and confessed that late at night he'd sneak to the pool and swim alone in the dark. He said that sometimes, leaning against the rail, he'd feel close to overwhelmed by the desire to dive into the sea. He spoke about the responsibilities of his job and the inspirations of travel.

As the days passed, the afternoon meetings between our mother and the engineer became routine. She would arrive on deck first, and he'd appear within ten minutes. He was pleasant, she thought. Perhaps a bit pedantic. The knowledgeable engineer from Ohio. She listened to him. She looked at him. Each day she looked at him more closely — at the delicate curl of his nostrils, the slight peak of his upper lip, his long lashes, the pinhead pupils in his eyes, the spray of dandruff on his shirt. She noticed that his breath smelled of peppermint, and the thumbnail on his left hand was a bruised purple. She was about to interrupt him — he'd been talking about Darwin, Darwin and pigeons — and ask him what he'd done to his thumb. But just then Mrs. Fugle came up to complain about the breakfast, from the soupy eggs to the cardboard bacon.

Claire and the engineer murmured in agreement. Mrs. Fugle settled in a chair beside the engineer and tilted her hat to keep the sun out of her face. Claire let her thoughts drift away from the conversation for a few moments. She experienced the kind of peace she associated with waking up from a good dream.

She decided that she'd misjudged Teresa Fugle. And the engineer from Ohio — was there anything he didn't know?

Only minutes later, they were all laughing because Mrs. Fugle admitted that Mr. Fugle had poured salt into his jacket pocket at breakfast after he'd overheard a man at a nearby table saying that a pinch of salt was considered good luck onboard a ship.

"And when you sneeze," said the engineer, "sneeze on the starboard side —"

"And not on the port side, or you make trouble," finished the first officer, who'd come up quietly behind them while they were talking.

"Ah, sir, welcome," offered the engineer.

"Officer, sir!" Mrs. Fugle snorted with laughter; she'd worked herself into a giddy mood and was finding everything and everyone ridiculous.

"Of course, you might have nailed a horseshoe to the mainmast for our protection, sir!" joked the engineer.

"All you need to do is cross your second finger over your first, ecco!"

"Or a hunchback. You should keep a hunchback onboard, sir."

"Or you can spit into your hat — that will bring good luck. Or strike your left palm with your right fist."

"Or break a piece of wood, here" — the engineer took a pencil from his shirt pocket and snapped it in two — "and you'll have a lucky break."

"A lucky break!" echoed Mrs. Fugle with another burst of laughter.

The officer touched the peak of his cap and strolled on, leaving the engineer and Teresa Fugle and Claire to sigh and acknowledge one another with friendly smiles. Claire felt as if she were sitting outside on a summer evening with neighbors. The engineer and Teresa were her neighbors on the ship, and Claire was grateful to both of them, to the first officer as well, to the other passengers, the captain, the stewards, to everyone who was making this trip so safe and wonderful.

First there were petrels wheeling overhead. Then porpoises swam for a couple of hours alongside the *Casparia*. Then the barometer dropped, the birds and porpoises disappeared, rain balls gathered overhead, and the squall began, sheets of rain lashing the deck, waves colliding across the stern, the wind whistling, the ship's bell clanging. At dinner the engineer told the others at the table about a North Atlantic storm so powerful it tore apart a breakwater on the coast of Scotland by ripping away an 800-ton slab and the 550-ton foundation to which it was bound. He said he knew the engineer who worked on the replacement section — a 2,600-ton block of concrete, which was promptly swept away by another storm.

Talk turned to tsunamis and tidal bores, gales and hurricanes. Mr. Fugle put a handful of marbles on the floor and sent us in pursuit when they rolled away. The vertical lights around the room flickered, making the bright walls look as if there were flames spreading behind the hammered glass. The motion made Mrs. Fugle queasy and she left early for bed. Claire drank too much wine. Murray did some card tricks for my brothers and me.

The storm passed without incident, and by the next morning the air was cool, the skies gray over the turbulent water. Shortly before breakfast, Claire took Nat and me out to get some fresh air, and we found the engineer on the sundeck. He was smoking a cigarette and watching passengers stroll by. When Claire saw that he hadn't spotted her yet, for some reason she couldn't have explained she started to move away in the opposite direction.

But just then Nat tugged loose from her hand and ran ahead, calling us to hurry up and come on. Claire carried me toward Nat, and a moment later the engineer joined us. Nat was already scrambling over the partition dividing the first-class terrace from the second-class promenade. Claire yelled at him to stop. The engineer climbed over the partition and grabbed Nat, who squirmed in his arms and tried to slip away. But when the engineer murmured something in Nat's ear, Nat abruptly calmed, as if he'd just been promised an extravagant toy. The engineer carried Nat to the far rail at the stern, and they stood there, watching the wide white expanse of the wake disappear into the mist.

That's when I felt my mother tense. She held me in the usual fashion, propped against her jutting hip, one of her arms supporting me, and I felt the hand resting flat against my belly tighten into a fist. I might be picturing what my mother has described to me, or maybe I do have some real memory of it: the salt spray, the wind, the rough sea, the knuckles of my mother's hand, the broad white wake spreading out behind us like ribbons of taffy. And a man in white trousers and a black jacket standing with his back to us, my brother in his arms.

Claire set me down on the terrace and hoisted herself over the partition, her knees stretching the tight cap of her skirt hem. She ran toward the engineer. I started to howl, for it seemed clear that my mother had discarded me. Claire skidded to a stop a few yards short of the engineer, who pivoted slowly. His expression was somber. His arms were outstretched in front of him.

There he stood, palms turned inward, my brother no longer between his hands. That's what my mother saw: a man in the pose of a priest who has just made an offering to the sea. Where my brother had been was the invisible outline of his form.

And then the engineer turned another degree and Nat was

there again — my brother, Claire's third son, a boy overjoyed at the thrill of flying high, effortlessly, over the open water.

Iron rings clanged against the flag mast. A dog barked on the deck below. The wind carried the sound of someone's cough. I heard all this through the sound of my own crying. Something awful had happened, I thought, and something worse was about to happen.

The wind. The sea. Shifting bodies. Shifting moods. Accidental minglings. *Pretend you're a bird. Pretend you're flying over the ocean. Like this!* The infinite water. *It's a small world,* my mother liked to say. *Sometimes,* she would add as an afterthought.

And then the man pivoted another notch, his arms like the gun of a tank, and lifted Nat back inside the boundary of the rail, setting him safely on deck.

Nat wanted to keep flying. He stomped his feet and beat his hands against Claire when she tried to pick him up. Nat wanted the mister to pick him up. But Nat must come with Mama. Wasn't it time for breakfast? Claire flashed a weak smile, unwilling to stir up new trouble by telling the engineer what she really thought of him, murmuring inaudibly that he'd given her quite a scare, muttering a little louder, "I almost thought . . ."

"What?"

"Nothing."

And that was that. Nat forgot about the thrill of flying and remembered he was hungry, and I forgot that I was useless. We left for breakfast. The engineer stayed behind to smoke another cigarette.

The rest of the day passed uneventfully. After breakfast Claire felt a headache coming on, so she retreated to a cozy chair in a deserted salon. She skipped lunch, and though she made an appearance at dinner she only ate the soup. The engineer seemed as animated by his knowledge as ever, but Claire made a point of avoiding any direct exchange. She decided it would be best not to tell Murray about how reckless the engineer had been with Nat.

By the next morning Claire felt better. She was buttering a piece of toast when she noticed both the captain and the first officer moving from table to table. They'd pause to speak quietly to the passengers and then raise their hands in a calming gesture. The murmur in the dining room grew louder as the news spread ahead of him. One woman shrieked. Men echoed each other: Good God, good God. One elderly man led his distraught wife from the room.

A woman at a nearby table communicated the news to Claire and Murray. Apparently, a passenger had jumped overboard during the night. Who was it? Murray asked, though by then Claire had already guessed it was the engineer from Ohio. The first officer approached their table. When he spoke his voice seemed to come from behind him. A terrible tragedy, he was saying. Yes, it is, it is.

Claire's face had drained of color. She could only shake her head stupidly as she imagined the engineer leaping off the rail of the first-class deck into the darkness, his heavy body gaining velocity and tumbling past the cigarette he'd tossed ahead of him. *The most dangerous thing you can do* . . . what had he said? *The most dangerous thing* . . .

Murray stared at the officer. Later he would confide to Claire that he couldn't help but wonder if at the last conscious moment, when a man is breathing in a lungful of saltwater, he'd have the wherewithal to feel regret.

OLLIE, FORGIVE ME FOR SAYING SO, but I wonder why you haven't learned from past mistakes. Your penchant for melodrama. I can tell you that no one shrieked that morning on the *Casparia*. No one was even visibly distraught. In fact, the concern passed quickly, and people sat and finished their breakfast. The stewards came around and refilled our cups with coffee. Newspapers were opened and read. I overheard two men arguing about Khrushchev. The news of the engineer had been noted. Those who had spent any time with him traded stories. Murray and the Fugles recounted conversations. Only six of us joined the chaplain for a memorial service that afternoon.

You say you've lost the ability to make up stories. You're done with novels, eh? I doubt it. You say you might as well write something that's true. Go ahead. I don't mind the disclosures. I have no use for embarrassment in my old age. But you don't mind, do you, if I correct some of the inaccuracies? The description of me shaking my head stupidly, for instance. Stupidly, indeed! It was almost forty-five years ago, but I remember exactly what I was feeling. I was feeling the opposite of stupid. I saw everything too clearly. The man who had thrown himself off the ship had almost dropped your brother overboard. He'd wanted to drop him. He would have dropped him if he'd stood there another minute. That's what I was thinking.

But I wonder, Oliver, if you really want to hear what I could tell you about this particular period in our lives. You are trying to understand what happened to our family on Elba, to sort out fantasy from fact. You say you remember the island as a place where your brothers and you had magical powers. But how much do you actually remember? What should I tell you, and what do you already know?

Here's something: did you know that I didn't learn to swim until I was a teenager? I was terrified of water. I had no reason to be terrified, no frightening experience behind me, yet for whatever reason, I had an intense fear of drowning. Then when I was fifteen my mother forced me to take swimming lessons, and I learned to stay afloat in deep water. But I didn't learn to enjoy it.

From my window here at home the lawn slopes to the seawall, which blocks my view of the narrow beach. When the tide's out the sand is full of driftwood and broken shells, seaweed and sponges — the yellow dead-men's-fingers kind that smell like sulfur when they're burned. The dock behind the Hunters' house is stained with guano from the gulls. The terns are back, nesting in the hedge between our yards, and they dive at me when I go to pull weeds. From Cannon Point sometimes I see the fins of bluefish passing in schools offshore. Emily, the little Hunter girl, said her father saw a Portuguese man-of-war floating in the water last week.

Every morning from May to the end of September I still take my swim. When I'm swimming or just walking along the beach, breathing in the sharp smell of the water, I remember my gratitude. I'm in good health. You boys look out for me. You see to it that my bills are paid, my gutters cleaned, my car serviced. You're fond of me, aren't you, the way people are fond of an old pet? I am lucky. Some mothers must continually prove their merit. My sons don't expect much from me. But you expect me to tell the truth, don't you? Family history as it took shape on the *Casparia*.

I told you the story of the engineer a few weeks ago at dinner. How for a terrible instant I thought he'd dropped my son into the ocean. The mistake of my perception. What I didn't admit was my own complicity. Not for spending time in conversation with the engineer, but for ignoring him. I was too self-absorbed to hear what that troubled man was trying to tell me. With each day on the *Casparia,* I felt happier, and pleasure made me complacent. I wanted to do nothing more than watch the color of the water change with the changing light and let the motion of the waves lull me into oblivion.

I'd been opposed to the trip. With Murray between jobs, it wasn't the time for us to go away. But on that grand ship I shared with your father a new sense of possibility. I could fill the emptiness around me with thoughts of the kind of life I would have lived if I had no responsibilities. And when that man held Nathaniel over the rail, some demon in me saw it as my punishment. If I thought he'd dropped my child into the water, it was because that's what I expected him to do.

I often dream of falling. Even if I wake without the memory of it, the ache in my bones tells me I've had the same dream again. When I push myself up out of bed, I'm still dizzy. I haven't told you about the dizziness before now, Ollie, because I didn't want you to drag me to the doctor for a checkup. I'm feeling fine enough to take a swim in the brisk cove water every summer morning, to go crabbing with my grandchildren off the Hunters' dock, to build a bonfire of driftwood and seaweed at dusk. Did you know that I'm the local expert on the origin of the waves at Morrow Beach? Waves with steep choppy peaks are young waves churned by storms off Block Island. If the waves advance in stately intervals, the rear bulging in a crest, curling, plunging into the foam, then they come from the South Atlantic, born on a far-away fetch.

Superstitions are the riddles we make out of mystery. And the mystery of the sea has to do with death. A person dies on land, takes a bullet in his heart, has a stroke, chokes on food, and his body, whole or torn, remains behind long enough to prove that he was once alive. A person falls overboard — he's there beside you, and then he's gone. When death is disappearance, you can't be sure there was life preceding it. One moment the emptiness in front of you offers any possibility you care to think of, and the next it is full of ghosts and monsters and angry gods.

But maybe it's easier for you to return to the past, and I'm mis-remembering the details. I consider myself adequately lucid, though there are some people who have a different opinion. Emily Hunter informed me that her father believes I have Alzheimer's. What is Alzheimer's? she wanted to know. Alzheimer's, I told her, is what happens when an old lady throws away her clocks and mirrors. Did I have Alzheimer's? Not yet, I said. Do old men get Alzheimer's? she asked. They do. Old men start seeing things that aren't there and confusing one thing with another — for instance, they might see a clump of seaweed and think it's a Portuguese man-of-war. Chew on that one, little Emily. She did, in contemplative silence. And then went home for the day.

There's something else I'd like to point out, Ollie: while it's true Murray wanted to take us to Elba because he remembered it as a place of great beauty, by the time we set out from New York on that muggy July day (the heat, Ollie, the stifling city heat — the white sun burning through the haze of clouds, a ventilator cowl nearby blowing hot air on us . . . ask your brothers if they remember the heat. . . .), by then, the seventh of July, 1956, it hardly mattered where we were going, as long as we were going far away.

SAY THE NAMES. Hold them in your mouth like polished stones: *Leviathan, Titanic, Queen Mary, Ile de France, Normandie, Mauretania, Conte di Savoia, Casparia.* There was a time when three quarters of their space was reserved for the upper classes. "The English Lines," wrote the travel writer Basil Woon, "perhaps have a more distinguishable air of disciplined smartness. . . . 'efficiency' is a word which fits United States Lines boats; Italian Lines err rather on the side of too much servility. . . ." First-class passengers could swim in Pompeian pools or drink chamomile tea beside marble fountains. They could play boccie or shuffleboard or miniature golf. The women could take turns dancing with the captain while the men enjoyed their cognac in the saloon.

My father's first experience on a luxury liner was as a soldier heading to Glasgow on the *Queen Elizabeth* in the early months of 1942. The six miles of carpeting had been stripped from the ship, along with the china, crystal, and silver, and in their place were twenty-millimeter Oerlikon antiaircraft cannons, rocket launchers, and range finders. The ship had been painted battleship gray and girdled in degaussing wire. The restaurant had been turned into a mess hall. Instead of stewards there were chow lines. Instead of brass beds in the staterooms there were bunks crammed on every wall. The ship had been built to carry 2,100 passengers. Lifeboats were provided for 8,000 men. Sixteen thousand troops were onboard. They sailed alone to the Firth of Forth, without convoy. Every man onboard knew that Hitler had offered the equivalent of a quarter of a million dollars and an Iron Cross to any U-Boat commander who could sink the *Queen Elizabeth.*

The ship made the voyage without incident, and Murray spent

most of the remainder of the war at a base in England overseeing the distribution of supplies, except for the one expedition in 1944 trailing the Fourth U.S. Corps up the west coast through the rubble of Grosseto and on to Piombino and then, after the island was liberated by the Ninth French Colonial Division, to Elba, where he stayed for over a month, not because there was work to do but because the army command simply forgot about Murray's insignificant division.

Lasting peace came first to Elba — or so it seemed to Murray during that lost month in '44, and when he needed a refuge ten years later, it made sense that he would return.

We were somewhere near the Azores when we almost lost Nat to the depths. Nat says that though he has no recollection of the engineer from Ohio, he remembers the sensation of being dangled high over the open sea. He remembers the tingling on the surface of his skin and another feeling more difficult to express, a feeling in his bones, he says, an impression that he was in danger, a sense of joy, a sense that he was experiencing a forbidden freedom. He remembers how the wind tugged at his earlobes as if to get his attention. And far below him he saw the churning, foaming, boiling water. He perceived the water to be deadly hot and had a passing impulse to escape the hands holding him and return to the safety of the deck. But somehow he knew that he should be still. For danger to be any fun at all, you have to trust the person in charge — he understood this instinctually and knew better than to try to squirm free.

I don't remember passing through the Strait of Gibraltar, but my brother Patrick does. Or at least he remembers watching two identical steamers surging past us, the ships so minute they looked like toys from the heights of the *Casparia,* their plumes of smoke like the white feathers of cockatoos.

And Harry remembers sneaking from the nursery and making his way to the galley, where a cook put him to work drying pots and then showed him some of the extra treats — hominy grits, cranberry sauce, and malted-milk powder — items so special they were only dispensed upon a passenger's request. Then the cook gave Harry a spoonful of tangerine sherbet and made him promise to go back to the nursery. Harry says he remembers lying across a soft leather ottoman in an empty salon, though he's not sure whether this was before or after he left the galley. He remembers watching our mother repack a trunk. He remembers asking for cranberry sauce at breakfast and being laughed at by our parents.

Our first day on the Mediterranean was unusually stormy, and the ship "rolled like a sick headache," as Mrs. Fugle described it. But among our family, only Meena the cat suffered the effects. She left little puddles of vomit in corners of the cabin, and Claire scrubbed the floor clean and then hid the dirty towels in a bin by the pool.

Our mother didn't let us out of her sight for the last part of the voyage. She ate her meals quickly and paid little attention to the conversations at the table. The Fugles and Murray talked at length about the engineer, speculating about his reasons for suicide. Teresa Fugle noted his obsession with stories of disaster. Walter said he'd seemed well-read. Murray had considered only after the fact that his wife had spent her afternoons in conversation with the engineer, but he decided he'd accomplish nothing by asking her what she really thought of the man.

The weather cleared, and we approached Genoa at noon on a bright, warm July day. After they'd packed and closed the trunks, our parents took us to a terrace to watch as the port slowly acquired form and detail. Beyond the clutter of masts we saw the black and white of buildings, the dark gaps of windows, the bulge of a cathedral's dome. The *Casparia*'s whistle bellowed salutes. A man in a glen-plaid ascot strummed a banjo. Stewards walked dogs along the third-class deck. It seemed as if most of the passengers hadn't noticed that our voyage was almost over, and my brothers and I, knowing nothing about the engineer's death, all shared the wordless disappointment that one feels when a party starts to peter out. Shouldn't there have been fireworks and a band gathered onshore to welcome us, after all the trouble we'd gone through to come here? Murray held me in one arm and carried Meena's cage with his free hand; Claire held Nat's hand, and she ordered Patrick to keep hold of Harry.

The gangway was jarred loose and lowered to the shouting of a dozen men, their commands neatly synchronic, as if joining in song. The sound was a welcome of sorts. But even better was the bagful of streamers Mrs. Fugle gave us. We flung the streamers over the rail and watched them unravel in long ribbons of color that stuck to the hull.

Once the ship had docked, the passengers began collecting their families and appointing stewards to take charge of their luggage. On a crowded stairwell Harry announced that he had to pee, so we returned to our cabin. Later, as we waited in the crowd funneling onto the gangway, Patrick started to whine that he was thirsty, which reminded me of my own thirst, so I began wailing, the cat began howling in sympathy, Harry yelled at Patrick to shut up, Murray yelled at Harry to shut up, and Claire told Murray to stop acting like a child. The faces of adults in the packed crowd were flushed and drenched with perspiration; one woman swooned; someone yelled for help, and at the front of the crowd the first officer called instructions through a bullhorn.

Mr. Fugle appeared beside us, his wife nowhere in sight. "It's not like the *Ile de France,*" he said. "On the *Ile de France* you were inspired to live merrily, if only for the moment."

"Mr. Fugle, I wanted to say . . ." Our father hesitated, and Claire peered at him angrily, as if she thought he were going to reveal some humiliating secret about our family. "To ask, rather, if you knew of a decent hotel where we might put up for a day and rest." Claire rolled her eyes and looked away. Mr. Fugle gasped.

"You have nothing booked, Murray? You have your whole family here and no place to stay?"

"I thought . . ."

"You didn't think is the truth of the matter. You'll have to come along with me, stick close, we'll need a fleet of taxis with your luggage and the five boys. . . ."

"Four. We have four boys."

"Four then, no matter. Now stay close. Teresa! Where is she? Teresa?"

We followed Mr. Fugle down the gangplank, followed his muttering voice when we lost him for a moment in the crowd, found him again standing miraculously beside Mrs. Fugle — *miraculously*, I say, because Mrs. Fugle had apparently lost twenty or so pounds in a matter of minutes and had dyed her hair black, powdered her face white, and shrunk in height a couple of inches.

Mrs. Fugle was, in fact, Mrs. Fugle's sister, Ida, who, Mr. Fugle explained, lived half of each year in Florence and was perfectly fluent in Italian. She would keep us from becoming gypsies, he said. They conferred for a moment, then Ida instructed us to take a taxi to the Hôtel Luxembourg, where the Fugles had already reserved a suite; we'd rendezvous in the courtyard, she said. Mr. Fugle secured two more taxis. He'd wait for the luggage and bring it along directly.

We left the Fugles just as Teresa arrived and embraced her sister. We crammed ourselves into a taxi with corduroy seats ripped at the seams, broken floorboards, and a driver who smelled like broiled flounder, and as we rode up the steep narrow streets of the old port, I whimpered because I was hot, Patrick whined because he was thirsty, and Murray remarked at all the stone monsters lounging above doorways, "Will you look at that!"

After nearly half an hour the taxi pulled up onto the sidewalk in front of the arched brick entrance of the Luxembourg, an elegant hotel near the Piazzale Resasco. When Murray reached for his wallet, the driver gestured behind him and said something about the signore. Claire and Murray understood him to mean that Mr. Fugle had generously paid our fare. They gathered us and Meena and the few small sacks we were carrying and headed into the hotel. A fountain graced by a bronze Pan gurgled in the courtyard, and Murray threw in a penny. Then we all had to throw pennies, including Claire. A maid swept the cobblestones, and the swish of her straw broom sounded like the wind onboard the *Casparia*. The broom, the fountain, the fragrance of orange blossoms, the blue patch of sky overhead, the warmth, the stillness, the uncertainty of the future, the certain fact of our safe ocean voyage — everything combined to lull us into calm. I stopped crying, Patrick stopped complaining, Meena curled up in her cage and fell asleep. We sat on the edge of the fountain's basin and waited for the Fugles and our luggage to arrive. We waited serenely for ten minutes, until a concierge approached and in perfect English asked if he could be of assistance. Murray went into the hotel to arrange for a room. Claire sat with her face turned up to catch a beam of sunlight. Patrick quietly counted to twenty in the Italian he had learned from the sitters in the ship's nursery.

Murray appeared, key in hand, and we continued to wait. Thirty minutes turned into an hour. I chased my brothers around the fountain. Murray went to see if the hotel had another courtyard. As each minute passed Claire's features grew tighter. Murray returned, shaking his head as if to shake away the irritating buzz of a fly. Claire coughed, and just as she was about to tell Murray to go back to the harbor to look for the Fugles, they heard the crunch of gravel beneath car wheels. Doors opened and slammed. Voices rose in argument. An engine revved, stalled, and revved again.

The Fugles had arrived, along with one canvas suitcase. The rest of their luggage, and ours, was in another taxi — a taxi that was supposed to follow the Fugles to the Luxembourg, a taxi with a black-eyed, bearded driver who turned off on a side street somewhere back in the centro storico and disappeared without so much as a parting honk.

Ida scolded Walter for not paying better attention during the drive. A bellhop fetched the concierge. The concierge and the Fugles' taxi driver conversed solemnly, while Ida turned her rage upon Teresa. Walter started arguing with Murray, calling him inept and irresponsible. Claire asked the concierge, "Does this mean our belongings have been stolen?" and the concierge, forgetting himself for a moment, started rattling in Italian, then bowed slightly and apologized "for the inconvenience."

The police would be called, the concierge promised, and hopefully the thief and our luggage would be found. Until then he trusted that we would enjoy our stay at the Hôtel Luxembourg. The other adults followed the concierge to the manager's office. No bellhop came to help us, so Claire led my brothers and me up to our fourth-floor room. We had a spitting contest on the balcony while our mother leaned back against pillows wrapped in colorful lace and dozed.

Or, rather, let her thoughts drift through the clutter of impressions — the bearded satyrs and fat-cheeked gargoyles decorating the buildings of Genoa, the delicate green-tipped fingers of the Luxembourg's Pan, the bodies surrounding her on the gangway of the *Casparia,* the annoyed expression on Mr. Fugle's face at the harbor, Teresa's impatient smile. The engineer.

The mysterious, doomed engineer from Ohio. When Claire thought of him now she felt something she wouldn't have wanted to describe to anyone. The engineer had taken the most desperate measure possible to escape his private agonies. That he had spared Nat was cause for a strange, uncomfortable gratitude. Claire wouldn't have called it gratitude. She wouldn't have admitted to feeling anything but sympathy for the unhappy engineer and his family.

Sympathy — and relief. Her four boys were alive. Amazingly, we were alive, safe, healthy, attentive to the world, full of hope, easily pleased. The Murdoch family had survived an ocean voyage, and we would survive the theft of our luggage. Who knows but that it was a necessary loss? In order to leave home behind, we had to lose what we'd brought along with us.

Still, Claire decided that we should postpone our journey and wait in Genoa while the police searched for the thief. In the meantime we'd shop and replace what we'd lost. We were already living off borrowed money. Now Murray would have to wire his mother in New York and beg for more. Convey his desperation in a telegram and wait at the Luxembourg for the reply, which would come eventually, though he'd have to suffer the wait while our grandmother borrowed the money from her brothers.

Such suffering, here at the top of the Luxembourg! The breeze blew through the balcony doors. The hills were the color of new leaves on a sugar maple. Claire could smell the ripe lemons in the garden.

She must have fallen asleep, for when she woke Murray was sitting on the chair in front of the dressing table, his face hidden in his hands. Claire heard Patrick talking to the rest of us out on the balcony. The only other sound was the chatter of a parakeet in a cage on the balcony next door.

"Any success, Murray?"

"We're lucky we didn't lose a thousand dollars' worth of diamonds and pearls like the Fugles did. Though if we're talking relative value, the Fugles lost a couple of shoelaces, and we've lost almost everything."

"Do you want to go home?"

"Yes. No." He rose from his chair and stood with his hands in his pockets, idly watching us through the open doorway. "I don't know. What a mess I've gotten us into. If I'd used the money as intended, I'd have my own office by now. Maybe a client or two — on the condition that I cut my commission by fifty percent. Why do I sacrifice every possibility of profit to incentive? You understand why I needed a break, don't you, Claire? A man who's going nowhere benefits from a change in routine. Some time away to give him perspective."

Of course she understood. We couldn't give up now. We lingered in Genoa. Mornings we'd stroll with the Fugles along Via Garibaldi, led by Ida Fugle, who took it upon herself to distract us all from the loss of our belongings. We dragged our open hands along the cold stone facades of palazzi as Ida told us the history of the local families. We crowded into a funicular and rode above houses built on streets so steep that they had doors cut into their roofs. We climbed up La Lanterna, the ancient lighthouse of Genoa. We shopped for clothes along Via del Campo. Murray treated himself and Walter Fugle to cigars from the Hobby Pipe at Via XII Ottobre and treated us all to marrons glacés. We ate licorice that stained our tongues black. Murray gave Patrick a taste of wine at a bar. We threw the last of our pennies to Pan in the fountain at the Luxembourg. One day in a gentle rain we sifted through the decade-old rubble in an area where new construction hadn't yet replaced a building destroyed in the war. Harry found a leather watchband. Patrick found the frayed end of a rope.

It took five days for our grandmother to wire us enough money to give Claire and Murray both the means and confidence to continue our trip to Elba. The Fugles gave up hope of recovering their luggage and left for Florence on the fourth day. We were content to stay on in Genoa. We were cast as royalty by the smiling, whispering staff of the Hôtel Luxembourg, who made it their goal to convince all the Murdoch boys to try the gianchetti they served as an appetizer at lunch. Gianchetti are tiny newborn fish steamed and coated with olive oil and lemon, and they stare up at you from the plate with the passiveness that comes with condemnation. My brothers and I would wrap handfuls of gianchetti in bits of newspaper and hide the wads in our pockets. We'd nod vigorously when the waiters gathered to ask in English, "You like?"

We fed the gianchetti to Meena, and over the course of the

week she grew strong, regal, fierce. She took to sitting on the rail of the balcony and staring at the parakeet that was owned by a widow who lived year-round in the Luxembourg. The parakeet would twitter — in panic at first, then weakly, helplessly — and Meena's tail would snap back and forth to the rhythm.

Bells rang through the dusk. Swallows fished in the sky for insects. Nat said we were in Fairyland. Harry said we were never going home.

Shortly after dawn on the morning of our fifth day at the Luxembourg we were woken by a scream. Or Murray and Claire and Harry woke; the rest of us managed to sleep as the widow on the balcony next to ours screamed, doors banged, and a maid called from the courtyard below.

Murray and Claire had been sleeping in their usual fashion, back to back, Claire's new silk nightgown bunched up around her waist, Murray in boxers, their rumps touching, one of Claire's legs sandwiched between Murray's shins. When Murray woke he clamped his legs together so Claire had to yank hers free, a movement which, as he'd later explain to Claire, reminded him of her angry, abrupt movements during early labor, and in the blurry haze of sleepiness he forgot where he was and thought that Claire was getting ready again to give birth. How many times had she been through it? How many boys did they have? Four? Or five? He remembered that someone had told him he had five sons. But the someone was a liar — Murray remembered that much. Who was screaming? What was wrong?

Claire had bolted out of bed by then. Murray stumbled after Claire, pulling on pajama pants. Harry followed Murray, dragging a blanket along with him. They gathered out on the balcony and found the old widow on the balcony next to theirs screaming something about a gatto, a gatto cattivo, weeping, shuddering, clutching the sides of the parakeet's cage. Inside, the little green bird lay on its side, button eyes without the flicker of life, legs twisted together like pieces of wire.

Cattivo, Claire heard, a word she mistook to be the Italian word for *cat,* and with her mistake succeeded in understanding the woman's accusation. *Gatto cattivo.* Cat something. Something cat. The parakeet was dead — that's what had made the old woman distraught, a dead bird, nothing more — and our cat, black-masked, velvet-pawed Meena, was the assassin. Or mere onlooker, perhaps, since the door to the birdcage remained closed. Or a medusa, which was the widow's explanation, Claire would understand later from the concierge, Meena having murdered Cerabella with her gaze, simply sitting on the partition and staring had driven the little bird into such a state of inarticulate panic that it had what the concierge called in English "an eruption of the heart."

Nothing more than a parakeet with heart failure on a balcony in Genoa with a view of the rose gardens edging the cimitero di Staglieno and the Ligurian hills beyond. Nothing more than two trunks stolen by a Genoese thief. Nothing more than a few polite conversations with a stranger on an ocean liner. Nothing more than the first two weeks away from home.

OUR FATHER HAD BEEN TRYING TO FIND a suitable job ever since he'd come home from the war. In ten years he'd talked his way into eight different firms — advertising, investment, and real estate — and then somehow managed to talk his way out, leaving behind him a history that his colleagues politely called *mixed.* Finally he decided to open his own consulting firm. His mother loaned him money. But before he'd even rented office space he felt he needed a break from work to consider his options, and he convinced his mother to let him use the money for a trip abroad. He assured her that he would secure a good job upon his return in the fall.

When our grandmother wired the extra money to Murray in Genoa, she warned him that this was it — he'd get no more. But it was enough to let us continue our journey. We left the hotel for the train station on a warm July morning when the clouds were still pink with dawn. We were going to Florence, though in the taxi Murray suggested that we get off the train in Pisa and from Pisa take a bus to Piombino and there catch the ferry to Elba.

"We're going to Florence," Claire said.

"Why not directly to Elba?" repeated Murray.

They argued in the taxi, though Murray knew that Claire would not change her mind. Of course we'd go to Florence, as planned, and Murray would travel alone to Elba to find us a suitable place to stay for the month.

"Wish I didn't have to go alone," Murray murmured.

"The whole point . . ." Claire was in the backseat with me on her lap. She let her voice drift off, leaving the obvious point implied — that Murray had chosen to take us to an island known to the rest of the world only as a place of exile.

When we arrived at the station our train was waiting, the rear cars already packed with passengers. Claire agreed with Murray that if we were going to find seats we'd have to travel first class. Murray, carrying the two new valises, went off to buy tickets. Claire led us toward the front of the train and lifted us one by one up the metal stairs.

The seats of our compartment were upholstered in red leather, the armrests were mahogany, and the perfume of the last passenger still lingered in the air. Harry, always the luckiest among us, found an empty ring-box covered in navy velvet beneath his seat cushion. Patrick offered to trade the rope he'd found in Genoa for the ring-box. Harry declined. Patrick sat on Harry, pinning him down, and tried to pry the box from his fist. Harry screamed. I started to cry. Claire grabbed her umbrella and raised it threateningly. Patrick's terror was fleeting; a moment later he was tugging at the umbrella, wrestling in fun with Claire. No one paid attention to the train whistle. Only when we moved forward with a lurch did it occur to Claire that Murray had been left behind.

"Boys, we have to get off!" But we'd just gotten on, Harry said. Claire gestured as if to wave off his stupidity and rushed to the door at the end of the corridor. By then the train was already moving fast enough to blur the platform, making it appear liquid. As the carriage passed a porter Claire yelled, "Stop this train!" The man cheerfully touched his cap and nodded. Jump, Claire thought to herself in desperation. We must jump. Of course we couldn't jump. It was too late. We were heading to Florence without Murray.

We rode in silence. The train's jerking settled into a smooth forward motion, and Claire sat with her hands crossed over the base of her throat — a position she'd assume in an attempt to ward off panic. The sunlight gave her eyes a milky sheen. She caught the smell of cigarette smoke drifting through from the corridor — Murray's cigarette . . . but Murray wasn't there. She jumped to her feet, snapped open her wallet, and poured the contents onto the seat, counting her lire too frantically to keep track. She had begun counting it again when we heard the conductor's sullen "Biglietti, prego," in the corridor. Claire separated coins from bills. She told us to keep quiet, though we weren't making a sound. A moment later the swaying of the train unbalanced Claire, and she tipped toward the door and into the arms of the conductor, who stood with the smirk of understanding on his face, his expression suggesting that he needed no explanation, he knew well enough about le signore like this one, le signore traveling without their husbands. Lonely signore and their clever mistakes.

Claire stumbled away and resumed her frantic search for money to pay our fares. The conductor watched her through the smoke of his cigarette. My brothers and I watched the conductor.

Six carriages back, Murray leaned out a window and watched the landscape, drawing a deep breath in an effort to inhale the scenery — the long single-arch stone bridge, the steep hillside rising above the tracks, a castle's towers in the distance, terraces of vineyards, perfect rows of cypress, a boy walking along a dirt road with a goat on a leash, morning sunlight turning a river gold. He nodded to a conductor and squeezed past with the valises into the next carriage. He opened each compartment door and checked to see if we were inside.

Where were we? If not in this first-class car then in the next one. Murray ambled on — or danced, yes, it felt like he was dancing to the music of the train. He tried to decide whether he wanted a cigarette. He didn't really want a cigarette right then, but he could strike up a conversation by asking someone for a light. How do you ask for a light in Italian? At this point Murray knew only words from a phrase book he'd brought along. *Piacere di conoscerti. Mi vuol passare il sale per favore.*

He looked around. This gentleman in the white linen suit, maybe he'd have time to spare, along with a light. "Pardon me, per favore, signore. . . ."

Of course he had a light. And he spoke a little English. He had a brother who lived in New York. Murray said he was from New York. Davvero? Sì, sì! Murray offered the man a cigarette. The man was from Genoa but was going to Florence to visit his cousin. He wanted to talk. If the signore could wait there, Murray would be right back. He had to find his wife and give her the tickets. *Va bene, va bene* — the man nodded him on. He'd wait there. They could talk about New York. The man had lived for six whole months with his brother in New York!

Murray continued down the corridor, checking the first-class compartments. When he finally located us, Claire had just finished paying the conductor for our tickets. Murray, a few inches taller than the conductor, peaked his head over the man's tasseled shoulder, and said, "There you are!"

"Murray!"

"Where were you?"

"Where were *you?*"

Claire explained that they'd had to purchase five tickets to Florence. But Murray had bought our tickets back at the station. He tried to give them to the conductor; the conductor would only accept a single ticket for Murray. It was too late, apparently, to return Claire's tickets. The five new tickets had been issued. We had eleven tickets for the six of us to travel from Genoa to Florence, at a cost equivalent to a night at the Hôtel Luxembourg, Claire pointed out after the conductor had left.

But she was too relieved to stay angry at Murray. We were together. We were coming from Genoa, heading to Florence, following a zigzagging route to Elba. There was no possibility of retracing our steps. We could only go on, go forward, continue to go away from the past. The speed of the train made our journey feel more than ever like destiny.

MOST OF WHAT I KNOW about my mother's experiences in Italy I know from her directly. We have talked at length. She continues to reminisce. She has shown me photographs and read aloud portions of her journals. Though sometimes she chides herself for her forgetfulness, her memory is far richer than any hazy story I might concoct.

On the other hand, what I know about my father's experiences I've had to piece together from a variety of sources. I've been back to Elba once and plan to go again. I've read history books and newspapers. From my mother and brothers I have a sense of what questions to ask. And thanks to my grandmother, who hoarded everything, I have the letters my father wrote to her from Elba.

As our parents had planned, Murray left us in Florence, in a dark, modest pensione on Via Faenza just around the corner from San Lorenzo, and he went ahead to Elba. In his first letter to his mother, he describes the blue sea cracked with white beneath the blue cloudless sky. He describes the sweet scent of lavender, the linked shale peaks of the mountains, the blue of periwinkles and the red of poppies rippling like scattered bits of silk in the grass. He says the island was even more beautiful than he remembered.

I picture my father standing on a balcony, watching a farmhand named Nino nudge open the door to a shed with his elbow. From another place in the yard came the sound of hammering. A nightingale hidden in an almond tree sang, paused, and sang again. A woman up on a vineyard terrace pushed back her straw hat and called, "Lidia! Lidia!" A small dog yelped in pain, and Murray saw it go skittering across the dirt yard.

Here in a villa on the island of his dreams. Here in the place that after a month-long visit in '44 had filled him with the desire to return. Peasants tying vines, cows chomping on wildflowers, a black dog running across the yard, as weightless as a tumbleweed.

In the distance Murray could see the lopsided orange roofs of the houses in Portoferraio. He considered how little had changed in hundreds of years, how what he saw was close to identical to what Napoleon would have seen during his year of exile. He imagined the little emperor in military garb wandering around the island, plotting his escape. The contradiction amused him: the island of Elba had served as Napoleon's prison, and yet Murray Murdoch had never been as free as he was now.

The summer ahead was like a picture on a screen gradually coming into focus. On Tuesday Murray had lunch with the hotel proprietor, whose friendliness made up for his poor English. Later that afternoon Murray fell into a conversation with a British historian, Francis Cape, when he was browsing in a little stationary shop in Portoferraio. On Wednesday Francis introduced him to Lorenzo Ambrogi, a local padrone, who invited him to stay at his villa. On Thursday Murray borrowed a car and visited Lorenzo's various properties, and by Thursday evening he'd decided upon a house, a sprawling, one-storied house amidst neglected vineyards in the hills midway between Portoferraio and Magazzini. Today was Friday. At one he would have lunch with Lorenzo Ambrogi and negotiate a rent.

Until then, what? Here in a villa on the island of Elba, without his family, with miles of fields and woodland to explore. He would have liked to linger just a little longer at the pocked pinewood table in the kitchen, where Nino's wife, Maddalena, served him a breakfast of hot milk and coffee and panini with fresh butter and honey. But Maddalena, who spoke no English, had chores to do, and she left Murray to finish his breakfast alone.

Afterward, he went for a stroll. He followed a shale path up to the vineyards. He paused at the end of a row and watched two young women tending vines. They glanced at him, turned to each other, and began whispering. If Murray had spoken their language he would have introduced himself. Instead, he left them to their secrets and continued along the path, up and over a verge, and down into a ravine. The broken shale gave way to slippery clay beneath his shoes. The perfume of lilies grew stronger, the vegetation denser as the path leveled. Velvety ferns bordered the path. The sun, still low in the sky, shone through a gap in the ravine's ledge, catching the glint of larkspur and daisies. The rock walls threw back the hollow echo of a trickling spring.

Murray sat on a flat-topped rock beside a pool. He would remember — mistakenly — feeling the tension of expectation, as though he'd been waiting for someone to join him. He listened to the water, the call of a cuckoo, the shush of the wind along the grassy shelves above the ravine. He sat without thinking. He sat for an hour, a day, a week. He had no idea how long he'd been sitting there, how long he'd been listening to the sound of soft humming, how long he'd been watching the girl work. She was pulling handfuls of clover from the flower bed along the opposite rim of the pool. When Murray realized that she didn't know he was watching her he found himself unable to move, as if after immeasurable time he'd grown rubbery roots that stretched around the rock and deep into the soil.

He kept staring at the girl; she must have felt the pressure of his gaze, for she looked up at him abruptly. But she just shook away the startle, shrugged, and went on weeding, as though she didn't mind having an audience. No, she didn't seem to mind at all.

She wasn't beautiful. Her hair was black, with short curls so fine and feathery that he could see the white of her scalp. Murray noticed the line of muscle in her thin arm as she tossed a handful of clover into a basket. She was unnaturally pale, and her cheeks had an oily glow, like marble lit by backwashed sunlight. She wore a simple white blouse and brown skirt, garb that didn't distinguish her from any of the other peasant girls on Elba. Yet there was something different about her, Murray thought, a refinement in her movements, perhaps, or a subtle haughtiness expressed by the tightness of her features. The girl wasn't just too pale, too fragile. Her condition seemed oddly revealing, as if she were sickly because she was selfish or devious or cursed by bad luck. And though she ignored him, she demanded his attention. Murray was certain that she wanted him to keep watching her. She was lonely, and yet — how did he know this? — she was responsible for her lone-liness. She fit the role perfectly. Eve in the garden, leaves floating, falling around her when a gust shook the trees. Just the fact of her presence was a temptation, and yet everything about her warned Murray away.

He stared at her, attempting to settle his impressions into un-ambivalent judgment, telling himself that she was in every aspect a plain peasant girl. He had nearly convinced himself when she stopped humming and spoke.

"You must be Signor Americano." Her voice threw him back into inarticulate confusion. Her English, though clearly a second language, was precise and had a British ring to it. He couldn't bring himself to ask how she knew about him. You don't ask witches and goddesses how they know what they know.

"Yes?" she prompted. Her grin was sly — a response to his con-fusion. He wanted to remind her that she should be careful with strangers. He wanted to pin her to a name but couldn't bring him-self to ask.

She brushed her hands against her skirt. He thought she was preparing to extend a hand in greeting. Instead, she dipped her hands into the water bubbling out of the rocks, and he watched as she drank from the bowl of her palms, his discomfort growing as it slowly occurred to him that her action should have been private.

"Excuse me," he said, pushing himself up. "I must be going." He was amused to hear in his own voice a false accent, an involuntary echo of her refined diction. At the same time he realized he wanted to copy her and cup fresh spring water in his hands. He wanted to linger. He wanted to talk to her.

"Good-bye, Signor Americano."

He hesitated. He didn't want to leave. He must leave. "Arrive-derci." He considered asking her for directions, but on second thought decided this would be silly since there was only one path leading out of the garden, and from the top of the ravine Lorenzo's villa would be in view. He went to tip his hat and then realized that he wasn't wearing a hat. "Piacere di conoscerti."

He left her laughing at him, with him, in sympathy, in ridicule, in spite, in imitation while he walked up the path. He laughed at himself for making this simple encounter into something more meaningful than it should have been. He laughed between puffs of breath as he climbed the steep, slippery slope. He laughed at her laughter. He laughed at his own voice that was returned to him by the rock chamber of the ravine. Echoes of echoes, shadows of shadows. Down in the garden, a girl was laughing. He laughed at himself laughing at her as she laughed at him.

We were in Florence for six days. Murray telephoned every day. He told us that the sea was as warm as a bath, and when he swam out fifty yards from Le Ghiaie he could see through the clear water to the sponges and shells scattered on the sand. He told us about the magnificent gardens and vineyards, the orchards full of sweet yellow peaches, the wild goats grazing on hillsides. He said he'd climbed into the mountains and found quartz, pyrite, and a black glassy crystal that a man at a bar identified as tourmaline. Tourmaline! Tourmaline didn't just come in the blue that he remembered. It came in black, in green and pink and red. The mountains were full of tourmaline. The whole island was a treasure chest for those who knew how to open it!

Murray called to say he'd rented a villa surrounded by vineyards in the hamlet of Le Foci, not far from Portoferraio. The padrone would deliver more beds to accommodate the six of us.

Murray called the next day to say that the beds were in place, and upon the landlord's recommendation he'd hired a cook, an Elban woman from Portoferraio, along with a young woman from the village of Capoliveri to be our nanny. Since when could we afford servants? Claire demanded. Since the padrone had explained to Murray that the fastest way to gain respect on the island was to become an employer. Wages were shockingly low, Murray said, so he'd offered to double them. He hoped Claire didn't mind. The expense was negligible, the advantages immense.

He called to tell us about Francis Cape, the Englishman who was writing a book about Napoleon on Elba. Francis Cape had been helpful in every possible way. He'd even driven Murray to Porto Azzurro, where Murray bought a little motorcyle.

Murray described how the mountains in the early morning mist looked like shadows behind shadows. He said he'd met a Swedish geologist who had done some temporary surveying work for one of the iron mines outside of Rio nell'Elba. The Swede explained to Murray that of all the precious gems to be found on the island, blue tourmaline was the most valuable of all. To find more he should look in the granite outcrops in the mountains. Murray said he was going to buy a rock hammer and chisel and get to work.

Come on, Murray urged. The island was ready for us. Hurry up and come on. Our father would meet us in Portoferraio. He'd take us to play football on the beach.

None of us remembers the uneventful trip from Florence to the port town of Piombino or the ferry ride to Elba. Among my brothers, the first memory of the island belongs to Patrick: he says he remembers waiting while Claire and Murray greeted each other, kissing and embracing as though they'd been apart for months. He remembers staring at the water sloshing against the edge of the quay. He remembers dropping a coin into the water just to hear the sound of the splash and then looking up to face an ancient, gray-bearded man, who scowled and shook a finger at Patrick for wasting good money.

I Fantasmi

ACCORDING TO HIS REPUTATION — SOMEWHAT EMBELLISHED by himself, I came to realize later — our father was a genius at persuasion. He could persuade men to hire him against their better judgment. He could persuade his mother and uncles to lend him money for a vacation they didn't think he deserved. He could persuade his wife to forget the family's debts for a while and enjoy life. And he could persuade his children to spend their time searching an island for treasures left behind by pirates and emperors when we already knew that such treasures didn't exist.

Our father's art of persuasion played upon the contrary temptations of risk and safety. Even as he'd emphasize the thrilling possibilities of an idea, he'd offer assurances and somehow make the paradox seem natural. *Trust me,* his smile would imply. Go ahead, give it a try, and trust Murray Murdoch to manage the dangers.

While my brothers and I only pretended to believe our father when he told us that the island's treasure would be found by those who knew how to look, we sensed that the proposition would make a diverting game. During our first days on Elba, we each searched in different ways, following our different inclinations, escaping from the watch of our new cook and nanny whenever possible.

Patrick looked for treasure by drawing detailed maps of the land around our villa. From an early age he'd understood that learning came more easily to him than to others — an ability that was as much a handicap as an advantage, since it threatened to set him apart from the rest of us. But he couldn't help it — he was our expert. He almost always knew more than we did, and when he didn't, he'd know how to find out.

Harry looked for treasure as if he were hunting for small animals. He'd move stealthily through the vineyards, sift through broken pottery, pick quartz from the gravel drive. He knew how to find whatever had been lost. He was our detective.

Nat, the bravest among us, looked for treasure by roaming. Treasure can't be easy to find, he'd insist. It wasn't enough to draw maps or collect broken rocks. We'd have to go far from home, up into the island's highest mountains. Every day Nat convinced us to go a little farther. Sometimes we went so far — across roads and meadows, through vines and abandoned olive groves — and became so engrossed in the search that we'd lose our direction. But then Patrick would climb up into a tree or to the top of a boulder and orient himself with landmarks — there was the port in one direction, the peak of Volterraio to the west, and there below him, right down there, the villa we already called home.

And since I was the most helpless and least visionary, I looked for treasure by doing whatever my brothers told me to do. Ollie, get me a shovel! Ollie, go find Harry and bring him here! Ollie, hold this, watch that, do it for me now!

We were eager, inexaustible, confident that even if we didn't find treasure we'd manage to prove the worthiness of our efforts. We were sure that there was no place more promising than the island of Elba, no time more appealing than the moment at hand, no adventure more exciting. Not once did we ask to go back to America.

It's as though we've stepped out of time, our mother would say in a dreamy soft-pitched voice. How easily the modern world disappears. She'd close her eyes and listen to the sounds carried like bits of debris by the wind — a ship's horn, the crowing of roosters and chittering of hens, the gabble of servants, the dry rustle of palm fronds, the humming of bees in the oleander. She'd open her eyes and see the scarlet bougainvillea spilling over the terrace wall, the roses filling each frame of the trellis. Inside the villa the marble floors were deliciously cold beneath bare toes. Claire would sink into a chair and stretch her feet out over the floor and ask in a voice rich with irony and pleasure: "What are we doing here? Who gave us the right?"

Murray would say we'd earned the right. Claire would shrug. They'd sip their wine, and when their eyes met they'd laugh a little, as though they were sharing a joke.

After the first quiet week, Claire was ready to spend the second week in the same fashion. She didn't need other company; though, predictably, Murray did. He needed the few hours of distraction that visitors provided, along with an excuse to mix up a pitcher of martinis, so on Saturday afternoon he rode his Lambretta into Portoferraio, where he found Francis Cape watering the geraniums on the stoop of his building, and he invited him to come out to Le Foci for supper.

Of course Francis Cape would come for supper. He would always come to supper, when asked, and he would arrive a respectable ten minutes early.

"He's here!"

"Who's here?" Claire had heard the car coming up the gravel drive but had assumed it was someone coming to visit Lidia or Francesca.

"Francis Cape, the Englishman!"

"What Englishman?"

"Francis Cape. He's the one I told you about. Francis Cape. He's here."

"You didn't tell me you invited him over."

"Didn't I? I thought I did. I meant to tell you. Well, he's come for a visit. You don't mind, do you? He's the one who put me in touch with Lorenzo. Francis lives in Portoferraio, you see. He's lived there for nearly ten years."

It was that soft hour of Elban dusk when everything solid hovered on the edge of transparency. My brothers and I had already eaten our supper and were in a bedroom sorting through the day's booty of rocks. Lidia, the cook, was clattering dishes in the kitchen while she rebuked Francesca for some new fault. Murray's voice trailed behind him as he stepped outside to greet Francis. Claire felt an odd, unsettling presentiment, probably because she'd been so content to have nothing to do and no one new to meet.

Francis Cape the Englishman was here for a visit. Claire heard his voice first out in the courtyard, a barking, confident voice, then Murray's, and then a third voice — the subdued voice of a woman, audible just for a moment before disappearing beneath the clamor of Murray's exuberance.

"Come in, please, come right in, let me introduce you to my wife. Claire, this is Miss Noddi, Adriana Noddi —"

"Nardi," she corrected. Narrrdi. Adriana Narrrdi. She was a young woman of about twenty, with milky skin and black hair clenched in wispy curls. There was something in her smile that struck Claire immediately as deceptive, tinged with private trouble, though when Claire extended her hand Adriana shook it with a confident, delicate firmness.

"Narrrrrrrdi," Murray echoed. "Adriana Narrrrrrrrrrdi, the family who owns the land adjacent to Lorenzo's property, if I'm not mistaken. . . ."

"That's right."

"Signorina, it's a pleasure to welcome you to our house, though you'll have to forgive me for speaking in English. I'm an idiot when it comes to languages. . . . Not like Francis, eh Francis? Francis, I almost forgot! Let me introduce you to Claire, my wife. Claire, this is Francis. He's the one I was telling you about, the historian. He knows more about this island than most people know about themselves, though you could say the comparison necessarily favors Francis, eh Francis? Please, let's sit down, relax, make yourselves at home while I get the drinks."

Adriana Nardi sat gingerly on the edge of her chair, pressed her knees together beneath the cloth of her dress — a plain, V-necked solid navy cotton dress. She played with the braided fringe of her white shawl as she listened to Francis Cape, who launched into an account of the Nardi family — one of the oldest and most notable families on the island, with ancestors who had dined with Napoleon and at one point had owned all of Monte Calamita.

Murray brought out the pitcher, stirring it with a wooden spoon as he explained that he'd picked up the Bombay gin for a song in Genoa. Had Adriana ever been to Genoa? As she nodded Murray rattled, "Of course you've been to Genoa. Genova, rather. Narrrrdi. More proof that I'm inept with languages. There's not a foreign name I don't mangle."

Murray poured four cocktails, but Claire noticed that the girl didn't drink hers after the first difficult sip. Nor did she speak much through the evening. Nor did anyone explain what she was doing there. Was she Francis's mistress? Was Francis taking care of her for some reason? Francis Cape spoke more about the Nardis, moving into a general account of the island's history. Murray joined in to talk about the Second World War and to explain how he'd come to Elba in the summer of 1944 and stayed for a month. "Do you remember the Americans, Miss Nardi? You would have been a child then. The Elban children used to watch us when we played football on the beach. A blissful month we spent in the middle of an ugly war, playing football on the beach at Le Ghiaie."

No, Adriana hadn't watched the Americans playing football, but yes, she remembered the war. Her school had been destroyed when the Germans bombed Portoferraio — a fact she stated with a simplicity that evoked a long, awkward minute of silence.

Francis finally broke the silence with a comment about the island's importance in history as a strategic location, "an island easily ignored until there's a conflict, and then everyone wants to claim Elba as his own. This has been true since the Etruscans began mining Elban ore. Isn't this true, Adriana?"

What is true, Adriana? Claire wondered to herself.

"It is true," she said demurely.

"You speak wonderful English," Murray said with an admiration Claire considered excessive, given how little the girl had spoken. "Your English is better than mine," he continued. "You could teach *me* some English. Maybe some Italian, too. That's if it's possible for an old dog to learn new tricks! I doubt it. What do you think, Claire? Is there any hope for me?"

Claire didn't bother answering, because right then Lidia came to the doorway, her presence announcing that supper was ready and the table set for four, though no one had warned her there would be visitors. Claire took Francis's arm and led the way into the dining room. Murray escorted Adriana with his characteristic gentility, which only ever seemed comical, an effect increased when Murray stepped on one of Harry's toy race cars and his leg swooped forward. He would have fallen if Adriana hadn't caught him and held him upright.

Much later, Claire would mark this evening as the beginning of the end of her idyll, for it had unsettled her, though why and how she couldn't explain, and could only blame herself for craving a tranquillity that excluded others. She didn't dislike the girl, but she found her enigmatic and couldn't entirely believe what she was told by Murray, who repeated what Francis had told him after supper: that apparently Adriana was assisting Francis in his research on island history in exchange for instruction in English.

They were a strange pair indeed. Still, when the visitors were preparing to leave, Claire readily invited them to return — and not just for Murray's sake. She had a sense that she had more to learn from the Englishman and his young friend. The more she knew, the more at home she'd feel. Not that Claire had any intention of settling on Elba. But over the course of the evening, listening to all the talk about the island, she'd become aware of what she'd started to desire in the week already past. She wanted to live on the island as though she belonged, to experience it as if she had no country of her own.

My brothers and I didn't have to waste our time getting used to our grand island empire because, from our point of view, we had earned the right to stay. After our long journey across the Atlantic, we believed that anything we found we could claim as ours and anyone we met was someone we might as well have already known.

After the first week we could gesture emphatically enough to promise Francesca that we wouldn't leave the property, meaning we'd go no further than the dry streambed separating our land from the neighboring farm on one side and the driveway on the other. As soon as Francesca turned her back, we'd take off. We'd cross the sandy ditch and head up into the terraced vineyards and from there into the hills.

On the edge of one field we saw a farmer sleeping in the shade of a cork tree every afternoon. Through the loops in a fence of chicken wire we'd watch an old woman milking a goat in a dirt yard and an old man weaving a basket shaped like a top hat. Every day we waved a greeting to the milkman when he rattled past us in his truck, and he'd honk his horn four times — a honk for each of us. High up on a rocky trail above the villa we'd shout just to hear our echoes. Down at the marshy shore below San Giovanni, Patrick and Harry would jump off the iron skeleton of a dock that had been left unfinished, and Nat and I, who couldn't swim, would throw sticks for dogs whose names we didn't know. The sun turned our freckles black. Salt streaked our brown hair white. Whenever Elbans spoke to us we would nod. Whenever they laughed we would laugh.

About midway through the month the words we'd heard as nonsense began to take on meaning, thanks in large part to the two women who worked for our family. Francesca had a bedroom in the south wing of our villa. At the end of July, Lidia, who'd been living in a house she shared with relatives in Portoferraio, moved into one of the outbuildings — an old chapel that was equipped with a wood-burning stove. She made it clear to our parents that they must surrender all decision. And she made it clear to us that if we wanted to be understood, we had to use her language, not ours.

Lidia, fat Lidia in her voluminous pleated skirts, treated us with the same wariness she demonstrated at the market when she prodded squids in a bucket. She'd poke our bellies after every meal, or she'd make a bracelet of her thumb and forefinger around our arms to measure the size of our muscles. She cared only that we were getting bigger. Children must eat in order to grow, and they — we — never ate enough to please Lidia. She didn't urge us with the typical *mangia, ancora* we'd heard at trattorias in Florence. Rather, she'd stand over us while we ate our meals at the kitchen table, her folded arms resting on the mound of her own belly, daring us to see what happened if we didn't eat every last noodle.

Francesca, our nanny, was far more forgiving than Lidia, more easily delighted by our jokes, and less attentive. It was easy to escape her watch, especially on days when her fiancé, Filiberto, rode over on his scooter from Capoliveri to help with chores.

We didn't need Francesca to watch us, and we could have done without Lidia's fish soup. We were hearty scavengers, as brave as the pirates whose trail we were following. We needed no more than a bit of stale bread and some water to shore up our strength, though a few pieces of milk chocolate didn't hurt, along with a handful of the jelly beans our aunt had sent from America.

Day by day, we learned everything about the sunbaked land that we needed to know in order to find Elba's secret treasure. None of us noticed that somehow, at some point, or gradually over the course of the month, we'd forgotten that the treasure didn't exist.

YOU SHOULD ACKNOWLEDGE the truth of privilege, Oliver. Privilege more than language set us apart from the Elbans. Even though we remained dependent upon Murray's family for money, we were lucky to be able to do as we pleased. We could travel first class on a luxury liner. We could spend an entire summer doing nothing. We could let our children throw money into the sea.

I'll remind you not to forget the privilege of being able to sit with a book. You mention *The Marble Faun* early on and then forget about it. But in those first weeks in Italy I saw the country through the eyes of Hawthorne's Miriam and imagined bearing her burden of secret knowledge, every sight tinged with the memory of a secret crime. I imagined what it would be like to see in the red cast of sunset the red of blood. Donatello's *Amore* made me think of Hawthorne's Donatello. I'd hear Hawthorne in my head as I wandered with you boys around Florence. I'd remember Hawthorne's observations: twilight comes more speedily in Italy than in other countries, the owls hoot more softly, and convent bells ring in a chain from end to end of the priest-ridden country.

And it wasn't just Hawthorne keeping me company. I'd brought along *The Magic Mountain,* at my sister's suggestion, along with *Anna Karenina* — long books useful for long trips, Jill said. I read *Anna Karenina* first. I was reading it during those days in Florence after Murray had gone on to Elba. Not that Tolstoy's novel had light to shed on my circumstances. But I think it's useful to note that at any particular point in our lives our minds are full not just of our own memories but of the experiences of characters from the books we've been reading. That's if we are lucky to have the education and leisure to read at all. And the curiosity. I've always had plenty of curiosity. Too much, perhaps. I have friends who make a habit of telling me I should mind my own business. These are the same people who tell me I shouldn't take my morning swims — not at my age, and not alone.

But I'm wandering. What was I saying? There's lots to tell you, Ollie. The way memory returns with a gentle nudge. You know how it is. Remembering twilight in Florence, Hawthorne's owls, Tolstoy's Anna. Do you need to hear all this? It's hard to know what to tell you.

I am trying to be candid. You shouldn't have to wonder if there's something I'm not telling you, though you'll understand that I must sift through many old memories, some of them vague, some of them irrelevant. Maybe *Anna Karenina* is irrelevant. Also, an awful night I endured back in Genoa, sickened from eating clams. You don't need to know about that.

I suppose I should tell you more about Adriana Nardi, the girl who came with Francis Cape to supper. She was, as I told you the other night on the phone, the same girl your father saw in the garden, though I didn't learn this until much later. When he saw her again so unexpectedly in our courtyard he didn't immediately recognize her, and by the time he did he was already welcoming her as though they'd never met. But I presume she recognized him. She'd recognized him when she'd first seen him sitting on a rock. Signor Americano. The Elbans were already talking about Signor Americano and his famiglia, their curiosity about us mixed from the start, I have to say, with some distrust.

We learned Adriana's history from Francis Cape. Adriana's ancestor Renato Nardi had been advisor to the ruler of Elba, Antonio something or other, in the 1790s. Antonio was duke when Napoleon's troops landed in — when was it? Around 1800, I think. French rule deprived Antonio of his territory, and he went to live in Rome, where he died a few years later. Renato Nardi stayed in Elba, and after Antonio's death he led the local resistance in Portoferraio. The garrison held out with support from the British navy. When

France and England signed a truce, Renato Nardi was acclaimed by Elbans as a great hero. And among his rewards bequeathed by Antonio was iron-rich land on Monte Calamita.

Not long after the siege of Portoferraio, Renato was one of the patrons who welcomed Napoleon back as king. It wasn't that he disliked the French any less, but he was hopeful that Napoleon's presence would have great material benefits for the island. And it did: for one year all of Portoferraio became a huge barrack filled with troops and gendarmes, courtiers, servants, adventurers. Napoleon made the Elbans feel like they were at the center of the world, and Renato Nardi, who became a confidant of Napoleon, was at the center of the center.

What does all this have to do with Adriana? Over the years, most of the Nardi family left the island and dispersed. By the mid-1950s, only Adriana and her mother remained on Elba. And they were the ones to inherit the archive — boxes of documents, contracts, elaborate land surveys of the island dating back to the seventeenth century, along with letters from Napoleon, one hundred years' worth of ledgers, drawings, a musical program with Renato's doodlings on the back, and a coffee cup, coarsely glazed — I've seen it myself — with bees painted on a white medallion and *NB* inscribed on the bottom.

It was because of the Nardi archives that Francis Cape became involved with Adriana. Francis, who was writing a book about Napoleon's escape from Elba, had met Adriana when she was a young girl. She would keep him company in the library while he pored through old letters and contracts, and he took the time to help her improve her English. Later, he would describe her to us as *intriguing.*

She arrived in our lives with a significant past, she was one of the very few Elbans who spoke English, and she was lonely. She was Signora Nardi's adopted daughter and her only child. Her birth mother was a Corsican girl who'd fled to Elba in disgrace, left her newborn baby outside the hospital in Portoferraio, and disappeared. We learned later that her father was said to have been a foreign sailor — a mercenary, according to the gossip, or a pirate.

At the age of eighteen, Adriana enrolled at the university in Bologna. She studied English, and after two years was encouraged by her professors to apply for a fellowship at St. Hilda's in Oxford. Her application was accepted. She would have gone to England the following fall, but for some reason no one understood, she began losing interest in her studies and didn't bother to take her exams at the end of the year. She returned to Elba, shadowed by the inevitable rumors about an unhappy romance.

So there you have it — a short history of Adriana Nardi up to the point when she entered our lives. It's hard to describe the effect she had upon people because it never seemed to be the same effect twice. Sometimes I felt she was made up of different people. Other times I thought of her as an empty shell, without a soul or self, like one of those conchs that washes up on the beach and Emily Hunter holds against her ear, mistaking the whooshing vibrations of her own circulating blood for the sound of the ocean.

We had Francis Cape to thank for Adriana's presence at our dinners. Francis Cape was a close friend of the Nardis and took it upon himself to introduce the girl to any English speakers he could find.

I remember one dinner in particular at a restaurant in Porto Azzurro. Francis, as usual, was entertaining us all with stories about the Turks and pirates, and then, in response to a question from Murray, describing at great length the screes of Elba and their yield of crystal and tourmalines, rose-colored beryls, red and gray and honey-colored granite. Francis himself had purchased a serpentine pedestal from a store in Portoferraio — he'd picked it up for almost nothing, he said, because the figure of the saint which it must have once supported was missing. He dated it from the seventeenth century and could tell from the quality of the stone that it came from one of the local quarries. He invited us to visit his home the next day to see it. Which we did, and found the poor man living in a filthy hovel in the shadow of Fort Stella.

But that's another story. I was telling you about the dinner at the restaurant in Porto Azzurro: with Francis Cape holding forth, I stole glances at Adriana. She struck me as frail in appearance and yet rigid in her manner. And she hardly touched the food on her plate, I noticed. Afterward, I found myself thinking more about her, and the more I thought, the more elusive she became in my mind. I asked Murray about his impressions because I needed confirmation that my apprehension was justified. I felt as if I'd met a ghost, or, more realistically, a clever actress who was used to pretending.

Murray felt nothing of the sort. He thought she was shy, or no worse than reserved. He enjoyed her company and worked hard to make her feel at ease whenever she was our guest, which turned out to be a frequent occurrence, since we spent so much time in those early weeks with Francis Cape, and Francis liked to bring Adriana along. Though the girl's ostensible goal was to practice her English, often in the quiet hour after pranzo Murray would encourage her to speak with Francis in Italian, and he would sit across from them with his eyes closed, happily listening without understanding a word.

My job during siesta was to keep you boys quiet and out of the hot afternoon sun. It was the only time of day when Lidia and Francesca did not expect me to be idle. They would retreat to their rooms, and I would read to you, or we'd work on puzzles or play cards before I'd turn you loose. I'd forget that I could hear the soft music of conversation out on the terrace.

For the rest of the day, Lidia was in charge of our household. She spoke a few decisive words of English and made it clear that she approved of me only when I didn't interfere with her work. Do you remember how she smelled of the fresh anchovies she'd cook almost daily? And Francesca smelled of lavender, like the island itself. Lavender grew everywhere — bordering the paths, sprinkled through the hills and in the village gardens. And aloe — you could take a deep breath and pull the silky taste of aloe down your throat. And rosemary, of course, and mint and honeysuckle.

And do you remember the winds? The powerful scirocco that caught the sunlight and shattered it into a glassy, spiraling mist. The damp grecale that followed a rainstorm. The harsh winter maestrale that brought two months of rain. Always the wind scraping against the side of your face. Always the sound of it. Moaning through cracks in the shutters, swishing over the vineyards, rattling the fronds of palm trees.

And the blue glimmer of the sea all around, as if the hills of Elba had been heaped upon a plate. And fresh fish to eat every day, sole and tuna, squid and shrimp. There was the time we came upon fishermen cutting up a manta that must have weighed a few hundred pounds. And one evening after supper in Portoferraio we saw a thirty-foot-long giant squid stretched out on a dock for display. And once Nino brought over a tiny monster, a viper fish, with its huge, ugly mouth held open with toothpicks.

I remember one beautiful evening, drinking martinis on the terrace. Francis Cape was describing in his usual vivid detail how the German and Italian submarines would cut their engines and use the inflow from the Atlantic to drift past the British blockades at Gibraltar. Once in a while they made it; usually they didn't. I remember thinking sadly that the engineer from Ohio would have enjoyed trading stories with Francis Cape.

But I couldn't stay sad for long. The wind would rise and whisk the past away. The sun turned Murray the color of half-polished bronze. My hair was so tangled I wouldn't bother to brush it for days at a time.

You see how happy I was? Go ahead and use the word *magic* to describe those first weeks. You remember wandering with your brothers in the hills. Have you forgotten that almost every morning Francesca would take you boys to a quiet cove where the clear water was as still as glass? Sometimes I'd tag along. You, Ollie, would stare in a trance into tidal pools, watching the tiny mouths of barnacles opening and closing — you thought they were the eyes of the rocks! The other boys would walk in bare feet across the slippery kelp. Harry always found something — a cork, sea glass, a pink anemone latched onto the back of a crab. Nat would inevitably wander off, and Francesca would go climbing across the rocks in search of him.

Midway through the summer, your father and I began talking about extending our vacation beyond August. The dollar was strong against the lira, and even with Lidia and Francesca as full-time help we lived cheaply. Our rent for a month was roughly the cost of dinner out for our family at a New York restaurant. For next to nothing, we could remain on Elba until Christmas. Harry and Patrick could go to school in Portoferraio. We could fish and swim and climb into the mountains to hunt for precious stones. Maybe we'd get lucky and find a big chunk of blue tourmaline. Who knows? Maybe tourmaline would make our fortune.

In the evenings Lidia would make a big bowl of soup or pasta, and we'd eat too much and sit with guests and watch the sun go down behind the mountains. Our circle of friends grew wider. Adriana introduced us to Mario Ginori and his wife, a wealthy local couple. Francis introduced us to Joshua Meredith, from Shropshire, who was doing research for a travel guide.

During those early weeks life kept me too occupied to anticipate any change. This has more to do with the proximity of the sea than with our routines, for the endless expanse of water makes one feel that nothing short of death is important, and nothing important can happen without nature's consent.

Nothing without natural propulsion. It's comforting to believe that our lives follow the patterns of nature. But it's a small comfort when we're faced with the violent outcome of human action.

OUR MOTHER READ THE BOOKS she'd brought from America, wrote letters to friends and family, and occasionally accompanied us to the beach, where she sat on a blanket looking like some sort of foreign luminary, a visiting duchess from the distant North.

Once in a while our father would come along for a swim, but more often he'd wander off on his Lambretta and spend the morning tapping away at boulders with his hammer and chisel, separating feldspar from granite, granite from quartz. Sometimes he'd bring home wishing stones — dusty, egg-shaped rocks belted by a full circle of quartz — but nothing more, nothing of real value.

The dust was rust-colored, black, brown, gray. Our father would return capped and coated with dust. Dust would envelope Francis Cape's car whenever he bumped along in his Fiat up our drive. Dust would hide Adriana Nardi from view until she opened the door and stepped away from the car. If she ever smiled a greeting at my brothers and me when she entered the house, we were too busy to notice.

July melted into the heat of August. August brought us closer to September. We didn't bother to ask when we would be leaving, and my older brothers didn't protest when our parents announced that they would be going to the local school.

We overheard our father describing to our mother what he'd seen in his expeditions. We listened carefully when he turned the subject to treasure. The land, he said, was the island's greatest treasure. The rich stock of Elban land. Land strewn with sparkling minerals, land rising in peaks and sloping down to the blue disk of the sea. Here on paradise, the value of land was rapidly increasing as the island's future as a tourist haven became more certain. While

Murray spoke, he let a match he'd used to light his cigarette burn far down its stem. The shock of heat against his fingertips roused him and he shook out the flame abruptly. We watched him relax into his cigarette as he continued. Claire watched him. An investor could take advantage of the trend, Murray said. He could invest in property. Developers were already scouting, and local farmers were ready to sell. If an investor were clever, he could be a middleman. He'd find the land that others wanted, stake his claim, bide his time, and eventually sell his property at enough profit to make the effort worthwhile.

Murray wandered the island on foot and motorcycle. He circled it by boat. He studied maps and topography charts. He even tried to make sense of the laws relating to property and taxes, but he found them as impenetrable as the rules relating to Italian grammar. He decided that there were some things he didn't have to know.

In order to calculate the value of land, he needed to know more about the island. Francis Cape brought him to the Nardis' villa, La Chiatta, to see the family's extensive archive.

The front drive cutting between Lorenzo's property and the Nardi olive groves was lined with oleander bushes, their blooms brown and faded from the heat. The villa itself was a tired orange stucco, with a high stone wall around the courtyard that blocked the view of the sea, though the shore must have been close — Murray heard the water slapping against rocks when he stepped from Francis's car.

Signora Nardi, Adriana's mother, met them at the door. She spoke English stiffly, self-consciously. She was a small, gray-haired woman with steely eyes that absorbed everything in a cold, consuming glance. Francis Cape had warned Murray about her, describing the woman as aloof. Murray had the immediate impression that she disapproved of him. Before he opened his mouth to speak, Signora Nardi already disliked him.

She said that her daughter had told her all about the American couple and their lively bambini. She hoped Murray would bring his family along for a visit one day. Murray promised to do so and added that he hoped Signora Nardi would come join them at their house for a meal.

The stiff way she smiled in response suggested reluctance. She motioned to Francis to lead the way inside. Murray followed Francis. Adriana met them in the library, at which point Signora Nardi left, having indicated that Signor Murdoch could examine anything in the collection relevant to his studies.

Studies, she'd said, as though he'd been presented to her as another scholar joining Francis Cape in his search of history. He wanted to laugh at the idea. He wasn't even sure what he was looking for.

Adriana showed him whatever she thought might interest him. Signor Americano wanted to know more about the island. Look at this — a cup made by a nineteenth-century Elban artisan for Napoleon. And this — a mine survey of Monte Calamita dating from the seventeenth century. You want to know about our island, Signor Americano? Here is a ledger from the Palazzina dei Mulini tracking the emperor's expenses.

While Francis Cape watched with a possessive pride, Adriana showed Murray brittle yellow documents signed by Napoleon, music programs from the early 1800s, and old maps of the whole Tuscan archipelago.

What else could Adriana show Murray? Could he come visit her again? Of course he could. What could she tell him about the island and its history? This beautiful, mysterious island. Would Adriana tell him that story again, the one about Napoleon laughing so hard he fell out of his chair?

Murray returned on his own to La Chiatta a few days later,

drawn there because the girl had made him feel welcome, though when he arrived he found the shutters closed against daylight and the courtyard eerily empty. He expected to meet Adriana's mother again, but it was Adriana who answered the door. It was Adriana who served tea brewed from wild mint and let him drink from Napoleon's cup. Murray watched her watching him from her chair across the marble-top table, her chin propped in her hands. Her eyes were a dull brown, the whites faintly bloodshot. Her fingernails had a yellowish tinge to them. Only the moist natural red of her lips suggested any vitality.

Adriana spoke briefly, concisely, about the first visit of Cosimo III to Elba in 1700, how he arrived at three in the morning and was carried by two slaves in a velvet-cushioned chair all the way up to the Stella. She told him a little about the Austrian blockade in 1708 and the civil war that ensued. They discussed the French Revolution and even got into a mild, fleeting argument about a statement by de Tocqueville:

"The King's subjects felt toward him both the natural love of children for their father and the awe properly due to God alone."

Murray accepted every word of de Tocqueville. Adriana declared Murray a fool. Murray scoffed at Adriana's arrogance. Adriana laughed at him, and then without warning she leaned across the table and with her thumb rubbed from his cheek what he assumed was a smudge of dirt or ink, her gesture more in the manner of a sister or daughter than a lover, but still it was enough to unnerve Murray. Before he could speak she'd left to refill the teapot in the kitchen.

After that they spoke in softer tones, laughed nervously to fill an awkward silence, looked away when their eyes accidentally met. He asked if he might return, and she just smiled in reply. He did return — a third and then a fourth time. They grew more formal in their exchanges and rarely let opinions clash. When Murray visited La Chiatta he tried to come prepared with specific tasks. He asked for Adriana's help in translating a newspaper article. He asked for her advice about the land. She told him he should spend his money on a boat.

He found himself watching the girl when he thought she wouldn't notice him, not because of any inappropriate desire but because she puzzled him. The deliberateness of her movements and the scripted quality of her voice provoked in him an imitative poise. He wondered if Adriana were suffering from some chronic illness, but she never mentioned it and Murray never asked. He studied her for signs either of deterioration or improvement. He told himself that his interest in her was as harmless and inevitable as his interest in all things exotic.

Though it remained hot through September, the quicker turn of dusk into night foretold the seasonal changes ahead. Our parents talked about staying on Elba long enough to experience the island in the guise of winter. They negotiated with Lorenzo a three-month extension of the Le Foci lease. Patrick and Harry dutifully went off each day to the elementary school in Portoferraio, and we spent our free hours scouring the sunbaked land for treasures. No one asked us to explain why we weren't going back to America.

Every morning Murray rose early and planned how he would fill each empty hour. At the end of the day he'd feel as though he'd passed the time in a stupor. Sometimes it seemed to him that all the islanders were plotting against him, luring him into a trap with their insinuative talk about the future. He kept asking Francis Cape for assurance.

One morning in October he lay awake in bed trying to remember a conversation from the previous day. They'd all had supper together — he and Claire, Francis and Adriana. He'd been listening to Adriana and Francis speaking in Italian. Somehow Murray had intuited that the girl was saying something he deserved to know, but he hadn't been able to bring himself to interrupt and ask for a translation.

Now, the morning after, he couldn't stand not knowing what he'd missed. He climbed out of bed, leaving Claire sleeping, and rode his motorcycle along the deserted road to La Chiatta. Only when he'd turned off the engine and paused to listen to the sea lapping behind the courtyard wall did he consider how early it was and how ridiculous he'd appear if he knocked at the door.

He snuck away as quietly as he could, though as he crossed the courtyard he had the prickling sensation that someone was watching him from an upstairs window. He resisted turning around to check. He pushed his motorcycle back up the long dirt drive. Doves cooed, hidden in the palms. Olive leaves rustled in the morning breeze. A silver moth fluttered around his head, bumping against his cheek as though to wake him.

The first moth in our Le Foci house was found by Nat floating in his cup of milk, its silver wings shaded gray by contrast. He picked it up by its soggy wingtip and laid it carefully on the table, then called the rest of us to come look. Lidia wasted only a quick glance and commanded Nat to finish his milk, which he did with gusto while the rest of us watched in admiration.

I found the second moth flitting above me when I awoke from my afternoon nap. I knew many Italian words by then, and one happened to be the word for *butterfly.* I announced its presence with a shriek of joy — "Farfalla, farfalla!" — causing both Francesca and Claire to rush to my bedside. They laughed when they understood what had excited me. Francesca threw open the shutters and the moth zigged and zagged across the room and drifted out the window.

Francesca, who was given every Wednesday afternoon off to visit her family in Capoliveri, had been about to leave to catch the bus, and now she tied a blue silk scarf around her head and excused herself. Claire picked up and folded my pajamas. I stared at the rectangles of blue sky and watched without a word as three silver moths flew into the room.

Three dancing moths. Before our eyes they became six, eight, a dozen and more. They were a mist of gauzy wings, a cloud filling the room, spreading down the hall like fog through a seaside village. It seemed as though a single moth had only to unfold its wings and release a haze of offspring. There were hundreds of moths, thousands, their silver, pink-lined forewings identical to hindwings, brown furry bodies the size of plum-pits, needle tips for eyes. Claire fanned them away from me with her hand. In such numbers their fluttering should have been thunderous — instead, they were eerily silent. But a moment later the silence was broken when the moths filled the bedroom where my brothers had been playing. They yelped with delight. The enemy force was attacking, quick, radio headquarters, call the troops, load, fire! Nat threw plastic soldiers at the moths, Harry trapped them in his cupped hands, Patrick batted at them with a rolled magazine. The enemy advanced. The allies were outnumbered, but still they held their ground. Duck, jump, run, stop, turn!

"Get out of the house!" It was Claire's order, but this time the urgency my brothers heard in her voice struck them as ridiculous, and they continued their war. Claire held me with one arm and managed to grab Nat and Harry by their wrists, and she pulled us to the door. Patrick kicked the floor as he followed, furious to have the best game ever interrupted.

Inside the house Lidia threw open shutters and closed closet doors. She found an old set of bellows and set about puffing clouds of moths from one room to another. Though she'd never seen quite so many moths at once, she remained grimly calm. The moths came every autumn to feast upon blankets and sweaters. I fantasmi — the ghost moths. They were arriving in multitudes this year. In some later year, they would come in even greater numbers. That was the way life worked in Lidia's scheme. The moths were proof that the future would outshine the past. Next year's storms would be the worst storms ever. Or they'd be the mildest. If the next summer wasn't the warmest, then the following summer would be. Or the one after. Every record set would be broken. Every war fought would be worse than the last. *Bella, horrida bella.* There were no surprises under heaven.

The season of the ghost moths. We loved them, loved to lose ourselves in the thick of their wings and feel the feathery wisps of their touch. We loved to hear them thumping against windowpanes and watch their shadows moving like the reflections of raindrops on our bedroom walls. Meena loved to comb her claws through their midsts or hop up and catch one with a gulp, swallowing it whole. Our parents hated them. They bought little metal fans for each room and set the switches on high to drive away the moths. But the fans only seemed to draw more moths. They'd fight their way toward the center of the air current like fish struggling upriver and then turn on their wings and flit off, as though it were nothing more than a game to them. The best game ever.

No one noticed them leaving. We just woke up one morning in late October, wondered for an instant what had changed, and realized then that the shadows on the walls were gone. Lidia said something we didn't understand about the sea. Francesca said that the little farfalle had turned into cherubini.

We would have been disappointed — rather, we were disappointed for a few hours, until Harry found the spider in the tub. It was black with white dots on its carapace and white chevrons on its abdomen, and it was about the size of Patrick's thumbnail. Harry trapped it in a cup topped with paper and brought it into the kitchen for the rest of us to see. We gathered round, marveling as Harry dumped the spider into a deep crease in the paper. He asked for a toothpick. Patrick brought him a spoon. Harry flipped the spider over, and we were astonished to see it somehow manage to flip back and right itself. Harry touched it with the spoon again. The spider leapt into the air and landed on the table, and it would have escaped if Nat hadn't crushed it with a rolling pin.

Harry pushed Nat in retaliation, pushed him right against the rickety table. The tabletop knocked against the shelf in a wooden cupboard. On the shelf the delicate glass flue of a lantern swayed drunkenly and then fell forward, shattering on the tile floor.

"Che è successo!" We heard Lidia's voice before we saw her. My brothers fled. I was frozen by confusion. Lidia swooped down, spanked me once, and scooped me into her arms, holding me over her shoulder as she marched down the hall to tell Claire what trouble I had caused.

I suffered my resentment in my room, alone, for the next ten minutes or so, until I heard my brothers whispering in the hall and went to find out what important thing deserved secrecy. Patrick was holding a milk bottle; Harry was securing a piece of paper with a rubber band to serve as a lid. "Shut up," Nat said when he saw me. I circled, preparing to kick him, but my attention was soon absorbed by the spectacle in the bottle — not just one striped spider but a whole clutch of them leaping toward the stick, bouncing against the glass and tumbling down upon one another.

My brothers had gathered the spiders from windowsills on the outside of the house. But they were all over the inside of the house as well. Now that we knew what to look for, we saw them everywhere — crawling on bookshelves, up flowerpots, across the tiles and planks of the floors, up walls, along ceilings. When we understood how plentiful they were, we began yelling with delight. Claire joined us on our hunt without understanding what, exactly, we were hunting for. When Harry showed her the mass of spiders underneath the living-room sofa, she herded us all out of the house again, and this time she wouldn't let us go back inside.

These were the zebra spiders — minute spiders that could leap from the floor to a tabletop and were as wily a prey as minnows. They weren't as beautiful as the ghost moths, but they were more interesting to us. To Claire, they were a new and worse kind of pest, somehow expressive of a mute hostility. If the house had an animate spirit, this spirit had taken a strong dislike to us, and with the moths and spiders meant to drive us away. And if the house were just a house, it was proving itself uninhabitable.

That same afternoon, Claire ordered us to stay outside until she returned, and she walked to Lorenzo's villa, where she put to him an ultimatum: he would see to it that the Le Foci house was free of pests or the Murdochs would break the lease. Lorenzo poured her a glass of wine and promised to help. If the villa didn't suit the Signora, he would find her another villa — *una villa più bella,* he assured her. He smiled gently, his mustache flattening across his upper lip. Claire felt startled by his kindness and recognized how excessive her distress must have seemed. She sipped her wine. When he offered her a cigarette she accepted, though she hadn't smoked for years.

The problem was easily resolved, thanks to Lorenzo's graciousness. For the same rent, he provided us with a new house in the hills between Marciana and Marciana Marina, with a magnificent view of the sea. Claire accepted before she even saw the place. And she made all the arrangements to move without even consulting Murray, sparing him from the distraction of life.

Some days the vibrancy of colors on the island astonished him; other days the clouds hung low to the ground, the air was thick with smoke from burning rubbish, and he couldn't understand what the Italians were saying to him. Elba held no certain answers. But Murray grew increasingly resolute. He didn't want to leave the island without taking with him a deed to Elban land. He hired a surveyor, Carlo Giovanni, who had recently lost his job in the local mining industry. Carlo wouldn't give Murray a straight answer. Either the land on the east side of the island was worth more than the land on the west side, or the land on the west side was worth more than the land on the east side. Either Murray would prosper, or he'd fail.

He kept mislaying maps and forgetting appointments. He heard some men in a bar in Portoferraio laughing, and he knew they were laughing at him. Still, he wasn't close to giving up. Often he didn't come home for pranzo and siesta. Instead, he'd trail Carlo over rock croppings and through chestnut woods. Francis Cape tagged along and proved so useful as a translator that Murray offered to pay him, but Francis said he preferred the status of a volunteer.

If Murray could only put a claim down, he'd feel better. There was plenty of land to buy and plenty of islanders who wanted to sell. But where to begin. When to begin? How?

Uncertainty was beginning to make him agitated. He was losing sleep. He rattled lame jokes for his guests in order to keep them at dinners that lasted for hours. He shrugged when Claire announced that we were changing residences. He wasn't home to help pack. And on the morning we were scheduled to move, he left the house early, before the rest of us had woken, he trailed the surveyor all day, and in the early evening he rode his motorcycle right past Marciana Marina and the cart road that led to our new house, and he returned to the villa in Le Foci.

It was a cool, clear autumn night. The light of a full moon filled the deserted rooms with a dim fluorescence; the fringes of curtains fluttered in the breeze. It took only a moment for Murray's eyes to become accustomed to the dimness and another moment for him to realize his mistake and remember that his family had moved to a different residence. The first wave of panic passed, replaced by a puzzling serenity. He'd always preferred chaos to simplicity, noise to silence, society to solitude. But he felt inclined to linger in the empty house and enjoy the inventions of his imagination. To imagine, without much effort, life without a family or friends. The freedom of solitude.

Alone, without responsibility, in a villa filled with moonlight. He could consider what he might do if he could do as he pleased. He didn't want to have to answer for his actions. He didn't want to think about his reputation. For a good long hour he sat there not thinking about his reputation. All the jobs he'd quit since he'd come home from the war. His mother and uncles. The people of Elba. Adriana Nardi.

The truth was, he hadn't seen the girl for weeks, ever since the early morning when he'd gone to La Chiatta. Sitting alone in Le Foci, he was trying not to think about her. He had no reason to think of her. She'd been busy, Francis Cape had said with a vagueness that had secretly annoyed Murray. But of course Murray had no right to know what she'd been doing. He didn't really care about what she'd been doing. Most of the time, she couldn't have been farther from his thoughts. And yet he experienced an odd sensation of unreality when he heard a noise and looked out the window to see the girl stepping from his mind onto the path beside the house, a mirage so vivid that he had to shake his head and look again. And she persisted, an apparition he'd conjured, making her way toward the front of the house, as real as the curtain he drew aside to watch her. He listened to the delicate crunching as she rolled her shoes over the pebbles, saw her wince when she turned an ankle, heard his own intake of breath, and knew exactly when she looked up to see him move back from the window.

He couldn't will her away, nor did he want to. He just needed to compose himself. He was surprised at how boldly she knocked. People who knock like that always have a clear purpose.

Is anybody home? Buonasera . . . Oh, come in, you poor girl. . . . Without a coat, no less. . . . Murray, it's Adriana at the door. . . . Put the water on for tea and fetch a blanket, will you?

She'd seen him at the window. And his Lambretta was parked in the drive. She knew — he knew she knew — that he was inside the house, just as she'd known that he'd come to see her at the break of dawn. Did she know he was alone? She knocked again and again. She kept knocking until he had no choice but to get up and answer the door, greeting the girl with a smile meant to convey calm, inviting her to come inside.

She hesitated, privately struggling to enact whatever scene she'd rehearsed in her mind. All at once he felt sorry for her; he understood why she was there. It's not easy to find the words in any language, Signorina, when you know you shouldn't say what you want to say. Come into the living room, Adriana, come and sit beside Murray on the sofa, talk, if you want, don't talk if you can't, let the two of you enjoy the sense of existing far away from everything that is familiar, let him hold you, Signorina, just this once, and feel you in his arms, the softness of your skin, the surprising strength of your limbs, this strange island creature making him feel at home in this distant place, bringing to mind the shadows of mountains in the mist, the color of the sea, the beach at Le Ghiaie, the brightness of the moon, the deep folds of a skirt, the tenderness of touch, her coyness, his desire, her resistance, his insistence, her building rage.

She snapped her thighs closed, jerked away from him, growled, "Let me go!"

Why, of course he'd let her go. And she was gone, disappearing into the darkness of the hall. But wait, Signorina, he'd thought . . . what? He'd assumed . . . wrongly. Was there ever a man as foolish as Murray Murdoch! All he had to do was open a door and he'd make a stupid mistake.

He hadn't meant any harm. He was a happily married man. He even found himself resenting Adriana Nardi for leading him on. At the same time, he wondered if what he'd accepted as a deliciously mysterious air about the girl could be attributed to a waywardness of mind. Maybe she seemed mysterious because she was insane. The prospect made satisfying sense. He thought of the engineer from Ohio. He considered how confusion can harden into desperate intention. He felt some real sympathy for Adriana but at the same time wished that he had kept his distance.

He returned to the window in hopes of catching sight of the girl leaving along the terrace path. But either she had taken a different path or she was still somewhere inside the house. He strained to hear a floorboard creak, a door close. Outside, a rooster's restless night cry sounded like a voice raised in brief protest. Or a shout sounded like a rooster's cry. He decided he'd heard a rooster. He brushed a bug from his arm, an ant — no, a spider, one of the harmless little spiders that had driven Claire from the house.

He waited by the window for what seemed like hours but would add up to less than half an hour in real time. Eventually he decided that she must have left the house through the front door and headed down the road to San Giovanni. He'd have to follow the same road west, toward Procchio. His Lambretta was low on gas. How low? Could he make it to Marciana Marina?

He decided he would wait for the length of time it took him to smoke a cigarette. He sat on the sofa, watching the smoke spread and disperse into the darkness, and was reminded of watching the *Casparia*'s wake at night. The smoke felt more than pleasant every time it filled his lungs — it felt like a much-needed affirmation of logic after the frustration of an unsolvable puzzle, a round peg in a round hole. And he was glad to find that the Sambuca had been left behind in the credenza. He sipped the liquor straight from the bottle. He smoked a second cigarette and watched the shadows of the curtains on the carpet, shapes undulating like the long hair of a woman swimming underwater. He caught a white bar of moonlight on his open palm, closed his fist, and studied the stripe of light across his knuckles.

As the hours passed he thought about tourmaline. He thought about the satisfaction he'd feel if he could only succeed in proving that all he needed to thrive was freedom from scrutiny. He wondered if there was anyone left in the world who would lend him money.

BEFORE YOU CONTINUE, Ollie, you might consider the influence of Francis Cape. Remember that Francis introduced Adriana Nardi to your father. Remember that Francis wanted to serve as translator. Remember that Francis didn't want Murray to do anything without first asking Francis for advice.

Francis Cape plays an important part in this story, so let me take the time now to tell you about him. He was a tall man, the skin of his face pitted above his beard, his white hair thinning evenly over his scalp, his flesh collapsing into every joint, making him look comically knobby. He had a lovely voice — slightly hoarse, precise in its elocution yet surprisingly gentle, without any pretension suggested in the speech. At first I liked to have Francis around because I liked to hear him talk. Sometimes I'd even let my mind wander and listen to the music of his voice without bothering to follow his meanings. But as I came to know him better, I began listening more carefully for hints that might have revealed something he wasn't ready to say directly.

As I mentioned earlier, Francis Cape lived in a hovel in Porto-ferraio, in the shadow of Fort Stella. He had a single room, a third-floor walk-up with two grimy windows looking up toward the south wall of the fort. He slept on a mattress on the floor, used the communal bathroom in the hall, and had no kitchen facilities other than a gas bombola. The room stank of his pipe smoke. The blankets were threadbare, the walls crumbling, the shutters warped. The knickknacks he'd collected were jumbled on top of his bureau. And there were piles of books everywhere — books of poetry in French and Italian, travel guides, history books, Shakespeare's plays, an incomplete set of the 1928 edition of the

Encyclopedia Britannica, and too many books to count about Napoleon.

Francis had come to Elba to write a biographical account of Napoleon's year of exile and dramatic escape. Ten years later Francis was still on the island and had written no more than fragments, some closer to fiction than fact, all of it handwritten on pages their author didn't even bother to number. He wanted to write the definitive book about Napoleon on Elba. He would begin writing, judge his effort inadequate, and try again, writing and rewriting for years in an attempt to do justice to a history that was of mythic proportion.

His frustration with his work first led him to Adriana Nardi. He'd been on Elba three years before learning about the Nardi collection. Three long years he'd spent, or wasted, wandering the island, prowling the passageways of Napoleon's villas and scouring documents in the local library, before an Elban acquaintance finally told him about the Nardi collection. The man, a schoolteacher, spoke the name of *Nardi* with obvious reluctance. Although every native Elban knew about the collection, they also respected the family's privacy. But the schoolteacher was a poor man and could think of no other way to return Francis's generosity after Francis had paid for his dinner.

You might visit Signora Nardi, the teacher had said with a shrug, and Francis had shrugged back. Signora who? Nardi, Nardi, in the villa called La Chiatta, on the road to Magazzini.

Signora Nardi received him graciously, even if her manner was cautious, as Francis would later report. Adriana was still a young sprite, not yet fifteen years old, and she was the one who showed Francis the collection — a collection that would have thrilled any historian and that overwhelmed Francis so completely that he had to cut short his visit and ask to come another day.

Was the collection made more exciting because of the presence of Adriana Nardi? The easy conclusion would be that Francis fell in love with Adriana, though Francis wouldn't have put it that way,

I'm sure. He'd have admitted, if pressed, to no more than paternal affection. But whatever the tenor of the experience within those walls, La Chiatta became both the source of inspiration for him and the impediment. After every visit Francis would begin writing furiously, desperate to do justice to the history. And every attempt would end within an hour, the historian's passion exhausted.

This went on for years. By the time we met Francis on Elba, he had a dazed look in his eyes, which I attributed to eccentricity. He didn't strike me as a defeated man. Rather, he seemed barely able to subdue his giddiness. Whenever he spent an evening with us, he would become the center and catalyst for conversation. And at some point he'd inevitably pause, lean back in his chair, and declare loudly, *I love this island!*

I suppose I became suspicious of his happiness when he invited us to his home. A happy man might have tolerated the disorder of that room, but not the squalor. I remember noticing crumbs of food suspended in cobwebs along the window ledge. I glanced at Francis, who looked away from me in what I interpreted as embarrassment.

Afterward, walking through Portoferraio with Murray, I expressed some concern for Francis; Murray looked puzzled. Such a hovel for a home, I said. He's a bachelor — Murray offered only this as explanation. But it couldn't be good for his health to live in such a place. No, Murray insisted, Francis was doing fine.

I didn't understand Murray's indifference. He liked Francis, but it seemed he didn't care what became of him, and he didn't want to know more than Francis was willing to tell. Francis Cape was one of the few men Murray was inclined to keep at a distance, though not because he didn't trust him. He trusted Francis more than I did and didn't feel it necessary to press him to reveal his secrets or even to offer him a room in our house. Which was all for the best, I suppose, since Francis wanted us to believe in his happiness.

Life on Elba was good — so good that Francis thought Napoleon a fool for leaving. Yes, life on Elba was very good, Murray would agree. They spoke with the condescension of men who considered themselves worldly. Their knowingness irritated me. I remember one evening when Adriana had joined us for dinner. I stepped into the kitchen to fill a pitcher with water, and I paused to listen through an open window while Murray and Francis praised the island. Didn't the mountains look like cardboard stencils against the blue sky? And what amazing sunsets. The flowers. The iron ore. The precious minerals. Heaven stored its jewels here, Francis said — porphyry and serpentine, beryls and aquamarines. And tourmaline, of course. And who knows but diamonds, why not diamonds! Carlo had told Murray that a small diamond had been found on the slope of Volterraio by German soldiers during the war. I said it sounded like a rumor to me, but Adriana insisted it was true.

Where there's one diamond, there are always more, said Francis. He yawned, stretched his arms toward the night sky. Isn't that right, Murray?

The Germans made themselves sick digging for diamonds on Volterraio, Adriana said. When they weren't training, they were digging. Day and night, digging, digging, digging. They were sick and weak when the Allies attacked. I think many Germans were killed because of the Volterraio diamond.

She spoke slowly, more in the manner of one who chooses to linger over words rather than as someone who isn't fluent in the language. I used the opportunity to watch Murray watching her. It was clear that she intrigued him, yet even then I was not suspicious. The fact is, I'd already come to the conclusion that Adriana belonged to Francis Cape, his possessiveness being of the mystical kind, the way God belongs to priests, and Murray could only adore the girl through Francis, in Francis's company.

Call me innocent. Or foolish. Or blame the distractions of the sea. In those days all I wanted to do was watch the sunlight dancing on the surface of the water.

I told you at dinner about what happened to Murray when we

moved to the villa in the valley below Marciana. On the first day at our second home, I didn't even finish unpacking one suitcase. Most of the afternoon I spent lounging on the terrace, taking in the magnificent view of the sea. Right from the start of our stay in that beautiful villa I became — how should I put it? I wasn't exactly neglectful — I would never forget my mistake on the *Casparia,* the way I let myself ignore obvious dangers. But if Lidia and Francesca were the opposite poles, then I was letting myself become more like Francesca by the minute.

Only after sunset, when the sea was hidden by darkness, did I begin to grow anxious. Night has always been my time for worry. It was at night when Murray's ambitions would seem ridiculous. It was at night when I would let myself get drunk and Murray would get drunker.

That first night in our new villa I did not get drunk. I ate dinner alone after putting you boys to bed, and I stayed awake waiting for Murray to come home. I was reading *The Count of Monte Cristo* — I'd picked up the novel at an English bookstore in Florence — and I remember reading the chapter about Franz's hashish dream while I listened for the sound of Murray's motorcycle. Eventually I felt too tired to read, too anxious to sleep. I made tea and sat wrapped in a blanket out on the terrace. As the night wore on, the full moon seemed to shrink, the stars became brighter, the constellations more clearly defined, with Hercules stretching toward the west as though attempting to seize the jewel of Vega in his hand. A nightingale sang briefly but was silenced by a barking dog. Occasionally a car would rattle by on the Marciana road, and I would listen for the sound of it pulling up our dirt drive to deliver Murray, whose Lambretta might have broken down — one possibility out of many. I would try to compose myself, to disguise my worry with fatigue so I could greet him calmly, but the car would continue down the road, and I would go on waiting for my husband to come home.

This is what I reasoned that night: if Murray's motorcycle had broken down, he'd have to hitch a ride. If he didn't arrive by midnight it meant he was lost. He might have misplaced our address. Then he'd have to go to Lorenzo's house and find out where we'd gone. If he did this, then Lorenzo would surely give him a ride — which meant Murray should be back sooner. But Lorenzo might have offered him a drink. This would have delayed Murray's return for a couple of hours. We had no phone, so Murray had no way to contact me. He would assume that I'd gone to sleep. Lorenzo would open another bottle of wine and interrogate Murray about his plans. With the Rio and Calamita mines failing steadily, Elbans could only welcome investment. The Nardi family owned the lease to the land mined on Monte Calamita — what would they do when the mine closed down? What would anyone do? By the end of the decade there'd be no iron-ore mining on Elba at all, Lorenzo had already predicted for us, and he'd offer this prediction again as a wager, a five-hundred-lire bet, if Murray dared.

One thousand. Murray would always counter by upping the stakes. It was one of his certain habits, like always putting his right shoe on first.

Two A.M. Three A.M. The moon disappeared, and the sky brightened subtly to the hollow gray-blue that precedes dawn. I saw a shadow moving on the terrace. The dark body of an animal. A wild animal. A rat. A ferret. A cat — Meena.

I called to her, clicked my tongue, watched her freeze. She tipped her head, then decided to ignore me. Away she slunk, toward the sound of a barking dog.

A prowling cat. A barking dog. Hercules fading into dawn. Where was your father?

Morning came, and with it arrived Murray, his excuse cast as self-mocking explanation — he'd forgotten about the move, forgotten to head to Marciana after work, forgotten to put gas in his motorcycle, and on top of that he'd fallen asleep on the sofa of the other villa, slept straight through to 5 A.M., hadn't even taken off his shoes. Then he'd set off on his Lambretta, run out of gas, and ended up walking three miles into Marciana Marina, where he had to wait another hour for a gas station to open.

He needed a shave, a bath, breakfast. He looked awful, not just physically awful but dispirited. Yesterday's explorations must have disappointed him, I thought. His hopes for investment were ridiculous, and he'd already wasted too much money. It was all he could do to drag himself to the bedroom to change his clothes and get ready for another day of work.

But by the time he came to the table for breakfast he'd regained his optimism, so much so that he reminded me of Francis, giddy with denial. There was something he couldn't tell me. What? I'm not sure I wanted to know. I was grateful to have Murray home. He whistled while he cracked the shell of a soft-boiled egg with the edge of his spoon, *tap tap tapping* to the tune of "Home on the Range," until my worry turned to annoyance, and annoyance melted into amusement.

As I told you during our last dinner, Murray remained alone at Le Foci after Adriana had left. I believe this to be the truth, though it took many months for your father to explain.

OF THE THREE QUALITIES WHICH determine the market value of a gemstone — beauty, rarity, and durability — the last quality is the easiest to measure. Durability determines the rank of mineral specimens. Durability is a stone's defense against the wear of weather. Durability transforms certain stones into treasures and turns treasures into legends. If heroes were to find defunct paper bills instead of gold and gems when they unearthed a buried treasure, there wouldn't be much of a story to tell.

While rarity is a more elusive quality, the connection between rarity and worth is simple. If new sources increased the world's quantity of available diamonds tenfold, diamonds would lose value. If synthetic production of a particular type of gem rivals the natural process, miners lose their jobs.

Beauty is the quality most difficult to measure, as well as the most important. To some extent, a stone's beauty is contingent. One year garnets may be in fashion, the next year, pearls. But the intrinsic beauty of a gemstone is determined by one factor independent of human whim: light. Light creates luster, and luster is what gives a stone its character. Without luster, a diamond would be no more beautiful than quartz, and gold would be pyrite's equal. Without luster, topaz and ruby, amethyst and sapphire would be as dull as granite.

The greater the amount of light reflected instead of absorbed, the more lustrous the stone. The most remarkable version of this property is found in hexagonal crystals, such as diamonds, calcite, and tourmaline, which double an image by splitting the light.

Tourmaline's alkali tints range from black to transparent, rubellite to brown. Black schorl was the most common form of tourmaline found on Elba. Other specimens tended to be pink, yellow, and green, and frequently parti-colored. From the 1930s through the 1950s, the crystals were increasingly coveted. Pink and green watermelon crystals were highly valued, and blue tourmaline was the most valuable of all.

With the money his uncles finally sent, Murray purchased five hectares of terraced land on a wooded slope in the Mezza Luna zone between Sant'Andrea and Monte Giove. Stone walls hidden among the chestnuts suggested that centuries earlier this had been cultivated land. But when Murray purchased the title from a family that had owned the land for generations, only a footpath connected the property to the coastal road.

What Murray's land had, though, was tourmaline. Little black sticks of schorl, which Murray broke from the granite rock face when he was surveying the land. Because of tourmaline, our father agreed to buy the land for a price he knew was inflated.

In the mornings our parents would confer in low, growling voices outside, Claire still in her bathrobe and slippers, Murray already mounted on his motorcycle. They would discuss bills, loans, and their increasing expenses. Later in the morning Claire would take a taxi to the bank in Portoferraio in hopes of collecting the last of the loan Murray's uncles had promised to wire. Murray's uncles, however, were keeping Claire and Murray waiting, and Murray had to ask Lorenzo for a month's respite on the rent. Claire explained the situation to Lidia, who kept down costs by cooking her cacciucco with grouper instead of swordfish. Francesca was given the month of December off. And our mother began calling agents for information about ships heading back to New York.

The weather grew colder. The clouds overhead were dark gray with ragged edges, and rain would fall continuously for three or four days at a time. Patrick and Harry claimed that they were being bullied by the Elban boys at school, so Claire decided to keep them home for a while. She gave them reading lessons that amounted to an hour spent deciphering articles in a week-old *Herald Tribune*, worked with them briefly on math, and then she'd bundle us in raincoats and boots and send us outside.

I turned five in the middle of November. Patrick, who turned ten on the ninth of December, was responsible for the safety of the rest of us — which translated into tyranny. He was the king, we were his servants, and if he asked us to pick the spiny balls off a sandbur or collect dried-flower sacs from the sedge, we had to oblige.

After the disappointment of paltry gifts at our birthdays, we weren't looking forward to Christmas. Somehow, though, our parents managed to satisfy our greed. The presents were abundant on Christmas morning — toy soldiers and trucks, puzzles, model airplane kits, and even books in English. Lidia had the week off, so Claire mastered the oven and cooked potatoes and green beans and roasted a chicken, which she tried to fool us into believing was turkey.

After dinner we collapsed on the floor in front of the radio that provided only fuzzy reception on a single channel. We listened to a broadcast of a Christmas mass, not caring that we didn't understand a word of it. Claire was in the kitchen washing up; Francis Cape — who either had mistaken a casual comment for an invitation or else had somehow invited himself to dinner — lit his pipe, Murray lit a cigarette, and they settled in their chairs for a good long smoke.

They smoked in silence for a few minutes. Murray said something about work being done on the road to Marciana. Knowing Francis's resistance to all development on the island, he launched into a defense of the new roads, insisting that not only would they open up the island to tourists, they would ultimately save the Elbans time and labor, giving them the opportunity to concentrate on intensifying production on their farms as well as improving their dilapidated houses. He was describing a house he'd seen in San Piero when Francis interrupted him.

"That's all fine, Murray. But there's something important I want to discuss with you."

Murray's immediate thought was money: Francis wanted to borrow money from Murray or lend Murray money or else he knew of a secret source for money. But Francis had only to say the name "Adriana Nardi," and Murray felt a draining presentiment. What about the girl? Adriana had disappeared, Francis said. She'd left a note explaining only that she couldn't explain why she had to leave. She hadn't been seen or heard from for more than a month. At first her mother kept secret the fact of her disappearance. She made inquiries with friends in Bologna but failed to find any evidence that her daughter had been there at all. After a few weeks she contacted the local police. They questioned fishermen, sailors, and harbor workers. In the week before Christmas, the police told Signora Nardi that to the best of their knowledge Adriana had never left the island.

After Francis finished his account, the two men smoked in silence for a long minute. Murray considered what he couldn't say: Adriana had disappeared because of him. He knew this as surely as he knew that his land would never turn a profit, the knowledge as certain as it was untested, a theory born from common sense. Adriana had disappeared because of Murray. If she never returned, he would be held accountable.

"Well then, Francis, where is she?" Murray asked abruptly.

"Why, for God's sake, why should I know?" Francis could only sputter in outrage at the accusation implied in Murray's question.

"Why should you know. Of course you don't know. You don't have any idea where she's gone off to. Somewhere on the island. She's hiding out somewhere on the island." The possibility of this gave rise in Murray to a strange excitement — the scientist's excitement at the thought of proving his hypothesis. "Have they looked in the caves? The bunkers? Of course they have. Where else? She knew the secret places —" He stopped, blinked in surprise at himself for using the past tense. *Knows,* he thought. Say, *She knows . . .* He couldn't say it, not with Francis peering at him through the screen of pipe smoke. Knew. Knows. Was. Is.

In the living room Patrick shrieked, "Idiot!" Harry threw a wooden block that hit Patrick in the head. As Patrick lunged at him, he kneed Nat in the back by mistake.

"Dumbface!" Nat cried.

"Jerk!" Patrick yelled.

Murray was grateful for the uproar because it gave him the chance to get away from Francis. He attempted to mediate an elaborate truce among us. He wanted to hear Patrick's account of the fight, then Harry's. He invited Nat to add his own version. Yes, sharing should be encouraged, but on Christmas day a boy doesn't necessarily have to share his new toy backhoe.

"Let's talk about sharing," Murray said, his cigarette still clamped between his lips, the four of us watching in fascination as the long ash grew longer and still didn't crumble.

When he finally returned to the dining room to rejoin Francis, Claire was there and had already heard from Francis a good part of a longer version of the Adriana Nardi story. Had Claire ever met the Signora? Francis was asking as Murray settled into his seat.

"Never," Claire said.

"She's a retiring sort," Francis said, "not much interested in life, as far as I can tell."

Or else, Murray considered, Signora Nardi was inordinately interested in life and had found ways to watch without being seen. Perhaps she knew how to keep an eye on her daughter and hired someone to follow her. An absurd idea — yet it had the force of a startling memory. Murray pictured the living room of his Le Foci house. The moonlight on the floor. Adriana on the sofa beside him. Someone watching through the window, just like someone had watched him from a window of La Chiatta as he wheeled his Lambretta from the courtyard.

Murray had become a potential suspect in a potential crime —

or maybe not. Maybe no one had given him a second thought. He attempted to return to his earlier mood. The satisfaction of a smoke after a good dinner. A glass of cognac. Adriana just an annoyance.

At least the girl knew how to keep a secret — you could see this in her face, her pallor, her evasive sideways glances. She'd learned as a child to protect herself with secrecy, every word and gesture designed to deflect attention. But here was the paradox: her evasive manner invited attention, as though — no, not as though, in fact, she wanted to be seen, admired, exposed, to confess what she had been trained to hide.

Unless she were mad, her shattered mind held together by a dark obsession. I'm here, Signor Murdoch. Go away, Adriana. I don't want to go away. Go away.

A woman's voice. A rooster's crow.

He watched Francis and Claire talking, listened to the liquid, indecipherable murmur on the radio in the living room. He let himself drift, imagined a Saturday afternoon in his backyard in America. Screech of a blue jay, smell of fresh-cut grass, buzz of a chain saw in the neighbor's yard, and the sound of children's voices from the tree house — not so different from the sounds his children were making in the next room, reminding Murray of where he was, in a villa overlooking the Mediterranean, lured here by the simple promise of change.

He'd have admitted to being a ridiculous man with ridiculous ambitions, but he had committed no crime and had no reason to run away. He looked across the table at his wife for confirmation. She was chewing her thumbnail while she listened to Francis describing what he knew about Signora Nardi. Murray reached for the cognac and refilled Francis's glass and his own. Claire looked at Murray, and when their eyes met Murray was surprised to feel a different manner of scrutiny — the searching glance not of concern but of suspicion.

"You think I have something to do with this?" he said calmly, setting the bottle back on the table.

Claire flinched visibly but remained silent, and Francis watched them both with his lips pressed tight in what Murray read as a grin. The silence was unbearable. "I mean," Murray continued awkwardly, "the girl might have told me back when . . . she could have indicated . . . but she didn't, you know. She didn't admit it. If she was troubled. Or something."

Claire worked the dry skin of her cuticle. "Something," she muttered. The scorn implied by her echo ordinarily would have goaded Murray into an argument. Instead it stirred in him the same cool indignation he would have felt if he'd been holding a worthless hand of cards and Claire were threatening to call his bluff.

Guilt sounds like the crinkle of aluminum foil. The clank of a knife against the half-open lid of a tin can. A gas burner hissing without a flame. A cat clawing at a sofa's upholstery. Dry leaves blowing on pavement. Scotch tape being crumpled into a ball.

Claire heard guilt in Murray's voice, though not the guilt of a man who is pouring another glass of cognac when he's already drunk, which is the only kind of guilt she would have expected right then. When she looked at him suspiciously, it wasn't, as Murray had thought, in connection with Adriana Nardi. Fine to be concerned about Adriana, but at that moment Claire was more concerned about Murray's drinking, trying to decide how much was too much as she watched him refill his glass.

The sound of guilt is a man asking his wife if she thought he had something to do with a girl's disappearance. With this, Murray introduced to Claire a new kind of suspicion, causing her to wonder above all why his voice was unnaturally calm, and next, why he had to ask such a question at all.

Francis stayed past midnight. By then Murray was slurring his speech and bumping his knuckles against his glass. Claire took his drunkenness to be a retreat from the conversation he didn't want to have. The possibility that Murray had something to hide was more unsettling to Claire than drunkenness. Drunkenness was no more than a lapse. Claire decided to wait until the next day to talk with him.

But the days following filled up too quickly for her to pull Murray aside. He would set off early in the mornings, and in the evenings he'd bring home friends — Lorenzo, Mario and Pia Ginori, Francis. There was no time for Claire to have the kind of talk she wanted to have, a talk that would lead in a direction she didn't dare predict. She didn't even bother to tell Murray that for the time being she'd given up making arrangements to book our passage home.

Murray's uncles wired more money in early January, bolstering his confidence, and he was able to afford the rest of the down payment on the Mezza Luna property. He even sent photographs of the land to his uncles and promised to look for other potential acquisitions. His uncles wrote back to ask Murray what the hell he thought he was doing, buying land with the money they'd sent to help cover his expenses!

But Murray was undaunted. As the days passed, Claire felt less inclined to disturb his good humor, and she made an effort to convince herself of his innocence. Maybe the worst her husband could be accused of was to be trapped by someone else's affection. Sometimes, she reminded herself, we get entangled by accident.

At the end of January, during the quiet of siesta on an unusually warm day, Claire was reading on the terrace when someone knocked on the door. Directly overhead a gull glided lazily in circles, as silent as the words on the page —

The town, the churchyard, and the setting sun,
The clouds, the trees, the rounded hills all seem,
Though beautiful, cold — strange — as in a dream . . .

The sea rippled in the distance. The sunlight warmed Claire's face. And then came the rude interruption of the three brittle knocks.

A moment later Lidia came to the terrace to announce that Claire had a visitor. "Who?" Claire asked. Lidia turned around and went back inside without responding. Either she didn't hear or she pretended not to hear, leaving Claire to assume that the cook judged the visitor of too little importance to introduce.

No — the visitor was of great importance, and Lidia had already invited her into the living room and left to make coffee. When Claire approached, the woman extended her hand without bothering to rise from her chair. Claire smiled uneasily. She pretended to be pleased — pleased to make the acquaintance of . . . *it must be Signora Nardi,* she said gently, adding *Piacere,* which the Signora countered in her gravelly voice, "Thank you, Mrs. Murdoch."

She had bulging almond eyes, heavy lids, a long nose, and metal gray hair tied up in a bun. She wore a black wool dress that hung loosely on her small body, with a black shawl embroidered with delicate flowers. Claire thought of the woman on the *Casparia,* the woman who'd been dressed in black linen on a hot summer day, the one Claire had seen weeping at the rail. It occurred to her only now that she'd never seen the woman on the ship after that first day.

She was sorry to hear about Adriana — was this what she should say? Or this: She and her husband shared Signora Nardi's concern. But Claire sensed that the woman would appreciate directness.

"What news do you have of your daughter?"

"No news, Mrs. Murdoch. My daughter has disappeared like water into the air. You call it . . . what do you call it?"

"Evaporation, you mean?"

"I ask for your help, Mrs. Murdoch."

"We'll do anything we can."

"You are American."

"Yes."

"You have contacts."

Contacts — the word suggested a secret truth, as if Signora Nardi knew more about her than Claire knew about herself. "What do you mean, *contacts?*"

"In the government."

Her tone as much as her words suggested paranoia rather than reliable information. Perhaps, Claire thought with some relief, the Signora had read too many spy novels.

"The American government? We don't know anyone in the government, not personally. Not even a state senator! We'd very much like to help you, Signora Nardi, but we're not the kind of people who have important friends."

"You have money."

Claire had to stifle a laugh. "We're barely able to make ends meet!" She wanted to go on — they had no savings, and the Averils were losing patience. "But that's not the point. The point is, we want to help you if we can. Let me think. We could organize a search party. Do you know what that is — a search party?"

Lidia was back with the coffee tray. She handed a demitasse to Signora Nardi, offered her the sugar and a spoon. Claire watched the woman tip back her head and down the caffè like a man swallowing a shot of whiskey. When she spoke again, her rattling voice had turned into a growl.

"I do not need your parties. I need you to find for me the American diavolo who has stolen my daughter."

Guilt is the sound of a Lambretta carrying a man home shortly after dawn. Claire looked past her guest through the window and at the terrace beyond, where she'd stayed up waiting through the night back in November.

"What do you mean?"

Signora Nardi's laughter came abruptly. She started to explain, "He — " and then thought better of it. "I want to find the American who can tell me where my daughter is."

"There are other Americans on the island," Claire said stupidly. "I met an American in Porto Azzurro just last week. He asked me for directions. If we knew the name of his boat, we might be able to track him down."

"He was a man much older than my daughter — that is all I know for certain. Buonasera, Signora Murdoch. Arrivederla."

"Arrivederla, Signora Nardi. We will ask around, I promise."

It was a weak promise, Claire admitted to herself after Adriana's mother had left. A dismissive promise. She sipped her bitter caffè and told herself what she hadn't been willing to say to Signora Nardi. Asking around wasn't good enough; she could do better.

"Signora, please —" Claire caught up with her as she was getting into the taxi that had been idling in the drive. Signora Nardi waited, holding the door open.

"You suspect my husband, don't you?"

"I do not understand."

"*Suspect* . . . the word . . . to *suspect* someone is to —"

"I know what it means. But I do not understand why you think I suspect your husband."

"That's why you came here, isn't it? To share your suspicion?"

The woman drew in a deep breath, and Claire braced herself for the release of fury. But the Signora let the breath escape in a gentle sigh that suggested sympathy instead of anger. "Signora Murdoch. How should I say this? If I spoke in Italian. Never mind. Signora, at no time have I suspected your husband. I have met your husband. And I know what my daughter said. She said he was a good man. Molto vivace. A silly man also, she said. She trusted him, and I trust him." She paused, studied Claire's face, and asked abruptly, "Do you believe me?"

Startled by the woman's candor, Claire said, "Yes, I do, I do —" though she was thinking the opposite.

Patrick went twice into the Mezza Luna zone with Murray. The first time, the day after Christmas, Murray told him to look for colored stones amidst the dirty white quartz. When Patrick found a pinkish wedge lined with cracks, Murray identified it as feldspar. That was the extent of Patrick's first geology lesson.

The second time Patrick accompanied Murray was on a bright cold Saturday in early February, and Carlo was there, to Murray's surprise. He'd come to look for a knapsack he'd lost back in December and was sitting on a boulder beside a shallow, muddy pool of run-off water, finishing the wine in his flask, when Murray and Patrick arrived. Patrick spoke more Italian than Murray did by then, and he accepted Carlo's offer to accompany him on a walk around the site.

As they crossed a gulch Carlo found a forked twig about two feet long. He whittled the tip to a taper with his pocketknife and then showed Patrick how to grasp the stick with his clenched fingers held toward the sky. If Patrick happened to step upon a patch of ground over a vein of precious mineral, the twig would begin to turn and twist, Carlo explained, mimicking the motion with his hips. Then he led the way up the slope, stepping carefully between the brambles of rock roses.

The divining rod shook at ten different spots, Patrick told us later, and though he didn't find any gems, he did, with Carlo's help, find a geode, which he busted open on a flat rock, shattering one half, leaving the other circle of crystal intact.

We were awed by the crystal, especially after Patrick repeated to us what Carlo had told him — that it was a piece of a meteor from outer space. And if it came from outer space it must be magic, Patrick said.

"Magic how?" Nat asked.

"Magic like in being invisible?" Harry asked.

Magic like sawing a person in half? This was my question, though I kept it to myself.

"Magic like the kind that shows you the future," Patrick said, with a confidence that suggested expert knowledge. The problem, he went on to explain, was figuring out how to make the magic work. We pondered the geode half, stared at its crystal peaks and shards, but failed to decipher its code. And since potential magic becomes boring more quickly than real magic, we hid the geode in the bedroom closet and ran back outside.

That day we played a new game, invented by Patrick, who had

heard from Carlo about a tribe of giant ants living in the mountains of Elba. They were bigger than foxes, smaller than wolves,
and when they dug tunnels in the sand they brought up nuggets of
gold the size of raisins. We used pebbles for the gold and long green
twigs for our antennae. Harry and I were ants. My job was to guard
the horde of pebbles while Harry watched for intruders. Patrick
and Nat would creep toward us from separate directions, taunting
us with insults from their hiding places. Harry and I would throw
handfuls of little pine cones at every moving shadow.

The game absorbed us. We played even when a misty rain
started to fall. The gold made us greedy; competition made us violent. Harry scratched Patrick with a stick, Patrick pushed Harry to
the ground, I hit Nat in the eye with a pine cone, Nat yanked a fist-
ful of my hair. No one cried or threatened to go home. If our gold
was depleted, we would reverse roles, and we, the giant ants of
Monte Giove, would try to steal the gold back.

Death to the ants. The ants must die!
We have come to take back our gold.
The gold belongs to us now.
The gold belongs to us.
Vai, vai!
Scemi!

We smelled the needles carpeting the damp earth. We saw
the black-and-white flash of a cuckoo against the dusky sky. We
formed a circle and pissed into the opening of a burrow. Rain was
as thick as syrup on our short hair. These are the memories I share
with my brothers. But there are other details none of us can recall
accurately. Was it Harry or Nat who climbed high into a pine tree
and leaped to the branch of another tree? Was it Nat or me who
tripped over an exposed root and knocked his head against the
hard ground, blacking out for a few seconds? Who decided to band
forces and collect more gold? We gathered striped granite gneiss,
coarse gabbro, simple, brittle quartzite. Who found the greatest

treasure of all, a mica schist with two little tourmaline crystals poking up from the side? Patrick says he found the schist; Nat says Harry found it. Harry doesn't remember.

Give me that!

It's mine and you're dead!

We didn't realize how dark it had become or how far we had wandered up the mountain until we heard our father calling for us. His voice was plaintive, without the tremor of impatience or the promise of punishment — the voice of a guilty man who blames himself for the disappearance of his sons. Which meant, if we were interpreting the tone correctly, we were blameless and could even add to our father's torment by hiding from him.

His flashlight beam was the searchlight of the giant ants, and we were their prisoners of war. We would attempt a perilous escape.

Follow me, shhhh. We slid on our bellies down the side of a gulch toward freedom.

Ouch!

Shut up.

You shut up.

Murray's flashlight beam swept over our heads, swung back, and centered itself on Patrick's face.

"Patrick!"

"Hi, Dad."

"Where are . . . there . . . two . . . three . . . four, you're all here, right? You're all okay, right?"

"Right, Dad."

Murray squinted through the rain and moved his lower jaw as if to chew a tough piece of meat. "Now tell me what the fuck you were doing."

"You said *fuck*."

"Get up here."

We'd misinterpreted Murray's tone of voice, underestimated his capacity for anger. He was furious with us. This man who until that night never had the rage or indignation to hit us raised his hand and boxed Patrick on the ear. We were stunned, all of us sharing with Patrick the shock of pain and, worse, humiliation. Murray reached for Harry to do the same, but Harry ran ahead down the path. Nat cowered on the slope of the gulch. I started to cry.

If Murray regretted hitting Patrick, he didn't admit it and instead kept grumbling curses at us as he followed Harry down the path. Nat and I flanked Patrick, who by virtue of his punishment had become our martyr. He was stoically silent. And with all that he'd had to endure, he was perceptive enough to realize that at my young age I couldn't manage the steep shale path in the dark without help. He held my hand.

Lamps were lit in all the rooms and in the mist the glow formed a yellow penumbra around the villa. When we arrived Harry was already in the kitchen in our mother's arms. She was clutching him and crying, and the scene made clear to the rest of us what trouble we'd caused by staying out so late. We'd been gone for hours. Our mother was sobbing for the children she thought she'd lost. We understood all too clearly that we were responsible for her distress. But we would never forgive Murray for hitting Patrick, smacking him like a dog, just like Lorenzo would slap his segugia bitch when it wouldn't stop barking.

If Murray hadn't been so cruel we would have thought our mother's reaction excessive and wondered if her grief had some other cause. Instead, we believed that we'd seen proof of an important set of truths. Our mother loved us; our father didn't.

Patrick still had the mica schist in his pocket, and later that night he hid it behind a bookshelf and swore us all to secrecy. We'd intended to give it to Murray. Not now. Our wicked father would never know that we had two perfect little towers of pink tourmaline — not the rarest kind, not nearly enough to make us rich, but enough to convince us that we should keep looking for more.

What are the limitations of sympathy? How much can we really understand about someone else? What qualities are genuine? To what extent is our perception of others inflected by imagination? What are the limitations of imagination? What are the risks of imagination? What are the rules of imagination? What does imagination have to do with sympathy? With suspicion? Why does a child run away from home? Why did it take so long for Claire to notice that it was past eight o'clock, dinner had grown cold, and her children were missing? Why did Claire blame Murray for this? Why did Murray blame Claire? Why didn't we answer them when they called into the darkness? Where had we gone? Where had all the children of Elba gone? Why did some come home and not others? When would carnivale begin? When would it end? Why were the children of Elba throwing fistfuls of flour? What was the meaning of flour? Why is celebration so similar to protest? What would happen to the children? Who will live a long full life and who will die in youth? Where was Adriana? How much did the mother know about her daughter? How much can any mother know? Claire, why didn't you ask Murray more questions if you continued to harbor suspicions? If your sense of foreboding was so strong, why didn't you say something to Murray later that night, after your children were safely in bed? Why did you avoid the subject? What didn't you want to know? What did you fear? Why were you so content during the day and so nervous at night? What were you thinking while you sat on the rocks and stared at the sea? What were you reading out on the terrace while we were wandering in the hills? What were you thinking when you had ten guests for dinner and everybody but you was talking at once? What is learned through conversation? What was to be gained by remaining on Elba? Why continue to invest in a worthless plot of land? What is the point of a gemstone? Why is a blue tourmaline, an indicolite, worth more than the red, rubellite variety? Why should Murray waste his time roaming the island of Elba when he could be back home drawing a salary? So what if tourmaline is vitreous, pleochroic, trigonal, and piezoelectric? Why go against sound advice? Why don't you just give up and go home, Murray? Why did you hit Patrick, Murray? Why wouldn't we forgive him? What was happening? Why was Murray becoming a stranger in his own house? Why didn't spring bring better weather? Why did it rain for twenty-seven days in a row in the month of March? Why did Claire stop giving Patrick and Harry their lessons? Who would loan us money? Why didn't Adriana come home?

The Undaunted

1 May 1814

What is my crime? No more than sharing with the people of France a fierce hatred of inequality. For this I was made emperor. For this I've been repudiated. For this I was forced to surrender to foreign commissioners. They say I am responsible for savage acts of violence. I say I am responsible for the freedom that my countrymen have come to consider their right. Three days ago I left Fréjus on what is supposed to be the final journey of my life. I insisted on appropriate honors. Captain Ussher refused. Colonel Campbell overruled him, and I walked alone up the gangway to the boom of a twenty-one-gun salute.

Did anyone stop to consider the name of the frigate? I am being taken to Elba on the Undaunted. I boarded the Undaunted at night, the music of cannon fire announcing that a great man was being expelled from the country he had tried to save. To Captain Ussher and his crew I am pitiable. To Colonel Campbell I am — he understands the coincidence — undaunted. And so he does his best to placate me.

I am a man who perspires profusely. I need no more than four hours of sleep a night. I am a great military strategist. And I recognize as well as anyone the Allies' stupidity at sending me to an island so near the coast.

I have only to bide my time and plan my course of action upon my return to France. Here on the Undaunted *I've been entertaining my hosts by answering any question they put to me. I've already explained to them that if Villeneuve hadn't gone off to Cádiz and joined Nelson, I'd have had my army in London within three days. If I'd conquered England, I would have made her the greatest power in the world. And yes, the Duchess of Bedford was a good dancer, but her mother was too fat.*

Francis Cape had arrived on the island in 1947, at a time when many Elbans felt the need to reinforce their isolation. And yet with the closing of the mines and a few years of poor harvest, they were beginning to weigh the benefits of tourism against the costs. Some Elbans made Francis feel welcome; others clearly considered him an intruder.

He stayed through the first winter at a small, spare pensione in Portoferraio, where he was the only guest for weeks at a time. His first inquiries about more permanent accommodations were met with shrugs. His early attempts to use his self-taught Italian and engage Elbans in conversation were met with condescending bafflement. Cos' ha detto? What did you say? On gloomy days in February he was almost ready to abandon his project and go back to England. But then he'd be walking along the beach at Bagnaia and the sun would pop out from behind the clouds, or he'd be wandering in the hills above Poggio and the bells of San Lorenzo would begin to ring. There was the young woman in the Café Medici in Portoferraio who would sprinkle cocoa on his cappuccino and with a toothpick carefully outline the shape of a heart on the foam. There was the old woman named Ninanina, who'd invite him into the rustic enoteca she ran with her husband and serve him a plate of grilled anchovies and a glass of wine for free.

And there was the extraordinary Nardi collection, unknown to most of the world. Francis paid his first visit to the Nardi villa in April of 1950. From that point on he lost his lingering inclination to leave the island. He found a small, serviceable flat in Portoferraio. He transferred his savings to a local bank. And he promised the Nardis, the signora and the signorina, that with his book on Napoleon Bonaparte he would do justice to their hospitality.

Adriana had turned fifteen years old in the spring of 1950. She was a reserved child, with a sweet but wary face that reminded Francis of the Madonna in Piero della Francesca's *Annunciation,* and Francis believed that she both craved attention and was filled with distrust. So he set out to win her trust. He brought her little figurines, porcelain kittens and mice purchased from the old woman who ran the enoteca in Portoferraio. Adriana accepted the gifts with a grim politeness that made Francis nervous. He decided that the figurines were too childish. He brought her colored pencils and paper but again felt from her cool acceptance that he'd made a mistake. He gave her a set of ivory coasters, which she understood to be a gift for her mother. He gave her a necklace of onyx beads but never saw her wearing it. He gave her a book of fairy tales in English.

The book was the first present that aroused any spontaneous response — a flash of a shy smile and a quick, probing glance, as if she were trying to find out how he knew what she most wanted. Though he'd conversed with her only in Italian, he'd assumed that, like her mother, she spoke some English and French — better French than English, as it turned out. But she wanted to learn English and told this to Francis by way of thanking him for the book, admitting her interest with a coyness that took him by surprise. She wanted to learn English. She said it once in Italian and repeated herself in English, embedding in the sentence a request: Would Francis teach her?

He began teaching her informally, stretching their ordinary conversations into lessons and reading with her through the book of fairy tales. She learned the words of a song sung by three heads floating in a well. She learned the words of a song sung by mermaids. She learned many useless things. But then Signora Nardi insisted on formalizing the instruction and paying Francis for one hour of lessons each day. He tried to refuse payment; Signora Nardi ignored him.

From the spring of 1950 through the next two years, Francis tutored Adriana in English. When he ran out of books he set her to work translating the letters in the archives and with her help deciphered passages he'd skipped or misread because of his limited Italian: a recipe sent to Napoleon's chef for a particular kind of fish soup the emperor had liked, an eighteenth-century account of unearthing the ruins of an Etruscan ironworks, and an exchange between Elisa Baciocchi, Princess of Piombino, and Antonio Buoncompagni about the bodies washing ashore at Gorgona after the sinking of the *Queen Charlotte.*

These were good, purposeful years for Francis. Besides tutoring Adriana he gathered voluminous notes for his book. He explored the island, befriended Elbans, and came to feel entirely at home, so much so that he began to resent the intrusion of tourists. In his opinion, Elba could do well enough without transforming itself into one big resort. He argued in favor of isolation, reminding the Elbans of their long history of self-sufficiency. When had they ever profited from affiliation? They could do no better than fish and tend their vines and keep their riches to themselves.

Adriana grew up, or at least older. In Francis's perception she remained a child — a stern, poised, mature child, but still a child — because only a child could continue to adore him as she did. She cast him as the father she had lost, and Francis accepted the role. He believed that she needed to adore him. He, in turn, was fond of her and took it upon himself to help her continue the education they'd begun together. Though he knew that Signora Nardi would disapprove, he secretly gave Adriana money to help make her life more comfortable when she went off to study in Bologna. And when she applied for the fellowship at St. Hilda's, he wrote a rec-ommendation on her behalf to a relative, a second cousin who had some sort of function — Francis wasn't sure what, exactly — at a college in Oxford.

And then Murray Murdoch arrived on Elba, and Adriana de-cided that Francis Cape was useless. In the weeks before she dis-appeared she took to receiving him with an indifference that was humiliating. He had only to look at her averted eyes to see what she didn't want to see: a stupid, pretentious old man who could do nothing for her.

An old, old man, with rotting teeth, sour breath, rheumy eyes, gnarled fingers, and a disgusting habit of burping repeatedly into his fist all through a meal. He wanted to apologize to her for being so old. He wished she were old, as old as the gentlewoman who painted her face in the poem by George Turberville. A Hecuba rather than a Helen. He wanted to tell her all about his childhood to convince her that he was once young. She wouldn't have be-lieved it. Francis Cape was never a child. He had been old long be-fore Adriana was born. He had always been old.

Napoleon died at the age of fifty-two on St. Helena. Francis was seventy-three. If he had died at fifty-two he wouldn't have learned Italian, he wouldn't have come to Elba, he wouldn't have climbed to the top of Volterraio, and he never would have stood on the cliffs at Capo Vit at sunrise. But he also would have been spared knowing Adriana Nardi.

Until he'd met her, Francis had never experienced the problem of loving someone too much. He'd been a solid, decent English bachelor, his past sprinkled with solid, decent relationships. He could have married any number of good women but for one rea-son or another had remained single.

He wouldn't have loved Adriana too much if he hadn't become aware of how little he could do for her. He tried to please her and win back her adoration. He brought her books, he gave her money, he complimented her, he gave her more money.

He worked frantically on his history of Napoleon, felt simultaneously impassioned by his mission and ashamed of his inadequacies. Napoleon became the excuse to write about the magnificent beauty of Elba. Why would anyone want to leave? How could the little tyrant have been so foolish? On paper he ruled an island principality but in effect he was the emperor of paradise. Francis wanted to write a biography of the emperor of paradise. He didn't want to write about Napoleon's escape, but history obligated him to try. Every day he'd write another page or two. And every day he'd set aside the work he'd done and start over.

When my parents met Francis Cape they took him to be the respectable English bachelor that he was still pretending to be. Our mother felt a little sorry for him. Our father felt grateful for Francis's assistance. Francis had introduced him to Lorenzo, our padrone, and helped him to find a place to stay on Elba. He'd served as a translator for Murray and told him whom to trust. And he'd introduced Murray and Claire to Adriana Nardi.

At first Francis didn't mind Murray's friendship with Adriana, for he saw that it was making her a little perkier, a little more interested in life. Whenever Francis told Adriana that he was going to see the Murdochs, Adriana was keen on going along. But soon enough Francis began to notice Murray's inappropriate interest in the girl. What did he want from Adriana? He said he wanted to know whatever she could tell him about the island. Why did he care? What was at stake? Francis wondered if there was something he'd missed in the Nardi collection — not just a tantalizing fact about Napoleon but some sort of information that could have more material consequence. Something along the lines of a treasure map. Murray kept talking about the value of tourmaline. Had he found routes to ancient mines, perhaps? To intact veins of precious minerals?

But it was jealousy, plain and simple jealousy, that turned Francis's worry into deep resentment. Murray had come to steal Elba's most precious treasure — the treasure named Adriana Nardi. By then it was too late to help her. She liked the American, she told Francis. She liked best of all his airy hopes. Coming to an island to buy land that no one else wanted and hoping against hope to make money. She, too, would have liked to hope for something impossible, or at least to know that she had the luxury to be foolish. In a middle-aged American investor, Adriana had found a model fool.

Francis told Adriana that Murray had been seen digging in the yard behind his house with a teaspoon. He told her that the American was convinced he'd find gold. Gold! He told her that people with nothing better to do like to dig holes and then fill them up. But Adriana didn't have much to say in reply. She'd laugh and shrug and toss her hair back away from her eyes. And once she reminded Francis that chunks of Elban rubellite as big as melons were said to have been found by the Etruscans.

The secret treasure of love. A girl as lustrous as tourmaline. A man who wants the treasure for himself. The story made such sense that Francis came to believe he couldn't alter the plot. He thought of himself as no better than a spectator — or no worse.

On the occasions over the years when Francis had spoken at any length with Adriana's mother, they'd moved back and forth between English and Italian, with some French thrown in whenever the subject turned to island history. At first Francis had found the conversations awkward and could only follow the Signora's lead. But once he realized that he could be the one to choose the language, he grew to enjoy the shifts.

So he was discomforted by the Signora's decision to speak only in English with him. English had been the language Adriana had preferred to use with him once she'd become fluent. But with the

Signora, the exclusive use of English made him feel more awkward than ever in her presence.

He tried to offer consolation. No, the Signora didn't want consolation. Her daughter would be found, she said. You don't console the mother of a daughter who will be found.

"Forgive me, Signora. I only want to help."

"Everyone wants to help and no one is helping."

It was a clear day in late March after weeks of rain, the air over the island was spiced with the smell of bonfires in the fields, the sea was glittering, the vault of sky a magnetic blue. But in the dining room of the Nardi villa the only light was the sunlight shining through the slats of the shutters, turning the darkness a pale gray and the walls the greenish color of a gecko.

Francis had taken to visiting Signora Nardi regularly in the months since Adriana had been gone. He was served English tea at the dining-room table, with powdery scones baked by Luisa, the Nardis' cook. Francis would talk with the Signora about her daughter, praising the girl for her facility with English, her quick mind, her perfect pronunciation. The woman would listen with an expression that suggested boredom, but she wouldn't tell Francis to stop.

It was Francis who had persuaded the Signora to seek help from the local police. And it was from the police rather than Signora Nardi that Francis learned about the possible involvement of a foreigner. An American man who went by the name of Murray Murdoch? It was such an obvious identification that Francis didn't bother to point it out. Everyone on the island knew or knew about the investor from New York and his interest in Adriana Nardi. So why wasn't Murray asked some probing questions?

Apparently, Adriana had been seen by a taxi driver talking with an older man somewhere on the road — the driver couldn't say exactly where — between San Giovanni and Lacona. Is that so? Francis Cape was startled, but only for a moment. He wanted to point out that Le Foci was between San Giovanni and Lacona. But the Signora was explaining that the man had been old. A rich old white-haired straniero, most likely one of the millionaire yachters who docked in Porto Azzurro — this was the type of man Signora Nardi wanted to find.

Why didn't she allow herself to harbor suspicions about Murray Murdoch? Francis wanted to ask Signora Nardi this but couldn't. It was impossible to ask Signora Nardi anything. He couldn't ask her about the search for her daughter; he couldn't even ask her if she was well. Tutt'OK? This was one of his favorite greetings, and he called it out to his Elban friends when he passed them on the street. Tutt'OK? Everything was not OK with Signora Nardi, he already knew this, and anyway, he was expected to speak only in English.

He wanted to help. You can't help, Mr. Cape. He wanted to —

"To what?"

"To . . ."

"To what, Mr. Cape?"

He heard the chatter of sparrows out in the terrace garden, a garden as harsh as the Signora, with bramble roses and juniper thistles and gravel paths winding between meager olive trees. But on the Nardi property was also the beautiful garden in the ravine that Adriana had tended when she was home. Francis had been there many times since Adriana's disappearance. Already the lilies were blooming, and the ground was carpeted with purslane and chickweed. He didn't bother to pull the weeds; he wanted to see them grow, spread, choke the garden, destroy it. He hoped that Signora Nardi wouldn't send someone to weed the rock garden. He wanted to suggest this. He wanted to suggest —

"To what, Mr. Cape?"

"To suggest . . ."

"Yes?"

"The American investor. Shouldn't you find out more about him?"

"I know what I need to know."

"He is American." He'd been wanting to say this to her — Murray Murdoch is American! He wanted to startle her with his insinuation. But she just smiled coldly and danced her fingernails with a clatter across the table's mosaic tiles.

"He came here many times. Excuse me for reminding you of this. But I don't understand why you —"

"He is not an old man. Now do you understand, Mr. Cape?"

What could she possibly have said that would extend the meaning she conveyed with her eyes? Eyes with mud-colored irises, eyes telling him that there was nothing he could do or say in his own defense.

How slowly she moved when she reached for her tea. As though she were underwater, swimming away from Francis, out of his reach.

She was an agile woman — he hadn't realized how agile until that moment. Nor had he realized that her hostility was isolated, directed at him alone. He'd mistaken her dislike of him for natural reserve. But she wasn't a reserved woman, she wasn't even un-friendly. She simply despised Francis Cape. She'd despised him from the day they first met, and now she despised him for having something to do with the disappearance of her daughter.

Francis was an old man. A very old man. Yet he wasn't an American. Signora Nardi was looking for a wealthy American man, not an elderly librarian from London. He was confused. Francis Cape was an Englishman. So why should Signora Nardi despise him? He only wanted to help.

Not knowing what else to do, Francis added another lump of sugar to his tea. He stirred and stirred, but the sugar wouldn't dis-solve. Looking into his cup, he thought he might have dropped in a pebble by mistake. Then he discovered he could dig the edge of his spoon into the lump and crumble it.

Francis said he hoped the bad weather was over for the season. Signora Nardi hoped so too.

Soon it was time for Francis to leave. He stood. She offered to show him to the door. He declined.

"Arrivederla, Signora," he said, knowing full well that she'd hear this as an insult. "Buona giornata."

His knees were stiff, his jaw ached, and he needed to fart. How had he gotten so old? How old was he really? he asked himself as he stood outside the Nardi villa. He was surprised to realize that with his thoughts in such a swirl he could remember the year of his birth but not the day.

How old am I, Adriana? Tell me.

You are very very very very old, Mr. Francis Cape.

It would be easy to cast Signora Nardi as a type of woman familiar to readers of Victorian novels. She was stern, dusty, stuck in the past, repelled by the present, indifferent to the future. I find myself picturing her in a decrepit wedding dress with an ancient, cobwebbed feast laid out on the table. But my mother insists that Signora Nardi was a woman you would think you could know at a glance, and then you'd realize you didn't know at all.

Signora Nardi was not what she seemed. Not dusty. Not stern. And not loveless. She was no worse than solitary. She chose to stay alone in the villa day after day in order to be available. It was good for a daughter to know that her mother would always be at home. Signora Nardi wanted her daughter to be free to fill her life with experience, to find out what she could about the world, to travel and make friends, meet men, find love, and all the while to enjoy the certainty that she had a home and her mother was there. She could leave home. She could come back. Her mother was waiting.

Our mother often thought of Adriana's mother waiting in her lonely villa for her daughter to return. She imagined the Signora sitting inside her dark house, flinching at every unexpected sound. She imagined the Signora as a child, a little dark-haired beauty romping through the vineyards and olive groves, light-footed, light-hearted. Claire imagined being that child.

She'd only met Signora Nardi once, had thought afterward of Miss Havisham, and yet was surprised to feel at the same time the discomfort of recognition, the sense that in this strange, lonely Elban woman she was seeing a version of herself. The Signora had come to our home seeking help instead of revenge. She was prepared to trust Murray. The fact of this sank in slowly. Signora Nardi was not the kind of woman who would have been flagrant with trust. She was cautious. She had every right to be suspicious of Murray and instead believed he was innocent. Such confidence of judgment. Claire wanted the Signora to persuade her of her husband's innocence. As the days passed she kept thinking about her, kept returning to the memory of their brief conversation, kept trying to imagine the thoughts of the Signora, kept trying and failing to understand why she felt such a profound connection to this woman after her single visit, and eventually decided that the only way she could understand the Signora was to see her again.

Delayed by the rain and her own reluctance, Claire didn't visit the Nardi villa until the end of March. Coincidentally, she went the morning of the same day when Francis would pay his last visit.

Signora Nardi didn't have a phone, and since Claire didn't have the courage to write to her she arrived unannounced. The cook let her in and showed her to the library — a room lined with bookshelves from floor to ceiling, with shuttered French doors, closed and bolted, that would have opened to the garden. A grand piano filled one corner. The room was lit by a crystal chandelier that seemed to Claire too ornate for the setting. Arranged without any apparent order on some of the shelves at eye level were stone carvings, masks, iron arrowheads, and spear tips. Other objects in the collection, including the porcelain cup from which Murray had drunk his peppermint tea, were kept locked in a cabinet at the back of the room. On the walls were portraits, one of a man in a tasseled uniform, another of a woman in Victorian dress holding a lapdog, another of a gray-bearded man holding a pen.

Claire browsed through books while she waited. She pulled down a dusty copy of Marco Polo's *Travels,* but the pages were fragile so she carefully returned the book to the shelf. She was trying to make sense of the Italian in the prologue of Boccaccio's *Decameron* — "Umana cosa è aver compassione degli afflitti" — when she heard a door shut down the hall.

"Buongiorno, Signora."

"Signora Nardi, buongiorno. Sono, sono, mi dispiace . . ."

"Speak in English."

"I apologize. For arriving here without warning. I've been wanting to come see you again. You've heard nothing from Adriana?"

"Nothing. Come sit with me." Signora Nardi led her to the chairs on the far side of the glass cabinet. The cook appeared and transferred from her tray a little pewter coffeepot, hot milk and sugar, and a plate piled with meringues and chocolate biscuits.

What did they talk about? Even as soon as the afternoon of the same day, Claire wouldn't clearly remember the content of their conversation. They talked of Adriana — her education, her talents, her fellowship at Oxford. Signora Nardi had said something about Adriana's sullenness — what, exactly? Talk had turned to the island economy. The struggling iron mines on Elba. Local quarries. The inlaid serpentine on the library floor. What predictions had the Signora made about the island's future? Claire couldn't remember. What had she said about her own health? Claire couldn't remember.

Strange for Claire to remember their first encounter so vividly, the second with such difficulty. If she'd gone to the Nardi villa in search of understanding, she came away with no better sense of the Signora than before. But if, in fact, she'd gone for reassurance, somehow she'd received a fair dose. She'd left feeling comforted, though why or how she couldn't say. She felt certain that the Signora was more than just a good woman. She was a deserving woman. And she was powerful. And, as Claire had already sensed, she was potentially impetuous. Despite what others said about her, Signora Nardi hadn't finished with the world.

Spring on Elba that year was variable, with the sun rising behind storm clouds, burning through noon mist, and sinking from clear skies. It was hard to believe during a crystalline afternoon that we'd woken that morning to the sound of rain spilling from the roof. Single days were broken into pieces by the weather. My brothers never went back to school. Everything seemed mysterious to us. If a week might last a month, how could we make plans? We could only make up ways to occupy ourselves from hour to hour.

Only Murray made plans. He planned to buy more land in Cavoli, Chiessi, Pomonte. He'd heard about a grotto filled with tourmaline outside of San Piero. He roamed the area for days looking for the cave but never found it.

He considered purchasing an old farmhouse and the surrounding land in the plain between Marina di Campo and Portoferraio. He wired his mother for money, but she refused and again advised him to come home. He wrote to his uncles. They didn't bother to write back.

After finding shotgun shells on his land, he posted NO HUNTING signs. He decided to build a fence. He hired two men from Portoferraio to work for him and paid them the equivalent of fifty dollars each for a week's worth of doing nothing, since the wire fencing was never delivered. The next week he put them to work building a stone wall around the property. They worked slowly. Their siesta lasted three hours.

Murray ran his Lambretta off the road on his way home from the bank in Portoferraio one day. He was able to get the motorcycle started again, and he arrived spattered with mud but absorbed by anticipation of the next day's work. He was glad to find that Claire had waited for him instead of eating dinner with the rest of us. After changing his clothes, he opened a bottle of sparkling wine. Lidia had left them a plate of anchovies and a round of bread. A sip of the wine filled him with warmth, the white flesh of the anchovies melted like butter on his tongue, and when he blinked he found Claire looking at him from across the table without the sharp query of suspicion in her eyes.

A spring night on Elba. Claire and Murray, tousled, half dressed, bleary from the wine, made love on the sofa and fell asleep in each other's arms. Nat woke up late, went to the bathroom to pee, and then trudged sleepily into our parents' room, climbed onto the bed, and fell asleep between pillows that he mistook for our parents. Meena, inadvertently locked outside, yowled in the night, but no one heard her. When the rain began she took refuge beneath a board leaning against the garden shed. When the wind blew the board away, she scampered back to the villa and shivered in the doorway. And when the man emerged from the darkness, walking up the gravel path with the stiffness of a stilt-walker, and pounded weakly on the door, Meena didn't bother to move, for she knew what would happen in a minute or two if the man just kept knocking.

The door opened, and Meena scampered inside between Claire's feet. Claire suppressed an exclamation. Without a word she led Francis Cape into the front hall, where he stood dripping, trembling, his lips moving in soundless words.

Murray appeared, wearing only his trousers and undershirt. "Francis?" he asked. Could it really be Francis? Old Francis Cape gone out of his mind?

"It's me, all right. I'm here as a friend, you know."

Claire and Murray exchanged the familiar glance that people share when they believe themselves in the presence of insanity.

"I'm here to warn you."

"Come into the kitchen, Francis. Have a cup of tea. You need to calm down, collect your wits."

"It's you's the one in trouble." Startled by his own slurring speech, he shook his head, clenched his hands together to steady himself, and said, "I mean to say, I've just come from Uccello's, you remember it, the enoteca, we've been there, all of us, back when." He stopped abruptly, leaving Claire and Murray to fill in the rest of the sentence: back when Adriana was with us.

"Sit down, Francis. Sit and catch your breath, at least."

"I'm fine."

"You're soaked."

"The rain came in at the last minute. And there I was without my car."

"You didn't drive?"

"My car wouldn't start. I walked."

"You walked!"

"From Portoferraio? All the way from Portoferraio? My God, Francis!"

"I don't mind a good walk. I never mind a good walk. It's something I do quite well, you know. I walk. I can walk five miles at a stretch. And I know the roads. The moon was out only ten minutes ago. Then the downpour, all of a sudden. The rain this season. I've never seen anything like it. We've had wet springs, dry springs, but never such weather as this." He paused, looked first at Claire and then at Murray with an expression that both of them read as directly accusing.

"I was at Uccello's," he continued, "and the little woman there — you remember, the one called Ninanina. Ninanina, who is said to have the power of foresight. Did I ever tell you that? Ninanina pulled me aside, and she said to me, she said, Tell your American friend to take his family and get off the island. Tell him he must go home. She said it in Italian, of course, but I am giving you an accurate translation. Tell your American friend to pack up and go home. In my neighborhood, you, Murray Murdoch, are my American friend. And according to Ninanina, you and your whole family should leave the island as soon as possible. There is trouble brewing."

He was panting from the effort of speaking. Murray and Claire stood in silence. Ninanina — Murray tried to recollect — was the kind old woman who once had given him a second bottle of wine for free. Claire remembered her as the woman who offered her cheek to Francis when they'd walked into her enoteca.

"What trouble?" Murray finally asked.

"There are rumors. That's all I know. That's all I could gather."

"I don't understand," said Claire.

"Neither do I," said Murray.

"There are rumors," said Francis slowly, "concerning the disappearance of Adriana Nardi. And the involvement of the investor from the United States."

"That's ridiculous!" Murray spat with a fury that would seem courageous to Claire when she later recalled it.

"I am only the messenger." Francis's voice had become measured, even velvety. And his obvious consciousness of his effect was taken in by Claire, who in an instant decided once and for all that she abhorred the man. But at the same time she knew that the news he was bringing made them dependent on him.

Murray was only enraged. He circled the front hall sputtering, mumbling, protesting, pulling at his ears, kicking the wall. He'd replaced Francis in the role of the madman. Inadvertently, Claire met Francis's eyes and shared with him the same sympathetic glance she'd shared with Murray only minutes earlier.

There was no more talk of tea, and when Francis reached for the door, neither Claire nor Murray tried to stop him. Claire was already heading for the closet where we kept the luggage we'd purchased in Genoa. Murray was still walking in circles.

They argued in quiet, fierce voices. Claire wanted to leave the island the next day. Murray insisted on staying. He said he would not be driven away by rumors. He would not be the scapegoat of people who had no better way to entertain themselves than to turn on a foreigner. The islanders were provincial, uneducated, bigoted.

They doubled their prices as soon as Murray walked into the room. Their children were bullies. Their police were abusive. And don't forget — they shared a recent bloody history of collaboration with their mainland brothers. How easily guilt transforms into hate. They needed a stranger to hold responsible for their own negligence, and they found him in Murray, who, even if not entirely blameless, had done no one any real harm.

Claire and Murray didn't go to sleep until long after midnight. Their argument deteriorated into a cold standoff. Claire said she'd take the children and go to Paris and from there book a flight home. Murray said he'd leave when he was good and ready to leave.

But by the next morning Claire's resolve to return to America had weakened. The sky was clear, the morning clouds tinged with pink, the sea shimmering, the breeze fresh, the oranges sweet and bloody. The barking of dogs set the roosters crowing — or vice versa. The bells of San Lorenzo were ringing. Lidia was knocking on their bedroom door.

FROM ANCIENT ROMAN TIMES up through the 1920s, Italy derived most of its iron from the mines on Elba. But when we lived there, most of the mines had closed or were in the process of closing. Older men were unemployed, the deep wrinkles on their faces permanently stained a rusty yellow, and the young men who had survived the war and returned to the island were commuting to mainland jobs. New hotels were relatively small-scale. While there were tourists on the island, they usually arrived in yachts and didn't wander far outside the harbors of Portoferraio and Porto Azzurro.

To our young eyes, however, Elba was an abundant haven. We had no more awareness of the poverty on the island than we did of the battles being fought around the globe. What we saw were plates heaped with polpo lesso and scampi, grapevines sprouting new leaves, barley stalks trembling as they grew taller before our eyes. Harry remembers in particular the cap of cream on every cup of fresh milk. Patrick likes to describe the bowl in the kitchen that was stacked high with plums in summer, persimmons in winter. Every meal lasted for hours, and one meal followed so quickly after the last that we forgot what it was like to feel hungry. My older brothers didn't have to go to school or help with chores. I didn't have to take a bath every day. None of us had to be in bed by any particular time.

We didn't care that Claire and Murray were inattentive to us. Back in America we would have considered ourselves neglected and wondered what could be more important to our parents than seeing to the care and well-being of their children. But on Elba it seemed right and good that we were given the freedom to wander on our own.

In the morning Francesca would make us promise to stay within calling distance of the house, and then she'd go back to her room and fall asleep. She never knew how far we'd climb up the east side of Monte Giove. We played our game of Giant Ants, perfecting the rules as we went along. We decided that our ants would collect rubies and sapphires and tourmalines, along with gold; only green twigs could be used as antennae; when we were within sight of the ants' horde of gold we could approach it only by hopping on our right foot; if we were touched by an ant's antennae we had to spin three times and then fall to the ground; if we were dead, we had to stay dead until that round of the game was over. We called ourselves Jako One, Two, Three, and Four.

Qui, Jako Three!

Dove?

Guarda!

Io guarda la treasure.

Stai ferma!

You — io getta you!

We took over from our father the belief that we could find our fortune in the solid, integral stuff of the earth. Patrick showed us how to look for glassy beveled cubes with faces that sparkled when you tipped them to catch the sunlight, alloys speckled with yellow, black metallic rocks streaked with silver. He identified the pieces of pyrite, quartz, fluorite, and argentite in our collection and convinced us to discard chunks of marl and limestone. We didn't find another geode, but Harry found a smooth, hard puddle of tuff. We chipped away at it until we each had a handful of shards. We found frothy, shiny gray rocks that were probably obsidian. And once we found a trace of what must have been indicolite, the valuable blue form of tourmaline, tucked between points of white feldspar on a piece of granite too big to lift.

We used a flat-topped boulder for cleaving crystals and pounding smaller rocks into chalk. We argued about what to do with the chalk. Harry wanted to collect it in jars. Nat wanted to use it to paint our faces. Patrick wanted to scatter the chalk in the wind.

Jako Four, you're supposed to stai dead.

Shut up.

You shut up, you're dead. Jako Four is dead and la treasure's mio mio mio!

Mio!

Mio!

You lose, you bigga fat loser!

We came to know the terrain from different perspectives. The vista from the stone terraces midway up Monte Giove was always strange to us, Elba always in disguise. Which way was Portoferraio? Was that Corsica or the mainland we were seeing? We weren't sure. Patrick and Harry disagreed about the island to the north. Harry said it was Capraia, Patrick said it was Gorgona.

But when we were scrambling up and down and across the slopes, the land seemed as familiar as the four of us were to each other. We knew everything that could be known about the earth. We knew the weight of a rock before we picked it up. We knew its hardness and cleavage. We knew what was valuable.

Lascia me!

Guarda, it's, it's . . .

Jako Three.

What did you find?

Io found la treasure. Follow me.

Who among us first noticed? And what did he notice, exactly? None of us can explain. I wonder if together we noted some change in the air, perhaps an odd shape in the clouds or a glory's rainbow diffraction when the sun shone through the misting rain. How quiet it was. So quiet we could hear a snake wriggling in the grass. *Jako One, come in. Are you scaredia? If you're scaredia, close your eyes and sing. What are the songs you know by heart? Ascolta —* four boys singing without making a sound. *Can you*

hear me, Harry? Io can hear you. Nat? Sì? Oliver? Sì? Patrick?
Donta mova there, donta speak. Now talk con me. You're talking
ma not talking. Think con me. We hear thinking!

None of us is sure what happened on Elba, but my brothers
and I all remember the sensation of finding ourselves suddenly
capable of miraculous power — the power to speak to each other
without talking aloud. Nat's explanation was that the mountain itself was magic. Patrick reminded us of the crystal he kept under
his bed. Harry wanted to know whether what we were experiencing was good magic or bad magic.

Whatever had happened, Patrick insisted that we must keep it
secret. The rest of us agreed. The need for secrecy was so clear that
we didn't even bother to seal our pact with blood and spit.

We cut our game short and went home early that day. As soon
as we reached the place where the path intersected with the dirt
road heading toward Poggio, we turned back into four ordinary
young boys babbling together so loudly that we scared a whole
flock of starlings from a telephone wire. They rose in a smoky
mass. We shouted and threw rocks that fell far short of their mark.
We picked up more rocks and threw them into the air.

The disappointment we felt at not bringing down a single bird
grew out of proportion. None of us had ever hit a bird with a rock,
but now we thought ourselves ridiculous for having failed. Even
stronger than our disappointment was our sense of shame. Four
boys against a flock of starlings, and we didn't have a single trophy
to show for it. Forgetting what had happened to us on Monte
Giove, we talked of nothing but the birds — how close they were
to us, how poorly we'd aimed — as we trudged up the stairs into our
house. We didn't speak to Lidia when we passed her in the kitchen,
and we didn't bother to wake Francesca to tell her we were home.

We gathered in the living room and waited in sulky silence for
our dinner. Neither of our parents was at home. We didn't care.
Lidia served us bowls of green gurguglione, which we ate for the
first time without complaining. Francesca and Lidia joined us for

supper. Francesca asked us what was wrong, but we were too tired to speak, and soon Francesca and Lidia were engaged in a stormy conversation we didn't even try to follow. We put ourselves to bed. I didn't want to be alone so Nat let me share his bed.

I lay close enough to Nat to feel his warmth without touching him. I felt better, the foggy, inexplicable sensation of shame was dispersing, and in my dopey state I remembered our game of the ants of Monte Giove. I looked forward to tomorrow.

When we weren't in the woods, our language was as coarse and plain as ever, but we wondered if our magic had left some visible trace on us. At home we would study the adults for signs that they'd noticed a change. As far as we could tell, they didn't notice anything. Lidia and Francesca had taken to whispering between themselves, and our parents spent much of their time away from the house. That Claire and Murray were absorbed in problems of great magnitude might have worried us if we had known, but no one bothered to tell us.

Money was one problem. No one, not even Francesca, who often shared gossip with us, told us that our father's mother had stopped sending money, and the uncles wanted Murray to justify the money he'd already spent. Lidia needed money to buy our food. Lorenzo gave our parents another month's grace on the rent, but when the month passed he began charging interest.

Murray, biding time, trying to make work for himself, put in a bid for more land in the San Piero zone but couldn't raise the money to meet the deadline for a down payment. He waited for other land to come on the market. Every farmer he met talked about someone else who was selling his land. But no one wanted to sell to the investor from America.

We had no idea what trouble our parents were in. We would go off each day to a different world and leave the bland, real world of adults behind. They could have their real world. We didn't want it.

A world worth only the value of its resale, a world without magic. That's what we'd been taught to think; no one ever bothered to correct us.

So we didn't know about the dreams. Everyone else on Elba seemed to know about them, but not us. Everyone was talking about the dreams, about the *peste di sogni* spreading across the island.

It was a fisherman in Porto Azzurro who had the first dream. He dreamt that he was in the crypt of the Parrocchiale, keeping guard at an open tomb. Inside, a girl was sleeping on a marble pallet. He recognized her as the Nardi girl. He felt no need to wake her. When a man, a stranger, came along with a bucket of wet concrete, the fisherman put his finger to his lips to signal him to be quiet. The man nodded. He set down the bucket and began mixing the concrete with a huge wooden spoon, stirring it like a thick pot of minestrone. Then he began stacking bricks across the entrance to the tomb and slathering them with the concrete. The fisherman tried to stop him but discovered that he couldn't move or speak.

Who was the man? his friends wanted to know after the fisherman had recounted the dream. The fisherman couldn't say. Was the man a stranger? Yes. Was he American? Yes, he must have been American because he was wearing the helmet worn by U.S. troops — a detail that had great weight among the listeners, since most of them remembered the American soldiers who came to Elba in '44, and they remembered their helmets.

At first, though, the fisherman's dream seemed no more than a fanciful concoction, and while the friends talked at length about it, they didn't presume the dream to have an importance worthy of sharing with others beyond their circle. But when one of the fisherman's friends happened to hear his sister-in-law's cousin talking about her own dream after mass two days later and the cousin said the name *Nardi,* the fisherman's friend exclaimed aloud at the coincidence.

The second dream, the one dreamt by the cousin, a seamstress from the tiny village of Lacona, involved fire. The seamstress had dreamt that she'd seen the glow of a fire on little Isola della Stella, and she'd swum all the way across the strait to investigate. By the time she reached the island the fire had burned out. She climbed over the rocks and found the charred body of a girl lying amidst smoldering embers. The girl was still alive, barely, but burned beyond recognition. The cousin asked her name, and she said, *Nardi.* Then she fell silent, and her eyes rolled back in death. The cousin started to run. She tripped over the outstretched legs of a man. He was sitting on the ground across from the bier, smoking a cigarette. The cousin begged him for help, but he looked at her with the blank look of a foreigner who doesn't speak or understand the language.

Two dreams became three. At Ninanina's enoteca in Portoferraio, one of the men who had worked briefly for Murray listened to the fisherman's friend finishing the story of the cousin's dream, and then he told about his own dream. He had dreamt that he'd been helping the American signore test explosives on a hill above Rio nell'Elba when he'd seen the Nardi girl wandering across the slope. He called to her but it was too late. There was the pop of dynamite, and thick smoke filled the air.

Someone else described a dream that he'd heard from the maid of Signora Claudia Patresi, a wealthy, ancient, bedridden woman who'd come to the island from La Spezia five years earlier to die in the company of her niece. She was dying slowly. In Claudia Patresi's dream, she'd been ice-skating on a long, deserted river — she hadn't been ice-skating since she'd visited Vienna in 1892! — and she'd skated up to a man who was fishing just as he was pulling a fish from the hole. But it wasn't a fish. It was a girl. The Nardi girl, her face the color of clay, her cheeks swollen by the grip of the hook.

Three dreams became four. Four became eight. But what are dreams? people asked. Dreams are hopes that have gone rotten. Dreams are your punishment for drinking too much wine. Dreams are the stories the devil whispers in your ear while you are sleeping.

Eight dreams became ten, twelve, sixteen. In Poggio, in Capo-liveri, in Zanca, Procchio, Carpani, people gathered to tell their dreams. Those who forgot their dreams upon waking drank black-berry tea to help them remember. People did not only dream of the Nardi girl. They dreamt that the sea was so thickly covered with dead fish that they could walk all the way to Corsica. They dreamt that Volterraio erupted. They dreamt of talking dogs and moving statues and church bells that wouldn't ring.

What are dreams? How can you tell a true dream from a false dream? Who's to say that everyone, from the fisherman to old Claudia Patresi, wasn't lying? Why would they lie? Why wouldn't they lie? And why not blame everything on the power of sug-gestion?

Twenty dreams. Twenty-one, twenty-two. The roar of argu-ment in the bars grew louder. What about life? Truth? Here, this, a hand in front of your face! What are dreams? Add a hundred of them together and you get nothing.

Francis Cape stood at the counter in Ninanina's enoteca and sipped his wine. He didn't say much, but he listened carefully. He couldn't believe what he was hearing. He'd admit this to Ninanina when she was refilling his glass, and she'd flash a dark look and say, "You know what dreams can tell us, Francesco, sì?" But when he said no, he didn't, she'd only shake her head.

What can dreams tell us? The people of Elba were divided. Most were skeptical at first, wary of confusing dreams and real-ity. A few of the most fervent believers were prepared to accept the dreams as revelations. Local clergy had nothing to say about the matter. The editor of Portoferraio's local newspaper attributed the dreams to xenophobia, but he couldn't publish an editorial about what amounted to no more than hearsay.

What can dreams tell us? Francis Cape, himself capable of the wildest, most impure, unspeakable dreams, had always thought dreams were no better than ridiculous. He was shocked to see his

Elban neighbors treating their dreams with increasing solemnity. They might have been a religious people, but their priests were adept at keeping superstition in check.

Whoever heard of dreams being responsible for turning hundreds of people against an innocent man? This was the gist of what Francis Cape wondered as he listened to the Elbans. And this was the question our mother asked our father after she finally went to see Francis Cape at his home and asked him exactly what he'd meant by his warning.

"Salem, Massachusetts," Murray said in reply to Claire, standing behind her with a tumbler of scotch in his hand, watching her reflection in the mirror. Her face was covered with her hands; her hair fell in a curtain. "Salem in the sixteen hundreds."

"Oh, Murray, come off it."

"They say that colorful dreams come from abstinence. Maybe that's the problem with these people. They're not getting enough."

"It's not funny, Murray."

"Dreams are funny. They are hilarious. Nightmares are the funniest kind. Harry dreaming last month he cut off Ollie's winky by mistake. Remember? And then there was Nat's dream about *gentilissima* Lidia cooking the cat!"

"Murray . . ."

"I love you, Claire."

"What's this about?"

"I'm telling you I love you."

"This is serious, Murray."

"Nothing more serious."

"Stop it."

"I haven't had a dream in . . . I can't remember how long it's been, it's been so long."

"Murray."

"You want me to stop?"

"Yes."

"Whoever heard of dreams turning people against an innocent man? You're right, Claire. It can't happen."

"We need to leave Elba. You need to stop this."

"Stop this?"

"Murray . . ."

"You want me to stop?"

"Yes."

"You really want me to stop?"

"Yes. No."

"You don't want me to stop?"

"No."

"It feels good?"

"Yes."

"You sure? I can stop if you want me to."

"No."

"You sure?"

"Yes."

"You do want me to stop?"

"No."

"You don't?"

"Don't stop, Murray. OK?"

"OK."

What are dreams? They are stories we tell ourselves when we are alone.

Then the body decides to return us to reality — the reality of stomach cramps, sore throats, swollen glands. The fact of pain. The necessity of food, oxygen, and water. The fact of fever.

It was Meena the cat who got sick first, though our parents hardly noticed. We noticed, but we couldn't do anything but watch her ribs pulse beneath her fur and her tongue twitch as she panted. She lay on Nat's bed for three days without eating or drinking. Her nose was hot. The insides of her velvety ears were hot. And then on the fourth day she dragged herself to her water bowl and drank until the bowl was empty. By the fifth day she was as sly and quick and aloof as ever.

Harry was the next one to fall ill. He complained of a headache, and when Francesca felt his forehead her hand jerked away from the shock of heat. She put him to bed and sent a neighbor, Marco Scozzi, to fetch our parents, who had gone into Portoferraio to have lunch.

Our mother came home with Marco; she left Murray in Portoferraio to shop for presents for Harry, whose birthday was the following Wednesday. She gave Harry half an aspirin, coaxed him to take a few sips of water, and let him sleep for the rest of the day. In the evening she put cotton balls soaked in warm olive oil in his ears. If he wasn't better in a couple of days, she told herself, she'd check with the pharmacist. If he took a turn for the worse, she'd call a doctor.

Patrick woke up with a fever the next morning. He and Harry stayed in their bedroom with the shutters closed because the light hurt their eyes. They weren't even interested in the comic books Murray brought them. Nat mixed dish soap with water and blew bubbles in the room, but Patrick mumbled for him to stop, and when he didn't, Harry called him an idiot. Nat left the room crying.

The first cause for alarm was Harry's complaint that the back of his neck hurt. Claire immediately called Lorenzo, who gave her the name of a local doctor. The doctor was in Pisa for the day, but his wife booked a home visit for the following afternoon.

By the evening I was sick. This was not like any kind of sickness I had ever known. My gut ached, my head ached, my ears throbbed with pain, I couldn't swallow or speak, and I didn't have the strength to squeeze my fingers into a fist.

In our Marciana house I shared a room with Nat. When I fell ill my parents moved a cot into Harry and Patrick's room for me —

"the sick room" it was called, Nat announced. He wasn't sick — hahah! He didn't have to stay in bed — hahah! His voice hurt my ears. Someday, I knew, Patrick would beat him up for this.

Damp washcloths were draped over my forehead. Warm cotton plugged my ears. I heard my mother's voice but I couldn't understand what she was saying. I wondered if there was ever a time in my life when I hadn't been sick.

In the afternoon someone unbuttoned my pajama top and I felt the cold of what must have been a stethoscope against my skin. Then a lizard started to crawl across my chest and up my neck, along my jaw, beneath my ears. I heard a man's voice, a voice inflected with Italian, calling my name. I didn't understand why he needed to call me when I was lying right there in front of him, whoever he was. I wanted to tell him to leave me alone. I wanted to sleep. I did sleep, but not for long. I was woken by a huge black glossy ant, so huge it could hardly squeeze through the doorway. I screamed, and my mother rushed into the room. As she approached me the ant faded and disappeared. But it had been there long enough for my mother to see it, so I didn't bother to explain my terror.

Through the next period all I perceived besides the pain were odors, each of them distinct: honey, olive oil, ammonia and vinegar and candied cherries and the perfumed residue of shampoo in my mother's hair. When I smelled her beside me I was angry — why wouldn't she quit bothering me and let me sleep? When I didn't smell her I was angry — why wasn't she with me, making the pain go away?

At some point I revived enough to know that I wanted to tell my mother she was stupid, I wanted to tell my brothers they were ugly, I wanted a sip of water, I didn't want a sip of water, I wanted to sleep but I didn't want to sleep because I was afraid the giant ant would come back. I didn't understand why no one was helping me. It wasn't fair. I was five years old, and I was supposed to get a glass of water when I wanted it. But there was water only when I didn't want it. Didn't anyone know that everything inside me was hurting? Where was everyone? I looked across the room and saw Patrick sleeping on his stomach, his covers tossed to his ankles, one arm dangling off the side of the bed. The sight reassured me. Patrick was here. Patrick would take care of me. Patrick, wake up! But he wouldn't wake up. Whenever Patrick wouldn't let me wake him up I knew he was just pretending to sleep. Patrick was stupid! Everyone was stupid and ugly, except my mother, who poured warm olive oil into my ears and made them feel better. I did feel better. The room was filled with light, Patrick was sitting up in bed reading a book, Harry was sleeping, and there was a bowl of orange Jell-O beside my bed. Jell-O!

We all improved abruptly. One day we'd been stiff with pain, the next day we were complaining because we couldn't run around outside in our bare feet.

Then it was Nat's turn. He'd spent the week feeling alternately proud of his good health and bored without the company of his brothers. Our parents were useless. Even Meena the cat wouldn't play with him. He told Francesca he wanted to be sick. She ignored him. He pretended to be too sick to get out of bed, and for a moment he had Claire fooled. He was pleased to see how angry he'd made her. The next day he really did feel sick, and he was surprised when Claire wouldn't rush to his bedside.

By the time Nat fell ill, Claire had a clear sense of the fever's trajectory — its abrupt climb and steady high plateau over a course of five days. We'd all had the same symptoms and been sick for the same amount of time.

We had to put off celebrating Harry's birthday, which upset the rest of us but not Nat, who was too sick to care. We all felt the justice of his illness. It was his punishment for taunting us. He deserved to suffer as we'd suffered. Hahaha, Nat. Look at you now. Poverino.

I'm not sure how we realized that Nat's sickness was taking a different shape. The light hurt his eyes just as it had hurt ours.

He'd ask for water then push it away when it was brought to him, just as we'd done. He was terribly sick. We'd been terribly sick. Poverino Nat. We taunted him. He didn't have the strength to do more than gesture with his hand for us to go away. We went away — but we'll be back, Poverino, we said.

We hadn't realized that Claire had been staying up with us and then with Nat through the night, snatching an hour here and there during the day to rest. Even when she went to lie down she couldn't sleep. Or she'd drift toward sleep and after a minute wake with a start. Once she woke to find a ladybug sitting on her hand. She'd stayed still for a long while, watching the bug, and then had sent it with a puff out the window.

Claire was so exhausted that at first she attributed her anxiety about Nat to her own fatigue. Day three of the fever. Day four still to go, she told herself. Day five he would be sitting up and eating Jell-O.

The doctor had prescribed a liquid antibiotic, but as far as Claire could tell it hadn't helped the rest of us. Still, she gave it to Nat in the proper doses, tilting his head back in her hand and pouring a teaspoonful into his mouth. Once she bumped her arm against the table and spilled the medicine across Nat's pillow. She blotted it dry but didn't bother to change the case, and when I came into the room I mistook the stain for blood pouring from Nat's ear.

The fourth day came and went and then the fifth, and Nat showed no signs of improvement. He huddled beneath the sheet, and when I touched the lumpy outline of his body, he'd shudder. Claire continued with the routine of his care. The doctor came for a second visit and prescribed a stronger antibiotic. Claire asked if they should take him to the hospital in Livorno and realized only by hearing herself ask the question that she was scared, as scared as she'd been when the engineer had dangled Nat over the *Casparia*'s rail. When the comparison came to mind, she could only stare at the doctor, stunned.

He said he didn't want Nat moved. Which meant he was telling her that her son was too sick to go to the hospital.

She collapsed in Murray's arms after the doctor left, and Murray was grateful for the chance to offer her comfort. He reassured her, promised her that Nat would be fine, promised to bring in another doctor, reminded her of the time Harry contracted pneumonia, what a scare they'd had, but he'd recovered, hadn't he?

Claire realized as she clung to Murray that they'd taken to escaping from their troubles into each other. The natural ease of their love had been weakened by suspicion. Lately, suspicion had been replaced by a narrow, consuming need for each other's company. They'd been neglecting their children. They'd been horrible parents. She was a horrible mother.

And even now, Murray's presence was enough to subdue Claire's rising guilt. He convinced her she needed to sleep. She was mistaking guilt for exhaustion. Of course she was exhausted. All right, she'd sleep and let Murray take care of Nat for a while. He helped her to bed and was going to help her slip under the covers, but she sent him back to Nat's room.

When she woke she couldn't tell whether it was morning or afternoon. Wandering through the quiet house, she felt like she did when she woke in the middle of the night, though daylight lit up the windows. In Nat's room she found Murray asleep on the edge of Nat's bed, but Nat was awake, and when he saw her he smiled weakly. She smoothed his wet bangs to the side of his forehead. His skin was cool to her touch — or at least cooler than it had been for seven days, and his eyes had lost their milkiness. Claire wanted to cry. She disguised her emotion with a little gulp of laughter that woke Murray. They spoke in low, calm, efficient voices about what would be best for Nat — orange juice or orange Jell-O.

It took Nat another three days to recover strength enough to stand up, and he remained disoriented in some ways. But he ate heartily, laughed when we made faces at him, threw comic books and spoons and even a full cup of water across the room at us when we teased him. He ate a big piece of the chocolate cake Claire baked for Harry's birthday party. He worked on puzzles. He played with Harry's new troop of toy soldiers. He called Patrick a dumbhead and me a snotface. And when he was finally allowed to go outside and play with us one beautiful June day, when for the first time in weeks we were able to roam in our pack of four away from the house and up the slope of Monte Giove, Nat resumed his place in our game of ants. *Jako Three, come in, it's Jako One here.*

Maybe the game kept us from recognizing that Nat had changed. When we were playing, scrambling toward and away from the secret horde of gold, the four of us were as close to being a single self as we would ever come. We didn't need speech to understand each other. In retrospect, though, we can point to signs that Nat was having trouble. At home when someone spoke to him we'd see a strange expression on his face, new furrows in his forehead suggesting deep confusion. He'd have to look directly at us, he'd ask *what*, we'd repeat ourselves, he'd ask *what* again, we'd repeat ourselves again, and when he still looked at us, confused, we would resort to pointing, or else we'd just give up.

He hadn't gone deaf, not exactly. What happened to Nat was stranger than deafness. The fever had left him with hearing that was fragile, like a long-distance line at the mercy of the weather. Sounds would be coming to him with a clarity that was almost painful, then they'd fade out, and for an interval lasting at least a few minutes and sometimes as long as an hour he wouldn't be able to hear anything at all.

Like the rest of us would have done in his place, Nat decided to keep his condition a secret. And he was good at deception. If he wanted to know what he'd missed, he'd wait until we'd forgotten that we'd already repeated ourselves. He'd fall asleep in front of the radio. He'd fall asleep on Murray's lap. He'd decipher Lidia's meaning from the expression on her face. He'd shrug when Francesca asked him a question. He was clever in so many ways that none of us caught on.

OLLIE, I'M LOSING TRACK. There's nearly fifty years of life between then and now, almost fifty years to clutter my mind. I don't remember the doctor prescribing a second antibiotic for Nat. I asked Nat about this and he says he doesn't remember either. Where are you getting your information? How do you know so much? That last exchange between Francis Cape and Signora Nardi, for instance. How did you know about that? I don't recall telling you, and you say you weren't able to find anyone during your last visit to Elba who remembered the Nardi family. But you're right — the Signora did give Francis reason to feel accused. I found out about this later from our cook, Lidia, who was friendly with Signora Nardi's cook.

The more I talk about Elba, the murkier my memory becomes. Did it really rain so much that spring? Did I roast a chicken for Christmas? You say we had a radio. I don't remember any radio. And did I tell you I was reading Keats? Not only have I forgotten what I did four and a half decades ago, but I've forgotten what I said to you when you were last here.

What do you know, and what are you making up as you go along? I can't discern the difference anymore.

You've told me you want to write something that's true. A true history of fact. You make me wonder. Are you running from your own life into the past, and from the past into a fairy tale? What you're writing about my life doesn't match my collection of memories. What do I remember? I'm not sure. What do I know? What do you know? Do you really know, Ollie, that Signora Claudia Patresi dreamed about ice-skating? Where did you hear this?

I don't remember knowing about you boys playing secret

games in the mountains. But I do remember wondering what you were up to. All the whispering you did. You took to talking in a peculiar concoction of Italian and English. Do you really remember it? I remember. You boys talking amongst yourselves in your own stew of a language. Not just an Italian phrase thrown in here and there. What I heard was an incomprehensible mix of sounds. Could it be that what you're remembering is not a magical means of communication but nonsense that you could only pretend to understand?

What do you know for sure? I've gone back to old journals and sometimes I can't even read my handwriting! But as far as I can tell I never mention anyone named Ninanina. I remember the tiny woman who ran the enoteca in Portoferraio. Her name was Ninanina? This rings a bell. But how did you find this out, Ollie?

We've had a full week of clear skies, but it's been so cold the snow hasn't even started to melt. The white snow, the white sun . . . and did I tell you that for the first year ever, the swans are wintering here? Every morning I see them drifting back and forth across the inlet. I've tried to feed them, but they're too vain to eat. They want to be admired, that's all. Lloyd Hunter next door tried to scare them off with a shotgun. He's worried they'll freeze. But the swans have decided to stay and that's that. A pop of a gun isn't going to change their minds. I told this to Emily, who told this to her father, who told Emily to tell me that if the swans freeze to death, it's my fault. Even if they don't eat the bread I leave for them, I'm the one responsible for deceiving them into thinking they could survive our winter — so says Lloyd Hunter. I told Emily to tell her father if he shoots that gun once more, I'm going to call the police. Lloyd told Emily to tell me that's it, I can find someone else to shovel my walk. Which is a peculiar thing to say, since Lloyd Hunter hasn't offered to shovel snow for me for years.

Now what do I really remember? I let my thoughts drift like those swans across the dark water, and I remember the hollow sounds of voices coming through the fog in Portoferraio. I remember the gritty black sand on the beach at Padulella. Looking out from the darkness of the stone chapel on Volterraio to the sea. Watching you boys running after Meena into the vineyard. Nat's tired smile after he'd been sick, the smile of a little boy who thinks he's just played a splendid joke. I remember watching Lidia squeeze a lemon over a plate of anchovies. I remember walking out of the Chiesa della Misericordia into the rain. The pink-tinged sky at twilight. Harry calling us to come see the dead mouse floating in a pail of muddy water. Patrick calling us to come outside on the first cold day of autumn to see our breath make clouds. I remember everything I did routinely as if I'd done it only once — drinking my morning caffé, walking to Marciana Marina, floating on my back in that salty sea.

I am an old woman, ten years older than old Francis Cape had been in 1957. Do you want to hear what your old mother remembers about making love? I'm not going to tell you. But when you discuss your parents' absorption in each other, you might consider the complexities of love. You might think about how passion can become cruel when it is defensive.

What else do I remember? Looking for a gold earring I lost on the street in Porto Azzurro. Watching six fishermen in a row pass along a single wooden match to light their six cigarettes.

Do I really remember any of this? The more I read about my life on Elba, the more I forget. Alzheimer's. Little Emily Hunter keeps asking me if I have Alzheimer's yet. No, not yet, Emily, but soon.

You invited me to go back to Elba with you this spring. I declined. But I wish your father were still alive to accompany you. It would have done him good to return. And you can imagine all he'd tell you. By the time we left Elba, Murray knew that island better than he knew any other place else in the world. He knew it inside and out. He'd have plenty to add to this story.

Imagine Murray and me trying to sort through our memories to come up with a single version of our past. Remembering together what happened, what didn't happen, what almost and might have happened. I often find myself anticipating Murray's objections. Claire, the black sand beach was at Topinetti. And the earring I lost was pearl, not gold — a present to me from Murray's mother.

I remember looking for diamonds on Volterraio. I remember Harry cupping a lizard in his hands. I remember Nat's sharp reply when I asked him if he was having trouble hearing. He could hear just fine, he said, and I believed him. I remember you, Ollie, running toward the end of the pier in Marciana Marina while I yelled at you to stop. I remember the fisherman who caught you and carried you back to us.

I don't remember ever threatening again to take you boys and leave Elba. I was ready to stay with Murray as long as he wanted to stay. Only guilty men run from suspicion, he insisted, and though I didn't entirely agree, I was afraid that if he did leave the island the police would concoct a formal charge against Murray in order to bring him back. We couldn't leave, no more than we could have unlocked a padlock without the key. There were days when I thought we'd never go home.

I close my eyes and remember the winter wind against my face. The summer wind. The warm green water of the Terranera sulfur baths. The smell of fishing nets drying in the sun in Porto Azzurro. The fresh schiacciata from the bakery in Poggio. The gift of goat cheese from our neighbor. The bundles of fresh thyme and rosemary and mint brought to us by Lidia's niece. The red poppies in the meadows. Dust rising as we trudged along the path to the beach at Lacona. Riding on the back of Murray's motorcycle at night after we'd finished off a bottle of wine at a restaurant in Capoliveri. Standing in a doorway, watching you boys fill a box with the toys you wanted to take back to America.

THE TRUTH, FRANCIS CAPE would have said, is a sequence of names and dates arranged as verifiable facts. The truth is a fingerprint left behind by a thief or a document signed by a king. The truth is something you see with your own eyes and remember forever.

The truth, Francis knew, was that Adriana went to visit our father in Le Foci one autumn night in 1956. She hadn't stayed long with him — just long enough to let him have his way with her. Wasn't that so, Adriana? No! Oh yes it was! Francis had been able to tell at a glance that Adriana's denial was a lie. By coincidence, he'd been out walking near our Le Foci villa that same night . . . except it hadn't been a coincidence at all. He'd gone to La Chiatta first, but after learning that Adriana was out for the evening, he'd wandered over to Le Foci, though not necessarily with the expectation of finding Adriana there. Really, he hoped he wouldn't find her there. No one was supposed to be at Le Foci. Hadn't our family already moved to another residence? Then why was Murray Murdoch's Lambretta parked in the drive? Francis Cape waited outside, waited for ten minutes, twenty, a lifetime, long enough for Murray and Adriana to enjoy their liaison, and when Adriana left the house and rushed toward the road, Francis hurried to meet her. Out of sight of the house, he'd grabbed her, said what he needed to say, kissed her, and slapped her when she tried to resist, and she'd fled.

Of course she'd fled. He was an old man and she a young woman in love with someone else. She wanted him to leave her alone. That's what she'd told him. Leave me alone, Francis Cape! How could he leave her alone after he'd loved her for years? She was like a daughter to him. She'd grown up as he'd grown old. He wanted her to be his wife — was this such a terrible desire?

He disgusted her. He offended her. He'd been the reason she left Elba early the next morning. He was a very very very old man and if he was lucky he'd die in his sleep before the week had ended. But he didn't die. Instead, he kept moving forward in time, away from the unalterable past. He hadn't meant to do anything wrong. He was as innocent as any sinner. The devil made him do it. No, worse. You can always find a woman to blame. Remember, Francis, where Plato writes that the worst punishment for a sinful man is to be reborn as a woman? Blame women. Especially young women. Especially young women who make themselves available through the poise of courtesy and then will have nothing to do with you when you need them most.

He blamed himself for causing Adriana to go away, but he blamed Murray for cheating him of the girl's affection. The American investor had taken advantage of Adriana. He deserved to be punished. Still, Francis was amazed by the plague of dreams. The Elbans were dreaming of Murray's guilt. How did they know he was guilty? Where were their dreams coming from?

Francis had dreams, too. He dreamed that he was rich, capricious, charismatic, virile, and Adriana Nardi was his willing partner. He dreamed he was Napoleon, and Adriana was his mistress. He was the emperor of paradise, in no hurry to leave his island. The girl would do anything with him, to him, for him. She loved him. He loved her. Why should he go back to France and resume the war when life on Elba was so splendid?

Night after night, Francis Cape fell happily asleep. In his dreams he was youthful but not stupid, handsome but not arrogant, carefree, unburdened by ambition. He was the great Napoleon, and he needed nothing more than a girl in his bed and a flask of wine to share with her.

Then to wake each morning to the reality of his life: there were no frescoes on his crumbling plaster walls, no gold-braided uniforms in his closet, no canopy over his bed, no young girl tucked against him. From bliss to sodden consciousness. He was learning to hate his life. It didn't help to blame Adriana in her absence, especially as time went on. It felt much better to blame the American investor. So he sought out our father and worked on him the way a doctor will work on a patient he loathes.

Soothing him —

"Rumors, that's all! They have no hard evidence."

Reassuring him —

"Stick it out, Murray. You'll be absolved sooner or later."

Pondering —

"They won't find any evidence against you if there's no evidence to be found. Unless they make it up. And why would they do that?"

Suggesting to him —

"I'll be the first to agree that this island is more beautiful than any other place on Earth. But is beauty worth such trouble? Don't you think you'd have been better off if you'd stayed at home? Aren't there other ways to get rich? I had hopes for you, Murray, I must say. Shall we open another bottle? Are you all right, Murray? You look a touch bleary. I've always found it helpful to imagine how it could be worse. In this case it would be something along the lines of a public accusation. Let yourself imagine it, Murray. You'll feel better if you imagine it. But then remind yourself that you're innocent. There can't be actual evidence against you. You weren't anywhere near the girl on the night she disappeared."

"What difference would that make? I mean, if I were —"

"Were what, Murray?"

"Were . . . I don't know . . . if I'd seen her. Just seen her at a distance. Caught a glimpse of her that last night."

"If you'd seen Adriana the night she disappeared? Now that's a different matter. If you'd seen the girl that night, you'd have some explaining to do. Did you see her, Murray? Did you go to her house?"

"No!"

"So you didn't see her. When was the last time you saw her?"

"I don't remember."

"One of our dinners, perhaps?"

"Yes, dinner. Some dinner in October. The last time you brought her along to dinner — when was that?"

"Oh, I don't recall exactly. A few weeks before she disappeared, to be sure. You didn't see her afterward? You didn't go to take another look at one of those old maps in the family's collection? Tell me, Murray: what was it you were looking for? Buried treasure? Montecristo's just down the road, you know. You Americans and your optimism. More? Later we'll try the grappa, sì? Now tell me, how are the boys? They feeling better? Are you all in good health? That's what counts, remember. Forget about suspicion. You and your family have your health. At my age, I know what it means to be healthy. I walk five miles a day. Every morning I walk out to the Rada lighthouse and watch the sky brighten with dawn. I haven't had to call for a doctor since I came to the island. A decade of good health. This following a decade during which I gave up hope of surviving. That's the way it was. Those grim days in London when we all thought the world was ending. And then to come here and sit for long hours listening to the little silver leaves of the olive trees crinkling in the breeze. It's a glorious place, isn't it? Not a place where you'd expect trouble. I'm told the island hasn't had a murder since the nineteenth century. To be sure, there have been casualties of war. Our Allied friends came to Portoferraio in '44 and blew apart a few stout vessels in the German fleet, I'm proud to say. And still I feel welcome here. If only I could press on with my book. First, though, I want to help you find a way out of this fix you're in. Tell me what I can do for you, my friend. I'd like to help, you know. I'd like to find a way to convince the Elbans that you are innocent. If only Adriana would come back. Where do you think she's gone off to? Why did she go away?"

Francis probed Murray, roused and reassured him. He offered more wine, grappa, gin. He kept Murray out late. As long as Francis was with Murray, Claire stayed away. She couldn't stand Francis Cape. She didn't trust him. But it was Francis who had come to warn them about the dreams, and for this reason alone Murray felt indebted to him. Besides, Francis knew the Elbans and could provide Murray with a daily report on their gossip.

Claire was scared. The fever had scared her. The darkness scared her. The soft, dry scirocco scared her when it puffed the curtains at night. She would have preferred Murray to stay at home in the evening and told him so, but he felt an increasing need to meet with Francis and hear what was being said about him. And in the midst of summer, they could enjoy a degree of anonymity. There were more tourists on Elba than ever before. Two new hotels had opened up in Portoferraio. Builders from Piombino came by boat each day to put up more concrete bungalows. With all the strangers on the island, Francis and Murray could sit together in a café in Porto Azzurro, and no one would recognize them.

Sometimes Murray would only half listen to what Francis was saying. Sometimes he wouldn't listen at all. Instead, he'd look around at the group of German tourists and wonder what they'd been doing during the war. Francis Cape had been hiding in a basement in London. Murray had been playing football on Elba. What were you doing? Murray wanted to ask the Germans around him. You, sir. Where were you?

Only a little more than a decade had passed since the end of the war, and already the nations of western Europe had united in an economic partnership. If a world war could be forgotten after a decade, Murray's involvement with Adriana Nardi could be forgotten after a year. She had been missing for nine months. When would her absence be explained?

What Murray feared most: Adriana had left his house that night back in November, walked to the cliffs above Cavo, and thrown herself off.

What Claire feared most: there was something crucial Murray hadn't told her.

What Francis Cape feared most: Adriana would come home without warning.

"If you don't know for certain why she went away, can you make an educated guess, Murray?"

"Francis, you're a friend, yes? I can trust you, yes? What if I told you that I did see Adriana that night? What if I told you that? What would you do?"

"Why, I'd only wonder what else you had to say."

"What if I told you that I was alone in our first house, you remember, that property of Lorenzo's, the one near Le Foci."

"Of course I remember."

"The day we moved, I went back to Le Foci instead of to Marciana. I wasn't thinking. I went home at the end of the day to an empty house. And I stayed there for a while. A long while. And Adriana came over."

"Good lord, Murray. Why didn't you admit this before?"

"Francis . . ."

"I don't understand why you've kept this to yourself. Unless there's more to understand. Unless you're hiding something, Murray."

"I didn't mean to . . . I don't know."

"You didn't mean to what? You didn't mean to hurt her?"

"No."

"What did you do to her? Murray, answer me. What did you do to that girl? You —"

"I am."

"You —"

"I . . ."

"You did!"

"No —"

"You did!"

"Wait! You've misunderstood me. I didn't do anything! Damn you, Francis, come back!"

This was on a summer night, the warm air perfumed with roses.

Francis left Murray sitting by himself under the pergola at the café, and he went home. He reviewed the conversation with Murray as he drove. He hadn't intended their dialogue to go in that direction and would have attempted to redirect it if he'd seen what was coming. Murray had forced him into the position of accuser. It wasn't Francis's fault that Murray had confessed. Confessed to what? Murray was confused. It wasn't Francis's fault that Murray was confused. And you couldn't blame Francis for the fact that Elbans across the island were dreaming about Adriana Nardi and Murray Murdoch. Francis hadn't actively incited suspicion. He really hadn't done much more than ask a few questions and offer to help.

What would be done to him? Murray asked himself. What had he done? Played with a girl's affections, then jilted her. Mr. Murray Murdoch, are you there? Yes I am, though as far as you're concerned, Adriana, no I'm not. Go away. She went away, threw herself off a cliff, and her body was sucked into greedy Neptune's surf — all because of Murray.

Ridiculous!

Really?

It's possible, isn't it? It's possible that Elbans believed the American signore was capable of murder. He, the father of four young boys. The Elbans were suspicious of him. Suspicion being the action of accusation held in suspense.

When you're suspicious you need a distraction. A wife suspicious of her husband will renounce suspicion when neighbors begin to grow hostile. A community suspicious of a foreigner could use the distraction of some great national calamity. Short of a war, a drought would be of some use. A forest fire. A flood. Anything to draw attention away from Murray Murdoch.

They'd be coming after him soon. If they didn't lynch him, they'd lock him in a cell and torture him until he admitted to a murder he hadn't committed. How are confessions drawn from innocent people? With cattle prongs, electric wires, water drops, pliers, knives, bottles, hoods, forks, acid. The extravagant art of pain. But can anyone say for sure that the dead won't return to take revenge?

The only other customers left in the café besides Murray were two German couples. Next year there would be more Germans on Elba. And French, Slavs, Swedes, British. And Americans. More and more each successive year. Proving that a nation can't blast its way to imperial rule — ownership must be bought, paid for with hard cash. Money money money. Murray no longer had hopes of making a profit or even paying the loan back to his uncles. All he wanted to do was go home and start his life over again. Yes, of course, and civilization wanted to start the century over again.

He wanted to be with Claire, to be alone with her. He didn't want to have to share her with the rest of us. He didn't want the responsibility of children anymore. Four sons were too much to handle. They wandered off into the hills after dark. They were rude. They bumped into people. They broke things. They spilled things. They got sick, and when they got better they wanted nothing to do with their father and didn't even speak the same language.

Who did speak Murray's language? Not the people around him. Even Francis, an Englishman, had misunderstood him to mean that he'd done actual physical harm to the Nardi girl. Only Claire spoke the same language. Mrs. Claire Murdoch. She needed to know what Murray had done — and what he hadn't done. He would tell her about Adriana's appearance that night in the empty house in Le Foci. He would ask Claire to forgive him.

He left, forgetting about the bill. He felt an unexpected, unfamiliar wave of relief as he melted into the shadows beyond the café lights. Darkness belongs to fugitives. He could almost taste it on his tongue. Though the alcohol in his blood made him lurch, he perceived his steps to be smooth, stealthy, buoyant. As long as he was still free, he would find a way to remain free.

"Signore!"

But if he were caught —

"Signore, per favore!"

If he were apprehended —

"Signor Americano!"

If he were chased by a young Italian man, a waiter who wanted nothing more than payment for the bill but who in Murray's mind became the leader of a mob, if he were chased and apprehended, he would be torn to pieces. So he must run. Run fast, Signor Americano! He must run from his accusers. A girl was missing. Suspicion was growing. Run, Murray! He ran, stumbled, and somehow, even in his drunken state, managed to stay on his feet and keep running. He ran along the flatlands road leading toward Portoferraio. At one point the wind was behind him, then, a moment later, against him. Eventually — he had no idea how far he'd gone — he heard only the echo of his own footsteps slapping the paved road. With a great wheezing breath, he slowed to a walk. He tried to pretend that he was just an ordinary man returning home from a drink with a friend. A leaden fatigue came over him. He had no idea what time it was. He expected to be startled at any moment by the beam of a flashlight on his face. We've found you, Signor Americano! But no one found him. He didn't know where to go next. He told himself that he shouldn't go back to the villa. He mustn't go back. But he wanted to go back. And so he did.

Of suspicion, accusations, confessions, and missing girls, my brothers and I knew nothing. We did not hear our father return home late that night, nor were we woken by our parents' fierce whispers. It was the night Murray told our mother that he was responsible for Adriana's disappearance, but we slept soundly, and when we woke the next morning, Elba seemed as fresh and promising as ever. The rooster crowed; the goats complained; the motorcycles and milk trucks passed noisily up on the road toward Poggio.

Of the four of us, Nat was the most tranquil — and the one

most indifferent to our parents' troubles. He was often the first to wake, and he'd go outside alone and watch the chickens scratching in the yard. He'd collect the eggs for Lidia, cupping each one between his hands to feel its warmth, and if the rest of us still hadn't woken, he'd walk down the road to the Scozzi farm and watch Marco Scozzi milking the goats. Sometimes he'd return with a round of pecorino, a jar of plum jam, a bag of peaches. Marco Scozzi called him Cherubino, and when Nat looked at him, confused, Marco pointed at the swallows swooping across the sky. There you are, Marco had said. And so Nat went away understanding that he was a little bird and someday would be able to fly above the clouds.

I am a bird. Nat would repeat this to himself. *I am a bird, a bird, a bird* — and this served as a ready explanation for the intervals of silence. Nat had become a bird. You don't have to die to become a bird. You just have to get very sick and then get better. And when you're better you will be able to see everything with such clarity that you won't need words anymore. You won't need much of anything besides a little bit of cheese and bread and jam and water, and maybe one of Marco's fresh peaches still warm from the sun. You won't even need parents. And though you won't have much use for your brothers, you'll tolerate them because without them you'd be bored.

Without any active insurrection, Nat usurped Patrick's place as the leader of our group. Little Nat, who was just six years old. We found ourselves following his orders before we'd even admitted to ourselves that he was in charge. With Nat as our captain, we all felt within us an increased sense of individual purpose. We were whatever we were supposed to be. Nat filled his role with the confidence of an experienced actor playing a part for the hundredth time. Harry was adept at finding pieces of transparent quartz we could use as diamonds. Patrick, the most knowledgeable, provided solutions to all mysteries. And I was the lookout, the one to warn of intruders and other dangers when we were playing.

After the night our father broke down and told Claire about his involvement with the Nardi girl, that regrettable embrace when she came to the house at Le Foci, both our parents stayed at home. Through the rest of the month, neither left the house, not even to sit outside on the terrace. It was beautiful weather — bright blue summer skies, with a soft, cooling breeze blowing off the sea, which we enjoyed after scrambling over rocks up the mountain. But Claire and Murray stayed inside, received no visitors, and ate their meals separately from us, behavior we interpreted as the expression of uselessness. Most adults had to pretend to have a purpose. Our parents had stopped pretending, and their indifference was affecting Lidia and Francesca. Francesca was growing fat; Lidia was growing careless and twice had dropped glasses on the hard tile floor of the kitchen.

We had enough sympathy to feel sorry for the adults in our household but not enough to want to help them. We took our cues from Nat, who led us farther and farther from the villa each day. He could run in bare feet up the rocky slope of Monte Giove as if he were flying, he could leap down steep inclines, and he could stand on a precipice and flap his arms and make the sunlight glitter.

Guarda! Look at me!

Look at him!

I'm a bird!

Birds can volare. Volare, Jako Three. Let's guarda you!

How deep was our confusion? Sometimes I wonder if the quartz crystals we found on Elba were really diamonds, the pyrite gold, and all the colorful feldspar blooming with tourmaline. The whole island was the treasure chest our father had promised it would be, and we'd opened it with a magical key. We could have done anything if we'd let ourselves believe completely in the power of our wishes.

Guarda! Jakos, guarda!

He's doing it, he's really doing it!

No!

Sì!

This is something I think I remember: blinking rapidly against the blinding sun, then staring wide-eyed as my brother Nat, just a dark silhouette bounded by light, flapped his arms wildly, then rose about six inches and hovered for a few long seconds in the air above the granite crag.

He did! Jakos, he really did volare!

He didn't. I was guarding and he didn't.

Did I? Did I really do it?

You did!

He didn't!

He vero did!

IN LA CHIATTA, HER VILLA sandwiched between olive groves and the sea, directly across the bay from Portoferraio, Signora Nardi waited for her daughter to come home. She waited with a calm that many considered unnatural, tending to the business of the Calamita leases with her characteristic placidness. From time to time she'd swing open the shutter above the table where she worked and look toward the meadow where Lorenzo's cows were pegged out to graze. She would glide her hand along the table's inlaid mosaic, smoothing the tiles. She would listen to her cook, Luisa, running water from the hose into the courtyard's stone trough.

There were some who wondered how a mother could be so calm in the face of her daughter's disappearance, and some who suggested that the Signora had never really loved her adopted daughter. Others scoffed at such contemptuous speculation and said that the Signora was only pretending to be calm for the sake of dignity. Was she as calm as she appeared? No one dared to ask her, for they accepted the family's privacy as a right earned by centuries of nobility. Elbans liked to think that they would have fought to protect the Nardi family, not because of the Nardis' wealth but because three hundred years of the island's past was preserved in the name.

The islanders, though, had failed to protect the daughter. For this they blamed the American. Of course they blamed the American. There'd been talk about others involved in the girl's life — romances she'd kept hidden even from her mother. There'd been talk that the girl was wild and desperate and would give herself to any straniero who flattered her. There'd been talk about the girl and Signor Americano even before she'd disappeared.

She'd been gone for many months. The police had long since

stopped searching for evidence. The people of Elba dreamed their dreams and whispered about our father. My brothers and I played our games. Signora Nardi went on waiting.

Her closest friends spoke of her with a sternness that suggested disappointment. They loved Signora Nardi and would prove their love with a lifetime of loyalty, but they couldn't understand why she didn't wail and cry to the Blessed Virgin for help and solace, why instead she chose to wait as calmly as a mother will wait for her daughter to return from a dance. Signora, her friends wanted to say, there was no dance. Your daughter has gone away and no one can say when she will come back.

Would she come back? Could she, Adriana Nardi, taken in like dirty wash when she was a young child, have no sense of gratitude? Her beauty was coarse — was it this that made her vulnerable to men who otherwise would have respected the family name? Or was it that the girl, raised to be a lady and educated to take her place in the world beyond the island, had been born to be a whore?

Vado via perchè devo andare via, she wrote in the note she left behind. She had gone away deliberately and just as deliberately she would return. Whatever faults she had, whatever confusions drove her from home, the girl wouldn't disappear forever.

Signora Nardi had taken every logical action to find her daughter and had contacted everyone who might have had news of her. But there was no news. There were plenty of rumors. There were strange dreams and gossip and suspicion. But there was no reliable news, and Signora Nardi could do no more than wait for the sun to cross the sky, the olives to darken on their branches, the rain to start and to stop again, the mail to arrive.

Only Luisa, the Nardis' cook for more than thirty years, understood that the Signora's calm hid a busy mind, and at any waking moment, whether she was alone or with company, silent or involved in conversation, she was engaged in recovering what she could from the past, sifting through memories of her daughter, looking for clues.

Absence asks for the return of memory. With Luisa's help,

Signora Nardi tried to remember any action or comment that might have revealed traces of whatever secret had caused Adriana to run away. The girl had said one day last fall that she wanted to visit the prison at Pianosa. What did it matter that she'd said this? Luisa wondered. And then Luisa remembered that Adriana had said she wanted to learn to ski. Why suddenly did she want to learn to ski? And why didn't the summer sun brown her this year as it had done in past years? Luisa wanted to know. No Elban girl should be so white! Was this evidence of something? Everything was evidence, as far as Adriana's mother was concerned. Adriana's hand bumping her forehead as she went to tuck a curl behind her ear — this was evidence. The distracted look in her eyes — this, too. And the faint rise at the corners of her lips as she smiled to herself, the hesitations in her voice, and the way she'd taken to drinking water in big, furious gulps.

And there was the pleasant, droning ronzio — the sound of humming. In the months before she'd disappeared, Adriana had taken to humming, barely audibly but almost constantly through her waking hours. Hadn't Luisa heard the humming? Adriana's old, sweet habit of humming?

Sì, sì, certo, Luisa had heard her bimba humming again, though she had to admit that she'd thought nothing of it. It was not unusual for girls of a certain age to make a habit of humming. But the Signora pointed out that she hadn't heard her daughter humming for many, many years. Didn't Luisa remember how when Adriana was a young girl she seemed to breathe music, the sound like the whirring of wings following her everywhere? Didn't Luisa remember how she used to hum herself to sleep and hum herself awake, how she hummed as she read and as she listened to stories? Remember, Luisa: she hummed the day the Germans bombed Elba in September, 1943, and she hummed through the night nine months later when the Allies attacked. Didn't Luisa remember that night?

Of course Luisa remembered. It was the night when Mario Tonietti, the widower of Signora Nardi's sister, who had died of cancer in 1935, ran all the way from Portoferraio to Magazzini in his bare feet to tell them to hide. Luisa recalled how the oil lamp had flickered and gone out when Mario Tonietti entered the parlor. She remembered the high pitch of his voice, like the voice of a boy, rising to be heard above the sound of sirens and distant explosions.

What wild stories people could tell about that night. Even as it was happening and windows lit up with the fires across the harbor, the stories were being told and retold. The story of a pregnant woman crushed by falling rubble as she ran from her home. The story of a man bubbling at the mouth with blood the color of blackberries. The story of a child shot in the back on the steps of Via del Paradiso.

The night of June 17, 1944, when the Allies attacked Elba, and the French, the Germans, the Africans, the Italians shot at anything that moved. And not just shot. They had dogs, people would say afterward, real dogs that breathed fire like dragons. And poison arrows that melted men into puddles. And little grenades the size of peas that they'd force down the throats of old women.

By the time Mario Tonietti arrived at La Chiatta, Massimo Volbiani and his wife were already dead. Irene Cartino was dead. Allegra Venuti was dead. Federico the grocer was dead. Cosimo the butcher was dead. They were all dead, killed for the crime of being alive. But there wasn't time to mourn — Mario Tonietti, bless him, had come to lead the way to a cave below Volterraio, where they could wait out the night in safety.

But Mario Tonietti's stories had taken too long, and by the time he'd finished what he thought Signora Nardi needed to know, there were already voices in the fields and the nearby scattershot of gunfire. It was too late to run from the house, too late to do anything but hide the child in the cabinet under the kitchen sink and wait, frozen with awareness of their helplessness, for the fighting to end.

What happened that night on Elba? No one could say for sure, not even the people who lived through it. No one could name the

men who grabbed fourteen-year-old Sofia Canuti, took turns rap-
ing her, and cut her throat. No one saw it happen. No one would
ever know for sure whether to believe crazy old Stefano Grigi, a
fisherman from Marciana Marina, when he said that he'd helped
bury the bones of a prisoner who'd been killed, cooked, and eaten
by a band of soldiers. Which soldiers, Stefano? He had to admit he
wasn't sure. No one knew what to believe. The shroud of darkness
made it impossible to distinguish between enemy and friend. The
best you could do was try to save your family.

For many years afterward, people came to Ninanina's enoteca
to trade the stories that had already been told many times. It was
here that Luisa came to help her cousin prepare food. She would
listen to the stories, and when she was tired of listening she would
tell what she remembered.

She remembered that Adriana had been a good girl that night
and had followed her mother's directions, huddling in the cabinet
in absolute silence even after Signora Nardi closed the doors. How
about that for courage! A child of ten spending the night in a dark
cabinet and not making a sound. At one point Luisa had heard the
distant shriek of what she'd thought was a woman but later
learned was one of Lorenzo's pigs that had been shot in the snout.
She and the Signora and Mario Tonietti sat around the kitchen
table, not daring even to whisper, waiting for the soldiers to burst
through the door. But the soldiers never came to La Chiatta. By
morning the sky was empty, the fields quiet, and when Luisa and
the Signora opened the cabinet under the sink and brave Adriana
tumbled out, they devoured her with kisses.

Elbans who lived through that night would spend the rest
of their lives remembering. There was so much to remember that
Luisa forgot about how afterward she didn't hear Adriana humming. Not for twelve years did she hear the girl humming. And
then, all of a sudden, she'd started humming again.

What did it mean, the humming? Ninanina asked. Luisa could
only shrug. Girls of a certain age make a habit of humming. It

probably meant nothing. But with Adriana gone Luisa shared Signora Nardi's regret that she hadn't listened more closely.

When she comes home, Luisa told Ninanina with a pride that struck witnesses as defensive, she will ask her bimba to sing for her. She wanted to hear the girl sing a whole song, clear as a bell, start to finish.

In the same house where she had waited with her daughter and cook and brother-in-law through the night of the Liberation, Signora Nardi waited for her daughter to come home. She knew how to wait. Through winter, spring, and summer, she waited patiently, deep in thought, though she was prepared to welcome most visitors, Claire among them, and would speak of her daughter as if she were expected home any minute.

Adriana was safe — Signora Nardi believed this not just because she wanted to believe it but because in her absence she had begun to piece together the nature of her secret. She didn't speak of this to anyone, not even to Luisa. Let the dreams continue and suspicion build against an innocent man. Signora Nardi had long ago concluded that Signor Americano was too foolish to be guilty of doing any serious harm. And perhaps a dose of suspicion wouldn't hurt him. It might even do him some good. Malcolm Murdoch, the father of four boys, the man who had dragged his family to the island of exile — he could learn something about himself in the process of deflecting accusations. At the very least, he could learn the value of caution.

Signora Nardi was an insightful woman. But insight didn't save her from the occasional misjudgment. She believed her Elban neighbors had a powerful sense of justice and would never do more than trade stories about their dreams. In this sense our father was safe. Any action taken against him would have to be legal, and Signora Nardi would ensure that it didn't progress to conviction. Murray had a protector in Adriana's mother, a good fairy who would swish her wand and rescue him from peril at the last moment. No one would hurt him. Signora Nardi might as well have locked him in a secret vault and dropped the key into the sea.

But as the engineer from Ohio had said at the first dinner on the *Casparia,* the most dangerous thing you can do is get out of bed in the morning. Signora Nardi, noble as her intentions might have been, confident as she was of the general goodwill of the Elban people and her daughter's imminent return, couldn't keep our father from getting out of bed.

The moon over Elba is whiter than elsewhere, and the sea breeze is saltier. The soapstone is as soft as goose down. Obsidian tastes of licorice. Wells are lined with melted gold. The bladders of gulls are filled with nuggets of jargoon. A goat born on the eve of Ascension Day has hooves made of tin-stone. Beryls grow on persimmon trees. If you crack open a chestnut during an eclipse, you'll find a fire-opal. If you wear clogs carved of peridot, you'll add ten years to your life. The eyes of feral cats are amethyst. The eyes of wild dogs are citrine. Inside every hailstone there is a piece of sapphire the size of a pinhead. The shells of gull eggs are made of thin alexandrite. The shells of hummingbird eggs are made of hiddenite. Cut open the bladder of a dying petrel and you'll find schorl. Cut open the beating heart of a pigeon and you'll find rubellite. Catch a falling star and it will turn to blue tourmaline in your hands. This is true.

If my father were here, I'd ask for clarification. What is true, Dad? He'd say, everything I tell you. He knew about falling stars turning into tourmaline because he saw it happen.

What else happened? I'd want to ask him. Is there anything that hasn't happened on the island of Elba? What is possible, and what will never be more than the mind's concoction? Where do people go on an island when they want to go away?

The rest, my father would say, I'd have to figure out on my own.

The Life of a Rock

BORN MALCOLM AVERIL MURDOCH INTO A FAMILY CLINGING TO its shrinking fortune, educated in private schools, contemptuous of his aristocratic friends but himself cursed with a prospector's greed. Destined to crave the freedom to mess up his life. Malcolm Averil Murdoch, called Murray. Six foot one inch, weighing 190 pounds, brown-haired, green-eyed, an awkward dancer, inept at cards, good at checkers, a modern prospector who would be remembered in family history as the guy who lost a fortune on Elba. Elba! An island known to the rest of the world as a place from which exiled emperors escape. Soot Island.

I'll show you what can happen on Elba.

He went ahead and left his job, borrowed money, and led us across the ocean.

Here we are! How did we get here? Onboard the *Casparia* from Genoa, from Genoa to Florence, from Florence by bus to Piombino, and then the ferry. But we must have made a wrong turn somewhere. This wasn't the island Murray had envisioned. There must have been some mistake. One mistake leading to a whole series of miscalculations. Claire, what went wrong? Claire, can we go home?

She held him. They made love, moving together. . . . How would Claire have described it? Energetically? Lustily? With a hint of ferocity in their antics? Afterward, Murray felt ashamed, as if he'd hurt her. He had hurt her. Disgraced her. Forced her to bear the weight of suspicion that cast him as the man responsible for the death of a young woman. You'll answer for your crime, Signor Americano.

Just as lapidary involves shaping a gemstone to reflect light, suspicion involves shaping the recent past into a probable story. The effort of bringing something to light. You, Malcolm Averil Murdoch, where were you on the night Adriana disappeared? Were you sealing her inside a tomb? Were you burning her on a pyre? What were you doing? Tell us.

I was just fooling around.

Coward.

Yes.

All she'd wanted was to talk with you. Just talk. You answered her with the pretense of understanding. She ran from you, ran to the cliffs above Cavo and threw herself off. Is that what happened, Murray?

Maybe. Probably. Suspicion feeding on probability. Suspicion growing against you. Suspicion growing inside you. Stop looking at me like that! Elbans all over the island waking up from dreams about the investor from America, telling their dreams to their friends, shaping the dreams into evidence.

Everywhere he went, people were whispering. That's him, that's the one. Signor Americano. Pss, ssss, wind in the pineta, surf against the rocks. Suspicion generated by the need to tell the perfect story. Testimony rendered secondary by the powerful shock of logic. The truth brought to light. It couldn't have happened any other way, of course. Of course.

And did you see the way Lidia looked at him? Why did she bother to keep working for his family? Because she needed the money. Why did Francesca smile so sweetly? Because she was afraid of Murray. The investor from America was a monster. Everybody knew what he'd done.

Psss, over there. That's him.

Signor Americano, wait! No, he wouldn't wait. He would run. If he kept running maybe they'd tire of the chase and give up.

Did you do it, Murray? Tell the truth. What is the truth? Like everyone else, he wouldn't know until Adriana had been found.

The contagion of dreams passed from neighbor to neighbor until finally, inevitably, it reached the Murdoch's villa. Murray Murdoch watched his wife toss and turn in her sleep. He heard her moan and grind her teeth. He caught her when she sat bolt upright.

"It was just a dream, Claire." Never say *just*, Murray. You should know better.

He didn't ask, and she didn't offer to tell him, what the dream was about. They both only pretended to go back to sleep. They lay awake, side by side, until dawn brightened the room and Lidia arrived with the coffee and frothy warm milk. Claire read a book as she sipped her coffee. Murray read last week's *Herald Tribune* only up to the second page, where there was an article about an explosion in Palermo. A car loaded with dynamite. Three bystanders killed, including a young boy.

Signor Americano needed a drink. He drank wine at lunch, but by late afternoon he wanted a tall bourbon on ice. Another one, prego. Another one.

"Murray, you're drinking too much."

"You always say that, Claire."

"I haven't said it since we left New York."

"You haven't needed to say it. You've thought it. I can always tell when you're thinking it."

"Does it bother you to hear it said aloud? You're drinking too much."

"So I'm drinking too much. What else? Smoking too much. Spending too much money. What else?"

"That's enough, Murray."

"Messing around with young girls. Is that what you were dreaming about last night, Claire? Me doing it with the Nardi girl?"

"I don't want to have this conversation."

"Why not? Because you don't want to know what really happened?"

"I already know what happened."

"Maybe there's more to tell."

"Like what?"

"Like about how I strangled the Nardi girl with my belt. And carried her body all the way to Cavo in a potato sack tied to my bike. And threw her off the cliff there."

"Nope. You hadn't mentioned that. Murray, if I were you I'd make that drink my last and go to bed. I'm going to bed. Goodnight, my dear. Don't stay up late. You could use a good night's rest."

Murray Murdoch loved his wife. And he loved his boys, he really did. He could prove his love by leaving them, sparing them humiliation. And at the same time he could make up for his earlier cowardice, offering himself as sacrifice. He imagined closing the door behind him and standing with his back to the villa, facing the angry mob. I'm the one you want. At least he'd die with the knowledge of his heroism. Instead, he had nothing better to do than finish the bourbon and try to keep his mind from wandering.

Focus, Murray. It might help to stand, stretch, look at yourself in the mirror. Notice how your reflection is just as distant from the mirror on the farther side as you are distant on this side.

But what about . . .

Don't think it, Murray.

Claire's dream last night?

Consider, Murray, how when light passes through a surface, rays are refracted at different angles of incidence, depending upon the medium.

What did Claire dream?

Think about light, Murray. The fact of an image. These are your own hands you're holding in front of you. The hands of Malcolm Averil Murdoch — lacking the luminosity of gemstones, lacking the beauty of tourmaline.

What happened to Adriana?

Think about something else, Murray.

He could use a drink, but the bottle was empty. Wine, then. There was no wine. Then he'd finish the grappa. Go ahead. Just a swallow left. Not enough to keep him focused, but enough to unbalance him. He teetered, rocked back on his heels, forward on his toes, and would have fallen against the glass if Nat hadn't appeared in the corner of the mirror holding an empty cup.

"Water," he said.

Murray put one hand on a chair back to balance himself. He went into the kitchen and poured Nat a glass of water from a pitcher. Murray let Nat sit on his lap while he sipped the water. They sat a long time together. Nat smelled the odors of Murray's skin, his sugary aftershave, his liquor. Eventually Nat finished the water in a gulp, and Murray carried him back to bed.

But Nat wondered why his father had been staring into the mirror in the living room. What was so interesting about a mirror? Nat went to see for himself. Murray was already stretched on the sofa again, his eyes closed. Nat positioned himself in front of the mirror and stared at his reflection. Bored with what he saw, he stretched his lips wide with his fingers and stuck out his tongue. That was better. He curled his upper eyelids inside out. There — that was even better. He made a fish face. He pushed up his nose to make a pig snout.

With the mirror on the wall adjacent to the entrance hall and the sofa against the perpendicular wall, Murray was not within the mirror's range, so Nat couldn't see him.

"Nat, go to bed. Nat! Nat, cut it out. I'm telling you to go to bed. Nat, I'm gonna be mad soon. Very soon. Nat! Nat?"

Nat the aardvark. Nat the platypus. Nat the vampire. Nat the wooden soldier. March in place, soldier! March march march march.

"Nat, honey, can't you hear me?"

If Nat opened his mouth very wide, maybe he could see all the way to his stomach. He tried. What was that hanging from the roof of his mouth? It was a tiny baby bat!

"I'm talking to you, Nathaniel. Nat, goddamn it!"

Understanding came to our father neither as a blast of awareness nor in increments. It came to him as subdued recognition, as though he'd already known what he was realizing for the first time. His son couldn't hear him. With everything else in Murray's life held in suspension, this was something irrefutable. Nathaniel couldn't hear. Of course he couldn't hear. Murray already knew this, had known without knowing that he knew it. Nat was deaf. Murray's son had been ill, and now he was deaf.

"Nat." Murray had crossed the room and was about to touch his shoulder when Nat whirled around.

"I'm not sleepy."

Murray turned his head so his son wouldn't be able to see his face. "How old are you, Nat?"

"I don't want to go to bed."

"Knock-knock. I said, knock-knock. Say *who's there*. Nat, it's your turn."

"What?"

"Forget it. Go to bed."

"What?"

"It's the middle of the night. Go to bed."

"What?"

"Bed. Go. To. Bed. Vai!"

You thought you could keep it a secret, Nat. Well, your old dad has found you out. You can't hear, can you? Can you? Nat!

"Nat!" He watched Nat shuffle down the hall in Harry's old pajamas, the pants long enough to drape over his toes. "Why didn't you tell us, Nat? We could have helped." Without answering, Nat turned the corner into his bedroom. Murray stared down the empty hall in hopes that Nat would pop out from the room and say, Fooled ya!

Nat, you little imp.

But Nat had already gone back to bed.

Murray took one last look in the mirror, tightened his tie, and left the villa through the front door. He considered only as an afterthought how the left hand becomes the right hand in a mirror reflection.

Signor Americano set out walking. There were no stars out, and the cloud bed was smoky gray and swallowed the top of the mountains. The breeze carried the puckering fragrance of grapes. A quick rainstorm had passed through an hour earlier, and the ground, dry for months, was springy.

Signor Americano was going away. Somewhere. Nowhere. Direction contingent upon absence. Our father had no particular route in mind. He just wanted to get away. Go on, Dad, we won't mind. Just be back by morning, okay? But how could he go back to the mess he'd left behind? A man decides to walk away from his family — one step after the other. His value contingent upon nothing, scarcity being the measure of worth. Signor Americano would make himself scarce for his family's sake. And go where? Home? Home was bankruptcy — money increasing in worth with rarity. Home was the Averils and humiliation. Home was the past, the absence of the here and now.

If not home, then . . .

Croaking and chirping of frogs from the marsh below the verge. Accordion music of a cuckoo. Signor Americano could sing as loud as he pleased and no one would hear him. In this sense Nat's deafness was inconsequential. A change in the weather . . . The value of song contingent upon the absence of an audience . . . A change of heart . . .

He wasn't crazy. He was just drunk. Not so drunk that he was seeing pink elephants, but drunk enough to believe he was doing the right thing by going away. He imagined running his finger lightly over the slope of Claire's nose, kissing her on the cheek, soothing her when she woke with a start. It's okay, Claire. I just wanted to tell you I'm leaving for a while. I'll be home in a few days. Don't worry about me. Take care of yourself and the boys. Good-bye. I love you. Love contingent upon absence. He kept forgetting how much he did love her. And now, remembering. His innocence and stupidity. Not unlike Orson Welles in *The Lady from Shanghai*. It's easy. You just pull the trigger.

He continued down the road toward Marciana Marina and from there picked up the coastal road. Outside of Procchio a truck full of fishermen rattled past, and one of the fishermen called, "Salve, Signore!" He waved back to show that he wasn't afraid. The truck slowed, stopped, moved in reverse. He remembered only then that he'd forgotten his hat. The fishermen offered him a lift to Portoferraio. He accepted and climbed up into the bed of the truck. He rode in silence while the fishermen sang melancholy songs.

In Portoferraio he wandered through the streets that were brightening with dawn and finally found the lane leading up the east slope of the hill toward Fort Stella. He was tired. He was still drunk and wanted to be drunker. And he could think of nothing better to do than to go and find someone who considered him a scoundrel, pound on his door until he answered, and stumble into the hovel of a flat shouting, "Tell me something! Anything! Tell me about Napoleon!"

Francis Cape, dressed in a tattered blue-and-white-striped

nightshirt, his white hair almost fluorescent in the dim light, held the door open. Murray stood in the center of the room. Francis asked him to leave. Wait — Murray wanted to hear about Napoleon. Was it true that during the year he was king of Elba, Napoleon passed a law to make his birthday a public holiday?

"You're intoxicated."

Signor Americano wasn't intoxicated enough.

"Won't you offer me refreshment?"

"I'm showing you the door."

"Yes. A door. That's a door. I know what a door is. This is a floor. That's a ceiling. What else do you want to show me?"

"Get out of here."

Francis might have been an old man, but he wasn't old enough to be exempt from human courtesy. Malcolm Murdoch would teach him a lesson. You're showing me a door. I'm showing you a man, Mr. Cape. Murray sat in the only chair in the room, an armchair with maroon upholstery as tattered as Francis's nightshirt, and folded his arms. I'm showing you human dignity. I'm showing you persistence. Resistance. Revolution. And you're showing me a . . . what is that, Mr. Cape? A butter knife?

"Leave now."

"Golly, Francis. I mean . . ." I'm showing you the reflection of yourself, Francis Cape. Light bouncing off the emotion of hatred to form an image at equal distance from the surface. Francis Cape and Signor Americano being, at that moment, equally ridiculous.

Neither meant to do what he did next: Francis swiping that ridiculous little knife in front of Murray's face, Murray leaping up, throwing a punch aimed at Francis's arm, successfully knocking the knife from his hand and sending it clattering across the floor, then continuing the motion, his fist cutting upward at an angle to bang against Francis's sternum. The old man so feeble that the thump sent him stumbling, and he tripped over his feet and fell, landing splat on his backside, where he sat with his legs stretched out in front of him, his white knobby knees bare below the hem of his nightshirt, the look on his face so comical that Murray couldn't help but laugh.

Francis looked up at Murray in confusion. Murray tried to shake away hilarity.

"Christ, I'm sorry, Francis. I shouldn't laugh."

Francis looked from Murray to the open doorway, from the open doorway to the ceiling, from the ceiling back to Murray. His expression hardened into accusation.

"Are you hurt? Here, let me help you up."

Francis used the fringed arm of the chair to pull himself up. The white pallor of his face had darkened to a sickly gray. He moved backward a step, wobbled, but remained standing. With stoical control that had a vaguely fatigued quality to it, as if he'd rehearsed the scene too many times, he rested his hand on his chest and said, "Get out of here."

"You're not hurt, are you?"

"Get out of here at once. Leave, I tell you, and don't come back."

An elderly scholar with an aching chest. An American investor in the middle of his life. As Murray rushed down the dark cement stairs of the building, he said to himself what he would have liked to say aloud: Francis Cape, you don't know how lucky you are.

Murray headed back the way he had come beneath a sky that was the color of Francis Cape's face. On the outskirts of Portoferraio, he boarded an empty bus. As far as he could tell, the bus was traveling south from Portoferraio. Somewhere in the hills between Portoferraio and Marina di Campo, he got off the bus and wandered up an unpaved cart road. He followed this past a shuttered farmhouse and continued along a footpath that cut through a barley field. The path ended, but he kept walking. In case anyone was watching, he walked in big bold strides, crushing the flower clusters beneath his shoes to suggest an urgent purpose.

He came to a gully and followed the edge to the bottom of a hill. He climbed through an olive grove, up the hill, and picked a single unripe olive. He gnawed it and spit out the bitter flesh and continued to suck on the pit. He saw a donkey standing in the dappled light beneath the branches of the biggest olive tree in the grove, its hide shivering over its barreled ribs, its ears scissoring angrily against a swarm of gnats. When Murray clucked, the donkey trotted farther away. Murray cupped his hands together as though cradling oats, and the donkey took a few lazy steps toward him and sniffed the air. Murray approached slowly. The donkey waited for him and nudged Murray's hands apart with its nose. But the animal had no reaction to the deception. It stood patiently while Murray climbed onto its back. Murray gave a good kick, and the donkey squealed, flared its nostrils, but wouldn't budge. "Yah, yah, andiamo!" The donkey flicked its ears angrily, took a step forward, and then paused to drop a little pile of manure.

Was that really you, Dad? Our father, Signor Americano. See what he did when he found himself in a pickle? He mounted an ass! The action relieving him, temporarily, of the awareness of his difficulties. Combine a donkey, mist, the smell of wild mint and thyme, maybe add the chime of a monastery's bells in the distance, and you'll have an experience that doesn't match up with reality as you thought you knew it.

But the donkey wouldn't take another step in any direction, so Murray climbed off. He slapped the beast's rump, sending it at a trot down the hill. Murray followed the grass path in the other direction, zigzagging across the terraces uphill toward Orello and Barbatoia, up into the region hidden by the mist, where the cultivated land gave way to barren outcrops, to eroded lava flows, to buttes and cones and ancient volcanic plugs. A region where a prospector belongs, the place where Malcolm Murdoch should have headed long ago.

There's no logic to the distribution of minerals, is there, Murray? The "perplexing irregularity in the outer crust of the earth" is how one geologist has described it. The best a prospector can do is to begin looking in an area where the rugged surface is bare of soil, the heart of rock exposed. Look, Murray. Keep your eyes open. As you walk along up into the mountains of Elba, look down at the ground for the shine of a lustrous surface, the glint of color.

He wasn't drunk anymore; he was crazy. Not so crazy that his imagination completely controlled his perception but crazy enough to make the deliberate choice to ignore the facts of his situation. He was hungry. He wanted meat. A good bloody piece of Angus covered with A.1 sauce. A baked potato smothered in sour cream. Green-bean casserole, the kind Claire made using frozen beans and canned onions.

He needed a bath. His head ached. He owned a worthless plot of land. He was a thirty-eight-year-old Caucasian American man who'd taken his four young children and his wife on an extended vacation. He was a brother. He was a cousin, a son, an heir. He was, unfairly, the object of suspicion. But he could no longer pretend that he hadn't done anything wrong.

He climbed further into the mountains, scraping the heels of his palms on the steep craggy slopes. He climbed to the plateau where the gods were sleeping after one of their long nights of carousing. He climbed past their marble temple. He climbed through the clouds. And there it was, high up on the mountainside close to the summit: a door cut into a scar of bare rock and a stony gallery leading deep into the heart of the earth.

Signor Americano leaned back against an outcrop of limestone and lit a cigarette. He told himself he didn't have to rush into the cave. He could take his time about it. He needed to collect his thoughts, make a plan. Hesitation uncharacteristic for this impulsive man. But he was on the brink of something big, wasn't he?

The earth inviting him to come under the surface and have a look around, at no expense.

He smoked slowly, thoughtfully. Hesitation the perfect state for him right now. Holding himself in suspense in front of the mouth of the cave. Discovery ready to swallow him up.

Javan, the son of Japheth, stubbing his toe against a lump of Cyprus copper. The glint of silver in a campfire in El Rosario. Gold in the sand on Douglas Island. Vanadium in the asphalt of Peru. The history of discovery a history of fortunate coincidences — and failures. "Because the goldesmithes and goldefyners of London and many other namyd counynge menn had made many prooffes of the ewer and could fynde noe whitt of goold therein." Frobisher, with his *Meta Incognita.* You know what they say: the chieftain was covered with mud and then dusted with powdered gold blown through tubes. The gilded king. Where is he? Somewhere in the mysterious wilderness, floating on a golden raft across a sacred lake. And suddenly his wife appears.

Hello, Claire.

Murray, look at you!

Do you like me this way?

You're . . . you're . . .

Yes?

Amazing! Beautiful! I can't believe it! Like she'd really say this. Claire always the one anchoring him to responsibility. Don't touch me, not until you take a bath, Murray.

Seriously. Let's back up, Dad. Tell us about Claire when you first met her. Following her from a party, watching her walking along Central Park West in the rain in her bare feet, holding in one hand high-heeled shoes that belonged to a friend and were too small for her. Claire, your boss's secretary. Shall I carry you? The way curiosity flares into hope, is dimmed by restraint, is relit, is confirmed. Married in City Hall to avoid the Averils. Time measured by the establishment of new routines — Friday's dinner, the weekend ahead, Sunday morning in the apartment, sunlight, sheets bunched at the foot of the mattress, haphazard toss of pillows, pulp of fresh orange juice, a paragraph from a newspaper article read aloud. The two of you. Then three, four, five, six plus a cat.

And then, on a lark, the island of Elba. What went wrong? The simple act of leaving home creating the possibility of leaving the past behind.

Up and down and quick, up again, and "I see stars," as the expression goes. But they don't look like stars. They look like fragments of diamonds drifting in clear liquid around my head. My back to the darkness of the cave. In front of me, the mountains making a bowl filled with daylight, the mist lifting, dispersing like steam from soup. Did I really ride a donkey this morning? Why? Why do I do anything?

I was a boy once, too. Hard to believe, eh? Your dad in pinstriped shorts held up by suspenders, sneaking off to school with a live mouse in his pocket! Four cats against a little mouse outside the 89th Street stable. Some images survive time completely intact: that little mouse cowering against the doorjamb and four scrawny cats pawing and pacing with devilish languor, stretching out the torment for as long as they could. Sorry to disappoint you, kitties. I caught the mouse by its tail. Monsieur Petit, I called him, with some pretension, for I was learning French. Turned out Monsieur was a Madame, and three days later my mother found seven little pink worms in my sweater drawer. The only time I ever heard her shriek.

My mother. My father. My wife. My children. The pronoun a convenient reduction of personal history. Your father. Your husband. Your son. Oh to have been in Bisbee in January of 1881, receiving a short option of one million dollars for the Copper Queen Mine. Our family suffering from what an uncle on the Murdoch side called congenital greed. Sires training their offspring to want what had been missed, overlooked, and lost, generation after generation. You'll see how it happens. First you laugh at your parents. Their ridiculous habits and hopes. Then you learn to want what they had. Then you learn to want what they wanted and didn't have. And then, after a series of misunderstandings, you leave the island and go home.

I am Malcolm Averil Murdoch. Did you know I am naturally left-handed but was forced to use my right hand in early grades? What else would you like to know about me? Here I sit, my back to a cave, my face to the sun, having reached the peak of indecision. What next? Trapped by an impressive record of misjudgments. Oh for the ease of Catholic absolution. Or the carefreeness of the Epicureans. But remember where Dante puts Epicure! I'd rather be —

Myself as I'd planned to be when I was a young boy looking forward. Instead I'm the ass riding the ass. Deterioration provoked by stupidity. The way the lungs turn black and calcareous, like the inside of a cave, from cigarette smoke.

What had he done? Excluding the last six hours or so, he hadn't done much. Misty island of misty dreams. What happened? Signor Americano couldn't say exactly. So why did he hit a feeble old man? Good question.

It wasn't an accident, was it, Dad?

No.

Your one decisive action since we left America. You went to see Francis Cape with the intention of hurting him.

Yes.

Why?

Consider the life of a rock.

Cut it out, Dad.

Sediment compressed to form sedimentary rock. Sedimentary rock heated to form liquid magma. Magma blown to the earth's surface, cooling to form igneous rocks. Igneous intrusion causing contact metamorphism. Igneous and metamorphic rocks eroded into sediment. Buried sediment compressed into rock. I'd put myself at the igneous / metamorphic stage. More igneous than metamorphic. A crusty, coarse-grained piece of gabbro.

Say what you mean, Dad.

Compare minerals to rocks. It's not their luster, their rarity, their hardness that makes them desirable. It's their chemical composition. They are what they are, unlike most everything else in the world. Why is a diamond the most valuable gem? Because it has the simplest chemical composition. Diamond equals C. Not much in the world is as simple. And now you can see my fundamental mistake. I thought tourmaline would prove my worth. What's tourmaline? Tourmaline is a mix of boric oxide, silica, water, iron, etcetera, etcetera. The chemical composition of tourmaline is longer than the alphabet. What's tourmaline? Everything and nothing. Tourmaline is what a man looks for when he doesn't know what he's looking for.

In fact, you didn't think any of this, did you, Dad? And you never got further than the mouth of the cave. For all I know, there was no cave. What you found might have been no more than a shallow gouge in the limestone outcrop. You didn't even bother to look around your feet for the broken shards of tourmaline that would have indicated a rich vein nearby.

You smoked a cigarette. Maybe you smoked another cigarette. You watched the day grow brighter. You fell asleep and slept for a few hours. You slept so soundly you didn't feel the gecko scuttle across the back of your hand on its way to a patch of sun-warmed rock.

Our dad, Signor Americano. Moses on the mountain. Jeremiah in the wilderness. Your one opportunity for discovery, and you slept through it.

When he woke the sun was already in the west, the air was dry, and he had to piss. He pissed into the mouth of the cave, and he headed down the mountain, intending to go right home.

But you didn't come right home — remember?

The walk was long, so he stopped in La Pila for a bite to eat and a glass of wine, and he got to talking with the barista, who didn't speak a lick of English. In his own poor Italian, Murray introduced himself, watching the man carefully to see what effect his name had. The barista had never heard of our father. Was that possible? He returned Murray's stare with frank curiosity. Murray told him he owned land in the Mezza Luna region. The man had never heard of Mezza Luna. Murray began to explain. The man interrupted, rattling something Murray didn't understand, and motioned to the kitchen. He disappeared for a moment and returned with a liter of wine. They drank together for a few hours.

Anonymity as unexpected as it was welcome. Murray had finally found his refuge in a little bar in La Pila. He asked the barista if he knew of a pensione nearby, and the man offered him the back room of the bar, a little room with a single cot, a curtained window looking out into a dark pantry, crates filled with onions and potatoes stacked against the wall.

So that's where you were.

Drinking some. Sleeping. Smoking. At Murray's insistence, the owner and his wife put him to work in the afternoon chopping vegetables. They ate all their meals together. They took great delight in watching our father drink. Ancora, ancora. There was no malice in them. What they saw was the gradual animation of a dreary Americano. He drank steadily from pranzo on. His host and hostess drank, too, both of them, not just wine but Amora and grappa and even rum. Yet as far as Murray could tell, they didn't suffer any effects from the liquor.

He slept deeply, but only for a few hours at a time. He'd wake, confused, in the middle of the night. The room absolutely lightless. Yet somehow he'd managed to continue to lie quietly in his bed.

Tick tock tick. Signor Americano was alone. He'd never really been alone before. Oh, he'd been by himself, but not alone like this. Discovery no longer an attraction. Only trying to subdue panic. Using thought to try not to think. Then your hand happens to brush against the velvet skin of a peach that your host offered you after dinner. A little orange peach you left on a saucer. And the next thing you know you are remembering the tiny velvet bear your oldest son kept on his bedside table when he was younger and you were still in the apartment on East 74th. A little brown bear, with nose and eyes and eyebrows inked in black. Patrick's glasses cradling the water glass. Harry still in a crib. The smell of a baby's scalp. Another son. As many as possible. This was back in the days when fathers would chew on unlit cigars in the hospital lounge while waiting for their children to be born. Your own father dead from heart failure when you were six. Buried in the cemetery in Queens. You don't even remember the funeral.

Darkness itself the cramping factor. You'd rather be sleeping than thinking, but oh the way the mind works. Thinking about what happens when you stop thinking.

Which of your sons started crying in the middle of the night because he was afraid of dying? Barely able to put words into a whole sentence, and he was fretting about metaphysics. Whatever. Nothing to say other than offering the hypothesis of Father, Son, and Holy Ghost. Let's consider the proposition of divinity. Who is God, Daddy? How should I know?

The proposition of heaven and hell. Life directed toward judgment. Don't you believe it. Hell no more than hatred of the dead. That's your punishment, in varying degrees. Devils stoking the fires of memory. What you did. And what you didn't do. You being the sort who always meant well. Claire knew it, didn't she? She knew you better than you knew you. Our father the prospector. You wanted to give us a future. A father's effort to secure a place in the paradise of memory. A life judged by its life in the memories of others. The salvation of eulogy. The dishonest pabulum of respect.

He wanted needed loved his wife and children. So why at every turn did he succeed in messing up their lives? The stupidity of ambition. There's gold in them thar hills! Come on, boys. Claire, I promise, you won't regret it. Me. Your willingness. The warmth of your body returning life to me in the dark hours of the night. How can anybody ever sleep alone? I am scared, Claire. What good does it do to think it? Or even to say it aloud. I am scared. Don't even remember my own father's funeral. If a tree falls in the forest. Failure written in stone. Destined to end with my pockets full of gabbro. Not a glimmer of tourmaline in sight.

We went to look for buried treasure. Our father's script for success a mishmash of fantasy and jest and showmanship. The prospector's doomed effort to prove the validity of his wild guess. One version among many of ambition. Bolstered by his family. The prop of us. Following one little crack in the foundation, the slow collapse. Not even a chance of finding what he was looking for. Scripted failure. Marked by destiny to be a man whose most useful function would be as a contrary example — a warning to others. Look what happened to Murray Murdoch, who hauled us all to Elba for no good reason.

Where is Elba?

I told you I don't know!

Darkness like the darkness of an unlit room seen at noon from across a street, across a yard, across a piazza. Darkness like the bottom of a well. Darkness flattened by distance. A dark so dark that it had no dimension. This was the dark in which our father lay, thinking.

Musty, earthy smell of potatoes. Velvet skin of a peach. I am underground. Hello! Can't anyone hear me? Enormous pressure developed gradually on the hanging wall. Surviving pillars gave way. Sudden propulsion of air shaking the whole tunnel. Excavated to a maximum depth of 200 feet. I am alone. He is alone. My brother. My mother. My wife. My sons. He couldn't even remember his father's funeral, though the many funerals he'd attended since then all felt like repetitions.

My turn. His turn. How do I want you to remember me? How do you want us to remember you? Monsieur Petit in your pocket. Your hat cocked at an angle. Clocking our sprints with the second hand of your wristwatch. Napping on the couch on Saturday after-noon. Mowing the lawn. Riding a motorcycle. Our father, Signor Americano. Too late. You are what you were, and now you're stuck in a little room in a little village on a little island, it's the middle of the night, and no one can hear you calling for help.

He fell asleep at last, woke at dawn, slept some more, and woke again shortly before noon. He ate bread soaked in olive oil, he chopped vegetables, drank wine, played cards with the owner and his wife. How could they possibly make a living from this bar with so few customers? our father began to wonder. And then on Friday afternoon the bar filled with men — young men smoking hand-rolled cigarettes, old men playing rapid hands of a kind of poker Murray had never seen before.

The owner introduced him as Signor Murdee. Signor Ameri-cano, sono io. Not a single man in the crowd of two dozen knew him or recognized his name. "Sono Malcolm Murdoch." Shrugs of "Piacere." He was the most infamous man on Elba, and they knew nothing about him. How was it possible?

Anything's possible on this island of dreams. When Napoleon wandered the island, he was sometimes mistaken for a common soldier. Now Signor Americano was being mistaken for an ordi-nary tourist. Possibly, he'd found a hamlet so isolated that the people here hadn't heard the rumors. Or possibly — time to con-sider this, Murray — there were no more rumors to hear.

Non ho capito.

Suspicion rises like steam from water as the air cools at night. And then disperses. Without evidence, suspicion always disperses. Murray, those dreams Francis Cape was telling you about — he wasn't making them up. Those dreams were being dreamt, told and retold, measured and compared. But for weeks, new dreams had been dreamt, dreams that had nothing to do with either you or the missing Nardi girl, dreams that weren't worth retelling. You were being forgotten.

There were grapes that needed to be picked. Figs, oranges, apples, lemons, pomegranates. Let's taste the Sangiovese, peel the chestnuts, fry the squid. Ciao, Alberto, come stai? Did you hear? Elena, the one who played the girl at this summer's festival in Capoliveri — why, she's marrying Marco, who played Barbarossa. Elena e Barbarossa si sposano!

Music, laughter, a machine spitting caffè. Wait — sono Signor Murdoch. I'm the one people are talking about. Cosa? You know — the American who can tell you what happened to the Nardi girl.

They didn't care what he wanted to tell them. But if he was willing to stake cento lire on the first game, he was welcome to play.

He ate spaghetti with them. He played cards. He laughed when they laughed, though he understood next to nothing of their jokes. He was the stranger, the foreigner, as exotic as the dollar bill he passed around. He'd come all the way from New York to play cards with them, and they were grateful.

He lost the dollar, along with the rest of his money, within three hands. He borrowed money from the barista. He played another hand and won — a sign that his luck was changing. Here he was, no longer a presence provoking whispers. His innocence accepted as a fact. His past a story too dull to tell.

He'd play one more hand and go home. But they didn't want him to go. Look at the rain, Signor Murdee. A deluge. Guarda. They opened the door to show him the rain spilling in a beaded curtain from the overhang.

All right, he'd stay. Bravissimo!

They sang, smoked, played cards. More men arrived. They stamped their feet dry on the boards, shook water from their hats. Antonio! Leopoldo! Massimo! Arnoldo! Tell us, who had the foresight to begin picking in time to finish before the storm? Who will make the best Aleatico this year? Who has a vat to loan Roberto?

They all had to crowd in the doorway to see Paolo's new motorcycle. And then they needed the warmth of grappa, more conversation, volley of jokes, and news of the world, courtesy of a one-legged, gray-haired man named Ricardo, who hobbled into the bar on his crutch just as some of the men were preparing to leave.

Come va, Riccardo? Clatter of talk, clatter of nonsense. The men who had put on their coats took them off again to trade news about weather, thefts, accidents. Murray gave up trying to understand what was being said and didn't hear Riccardo report that an old Englishman had been found dead in his room in Portoferraio. Apparently he'd been dead for a few days.

An Englishman. Molto vecchio. Did Signor Murdee know of him?

What?

Antonio rattled a version of what Roberto had reported. There were only a few words that Murray understood, words such as inglese, professore, solitario, vecchio, and morto. But they were enough to draw a nod of dumb comprehension that continued even while the other men genuflected for all the anonymous dead of the world and then pressed on through other news — the price of tuna going up, the price of swordfish going down, and a new hotel being built in the hills above Procchio.

Spodumene, iolite, benitoite. Euclase, phenakite, enstatite. Oh give me some sphene, Gene. A little dioptase in your coffee? How about some fibrolite on your scapolite, Willemite?

It is evidently desirable that you should be able to resist the chemical actions of everyday life. Having failed to. You demantoid, you. Mister Malcolm Averil Murdokite, specific gravity 3.10, strongly dichroic. What do you have to say for yourself?

Um. Did I ever tell you about the time I was walking along East 29th in Manhattan and a woman ran up to me, thrust a package into my hands, and ran on? A man in a dirty apron ran after her, past me. The package. Raw sirloin inside the wax paper. Me and Claire cooked and ate it for dinner. And the time Patrick, just learning to talk, called a man on a bus a boll weevil. C-A-T spells cat. Where did you learn boll weevil, kiddo?

Make like a frog, Granma. Why? Because Daddy says when you croak we'll go to Florida. Ain't he a darlin'? Claire, will you watch the kids for a while? I'm going to mine for tourmaline. I guess I forgot to mention that I've always wanted to try my hand at mining. That and earn enough money so I have plenty to give away. None of which.

Unknown to the world at large, the industrial manufacture of precious stones. Man's restless efforts to bridle nature. Unrighteous products of alchemists. Murray Murdokite should have been an alchemist. He and Faust. Homemade sapphires. There's no limit to delight, ladies and gentlemen, with the purchase of my little machine here.

In 1837, Gaudin produced a few flakes of crystallized corundum. In 1877, Fremy and Feil lined a crucible with homemade flakes of ruby. In 1904, Verneuil and his blowpipe. Oxygen admitted at C, passing through the tube, E, E terminating at D. *Tap tap tap* goes the hammer, A, onto disc B. Coal gas plus oxygen in a blowpipe equals a beautiful pear-shaped crystalline alumina. If only you'd gambled on manufacturing instead of nature, Murray. Now look at you. The reflection your inversion.

Never caring that he never had a chance to:
1) Wade through high water at night in Venice. The challenge of figuring out where the flooded street ended and the canal began.
2) Run for office.
3) Witness the birth of a child.
4) Witness the slaughter of a lamb.
5) Talk with us. To us. You never really talked to us, Dad. Other fathers. Oh, forget it.

Here I sit, imagining you as you were before I remember you. The melting of sedimentary rock into magma. Once a man looking forward. Afterward, a man looking back. Every investment a mistake. Every casual gesture a provocation. Your habit of looking for friends in the wrong places. One thing leading to another, and the next thing you know a girl is missing, your son is deaf, and il professore è morto, flattened by a punch meant to deflect a butter knife. Then and then.

A nun inside her cloister for seventy years. Bliss of faith. Compare her to, say, Nietzsche, and his ascetic ideal derived from a degenerating life. What's the point of thought? Dad wondered, walking along a road in the rain at night. And for that matter who decided for us that cut stones are more beautiful than stones broken through some convulsion in the earth's crust, roughened by attrition, carved by solvents?

There he goes, walking away from La Pila toward wherever. Drunk again. Geez. Don't you know when to stop!

How dare you.

I'm just pretending, Dad. A little game I'm playing here on the page. My review, having watched the video of your life. The night we almost lost you forever. At last, having reached the place you'd been heading toward and having found what you were looking for. The transformation complete.

You have no idea, Ollie.

No more than scraps of possibilities. It's possible, Dad, that the thought of Nietzsche crossed your mind when you were heading away from La Pila after learning about the death of Francis Cape. It's also possible that you were exercising your mind, trying to remember a long sequence of numbers, moving backward from the end. Flexing your corrugator supercilii. Or maybe you were thinking about Giorgione's *Three Ages of Man*.

You will never know.

And so I am forced to make an educated guess, Dad. You. He. Thinking about that sweet little natal cleft between his wife's buttocks.

Stop it, Ollie.

Walking at night through the rain. Like any man upon realizing that he will never be innocent. Programmed to generate the events that would result in this state of mind. Setting off for Elba in order to become what you became. Our father, Signor Americano. Walking. Releasing himself to madness. Howl, spit, eek, suffamoaninacheron. Who out there wants to go mad with me?

Voices.

I wasn't hearing voices, Ollie.

Skin pricked by the nibs of invisible quills.

Not that, either. I walked. That's all. No thunder, no lightning.

Just walking along. The rain letting up. The rising moon glowing behind a silky mist. He was just walking along. A little more than a year after arriving on the island. Shrug. Nothing much to say about it. Shrug. Doesn't it feel good to shrug? A gentle tightening of the trapezius. Oh, there was that thing with the Nardi girl. Didn't amount to much. Shrug. Some money he owed — shrug. That bout of fever. His son having trouble hearing. They'd take him to the doctor tomorrow. Shrug. And the old man they'd known — Francis Cape. Heard he'd passed away a few days ago. Rest in peace. Shrug. That's all. A short history of Nietzsche's sickened soul.

Listen to the gods. Their catcalls.

That's me whistling. Shrug.

As though nothing had happened.

Nothing out of the ordinary scheme of things.

You being an ordinary man who once upon a time wanted to be more than you were. The prompt of your ambition. Before Elba, you were the one who rounded us up and ordered us to live, live well! Show me what you're made of! On your mark, get set, go!

You see, it's not my fault I use too many exclamation points. My tendency for exaggeration a gift from my father. He was like so many others — men and women who, in resigning themselves to their fate, must forfeit their spirited ingenuity and become ordinary. Not even madness to enliven their story. They are the ones left out of history, the explorers, inventors, artists, teachers, doctors, electricians, ophthalmologists, chimney sweeps and plumbers, bus drivers and farmers and lab assistants, etcetera, etcetera, who set out to accomplish something extraordinary, and after a series of setbacks just gave up.

You can write whatever you please, Ollie. But if you publish it, I'll —

Our father, Signor Americano.

You'll never know what happened to me that night.

Holding yourself responsible for everything else. And now for the death of an old man.

Do this, Ollie. Cup your hands over your ears. Close your eyes. Imagine a girl's muffled sob.

I did. And then a car backfired on the street below, and I blinked and saw a flock of pigeons rise and curl, silver swirl tilting into a white arc around a tree.

Always the interruption of the world. Proof that no matter how hard you try, you will never be able to imagine your way into my mind.

Night. Fog. And out of nowhere, the snuffle of a girl. A girl crying softly to herself. Hidden amidst the stalks of barley. In the gorge. Behind an empty military redoubt. Behind the crumbling stone wall. Between two rocks. Her face bruised, her lips bloody. Signorina, where are you? Where? Sweet child. I'll find you. Are you there? Where? A wayward girl is easy to charm, to use, to beat and leave for dead. That old tale. If only you'd cry out, I could find you. The gray darkness of a misty midnight on the island of Elba, and somewhere in the mud, an injured girl. I'll find you. In the grass. Beneath a bush. If you're not over here, then you're over there. Where? What girl? On a night like this. I must be mistaken. But how could I mistake the unmistakable sound of a girl crying softly in the dark? Me, a father, a husband, a soldier afraid of war. You must be cold, Signorina. Hungry. What good does it do to cry?

Don't cry, Signorina. I'll find you, if you're there to be found. If you're not. But I heard you, I'm sure I heard you. A sound without equivalent. Puff snuffle of a cry. A girl in the night, unable to sustain herself without help. I'll help you. First I have to find you, then I'll help you.

What in the name of God am I —

I'm looking for a girl.

What girl?

How can I answer that until I find her? Signorina, where are you? And when I find her?

I'll take her home.

Where's home?

Puff snuffle. Come on, Signorina. You're here somewhere, I know it. I can feel you in my bones. On my hands and knees in the mud, looking for a girl. A night like this. Sting of nettles. Clothes soaked through. I'll do some good yet. Where are you, Signorina? If the Averils could see me now.

Stop it!

Dad?

Stop it this instant.

Geez, Dad, I'm sorry.

The boundless foolishness of your imagination, Oliver.

That's exactly what I was hoping you'd say.

As if I'd lost my mind.

I'm way off, aren't I? You weren't crawling around on your hands through the mud that night and through the next day looking for an injured girl. Of course you weren't. But what were you doing? What happened? Something happened. I'm trying to understand but am hampered by the boundless foolishness of my imagination. My penchant for exaggeration. The distortions. Unreality a temptation for those of us used to fiction. At least tell me what you were intending, Dad. Tell me the truth. If you tell me, I promise I won't write it down.

Josephine loved Napoleon and was beloved. She pleaded with him, "Dearest, do not forsake me. Recall my skillful conduct during your Egyptian expedition." Still, he divorced her in December of 1809 and a few weeks later asked for the hand of the archduchess of Austria, Marie-Louise.

He met his betrothed on the road to Soissons and introduced himself. Her immediate emotion was plain relief.

"Why, Herr Napoleon, you don't look at all like your portraits!"

He was there at her side while she groaned her way through the difficult birth of their son.

"Emperor," asked the accoucheur, "which life should be sacrificed, in the event such action must be taken?"

"Why, save the mother, of course," said Napoleon. Not because he loved his wife but because he considered it her right to live.

And then the son: voilà, the king of Rome.

And then banishment.

The dust rose behind the wheels of his carriage. Seven hundred infantry and one hundred and fifty cavalry of the imperial guard volunteered to accompany the emperor into exile, along with a ten-man band and fourteen drummers. But where were his wife and son?

Tub-dum, tub-dum. In exchange for his empire, he was given an island. Long live the king of Elba!

The great grand king of Elba. "We will live because it is our right to live, my people! I bid you welcome. Your beautiful island is mine to share, and I will reign justly."

Turning a map of the island on its side so the west coast was at the top, he saw in it the silhouetted bust of a hatless man. Capo Sant'Andrea the brow. Punta del Nasuto — why, the nose, obviously! The long cravat extended between Marmi and Acquabona. And the bulk of the pedestal between Capo della Vita and Punta dei Ripalti. The bust of a king. The land a shadow of himself. His dukedom in a poor isle, and all of us ourselves.

To the captain of the ship that had brought him here he gave a snuff-box with his portrait set in diamonds. To the crew he sent wine and money. He wandered the island, and in three weeks he knew every foot of it. He fortified the garrison at Longone, strengthened watchtowers, disbanded the coast guard and replaced them with his own soldiers.

Meanwhile, the Allies, seeking a comprehensive settlement, gathered in Vienna. Among the group were two emperors, four kings, one queen, two hereditary princes, three grand duchesses, and more than two hundred heads of ducal houses. Balls and banquets were given nightly. There were pantomimes and balloon ascents and a performance of Fidelio conducted by Beethoven himself.

The last great party of the crowned heads of Europe, and Napoleon missed it. He could do no better than build a wooden ballroom in the Piazza d'Armi and entertain the Elbans with fireworks.

The grand king of Elba. This cell's my court. A compact man, impeccably turned out, with nothing much to do.

What time is it?

What time is it now?

Able was I ere I saw Elba. From a hill above Portoferraio, looking up at the peaks of Capanne and Giove, north to the sea, east toward Volterraio, he is reported to have said: "It must be confessed that my island is very small."

Or else, Francis Cape had considered on more than one occasion, he could begin with a description of the Palazzina dei Mulini, with its pinkish-white plaster facade, green shutters, and the long wing extending on the seaward side toward the cliff edge. Napoleon had lived in the cramped, dark rooms on the ground floor and slept on a collapsible bed. Upstairs, prepared for his wife and son should they ever join him, were the brighter, grander apartments, with gilded canopied beds ringed with carved swans and faded drapes bunched with golden tassels.

Or else Francis could begin with the end — Napoleon on his bed at St. Helena, groaning "tête d'armée," his last words before swooning into death.

It must have been then, at his last conscious moment, that Napoleon had recognized the mistake he'd made by leaving Elba. Francis Cape would never leave Elba. He didn't even have the inclination to leave this room he called his home. There was a time when he'd hoped, upon finishing his book, to reward himself by building a modest house of his own, a villetta with a drive flanked with limes and stone pines and a courtyard leading to a garage, behind which would have been the rabbit hutch and a small garden, where he could plant a few vines and olive trees. And keep a tortoise. A villetta with a garden, a garden with a tortoise. That had been his vision of completeness.

But the knowledge that he'd reached the end of his life without either finishing his book on Napoleon or building his house was by no means unendurable. He'd found happiness on Elba. He'd discovered pleasure.

There was one afternoon in particular. Was it April of '52 or '53? Bored with his work, he'd gone to visit Adriana, though they didn't have a lesson scheduled that day. Still, she seemed delighted to see him. Lorenzo had invited Adriana and her mother to come taste his Sangiovese. Signora Nardi had declined. Adriana suggested to Francis that he accompany her in her mother's place.

On a warm spring day in the dusty light in Lorenzo's cantina, he'd watched Lorenzo expertly flick the oil from the top of a demijohn filled with red wine. Six months from vine to glass, six months to the day, Lorenzo insisted, makes for a wine that sings of Earth and Sun.

Salute!

Adriana, her cheeks flushed from the wine, her long dark lashes lowering as she took another sip. The simple, correct pleasure contained in Francis's respectful love. He hadn't wanted anything more than to admire the child and watch her as she grew up.

Just as a father will admire his own daughter, watching from the distance of propriety the slow transformation of the body. Nothing wrong with that, is there?

It hadn't been wrong until Murray Murdoch came along. Americans have a special talent for turning paradise into a wasteland. They drill and pound and blast, ransacking the earth, and then they go away without bothering to clean up the mess. Like Murray had gone away after giving Francis Cape a good whack in the chest.

That was . . . when? Francis had lost track of time. No matter, now that time had lost track of him. Nor did it matter that he hadn't completed his book. Or married. He was, at long last, without regret. It was as if Murray had beaten out the demons that had been assaulting him of late. Francis was at peace. Looking back, he could say with confidence that in the last decade of his life he'd finally learned how to live.

And if everything wasn't as perfect as it had been, eventually it would be. Francis had only to be patient. Napoleon's great fault, it could be said, was not ambition but impatience. Desire lit by the *ticktock* of a pocketwatch. Whatever the king wanted he wanted right away. Not even a year had passed and he set sail on the *Inconstant* for Corsica, the island of his birth, and from there to France and Fontainebleau. And the next thing you know:

The English front in a concave line of columns four deep, pouring forth a ceaseless storm of musketry. The desperate cry of "Sauve qui peut!" drowned out by the explosions. And all the while a little man with a spyglass watching from the heights of La Belle Alliance.

The answer, as Francis Cape could have told Monsieur Bonaparte, was to stay put once you've found paradise. Don't move. Don't even get up out of your seat. With all the contingencies within and without, you don't want to take any chances.

After Murray had left, Francis sank back in his chair, and that's where he stayed. With the chair positioned at an angle so the right arm was adjacent with one edge of the single small table, Francis had only to turn his head slightly to see out the window. Luckily, he'd left one of the shutters open to let in the night breeze, giving him a view of the brightening sky. Unluckily, he hadn't bothered to put up the netting, so a mosquito — one of the wicked Mediterranean *zanzare* that are impossible to trap and kill — flew in and proceeded to torment him by buzzing relentlessly around his ears.

The place on his chest where he'd been hit no longer hurt him. Nothing hurt him anymore. The pink sky, the aroma of caffè drifting up from the bar across the street, the traffic noise increasing as the hours passed — it was all so pleasant. Only the zanzara's zanzaring — *zanzanzanzan* — to bother him. It was the kind of annoyance he'd totally forget once it had passed. *Zanzanzan.* But he could still relish the tranquillity of soul and setting. A kind of nirvana inflected by pride. He was proud of his patience. *Zanzanzanzanzan.* No matter. He could wait. He could wait forever.

Breakfast at ten, dinner at eight. I am a man of plain tastes. I prefer fresh water to coffee, unsalted bread, sauceless meat, boiled peas with no more than a sprinkling of chopped mint. I drink two glasses of Chambertin in the evening. Look at me. I am the general who walked on foot by the side of the sick as we crossed the fierce hot sands from Jaffa to Cairo. And I am the willing sacrifice to the hatred of the enemies of France. May they prove sincere in their declarations and only have aimed at me!

The day, it appeared, would be overcast; the pink was dulling to a creamy gray. But the wind was gentle, the sea calm for the fishermen. Francis Cape went on waiting. After a while he began to ask himself what he was waiting for. Or whom. He would have admitted, if pressed, that he'd grown tired of seeking out others. The company he kept was always the company he earned with the exhausting effort of courtesy. Fortunately he'd made plenty of friends on Elba, and he knew how to make himself useful. It was Francis, remember, who introduced Murray Murdoch to Lorenzo. Wasn't he the one who bridged the divide between locals and *stranieri*? With a foot in both camps, he kept communication open. And when Adriana Nardi had come to him wanting to learn English, he hadn't turned her away.

Good Francis Cape. *Zanzanzanzanzan.* He sensed that his manners were considered by the locals to be old-fashioned. In contrast to most foreigners, he was gracious, respectful, and, above all, patient.

Just look at him. He could wait and wait and wait without complaining. Doing no more than offering to the world the opportunity to come and visit him. Francis Cape was a gentleman. There weren't many gentlemen left. The kind of wars that must be fought in this century had reduced the numbers. In modern war, all actions taken had to be as quick as they were cowardly. But back in the days of Waterloo, battlefields were, on the whole, open and fair, and it paid to be patient. Had Napoleon successfully learned how to be patient, he might have triumphed. Instead it was brave old Blucher, who, after having his horse shot under him, was able to get up, brush himself off, and lead his regiment in such a skillful retreat that Napoleon did not know until noon the next day which way he had taken.

Who were the gentlemen left in the world? Recently, Francis had read in the *Tribune* about a man named David Strangeways. Mr. Strangeways had been in charge of Deception Operations in northern Europe during the war. As one of the leading military strategists in England, he was appointed to command the task force overseeing the nuclear tests at Christmas Island. The good man, absolutely opposed to the bomb, was forced to weigh his conscience against his duty. He refused the appointment, quit the military, and went off to take Holy Orders.

There's a gentleman for you. An oddity, certainly. The appropriately named Mr. Strangeways.

Francis recognized that he himself had been less than a gentleman in recent months. Suspicion does not allow for much gentility. Suspicious of Adriana's involvement with Murray, Francis had been forced to act in ways that could only be described as cowardly.

Yet from this tranquil vantage point, looking back over his life, he could say with confidence that though he'd made mistakes of a moral nature, he'd never done anything terribly wrong. Not like Napoleon, who would have improved his state of mind, along with his eternal prospects, if he'd asked to be forgiven —

For the murder of the youthful d'Enghien: convicted of capital crimes against the Republic, he asked for nothing more than an interview with me. I refused and ordered the prisoner immediately remanded, led to a ditch outside the castle, and shot by a party of elite gendarmes standing on the parapet above him. His body was thrown into a grave without a funeral.

For the murder of the humble Palm, bookseller of Naumburg, convicted of libel after publishing an inciting pamphlet and shot immediately.

For the murder of Stabbs, son of a clergyman. The officers of Pavia. And all the male inhabitants massacred at Lugo.

Even for the murder of the twenty bystanders in the Rue St-Nicaise, who were blown up in my place.

Napoleon, it must be admitted, was a confused man. Had his army been defeated early on, he would have lived to be a gentleman. That's what he'd aspired to when he was a youth on Corsica. But for a powerful man, tyranny will always be easier than gentility.

Francis Cape had never been in a position where he was burdened with great power. At best, he could be described as distinguished. His Elban neighbors called him il professore. He liked the title, even if it wasn't accurate. The only teaching he ever did was of elemental English to a young Italian girl. And really, it must be said that she ended up teaching him far more than he had taught her, though what she'd taught him could not be put into words. What he'd learned — *zanzanzanzanzan*. What he'd come to understand. Now that he was in a position to reflect upon the wisdom he'd gained from experience, he couldn't begin and didn't want to try to describe it. And he in no way minded being at a loss for words. This new serenity — it was most welcome, after the past year. He understood without really understanding what it was he understood. Murky certainty was good enough for him. Knowledge that exceeds the capacity of the language to articulate it should be respected. This was similar to but not the equivalent of faith. God being the mysterious subject of faith, knowledge being the definite content of a subject.

Silence was a form of respect. Patient silence. Francis's happiness was contingent upon his ability to experience pleasure without giving in to desire — a formula easily mastered. If he spaced his meals as Napoleon did — breakfast at ten, dinner at eight — if he ate heartily but simply, he could avoid the pangs of hunger. Similarly, he could love without needing to possess the object of his love, simply by enjoying the feeling of respectful, patient admiration.

Deprived of my pension, I had to cut the number of my servants by one-third and pay half of each salary with promissory notes. I've even replaced my Chambertin with a coarse local wine. I am forced to do almost everything for myself — soon I will be going to the market and cooking. If I plead poverty, it is out of justified concern.

Francis was beginning to feel mildly hungry. Though he would have preferred a panino made by Ninanina, he heated himself a can of soup on his gas bombola and, after eating, resumed his position in the chair and continued to wait.

Sooner or later, someone would have to come visit him. The postman, if no one else. On days when the postman didn't find him enjoying the sunlight from a bench on Piazza Repubblica, he'd come find Francis at home.

The clamor of the town had quieted with siesta. Francis went on waiting. The coo of pigeons outside his window returned to him as the sound of his happiness — the purr of a contented man.

It amused him to think of Napoleon reduced to shopping at the market, arguing with fishmongers over the cost of octopus.

Murat, where are you? Soult and Bernadotte? Where has everybody gone? Marie-Louise? My incomparable Josephine?

This foolish little king who was destroyed by his own ambition. Had they been included in some artist's scheme of heaven and hell, Francis would have been floating on a puffy cloud, looking down, and Napoleon would have been impaled on fiery prongs, looking up.

Taking whatever I could gain by force or art. The fullness of my presumption, some would say.

Napoleon had learned next to nothing from life. Francis Cape had learned enough to rise above life. Having spent the past year wrenched by emotions he shouldn't have allowed himself to feel, and having reached the peak of these emotions this very morning, Francis Cape was left drained. And with emptiness came invulnerability. He no longer could feel any kind of pain. He'd feel only what he wanted to feel. Pleasure. A serene anticipation. Pride.

It was amazingly easy to conjure happiness. He wanted to be happy; therefore he was happy. He was happy just sitting there. He was happy thinking about what he'd done with his life. He was happy knowing he needn't be burdened with regrets.

Hurry up, let's go, while Campbell is away!

Zanzanzanzanzanzan. This mild irritation the only threat to his happiness. Just when everything's right in the world, along comes a mosquito. *Zanzanzanzan.* Senza la zanzara, everything would be perfect. If only he'd remembered to put up the netting. He could close the shutters, at least. How did it get so late? Already dusk was dulling the evening light. Soon it would be time for supper, and Francis had forgotten to go out and get some bread. No matter. He had biscuits in the cupboard, along with spaghetti and sauce. That would do. He could even offer a portion to a visitor, if anyone came to see him. Why hadn't the postman come? Was it a holiday? What saint was martyred on this day?

No matter. In truth, Francis didn't really want a visitor. A single mosquito was bad enough. *Zanzanzan.* How irritating. How irritating? Hardly irritating at all. Francis was on the verge of being beyond rousing. Unlike Napoleon . . . yes, he was unlike Napoleon in every way. The king of Elba had never stopped wanting to possess whatever he desired; the professor of Portoferraio could desire with complete passivity.

Happy, happy Francis. He pictured in his mind twelve monks in Villeneuve L'Archeveque, dancing in the darkness around an olive tree, stopping only for a moment to watch the lawful king of Elba gallop by, alone, in the direction of Fontainebleau.

Nothing could shake his belief that he was yet in time . . .

The bells tolling vespers. *Huzza, huzza* for the fallen king. He wants his throne back. You can't have it, Monsieur. He wants his pension. In contrast, Francis Cape, content with his one simple chair, wants for nothing.

What could I say? My stomach filled with tumor, my spirit melancholy, my strength rapidly declining. I was and always had been, it must be admitted, unequal to the effort life requires.

Not Francis, whose mildness was turning out to be its own reward. Nothing remaining of last year's turmoil but a single mosquito buzzing around his head — *zanzanzanzan.* If he could only swat the bug and kill it, he'd be utterly free to enjoy his happiness.

Any intrusion unwanted, now and forever. Please do not disturb. After Murray had left, Francis had waited patiently all day long for someone to come see him. No one came. No matter. He no longer wanted company. He preferred to be alone. An old man sit-

ting in a room above the dark streets of Portoferraio, wanting nothing more than to be left alone. *Zanzanzan. Knock knock. Zanzan.
Knock knock.*

Who's there? Francis, you're supposed to ask who's out there.
Or just go ahead and open the door.

Was there really someone knocking? If someone was knocking
at this time of night, who could it be? It could only be Murray
Murdoch — *zanzanzan* — the mosquito in Francis Cape's life.
Francis thought he'd gone away. But he'd come back. Why had he
come back? To torment him some more. Signor Americano, like
Napoleon, always wanting more than he would ever have. Francis
Cape floating in heaven above them both.

Knock knock. Answer the door, Francis.

What? And let that devil back into his home? No, thank you.

Rattle of knuckles against wood. Buzz of a wicked *zanzara*.
Demons clawing at the floorboards. Francis Cape was at peace
with himself, unlike everyone else in the world. And in order to
stay at peace, he must not open the door.

But someone is knocking, Francis.

Zanzanzan.

*His favorite toy, they say, was a miniature brass cannon. And his favorite place to
play was a seaside grotto about a mile from the Corsican village of Ajaccio, where
he used to gather mussels and crack them open and eat them there on the spot.*

Everyone else is burdened with conflicting emotions. Not Francis
Cape. Everyone else is trying in some way to conquer the world.
Not Francis Cape. You'd do him a great favor if you left him alone.

Knock knock. Hello in there. *KNOCK KNOCK!*

"Go away!"

What did he say? Did he say, go away? That's exactly what he
said. Go away. And you thought he was a gentleman.

"Francis, it's me, Adriana."

It must have been about half past eight by then. The sky, still
overcast, couldn't hold the glow of the setting sun. But as often

happens late on a damp day, the smells were magnified, and up from the streets of Portoferraio drifted the aromas of fish: of trash cans filled with fish heads and fish scales, fish stock simmering over a low flame, fish fillets baking beneath a blanket of tomatoes. Fish, fish, fish. Though Francis had closed his shutters, he'd left his windows open, and now, though he hadn't eaten fish all day, his room smelled like a pescheria. Everywhere, the smell of fish. In the streets. In his room. In the hall, where Adriana Nardi was standing, waiting to be let in.

Francis had told whoever was knocking at his door to go away. Having identified herself, Adriana waited for a different kind of reply. She listened for the rattling sounds of an old man trying to put his disorderly home in order while he called to her, Just one moment, I'll be right there, vengo subito. She waited for the door to open wide. She being the kind of girl who, Francis knew, wouldn't wait for long.

He wanted to match his actions to her expectations, he really did. He wanted to get up and throw open the door. *Zanzanzan.* And say, My God, I wasn't expecting you. Why are you here? Why have you come to see me?

Giving her the chance to respond, I've come to apologize.

You, apologize? But it is I who should —

But I —

No, I —

Unless she greeted him with an expression so stony in its aspect that he felt the coldness of stone inside him.

Go away. That's what he'd said. He wanted to take it back. But you can't erase what has already been heard. Go away. Don't go away, Adriana. *Zanzanzan.* He desperately wanted to open the door and greet her — *zanzanzan.* He wanted to push himself up out of the chair and was just at the point of mustering what was left of his strength, anticipating — *zanzanzan* — the shock of what he was about to see — *zanzanzan* — the awful, wonderful shock — *zanzan* — her skin the creamy color of a peeled chestnut, her black hair, her lips, her hands too thin, her fingers gangly, that tiny mole above her right eyebrow, the collar of her maroon blouse cut in a high V, no necklace, her torso always seeming to teeter slightly, her waist too high, her legs too long, her nose too sharp, her eyebrows too thick, her teeth too small, her smile never wide enough, her eyes always mischievous, always full of spirit, full of life, little rubies in her ears reflecting the lamplight from his room, blinding Francis, so at the instant prior to the encounter that would have been, he believed, too momentous to survive, he couldn't —

Paolina? Maria? Josephine? Marie-Louise?

"Francis, it's me, Adriana." Did he even care? What did he care about? He cared about making others care about what he cared about, most importantly, a little man in a black cocked hat and Hessian boots who was said to enjoy picnics.

We can picture him resting under a lentisk tree. From a distance, he looks entirely approachable.

Why not, then, take advantage of the situation and confirm once and for all that Napoleon is indeed the author of the following sentence: "In the final analysis everything that is human has its limits."

And why, sir, did you want your regiment of young scouts to ride horses that only had their front hooves shod?

A man who has a strictly logical mind is a man to admire. Still, it occurred to Francis that, taken as a whole, the character made no sense.

The sky was weighted with rain clouds. Bicycle wheels rattled over cobblestone. Doves cooed. Men argued in the street.

Hai detto che —

Cosa?

If in doubt, advance to meet the enemy. Keep a cool head. Receive impressions of what is happening and never fret or be amazed or intoxicated by good news or bad.

History, it could be said, is the story of logic colliding against itself.

All persons who have committed excesses, and stirred up rebellion, either by setting up any rallying signal for the crowd, or by exciting it against the French, or the government, must be brought before a military tribunal and instantly shot.

First there were the Ligurians. Then the Etruscans. Then the Romans, the Pisans, the Genoese, the Medici, the Spanish. Then at the Treaty of Amiens the island came under French rule.

There was a lot that could be said.

One might consider the impact of the Turkish threat. One might consider many things. Sitting in the Chiesa della Misericordia, one might consider whether the king of Elba would really want a mass said annually for his soul. The same man who, faithful to his oath, declared that he would descend from the throne and quit France.

He agreed to exile, don't forget. He could have fought to the end. Instead he stepped down from his throne and left France without much of a fuss. Twice. But wherever he was, he always accepted visitors.

Which reminded Francis that he should have told Adriana to try the door. It wasn't locked. It wasn't ever locked.

Ricordate: He'd relinquished his title. He'd quit France and even offered to quit life, if such an action would have served the good of his subjects.

In another mood he might have begun, *C'era una volta un piccolo re.*

He knew himself to be a good man. It was as simple as that. The kind of man who sat in the shade of a lentisk tree. And who wouldn't even raise a hand to kill the mosquito buzzing around his head. *Zanzan.* The kind of man who wouldn't swim in the sea because he was sure that the outgoing tide would pull him in exact proportion to the force of his will to return to shore, and he would get nowhere.

He'd declared that he was ready to descend from his throne —
against his own best judgment. And quit France. Good riddance.
Zan. They hooted as his carriage rolled away from Fontainebleau.
They called him the great proud.

Go away, he'd said. The stupidest thing he'd ever said. *Zzzz.* Go
away. What he'd meant to say was that he was ready to give up
everything for the good of others and thus, with a few simple
words, to secure his place in heaven.

He didn't bother to get out of his chair because he was sure
that gravity would push him down in exact proportion to the force
of his will to rise to his feet. Instead, he felt like closing his eyes for
a while. At the same hour when our father was helping the barista
in La Pila finish a bottle of wine, Francis Cape closed his eyes. Leaving Adriana to return home in a rage because bruttissimo Francis
Cape had refused, if you can believe it, even to open the door!

NAPOLEON BONAPARTE, KING OF Elba. Francis Cape, scholar of Napoleon. Malcolm Murdoch, Signor Americano. Is it my turn again, Ollie? You say you want to know what I believe really happened on Elba. I was a young mother then. I am an old woman now. Have forty-five years passed? This is the part of the story I find most difficult to believe. The simple fact of passing time. Someone we love is here in time and then not. Not. Your father, my husband. Was that him peeling potatoes at a bar in La Pila? Was that him walking along a deserted road in a drizzle on an autumn night in 1957?

You know, instead of fretting about the mysteries of death, we should try to understand what we lose by staying alive. We lose someone we love, and we lose with him a good chunk of experience. We need the mingling of minds in order to know what is real. A story becomes true with recognition. The joy of recognition. The surprise of it. Someone else to recognize what you remember.

I want my husband to remember with me that first morning in Florence when we were woken at seven by the bells. The murky darkness of the shuttered hotel room. Our bodies sharing the damp heat of that warm morning in the summer of 1956. One of us to recognize what the other recollects. If he didn't remember the bells, he'd remember the heat. He'd remember the feather mattresses in our Le Foci house. Stopping to watch an old man in a doorway weave a basket. Drinking the new olive oil by the spoonful. Lines of sunlight falling across the papers on the desk when the windows were closed and the shutters opened. I remember. Murray would recognize these memories, even if he didn't share the details of them.

The memories that you children share. The memories I share

with you and you with me. All the memories I've lost because Murray isn't here to remind me. All that we'll never know for sure.

Dear Ollie, you say you want to know what I believe. What I remember. What I know for a fact.

Fact: we embarked in July of 1956 for Genoa.

Fact: we accumulated a debt of over 10,000 dollars during our fifteen months on Elba.

Fact: Francis Cape is buried in Livorno.

Fact: your father spent two nights, not three, at the bar in La Pila.

Fact: for four days I did not contact the police to report your father missing. I was afraid his absence would be interpreted as evidence of terrible guilt, so I did not contact anyone. I waited. I thought I'd learned how to wait from Signora Nardi's example.

Fact: Adriana Nardi came home the day before your father left us, as I told you. But I didn't tell you that when she went to see Francis Cape, she was not alone. Her mother was with her. Signora Nardi intended to surprise Francis when he opened the door.

Fact: I cannot account for the third full night your father spent away from home. You boys went looking for him on the fourth night.

Fact: Even Meena the cat was lost for a few days. But you all returned safe and sound — or, as it seemed to me then, you were returned, the way possessions are returned by the kind of thieves who only intend to borrow. We even got Meena back. Meena, along with those four kittens, all of them odd little flat-faced, long-haired creatures. Do you remember? The night Patrick insisted on keeping one in bed with him and then rolled over and crushed it in his sleep. Do you remember? Does Patrick remember? Have you asked him?

Elba, 1956–1957. Sixteen months in the life of an island. We were home by Christmas. We would have come home much sooner if your father had never met Adriana Nardi. But whether we remained on Elba during her long absence because your father needed to clear his name or because he needed to satisfy a secret longing in his heart, I'll never know for sure. If there's more to the story you've been writing, Ollie, if there were encounters your father kept hidden from me for the rest of his life, if, in fact, he did love Adriana, I can only believe that it must have been a destructive, frivolous love, prompted by his search for a haven where he couldn't disappoint the people he loved most.

Signora Nardi, having recovered her daughter, came and sat with me while the police searched the hills for you. I didn't want her there. I didn't want anyone besides my husband and children. She forced me to talk to her. I remember hearing myself admit, against my will, that I was afraid of my husband. And then, seeing her confusion, I explained that I wasn't afraid of what he'd do to others but what he would do to himself. It was some comfort to consider my children's self-protective instinct. But my husband was a self-destructive man. What would he do? She wanted to hear more, but I'd already said enough.

If I wouldn't talk, then she expected me to listen. I didn't want to listen and was about to say so, but she spoke rapidly, swearing me to secrecy before I could beg her to leave me alone. Of course I didn't want to be alone. I wanted her to sit beside me and stroke my hair and tell me something significant enough that it would require a promise from me never to repeat it to anyone. I gave her my promise, Ollie. Now, these many years later, I am breaking this promise for the first time with much regret.

The story Signora Nardi told me that night was the story of her daughter. And this is the story you deserve to hear. The true story of Adriana Nardi. She was not the coy young girl I'd taken her to be. She was not in love with Murray. Nor was she afraid of Francis Cape. She was a lonely girl bouncing from one heartbreak to another when your father first saw her in the Nardi garden. Yet she was far more capable than any of us realized.

As I told you months ago, Adriana had dropped her university studies and come home shortly before we arrived on the island. As many people who knew her guessed, she'd been involved — to the point of being secretly engaged — with a young professor there. He'd broken the engagement off abruptly; she came home to Elba, where, in a naive effort to reclaim her life, she threw herself into a brief affair with a brutal young man who worked at the prison on Pianosa. All of this Adriana hid from her mother while it was happening. And by the time the early symptoms of pregnancy had begun and the prison guard had deserted her, Adriana was too ashamed to go to her mother for help.

Imagine her that night at our villa in Le Foci. Honestly, I don't think she expected to find Murray alone. I don't know why she was there. Maybe she'd come to talk to me, just like her mother came to me, both of them mistaking our presence on the island as evidence of our influence. Maybe she just wanted to unburden herself. Maybe she wanted to test Murray's capacity for sympathy. She wasn't there, you can be sure, to test her powers of seduction. Murray misunderstood. And then, after leaving Murray, she'd met Francis Cape. Il professore. He wanted to keep Adriana to himself — a justified want, he'd thought, since it was inspired by love. He wanted to marry her. He wanted to kill her.

Il professore, the same pathetic man who tried to stab Murray with a butter knife. He could have done better than a butter knife. He could have wielded a good sharp knife with a five-inch blade. I'm sure he wished he'd had a better weapon ready when Murray came to see him. And I suspect he'd regretted not bringing a knife along when he followed Adriana to Le Foci.

Do you understand what I'm telling you, Ollie? Francis Cape wanted to marry Adriana, and when she refused him, he wanted to kill her. He would have killed her if he'd had the means. Instead he tried to slap sense into her so she would recognize that he was serious. Francis Cape was always serious. Francis Cape only ever told the truth. And all Adriana could do was laugh at him.

A life held in balance. Think of all the outcomes that are possible at any one moment. Adriana could have been killed by Francis

Cape that night. But he was an old man and she a swift girl. She fled down the road before Francis could stop her.

Adriana was seven weeks pregnant when she left Elba. She made her way to Paris and there had the pregnancy terminated. Not an easy thing to do back in 1956. The ordeal could have destroyed her. Instead, it enhanced in her the same ferocity her mother was known for. She struggled, survived, prospered. And while I don't know for certain what's become of her over the years, I expect she'd say now, so many years later, that Malcolm Murdoch and Francis Cape both played only smart parts in her complicated life.

But you want facts, you say. Facts, like the banded ironstone we found on Volterraio. The flint and sandstone and chalk. All the coarse, worthless breccia.

Facts as certain as the warmth of my husband's body in my arms. Nothing I could say to persuade him that he hadn't done anyone any real harm.

Facts, such as the stupidity of a drunk.

Patrick, have you seen your father? Lidia, mio marito — dov'è andato? Has anyone seen Murray? Did he leave a note? Is he back yet? No, grazie, Lidia, niente. Aspetto per Murray. What time is it? Has he called? No, Harry, stay here. I don't want you boys going out this afternoon. Un po' di minestra, sì, that would be fine, Lidia. You know, Murray, I can't fall asleep without you beside me. Where are you? Is it too late to find you? Did you come to this island to do whatever it is you've already done? It is over? Has it happened?

My husband. And then my cat. And then my four young sons. Ten o'clock at night, and my sons were missing, and Murray wasn't there to go out in search of them.

You know what I did then? I felt my head grow unbelievably heavy, my eyes blur, my mouth go dry, my pulse slow, and I fell asleep. Amazingly, I fell asleep. I'd hardly slept for three days and nights. My sons were missing. My husband was gone. And I fell asleep. And dreamt, of all people, about the engineer from Ohio, the one who'd thrown himself off the *Casparia*. I dreamt only of seeing him leaning on the ship's rail, a cruel smile on his face. When I woke up my eyes were dry from staring without blinking. And Lidia was leading Signora Nardi into the room.

Signora —

Signora —

Talk in English. Talk in Italian or French or Latin, for all I care. Don't bother me. Don't stay. Don't go. Don't leave me alone. Tell me a story, Signora. I'll tell you what could happen. You tell me what did happen. Tell me that your daughter's freedom is as important to you as her safety. You let her make her own mistakes — trust being the one absolute of love.

She didn't say any of this when she sat up with me through the night. Instead, she offered me the story of her daughter as proof of the necessity of trust. See what happens when you trust someone? She is always with you, and you with her. With him. With them, Signora Murdoch. You trust them to do what they believe they have to do, even if they are mistaken, even if they try to hide their mistakes from you. They trust you to welcome them back, no matter what.

We will wait together, Signora. We will keep the lights on and tell stories to pass the time. The story of my daughter. Do you want to hear it? You must promise never to repeat to anyone what I tell you, Signora. I will tell you what my daughter told me. My daughter roaming the world while I waited for her to come home. I will tell you. My heart like a bird fluttering inside a box. If I could have, I would have ripped open my chest and let the bird fly away. I will tell you. You will understand. And when morning comes we will see what we will see.

When my brothers and I left our villa that tranquil October afternoon, we were not going to look for our father. Though we hadn't seen him for a few days, we didn't really understand that he was missing. Murray always had come back; therefore he would come back again when he was ready. And so would we. But just in case we were gone longer than we expected, Nat filled a thermos with water, and we each carried a sack with an apple, a piece of bread, and some cheese.

We set out that afternoon during the quiet hour of siesta. It was a beautiful day, the blue of the sky the pure royal tint of sapphire. Patrick, who had hunted for minerals with Carlo along the far slope of Monte Giove, knew to direct us west. As we walked along our regular route toward the path leading up the mountain, we shared the feeling that we were on the mission we'd been training for. Our games had been nothing more than practice.

Over the past months we'd learned a fair amount about valuable stones and their histories. Patrick had a list and would tell us, and when we forgot he would remind us, about diamonds weighing more than a pound, diamonds that had been stolen, diamonds that had started wars, diamonds that had been found by shepherd boys in the mud of a riverbank and sold for the price of 500 sheep, ten oxen, and a horse.

We would have been satisfied to find any gemstone that would have made us a profit of one horse. We wanted a horse. And a boat. Anyone who lives on an island needs a boat. A horse, a boat, and maybe an electric train set. We'd left our trains back in America. A horse, a boat, electric trains, and snorkeling masks for each of us so we could explore the world below the surface of the sea. It hardly mattered that Nat and I didn't know how to swim. We could float on an inflatable raft. We needed a big inflatable raft. A horse, a boat, electric trains, snorkeling masks, and an inflatable raft in the shape of a beluga.

We didn't tell anyone where we were going because we didn't know. We just knew we were hunting for something valuable. Something that someone else would want. The Star of Elba.

After a few days of mist and rain the air was fresh, the breeze soft, the fields a velvety green speckled with patches of white — perhaps orchids or fuchsia. We walked quietly, hoping to spy a wild goat. We didn't see a goat but we saw a strange bird — a heron, it must have been, with a black velvet stripe along the underside of its long white neck and white feathers hanging from its breast like strings of pearls. Harry spotted the black eyes of a green lizard hidden in the grass. And we caught a glimpse of a mottled snake as it slid across the path.

We climbed through the woods up Monte Giove and along the rocky ridge at the summit. We rested against a granite boulder on the northern slope of the mountain. In the distance we could see dozens of colorful sails mingling at what must have been the finish of a regatta.

For the first time since we'd been on the island, we continued over the peak of Monte Giove and climbed down the western slope, out of sight of Marciana. Patrick led us into the hilly terrain of Mezza Luna. To our east was the peak of La Stretta. We continued south, watching the ground carefully for the glimmer of a gem.

We didn't find much that was worth keeping — only a few small pieces of what was probably pyrite and a clump of snowy calcite. We kept walking. The heat of the sun increased as the afternoon wore on. We passed our thermos between us.

We walked west toward Punta Nera. When I was too tired to walk, Patrick and Harry took turns carrying me on their backs. We climbed another, smaller mountain we'd known only from the view at the top of Monte Giove. We kept walking, following a shallow gully wherever it would take us. Eventually we came to a small creek that we hadn't known existed.

The valley was filled with holm oak and a green patchwork of myrtle and ferns, and there was a great scattering of huge boulders, some half cleaved with the crevices worn smooth by wind, others with buttresses and chimneys and deep openings that looked like windows. It seemed as if the rocks had tumbled down from the mountains after some great quake, as if the whole universe had shuddered over the chaos of love and picked up the earth and shook it violently, trying to force from the silent ground a confession.

Once upon a time the universe had felt . . . what? What did we know about the chaos of love? Nothing other than the evidence of its effect around us — broken stone, surfaces worn smooth by wind and rain, ancient gouges in the soil filled with green that were no less than proof of the world's ability to repair itself and endure.

Goldfinches flew between the trees, flickering like light reflecting from a tilting mirror. We inhaled the dusty smell of moss warmed by the sun. We waded with our shoes in the shallow water. We felt the silky sensation as schools of minnows bumped against our ankles. We grew giddy and loud. We splashed each other, slipped and fell, and returned to shore drenched.

We rested against the trunk of an oak and ate what was left of our bread and cheese. We finished our water, then refilled the thermos with water from the creek before moving off in different directions. Without saying it, we knew to stay within calling distance of each other, as well as to stay close to the creek. We knew that we couldn't get lost if we stayed within sight of flowing water.

Nat headed south toward Capo Sant'Andrea. Harry went in the same direction but on the other side of the river. Patrick crossed the creek and headed toward La Stretta. I headed back in the direction we'd come.

A frog began chirping and was answered by another frog. The coarse oak leaves hissed with each gust of wind. As twilight came on, the greens of the valley darkened to gray, and whatever was lighter than green became phosphorescent. White blossoms, gold birds, pink quartz — they glowed as though lit from within. Their colors mesmerized me. But when I'd try to approach, the object would disappear like a mirage.

The evening air was still warm, with a cool intermittent breeze. The sky overhead was a deep, metallic blue. Across the creek I saw Patrick's flashlight wobbling between saplings. I tried turning on my own flashlight but couldn't make it work. I tried to think a greeting to Patrick. He didn't answer. I shouted, and he shouted back, "Shut up, Ollie!" I watched him as he bent over to pick up a stone. I saw the quick arc of his arm when he threw the stone into the water. The clatter and splash scared the frogs into silence.

I'm not sure how long we searched in the darkness, but the sky had darkened to a dusky gray when we heard Harry yelling for us to come quick. I saw the beam of Patrick's flashlight on the opposite bank wobbling ahead of him and thought I saw Harry ahead of me, but it turned out to be the pale face of a rock. I tried to keep up with Patrick. When he ran ahead I called for him to wait. He ignored me. I followed the sound of Harry's voice and tried not to lose sight of the beam of Patrick's flashlight.

When I caught up to my brothers, I found Harry standing knee-deep in the creek, his face a ghostly alabaster in the glow of Patrick's flashlight. We all shared the startle of déjà vu. Once before, and now again, I followed Patrick into the creek to join Harry. The water seeped into our sneakers. We stood without speaking, staring at the wet rusty pipe that Harry was holding. We became aware of the silence. The frogs and birds were silent, the breeze was still, and we were hardly breathing. Only the little creek made any sound — the murmur of shallow water flowing over rocks. We pressed close to Harry to see what he was holding. The sky grew darker. Time passed. We might have stood there all night if Patrick hadn't finally found his voice.

"Big deal," he said. "A stupid old pipe."

"You think so," Harry retorted.

"Let's go, Ollie."

We were not playing. We were not Jakos One through Four who could make ourselves understood without even speaking aloud. We were not at all inclined to mix nonsense and different languages. Patrick shrugged. I couldn't decide whom to side with. I let Patrick take my hand in his, but still we just stood there.

"Stupid old pipe," Patrick said.

"Look, Patrick. Just look inside, will you? You dumbhead." Harry turned the pipe so one end faced Patrick and inserted his flashlight at the other end.

"Jeepers!" Patrick clutched the pipe to steady it against his glasses.

"Let me see!" I tried to shove Patrick aside. "It's my turn. Patrick, come on. Patrick!"

"Holy cow."

"I want to see!" I stomped, splashing all of us with water, but still my brothers ignored me.

"Wow!" Patrick peered into the pipe as though into the lens of a telescope. What was so amazing? Patrick was looking at a star. On the star was a colony of martians. The martians waved at Patrick. I waited for Patrick to wave back.

"It's a diamond," he whispered. Harry smiled smugly while Patrick stared into the pipe, mesmerized. I didn't know what else to do but curl myself into a powerful bundle of five-year-old fury and head-butt Harry in the stomach. He held himself upright. I slipped and fell into the water.

"Pigsnot!"

"Shitface!"

"What trash can did you crawl out of?"

I reached for Harry's ankle, he grabbed Patrick, and to my immense satisfaction they both lost their balance and fell.

I decided it was time to start crying. Harry said he'd hit me if I didn't shut up, so I cried louder. As we waded back to shore, Harry mocked me with his imitation wailing. Patrick joined in. We were all crying. We were all pretending to cry. We were laughing, the world was ridiculous, we were ridiculous, it was an October night on the island of Elba, we were soaked, the moon was shining, and we were having fun.

Patrick had held on to the pipe, but his flashlight was drenched, and when he shook it, the light flickered and went out, leaving one working flashlight between us. Patrick blamed Harry. Harry blamed me.

We took off our shoes, and while Patrick wrung out our socks, Harry let me look into the pipe.

What had Patrick said? Jeepers. "Jeepers," I said.

There was a star trapped inside the pipe. Not a star with martians. Rather, a crystalline star that absorbed the beam from Harry's flashlight but still glowed with its own light. It had no color. Instead, it emitted a mysterious gleam both from within and from the surface of the facets. A lustrous mosaic of atoms, like water frozen into ice, ice congealed by extreme conditions and transformed into a permanent, uniform substance. The star of Elba.

Harry shook the pipe gently but the star wouldn't come out. We argued about how to dislodge it. We considered carrying the pipe home and cutting it open, but we were too impatient. Harry inserted a twig into the pipe and tapped it against the crystal. The twig snapped in two. Patrick found a sturdier stick, which Harry plunged into the pipe. Nothing happened. He tried again. There was a loud popping sound, and Harry threw the pipe aside. We didn't see the splinters of glass flying out the opposite end, but we saw them scattered when Harry shone his flashlight on the ground. Glass, not diamond. Just pieces of glass, an old bottle or jar, that had been lodged inside an old pipe.

We stared at the ground rather than meet one another's eyes. Luckily, we were far away from civilization, and there were no witnesses to our stupidity. Not even Nat.

"Nat!" Patrick said.

"Where's Nat?" I asked.

Had anyone seen Nat? No, Patrick hadn't seen Nat. Harry hadn't seen Nat. I hadn't seen Nat. Where was Nat?

Strange that he hadn't been drawn by Harry's shouts or the noise of our fighting. We listened for his footsteps. We waited in silence for a moment, and then we began calling for him.

"Nat!"

"Nat, we're over here."

"Nat, come on."

"Nat, where are you?"

"Nat!"

"Nat!"

"Nat!"

We still had no idea that ever since the fever his hearing had been erratic. We assumed that if he were near enough, he could hear us.

"Nat?"

"Nat!"

We left our shoes and socks drying on the grass and headed together in the direction Nat had gone, beyond Monte Giove toward Capo Sant'Andrea. We had to walk slowly in our bare feet. I held Harry's hand. Patrick led the way with Harry's flashlight.

At one point we heard a noise of paws scrambling over pebbles. Patrick swept the light across the slope rising to our right. The beam illuminated the eyes of some animal — a wood rat or squirrel crouched in a clump of heather. The animal stared at us for a long minute, we stared back, then it slipped away, melting into the earth.

We were chasing a ghost. No, not even a ghost. The idea of a ghost. The farther we went, the more hopeless we felt. I began to feel itchy all over and kept having to pause and scratch myself. Harry tugged me along. I was hungry. I was tired. I was preparing to cry, but Harry cut me short: "Whatever you do, Ollie, just don't start crying, okay?"

Where was Nat? I wanted to find Nat and go home.

"Nat?"

We were all thinking the same thing — how right it was that of the four of us, Nat was the one who'd gotten lost. Nat's fate had always been clear. We'd always known that Nat was destined for trouble. The question we asked ourselves as we wandered along in the dark was, What kind of trouble?

"Nat!"

"Nat!"

"Nat, come on, it's not funny anymore!"

Nat, we found out later, hadn't lost his way at all. He'd followed the creek toward Capo Sant'Andrea just like he'd said he was going to do. And after twenty minutes or so, he'd heard Harry calling behind him. He was pleased to find that for the time being he could hear with perfect clarity. He heard his brother calling his name. But he also heard something else, something he recognized as the sound of someone breaking rocks, the clacking of stone against stone.

Nat headed away from the creek and up the steep bank, across an empty road, across a field, between rows of cypresses, and along a narrow footpath. At the end of the path he came to a segment of the unfinished stone wall marking our father's land.

In the center of a clearing was a wide, brackish pool. Opposite the wall, on the other side of the run-off water, beside a sheer granite wall glittering in the fading light with specks of quartz, was our father. He balanced on one knee. With a rhythmic, mindless motion, he was knocking a stone the size of a baseball against the granite.

On an island measuring 223.5 square kilometers, in the gray of twilight, in the middle of nowhere, Nat Murdoch happened to find his father breaking rocks in the woods of Mezza Luna. Nat couldn't believe what his eyes were telling him, and he staggered back in astonishment, fell into the dirt, and sat there, trying to sort out his confusion.

Only if something is possible can it be true.

"Dad?"

But reality, as our year on Elba had taught us, is full of surprises. Nat liked a good surprise. He decided that the scene of our father pounding rocks under a rising moon was more of a surprise than a coincidence.

"Dad?"

One. Two.

"Dad, hey!"

Three. Four.

"Dad!"

"Huh?"

"Hi."

"Nat?"

"What are you doing here?"

"What are *you* doing here?"

"I asked you first."

"It's late. Does your mother know you're here?"

"No."

As Murray rose to his feet, dust blew in ribbons around his ankles. He was barefoot, dressed in a T-shirt and suspenders, his left eye was swollen, the lid bruised, he had a sore crusted on his lower lip and a stripe of black bristles on his chin.

Nat started to unlace his shoes. Murray called, "Don't you dare."

"Why not?"

"Go home, Nat."

"No."

"I am your father. You are my son. Fathers tell sons what they can and cannot do."

"Yeah?"

"Yeah."

Murray slowly waded across the shallow pool toward Nat. He caught his toe against a rock, winced, but managed to pull himself out of the water. He collapsed beside Nat, who was still sitting in the dirt with one shoe off, one shoe on.

"Nat, something occurs to me."

"What?"

"I thought you had some trouble with your hearing."

"What do you mean?"

"I thought you couldn't hear."

"I can hear fine." Nat could hear fine. He could hear what he wanted to hear. Some of the time. Most of the time.

"You can hear me now. And now? And now?" Murray let his voice soften into a whisper.

"Yeah and yeah and yeah. Stop bugging me."

"I'm allowed to bug you. I'm your dad."

Murray leaned back, resting his folded hands on his belly, and gazed into the night. Nat asked Murray what he was thinking. Murray grunted. Nat stretched out beside him. After a while Murray began to speak aloud. He used the formal tone of someone delivering a lecture, though he didn't seem to care whether or not Nat was listening.

He said something about Babylon. Which made him think of Balthazar. B-words. Any old B-word snatched out of the blue.

What is Babylon? What should Nat already know, and what was Murray trying to teach him?

He rattled on about Eros and Erasmus. Epistolary jests. Expression and imagination. Something along those lines.

"Dad, umm . . ."

I-words. I I I I I.

M-words. Man. A man. Amen.

N for *no.* No . . . ah. Drunken Noah, ho ho ho.

Here was a name Nat recognized: Noah, like in Noah and the Ark!

Murray said something about Pan. Something about Proteus. Something about Pico. P-words. Something about Pico boasting that what he'd written would only be intelligible to a few. Something about parabolic fervor. More P-words. Late-antique Platonists. Mysteries cease to be mysteries when they are promulgated.

"What's *promulgated?*"

Murray told him to look it up. Nat reminded Murray that he didn't know how to read.

Murray said, "Learn to read and then look it up."

Paradigm. Purtroppo. Proud. Murray must have felt a last little stab of pride as he rested on the grass with one of his four sons beside him. Fathers and sons. It was then that he remembered that scene in Turgenev's *First Love,* where the son glances down a lane and sees his father slap his mistress.

Pretension.

"Personally I never had much of a taste for Turgenev."

"What's Tur . . . tur . . . turga . . ."

"Turgenev. Russian author of the nineteenth century."

T-words. The taming of the passions. Tripartite life. Tiresias. Trinity. Tourmaline.

"Tourmaline. I know what tourmaline is."

"You do, do you? Tell me, my young sage."

Tourmaline is unsurpassed even by corundum in variety of hue, and it has during recent years rapidly advanced in public favor. G. F. Herbert Smith. *Gemstones.*

"Tourmaline is a kind of rock you can find."

"Mmm. What else?"

"It's pretty, I guess."

"How is it pretty?"

"I don't know. It's just pretty. All rocks are pretty."

"Why?"

"Because they are."

Think about it, Murray. The beauty of rocks. The stuff of the earth, whether abundant, generally available, or rare.

Pause. Hmm. Dad was gathering himself, preparing to say something of great significance, something he'd been wanting to say for a long, long time.

"Nathaniel. Nathaniel, listen."

A subtle warning embedded in his father's tone of voice. The double click of Nat's name. Nat sat up as if on an elastic hinge.

"Nathaniel, I'm —"

Don't!

Don't what?

Our father was about to say something he shouldn't say, something Nat didn't understand and didn't want to know. How could he be stopped? The best Nat could hope for was to distract him, keeping him occupied until . . .

"Dad, I —"

"— was going to say —"

"— there was this rock —"

"I have to —"

"— this rock, you know, we want to find it, well, there's lots of rocks we already found, actually Harry finds them, he finds everything, it's not fair, every time we're looking for something Harry finds it."

"— to say —"

"And then there was this one rock, you know, well Patrick thinks it's tor . . . ter . . ."

Funny how often a word slips from your mind when you need it. Nat looked to Murray for help. What had they just been talking about?

But Murray was trying to explain that he —

Nat interrupted, saying anything that came into his head so he wouldn't hear what Murray was trying to tell him. "And then we, you know, um, we were just, then Patrick, I don't know, that's just what he did, and Ollie, he's such a brat because, that time we found the spiders, actually it was Harry, he's always finding things, you know, Dad, but still I don't see why we have to be brothers all the time, I wish I didn't have any brothers. If I didn't have brothers . . ."

Ei fu. "What I'm trying to say . . . what am I trying to say?"

Keep talking, Nat. Don't give Dad the chance to —

"Actually there's not a law, we don't have to if we don't want to, but since, I don't know. Dad, tell me about something. Dad? Dad! I want you to tell me about, oh, any old thing, or else I'll tell you."

Able was I.

"About once, you know, when, you know, um, well, so, Dad, are you listening, you have to listen, you have to pay attention."

They kept at it long into the night. Whatever nonsense Nat threw at Murray, whatever nonsense they exchanged, was from Nat's point of view merely a way to buy time. As if — and this thought only came to him much, much later — as if, with enough time, he could succeed in paying off our father's debts.

"What'll Mom say when we tell her?"

"Maybe we don't have to tell her."

"Yeah, like she's not going to notice there's three of us instead of four."

"We can say we weren't there."

"Where?"

"Here."

We were sitting on the narrow beach at the edge of Sant'Andrea. Behind us the stack of boulders rose up steeply, though only for a few feet. At the top of the rocks was an area cordoned off by a chain-link fence, and sleeping gray gulls bordered the edge.

While we talked we picked up little stones and threw them one by one into the sea. Whatever we happened to be saying, we'd pause whenever a stone was in midflight and listen for the splash.

Cluck, chuck, silence, splash.

"Is Nat lost forever?" I asked.

"Shut up, Ollie."

This was a sadness I'd never felt before, sharp and clear and deserved. Nat was gone. Nat had been a little bit bigger than me and a little bit smaller than my big brothers. Without Nat I felt unbearably small, as small as the pebbles disappearing into the dark sea.

A sob shuddered through me. Harry shoved me so I toppled over into the wet sand. I cried louder. Patrick clamped his hand over my mouth and promised I'd get it good if I didn't shut up. Why did everyone everywhere always have to tell me to shut up?

Most of the houses on the point were boarded up for the winter, but a few were lit with a warm orange light. Wouldn't it be better if we were inside one of those houses? How would we ever get home?

Patrick took off his glasses and rubbed the bridge of his nose, a gesture that made him look ancient to me. I wondered how he had grown up so fast.

"Some day," he said.

"Some day what?" Harry prompted.

"Some day we'll remember this and it will all be like it never really happened."

"Why do you say that?"

"I don't know."

"Penso —" Harry began, but Patrick barked, "Speak in English!"

"I think we need a plan."

"Like what kind of plan?"

"Like a plan to find Nat."

"The question is, will we find him before the wolves eat him up!"

I started to cry again. Harry hit me. Patrick hit Harry. Harry said, "Race you!" I ran after Harry. Patrick just sat there. We taunted him. He threw fistfuls of sand at us.

The night wore on this way. We kept meaning to resume our search for Nat but kept forgetting about him. We fought, we played, and eventually we flattened a patch of sand to make a smooth broad bed. We stretched out side by side. As we grew drowsy we counted the stars. There weren't many that night because the moon was so bright, like a bowl of liquid light. We remembered the glass star Harry had found inside the pipe. Idly, we wondered if the real star of Elba even existed. Sometimes it's hard to tell the difference between what's real and what's fake, Patrick pointed out. I gazed at his face. He'd put his glasses on and looked very wise.

Sleep crept from our toes to our ankles to our knees.

"Poor Mom," Harry said quietly.

Patrick yawned. Harry and I yawned.

"Let's pretend we're in a war," I said.

"OK," Patrick replied. His eyes were closed. Sleep had reached our elbows. Our necks. We could hear the explosions of battle. Enemy soldiers were advancing, but we were well-hidden and well-armed. The calcite in Harry's pocket was a bomb so powerful it could blow the entire island to smithereens. Imagine that. In the place where Elba had once risen out of the sea, there would only be water carpeted with the refuse of wood and metal, flesh and bone.

As sleep reached our ears, I felt, and was ashamed to feel, that I'd always remember this night as one of the best nights of my life.

And while you all were having such a swell time, I was trying to drag Dad back into the world of the living.

Sorry, Nat.

Even if Murray didn't say outright that he was ready to quit, he was thinking it.

He'd been thinking it for a long while. He came to Elba in order to allow himself to think it. Came so he could get away. Came to escape. There he was, trapped by the wish to escape from the wish to escape from the wish.

Whatever. I was just a dumb kid and didn't put two and two together. Our old man was drunk. Really drunk. It was the first time I'd seen him this way, and I didn't understand. But at least I could tell he needed help. He'd scraped his knuckles raw, his hands were bloody, his words were slurred, and his eyes had a weird foggy glare. Turns out he hadn't eaten anything since the evening before, but he'd forgotten he was hungry. I thought if I could get him home, home to the villa first, then home to America, everything would be okay. I did my best to convince him.

What did he say to you?

I've told you what I remember, Ollie.

Nothing else?

No.

And so we're left to imagine.

That's your job.

You telling Dad what it was like to be a small boy on an island in the Tyrrhenian Sea.

Whatever.

Dad telling you about Balthazar and Erasmus and Pico.

Whatever.

You telling Dad about quartz and pyrite, calcite and tour-tour-tourmaline, Dad telling you about the Guelphs and the Ghibellines, Garibaldi and Galileo, you telling Dad that the first thing you were going to do when you got back home to America was set up your trains.

Maybe.

Dad explaining that there are things a father can say only to his son, you telling Dad about an old episode of *Popeye,* Dad telling you something about the something he'd been wanting to explain, something having to do with the Nardi girl, you telling Dad about the time Popeye went overboard with his anchor, Dad warning you about the explosion of nothing into something, all you have to do is look at a girl for the fun of it, you reminding Dad about the BB gun you'd been promised, Dad reminding you that there are confidences a father can share with his son, his wife never needs to know, no one else needs to know what the father says to his son on this balmy moonlit night on the island of Elba after too many days of rain, you telling Dad you were kind of tired, asking, Can't we go home now and if we can't go home, do you want to play Ants? Dad asking, Why the hell did we come here anyway? but you weren't sure whether he was asking why did we come here to this place in the woods or to this island, Dad pointing out that we could have gone to Mexico or Alaska or Louisiana while you tried not to yawn and to keep yourself awake you decided to explain what a periscope is, Dad cursing his Averil uncles, you reminding Dad that your birthday was in ten-and-a-half months, Dad reminding you that you were an innocent child, you telling Dad that unlike your brothers you don't actually fall asleep, you just lie in bed thinking about sleep, Dad saying that even if you didn't understand what he was saying, it sure felt good to talk, what a relief just to talk, father and son, you unable to suppress a great big yawn, Dad giving a sad chuckle of resignation and cuddling you against his chest, you hearing his laugh as a crackle echoing from the cave of his ribs, Dad shifting you a little so he could free his arm, rubbing his face as if he had a towel in his hands and were blotting his wet skin dry, you lying there thinking about sleep, Dad saying, if only, you telling Dad you were cold, though you weren't cold at all, you just wanted him to put his arm around you again, Dad saying that what he'd like right then was a scotch, you thinking lazily about blowing the fluffy parachutes from the head of a dandelion, Dad repeating, if only, you enjoying the vibrations of his voice against your ear, Dad telling himself, if only he hadn't come to Elba, getting only this far in the hypothetical, Elba being the place where his troubles began as far as he could see, and he couldn't see very far, not in the dark, not with his son asleep across his chest, not with his head aching as the evening's alcohol dissolved, not with regret fogging his vision, regret an effective cover for the terror of self-knowledge, the story he could tell himself the story of an American guy who fucked up, don't we all fuck up sooner or later, he's sorry, Claire, he's sorry, Adriana, his deception, her deception, his coward-ice, Francis Cape, all of which kept him from considering his orig-inal purpose in leaving home and thus he was able to make the decision to feel nothing worse than guilt, which manifested itself visibly with the hint of a smirk, a smirk which would never en-tirely disappear from his face, marking him as the kind of person who, with a shrug, was always ready to acknowledge his potential for fucking up, no matter what he did he kept fucking up, sorry about that, girls, regret lit with the soft glow of virility, that radiant Y chromosome, that sexy X, the story such people could tell always the same story — Sir Winston who loved Lady Jane who loved the Duke who loved Lady Jane's sister who loved Sir Winston, never more than that, never less, you know the kind of people I'm talking about, the edge of their personality a little dulled, their eyes a little blank, ambition a little muted, and always that smirk to signal to others that they'll never be registered saints and, guess what, they don't give a damn, let someone else rise to the challenge, they can have it along with all the trouble, the confusion, the uncertainty, the suffering, the intensity of thought and feeling, no thanks, Malcolm Murdoch is going to ease himself into sleep by thinking about the only thing that really matters to a man who hasn't eaten for twenty-four hours, the antidote of food, in particular, a bloody steak just off the grill, green-bean casserole, and the well in a mountain of mashed potatoes filled with steaming gravy.

The Inconstant

M ORE THAN ONE HUNDRED ELBANS CAME TO FRANCIS
Cape's funeral, though not because they'd ever cared about
the Englishman while he was living. They came because they were
curious. They wanted to see for themselves the body that was said
to have turned miraculously into wax. Francis Cape had died of
heart failure a full five days earlier, the coroner had confirmed. But
instead of deteriorating with the usual rapidity, his body had remained unchanged, emitting no trace of fluids, no blood or excre-
tions, and no foul smell, according to those who'd helped transfer
the corpse to the little morgue behind the customs station in Portoferraio.

Signora Nardi paid for the service and burial. She ignored the
rumors about the mummified body of il professore and went
about the ordinary business of arranging a funeral. First she sent

cables to Francis's relatives in London, which went unanswered. Then she contacted an Anglican minister, the Reverend Nigel Fink, who lived in Livorno. And she managed to convince the parish priest of the Chiesa della Misericordia to allow a Protestant service to be conducted in his church.

The coffin was high-quality cherry wood, but the mourners were disappointed when they arrived to find the coffin closed and Francis Cape's uncorrupted body hidden from view. Some of the guests snuck out through the side door and went home. Among the mourners who remained were Lorenzo Ambrogio and his wife, Carlo the mine surveyor, Ninanina of the enoteca and her husband, Massimo, our cook, Lidia, Adriana Nardi, our mother, our father, and of course Signora Nardi herself, who sat in the front pew beside her daughter, both of them wearing black Burano lace veils that were said to have belonged to Napoleon's sister.

The maestrale had blown in cool, bright weather for the day. White chrysanthemums lined the aisles and the base of the altar and filled the Chiesa della Misericordia with their sweet dusty fragrance. Candles cast flickering shadows on the nave columns. People blew their noses frequently, not because of strong emotion but because the winter's respiratory viruses were beginning to spread. Reverend Fink said the Evensong and read the Absolutions of the Dead in English. "He cometh up and is cut down like a flower, he flieth as it were a shadow, and never continueth in one stay." Lorenzo delivered a short eulogy in Italian in which he praised Francis for his dedication to history. He quoted Aristotle, St. Augustine, and, of course, Napoleon — "Do not be surprised at the attention that I devote to details: I must pay attention to everything so as never to leave myself unprovided."

Francis Cape had been a man of detail. In recording a small segment of history, he'd wanted to include everything that could be known. Elbans would remember him for his noble effort, if not for his accomplishments.

Too bad he was Protestant, people whispered. If he'd been Catholic, they might have let themselves believe that his body truly had been the location where God chose to work a miracle. But in fact, they pointed out, refrigeration will keep meat fresh. Taking into account the cool weather . . .

Mamma mia, what disrespect. Shhhh.

People whispered about many things. Gathering outside on the steps after the service, they whispered about the solitary professor who had been dead for days before anyone bothered to check on him. They whispered about the consequences of loneliness. They whispered about the stealth of heart disease. They whispered about our father as he and our mother walked past them, holding hands. They whispered about Americans and their love of drink, for by then everyone had heard about Signor Americano's four-day spree that had taken him across the island from Marciana to Portoferraio to La Pila to Sant'Andrea. They whispered about American foolishness and American greed. The rumor passed among them that Malcolm Murdoch had paid five times for his patch of Elban earth what they knew it to be worth. They speculated about when he would take his family and go home.

And they whispered about Adriana Nardi. Though she mingled among them out in the piazza, she said little about her year abroad, despite the direct, probing questions put to her. And when she was out of range the Elbans made up stories to explain her absence.

They said that she'd run away to Paris with a lover, but the man had abandoned her, as men will abandon all women who are too willing, and she'd gone on to England alone, to London, where she'd worked as a servant for a wealthy family. A Nardi working as a servant! Impossible! As a lady-in-waiting, then, yes, who knows but that she worked for the queen herself! Absurd, though it was fun to pretend. And listen to this: the lover had left her pregnant. She'd had a child — delivered it right there in the royal palace and then had given the infant up for adoption. No! Yes! You can tell from the hips of a woman if she's birthed a child, and you can tell from the look in her eyes if she's had to give the child up.

Where was the child? In an orphanage in London. Sleeping in a gilded cradle in a palace. Wrapped in a threadbare blanket in a basket left to be claimed at a train station. Adriana, what happened to the child? What did you do with the child?

Another pressing question was the identity of the lover. If not the American investor, then who? Who took Signorina Nardi to Paris? Who lured her away from Elba? Who, Adriana? Tell us his name.

People watched Adriana carefully. They watched her when she shook hands with our father and mother on the steps of the church. They eavesdropped but failed to make sense of the English words our parents and Adriana quietly exchanged. The conversation seemed cordial, though of course they all knew that courtesy could be even more effective than silence as a cover for turmoil.

The funeral procession wound down to Via del Paradiso toward the quay of Portoferraio, where Francis Cape's coffin would be loaded onto a boat bound for Livorno. Reverend Fink led the way. The coffin, blanketed with chrysanthemums, rested on a carriage pulled by Claudio Baldi's sturdy dappled pony. The mourners followed, and behind them a little boy scoured the street for coins that with any luck would fall out of purses and pockets.

Adriana was flanked by Lorenzo and her mother. Our parents joined the rear of the procession. The mourners had to walk quickly to keep up with the bright-stepping pony. Shutters flew open and women leaned on windowsills to watch. Men repairing a lamppost stopped working and took off their caps. A dog chained inside a yard lunged at the gate and barked.

One of the mourners — Massimo, the husband of Ninanina — broke off from the group and wandered up the steps of Via della Lampana. Ninanina caught him and pulled him back into the procession.

Our father and mother walked arm in arm. Although it was difficult to see in the shadow beneath his hat, Murray's eye was still discolored, though less swollen. He rested against Claire in an effort to disguise a slight limp.

He'd been home for two full days and nights and had shaved, bathed, and put on a clean suit, but still he looked haggard, with new strands of white salting his hair. Claire, in contrast, looked serene, as if she were confident that the troubles were behind her. Or in front — in the cherry-wood coffin of Francis Cape.

Clippa clop clippa clop went the hooves of the pony on the paving stones.

The story Murray told Claire when he came home was that he'd visited Francis Cape early in the morning, they'd argued, and Murray had struck him down and left him for dead. The story Claire told Murray was that Adriana Nardi had visited Francis that evening and found him still alive enough to tell her to leave him alone. Murray couldn't have killed Francis. Nor could he have done anything to harm Adriana. He was exonerated. But he felt no relief. He needed the guilt, Claire sensed. Guilt provided useful comfort. All right, Murray Murdoch, everything is your fault, if that's what you want to believe.

There went Ninanina's husband again, up through an open doorway to see what was going on inside the courtyard. There went Ninanina after him, muttering, *Merde, merde, merde.*

Clippa clop clippa clop.

The story we told Claire was that we'd gone looking for our father and had found him on the property in Mezza Luna. Since by then it had been too late to make our way home, we'd stayed the night in an old military redoubt we knew of on the road to Sant'Andrea. And we were back home in time for breakfast, unharmed, though shoeless.

The rest of the story Murray told Claire was basically true — how he'd wandered around for a while, made his way to La Pila, and for two nights and three days had earned his keep chopping

vegetables in a bar. He'd left La Pila after losing at cards. He'd wandered around some more. Of the night and the day after La Pila
and before Nat found him, our father remembered nothing.

Clippa clop clippa clop. Ninanina's marito had stopped to talk
with Gastone of Bivio Boni, who was on his way home.

"Gastone! Come va?"

Clippa clop clippa clop clop clop cloppa! The pony shied when
a small raggedy terrier ran across the road in front of the procession. Reverend Fink helped Claudio Baldi steady the pony.

Clippa clop clippa clop.

Now where had Ninanina's marito gone this time? Massimo!
Had anyone seen him?

The story Signora Nardi told others was that her daughter had
fallen in love. Nothing worse. Her daughter had fallen in love.
Wasn't this a sufficient explanation? What else could Signora
Nardi tell her curious friends? Yes, she knew the boy's name. No,
he was not Italian. Yes, they would be married soon.

Clippa clop clippa clop.

Massimo?

There he was — in Armando Scarlatti's garden in a cloud of
hen feathers. Why were Armando's hens plumper than everyone
else's? Massimo was going to find out while Armando was inside
listening to his radio.

That Massimo!

One of the mourners called, "Salve, Armando!" to alert him. But
Ninanina led her husband back to the procession and planted him
beside the reverend before Armando arrived outside.

Hurry up, good neighbors. Attenzione! There's a dead man in a
coffin. The sacred vessel turned to wax, the contents emptied, the
soul gone . . . where? A soul that through the body's senses would
have taken pleasure in the shreds of clouds pasted to the blue canvas of sky, doves cooing in a garden, the two little girls swinging in
a string bed. A dead man who loved this island as only a foreigner

can love it. Its beauty endlessly strange to him. As strange as Adriana Nardi.

Did you ever consider, Francis Cape, that someday Adriana would be the escort for your coffin? Even if she never learned to love you, she forgave you. Is that enough?

Waxworks. The bronchial tree shriveled, the aortas crusty, the intestines hard, the veins collapsed, his skin without elasticity or temperature.

Not waxworks. Just an ordinary dead man to remind us that it's good to be alive.

Clippa clop clippa clop.

You're leaving Elba, Francis.

Ninanina's husband whispered something to the reverend. Everyone walking nearby could see that the reverend was trying not to laugh.

That Massimo!

Our father leaned on our mother's arm. He couldn't see the coffin through the crowd of mourners but he could hear the pony's hooves. He imagined himself in place of Francis Cape. He imagined waking up from a dreamless sleep to find himself nailed shut in a box. Hello, hello, is anybody there, help me, please, let me out! His voice so muffled that only Adriana, walking directly behind the coffin, would be able to hear. She'd hear him calling, and she'd ignore him. She had every right to ignore him.

Claire imagined Francis Cape alone in his hovel of a room at the moment when he knew he was dying. The pitiable man. How terribly alone he must have felt. Yet he never admitted he was lonely. Not to Claire, at least.

Clippa clop clop clop. The pony bounced awkwardly down the steep sloping road. This was the same pony that led the baldachin at the Festa di Santa Chiara every year. He was a strong little gelding, still spry at the age of seventeen, though, who knows, perhaps he felt an increasing need to prove himself capable. *Clop clop clop . . .*

Down through the streets of Portoferraio wound the funeral procession. Processions didn't usually come through the Medeceo quarter. The cemetery was in the opposite direction. Who was in the coffin? people wanted to know. Francis Cape. Who was Francis Cape? An Englishman.

Ninanina's marito started to —

Massimo Massimissimo, don't even think about it!

Adriana Nardi walked proudly — too proudly, some people thought — between her mother and Lorenzo. What secrets did she have to tell? No one really believed that she'd lived and worked inside a royal palace. But the business about the child — there must be something to it, people whispered. She'd been gone from Elba for eleven months. Why eleven months? Why not six months? Eight months? Girls who birth bastards go away from home for eleven months. And then they come back, trying to pretend that nothing has happened.

Clippa clop clop.

There would be a repast at the Nardi villa. Everyone knew and admired Signora Nardi's cook, Luisa. Luisa had been working in the kitchen for two days, preparing a feast to feed the mourners. There would be acquadelle and langostini, risotto and patate and a dozen different kinds of sweet cakes. Just the thought of it made Ninanina's husband hungry. "Are you hungry too?" he asked the reverend.

A dead man inside a coffin. Francis Cape. Who was Francis Cape? A professor of history. A scholar of Napoleon. An Englishman who once told Lorenzo that leaving England at the age of sixty-three was like checking out of a hotel. An old man who never spoke about his family. A careful man who never locked his door. A nattily-dressed man who lived in a filthy room. A solitary man. A bachelor who smoked a pipe.

Clippa clop clop clop.

Who was Francis Cape?

What do you care?

Massimo, you'd better get back into line or your wife will be —

There she goes, hitting her marito on the head with her purse again.

A dead man inside a coffin. A wooden box to signify the security of death.

Hai finito?

Sì, sì.

When will it be my turn? Murray wondered.

When will it be my turn? Lorenzo wondered.

When will it be my turn? Reverend Fink wondered.

Clippa clop clippa clop.

"Ciao, Roberto!"

"Ciao, Massimo!"

Please, people. There is a dead man present.

Who?

His name was Francis Cape.

What did he do?

Not much.

Whom did he love?

He loved the island and its history. He loved Adriana Nardi, Claire knew.

And who loved Francis Cape?

His mother, presumably. His father.

Adriana certainly didn't love him. Adriana was in love with a boy her age. Good for her. She would marry and have children, molti bambini to fill the Nardi villa. Good for her. And while she's at it perhaps she could give the archival material to a museum for safekeeping. An antique cup that once belonged to Napoleon did not belong in a house full of children.

Ninanina's husband pointed to the butcher's shop. In the window was a pig's head wearing sunglasses and a bright red visor. Bravo!

Massimo, stop it! Attenzione!

The mourners had never processed in a procession like this.

Down toward the quay instead of to the cemetery at San Giovanni. For a Protestant, no less. Mother of God, spare us.

Who was Francis Cape? A man who felt obliged to explain to the fishermen of Marciana Marina that what the ancients thought were the voices of sirens were, in truth, the cries of the gabbiani echoing in the Cove of Barbarossa at twilight.

Clippa clop clop clop.

The procession slowed to a halt. They'd reached the quay, where there should have been a boat waiting to transport the coffin and the reverend to Livorno. There was no boat. Massimo, Lorenzo, Carlo, and a dozen other men gathered by the harbor master's hut to argue about what should be done. Children approached the coffin. One girl took off a chrysanthemum and put it in her hair, but her older sister plucked the blossom free and returned it to the coffin. The mourners stood quietly, waiting for Reverend Fink to indicate the next course of action. The reverend looked at Signora Nardi for a suggestion. Signora Nardi blinked, startled at the awkward situation. People thought she looked vulnerable and gentle, and they were reminded of how much they had admired this woman over the years.

But it was time for the mourners to go on to La Chiatta. Motorcycles and bicycles suddenly appeared out of nowhere. A couple of taxis started their engines. The mourners bid Francis Cape a safe journey to his final destination and began to disperse — and then stopped, for they noticed, or were told to notice by their friends, Murray and Claire Murdoch, i signori Americani, approaching the coffin.

The Nardi women were standing nearby. Our parents had already let it be known that they would not continue up to La Chiatta for the meal. They had to get back to their children.

"Arrivederla," said Claire softly. People watched as Signora Nardi and Claire exchanged a warm three-point kiss. They watched as Claire and Adriana kissed twice. Murray just stood there. Signora Nardi offered him her hand. He pressed it weakly. Adriana offered him her hand. He held it. People watched as Adriana and Signor Americano politely shook hands. They watched as Murray bent to whisper something in Adriana's ear while Signora Nardi and Claire stood by, patient and expressionless. They watched Adriana give a slight nod, indicating plainly that she understood. They watched as Murray kissed her lightly on the cheek and then turned toward Francis's coffin. He bowed his head, touched the wooden lid with his fingertips.

"Good-bye, my friend."

A tear shed. A touch of sarcasm visible in that shadow of a smirk. Claire put her hand over Murray's, held it against the wood as though she wanted him to feel a heartbeat.

Good-bye, Francis Cape.

Our parents took a taxi back to Marciana. The rest of the mourners made their way up to the Nardi villa. The Nardi women waited with the reverend and Lorenzo while the harbormaster found another boat willing to take the coffin as cargo. Reverend Fink himself had to help carry the coffin, unadorned by flowers now. It was a difficult effort with only four men, and at one point the reverend lost his grip and the back end of the box banged down on the pier, splintering the wood at the corner. The harbormaster came to help, and the coffin was loaded onto the boat.

At last, Francis Cape was leaving the island.

From henceforth, blessed are the dead which die in the Lord: even so saith the spirit; for they rest from their labors.

Good-bye, Francis Cape.

He did not want to go.

Good-bye, Francis Cape.

Later that evening Nat and Harry and I were in the bedroom building block towers. Patrick, hidden in the darkness of the hallway, was spying on our parents, who sat across from each other in the living room, sipping wine and talking in quiet voices that grew more animated as the evening wore on. When he'd heard enough he returned to the bedroom.

"Hello, I have an announcement to make." Patrick stood in the doorway, looking imperious.

"We're going home," guessed Harry.

"I was supposed to say that," Patrick wailed. Harry smiled wickedly. Patrick jumped on him. Nat jumped on Patrick.

I realized only then how tired I was. I pulled my pile of blankets to the corner, planted my thumb in my mouth, and watched my brothers fight.

I don't remember who broke up the fight or put me to bed. I woke once to throw off a blanket and then went back to sleep, tumbling into the middle of a dream that seemed to have started without me. I found myself alone, lost in the woods — not in the pineta of Elba but in the suburban woods of Connecticut. It was winter, cold enough for my breath to cloud in the air, and though there was no snow the grass was brittle with frost and the brook I came to had a fringe of ice. I remembered my brothers telling me that if I followed flowing water I'd always get somewhere, so I walked along the bank through the woods. Eventually I came to a yard, which after a moment I recognized as the backyard of our old house. The lights were off, everyone inside already asleep. I went in through the kitchen door and up to the bedroom I shared with Nat and climbed into bed with him. I fell asleep.

That night Nat dreamt that he was asleep in our old house in Connecticut. A loud bang woke him. He climbed out of bed, careful not to disturb me, and went to the window. The moon was out, shining brightly, yet gale winds were shaking the trees. He tried to close the window but couldn't budge it. The wind blew into the room, swirling papers and books and clothes into a funnel.

Harry dreamt that he, too, was in our old house back in America. It was late at night when he heard the crash of books in our bedroom. He tried to open our door but found it locked. He heard Nat shouting for help inside. He ran to our parents' bedroom, but though the spread had been pulled loose and the pillows dimpled, our parents weren't there. He ran through the house looking for them.

In Patrick's dream, he was reading a book in bed when he heard the branches scraping against the house. He looked out. The moon was shining, the wind blowing. He saw Nat blow by like a cobweb being sucked into a vacuum. Patrick watched him disappear above the trees, then he returned to his book.

In my dream, I woke up and found the room in terrible disarray, as if it had been turned upside down and shaken hard. Nat was gone. I started to cry.

In Harry's dream, he heard me crying and ran back upstairs. He banged on our bedroom door. He called to me, told me to unlock the door. On the other side I pulled and banged the knob, but the lock was jammed.

In Patrick's dream, he was reading a book about wild horses roaming the hills of Wyoming. The thought of Nat flying across the sky filled him with envy. Lucky Nat, he figured, had gone to Wyoming.

In Nat's dream, he sailed through the air high above the town. He felt gripped by both fear and pride. He shouted. He wanted witnesses.

I was woken by Harry pounding on the bedroom door. Harry said he'd been woken by my stupid crying. Patrick said he'd been woken by Nat's shouts. Nat said he'd been woken by the whistle of wind as he plummeted from a great height toward the earth.

At breakfast we whined and protested when Claire told us we would be going home soon — home to America, home, hopefully, to the very same town in Connecticut where we'd lived before Elba. We said we didn't want to go home. Harry told Claire about his nightmare. I was going to tell her about mine next but was silenced by her response to Harry.

"A dream," she grumbled. "What are dreams? I'm sorry, puffin, but I don't want to hear about dreams for a while."

MURRAY WENT ON AHEAD of us by train to Paris and by plane from Paris to New York, where he would immediately start looking for a job. Once he found an adequate job, he'd find a house to rent. Once he found the house, he'd send for us.

Our cat had returned after wandering off. Harry found her in the old cantina on our property. She'd made a nest for herself with a bundle of tarp behind a rusty vat, and she was nursing four new kittens. They were longhairs, with wisps of blond woven with red and black — odd offspring for our sleek, dignified seal-point Siamese.

Before we left Elba we gave the three surviving kittens away — one to Lidia's ten-year-old niece, one to a neighbor, and one to Francesca. Meena, in outrage, would sit outside in the yard and yowl through the night.

In the weeks remaining, we returned to Monte Giove at every opportunity. Although our mother had given Francesca strict orders to keep us in her sight, we took advantage of the long pause of siesta, when all the adults closed themselves inside their shuttered rooms. We promised to stay inside, too, but as soon as the house was silent, we went outside.

Up the dirt path behind the villa, up into the woods, then off the path and up the rocky slope toward the summit. The gulls drifted lazily overhead. We discovered that if we made the right scratching sound with our fingers in the gravel, the lizards would stand still for us. We always saw the same lone blackbird perched in the bare branches of a dead cork tree. It would watch us with a look that suggested it was only reluctantly giving us permission to pass. One day Nat cawed at it, and the bird squawked back in obvious indignation, then flew off with a noisy, heavy flapping.

Jako One, smettila!

No!

Our attempts to revive the magic of our game was halfhearted, our success limited. Were we hearing what we expected to hear, or were we still able to hear the sound of thought? We hardly cared. We knew we couldn't take the magic of Monte Giove away with us. We were going home. We belonged to our parents, not to this island.

One afternoon we climbed up to the shade of Madonna del Monte, to a stone table and blocks of granite seats where, according to a sign, Napoleon had sat during his year of exile.

"What's the big deal about Napoleon?" Nat asked. Nat the bird. I wondered if he would ever fly again. I didn't wonder if he could hear us when we spoke to him because I'd never known that he'd had any trouble hearing. The mysterious problem had resolved itself, and he could hear perfectly well. We didn't realize anything had changed.

Harry shrugged. Patrick began to reply, "He was . . ." and then fell silent.

"What?" Nat asked.

"I'm not sure," Patrick said.

I thought about this. I thought about other things I wanted to know.

"Why don't we come back next year?" I asked. My brothers gave me looks implying that my stupid question couldn't possibly have an answer.

I meant to urge them to reconsider and started to say, "Hey, Jakos," but somehow it came out "Jackass." My brothers hooted with laughter. Harry laughed so hard he fell off the stone bench. Harry lying splat on the ground with his feet in the air was something I could laugh at. I joined my brothers.

What was Napoleon? He was. Heehaw, heehaw!

Four little jackasses, our ears forever tipped with fur. Four little jackasses on the terrace where the king of Elba once sat, writing the future in airy words above the sea.

Those were serene weeks for our mother. After helping Signora Nardi dismantle what was left in Francis Cape's apartment and put his belongings into storage, she began sorting through our own accumulations. What we wouldn't take back with us she planned to disperse between Lidia and Francesca — except for the various minerals Murray had brought home, most of which he'd never even bothered to identify. These she'd give to a collector Signora Nardi had told her about, a man up in Sant'Ilario.

Claire and Signora Nardi spent most afternoons together, both of them relishing each other's company with an energy neither could explain. They talked at length, in private, about Adriana. The great consuming love that the mother felt for the daughter was returned by the daughter in her abiding loyalty. That Adriana hadn't come to her mother for help remained a source of deep pain for the Signora. No matter what her mother could say to reassure her, Adriana would always believe that she should spare her mother from her own troubles. In the girl's scheme, secrecy was protection. Adriana, like so many people who know they are beloved, was determined to be happy for the sake of someone who wanted her to be happy.

And now she was happy. Happy to know she had the freedom to go away and always to be welcome at home. Happy to have fallen in love with a good man, a young Englishman who arrived on the island in the last week of November.

"Piacere, Paul."

A man who would never hold her past against her. You could tell by the way he looked at Adriana, the way Adriana looked at him. Love enriched by some secret understanding of what each had endured. The secrets children try to keep from their parents,

Claire thought, watching the two of them sitting without awkwardness or the performance of affection on the sofa in Signora Nardi's living room. They were in love. Love born from heartbreak. Love repairing the damage of love.

If Claire stayed, she and the Signora would teach each other the nuances of their languages, the energy of their friendship opening up the subtleties of words. But she wasn't staying. Signora Americana was going home, and though she promised to write, she knew their letters would be too formal to sustain this intimacy.

As they kissed good-bye, Claire's premonition of this friendship fading with the rest of the past — life going on, memory blurred by experience — sharpened into understanding of the way fierce love provokes loyalty. The daughter's loyalty to her loving mother had cast a veil of secrecy over her life. Adriana feared disclosure, not because it could lead to accusation but because it would lead to sympathy. The mother's protective love for her child would continue to generate the daughter's determination to protect her mother from pain.

The mysterious nature of love and all its unpredictable outcomes. Now we know better, you and I, Signora, how to be patient. Both of us a little wiser, Claire told herself, comforted by the cliché, resisting the urge to turn around as she walked away from Signora Nardi, and then giving in to the urge, turning, facing the Signora, who was still standing at the door, and declaring, "Tu sei magnifica!"

Two taxis came early in the morning to take us to the ferry. It was a gray day, though not yet raining. Nat refused to get dressed, and Francesca had to hold him while Lidia pulled his clothes on. Harry hid in the cantina. He was found and dragged back to the house by Francesca's fiancé, Filiberto, who would accompany us as far as Genoa to help with the luggage. Patrick appeared with a pillowcase filled with rocks.

Four boys — Oliver, Nathaniel, Harold, and Patrick. Sir. All accounted for, Sir. Ma'am, rather. Here we are, Mom. All four. All of us except —

"Meena!"

It was my fault. My crime. My stupidity. One of the many foolish acts I've never been able to live down. I'd opened the door of Meena's cage to give her some grass. Good Elban grass. She needed some grass for the long journey ahead, I'd decided.

Spark of tawny fur, black tail whipping through the air, paws outstretched, body low to the ground as she wound up the path toward Monte Giove, and she was gone.

"Meena!" Patrick ran after her. Harry ran after Patrick, Nat after Harry. Francesca kept a firm grip on me.

"Boys, get back here! Filiberto, help!"

Filiberto Boschi to the rescue. Filiberto Boschi and his dog. "Vai!" The dog racing up the slope past my brothers, up along the path where Meena had gone, up Monte Giove. Look, there she is! A glimpse of cat, a dog, a dog chasing a cat.

"No, no, Rosella, vieni qua!"

A big dog chasing a little cat up into the mountains of Elba while my brothers shouted in desperation. It was no use. They'd never catch her. They headed back to our garden while Filiberto raced past them.

"Rosella!"

My brothers and me — the four of us. Attenzione! Was there ever a kid as stupid as me? My brothers, our mother, the taxis and their drivers, Francesca, Lidia, and, at last, Filiberto with his panting, slobbering hound named Rosella. The bliss of pursuing a creature smaller than yourself. Proud Rosella.

The grownups clucked and called in a pathetic attempt to lure Meena home, but she was gone, and we had a boat to catch. We were herded, sobbing, into the taxis. We weren't going to leave Elba. We vowed to jump off the ferry and swim back to the island.

We insisted that we couldn't leave without our cat. We couldn't. We just couldn't.

We did — traveling to America on a ship called the *Roma* in another first-class cabin paid for with borrowed money, because Murray said we deserved the luxury after all we'd been through. We were home in time for Christmas.

LOOK AT THE SURFACE of the water. Look carefully. Look at the words on this page. Look at the tip of your pen. Look up at the clouds. Look down at the clover growing in the cracks of the sidewalk. Look at your hands. Look at a map. Look at a painting. Look at a clock. Look at the ceiling, the wall, the floor. Look at a piece of honeycomb. Look at a sign. Look at these photographs, Ollie. We've looked through them before, I know. But I want you to look at them again when you have a chance.

Here I am — 1956, in Marciana Marina, framed by the lens of the camera your father held. It must have been September or early October.

Look at me. My hair pulled back in a ponytail, my glasses propped above my forehead, a bra strap showing where the sleeve of my dress has slipped down my arm, my lips dark with what must have been plum-colored lipstick.

I don't remember me. I don't remember what I was thinking when Murray took the photograph. Probably I was thinking I wanted to look better than I knew I looked, but I'm not sure.

Look at me, Ollie. What do you think I was thinking?

Here we are, the six of us, on the beach. Lidia or Francesca must have snapped the picture. Your father in his striped boxer suit. You, Ollie, plump and brown and naked, straining to pull away from the grip of Patrick's hand around your arm. Harry looking at something to the right of us. Nat making a silly face.

Here is Lidia, stern, stout Lidia. We could never get her to smile for the camera.

You and Nat in the little wooden cart Lorenzo's farmhand Nino built for you. You're on the terrace of our first house, the one in Le Foci. I think that's Francesca's arm cutting across the picture, reaching over to steady you, Ollie.

Look at you. What were you thinking? What are you thinking now?

Here's the picture I thought we'd lost. A little blurry, but it gives you an idea of what our Mezza Luna property consisted of. Not much more than thick sloping woods surrounding the pool of run-off water and the gouged granite rockface in the background.

Here — these are out of order — a picture of the four of you eating gelato in Piazza Signoria in Florence. Look at all of you. Your faces masked with chocolate. Look at how happy you were.

This is Francis Cape. Old Francis Cape on our terrace in Marciana. He looks startled, doesn't he? As though he wasn't expecting the pop of the flashbulb.

This — oh, this is Mom and Jill on a trip to Niagara Falls. How did this one get in the box?

Here you are asleep on Murray's lap. Murray is asleep, too. No, he was only pretending to sleep, if I'm remembering correctly.

The four of you dressed in your darling pinstriped jackets and shorts. We didn't go to church while we were on Elba, and I'm not sure why you were dressed up. Maybe so we could take this photograph.

This — your father and me in a restaurant. Our faces lit from the glow of the candle in the cake. It must have been my birthday.

This is the view of the island from the castle at the top of Volterraio.

This is our garden in the second villa. The wall of sunflowers, the jungle of Lidia's tomato plants. We had fresh tomatoes all year round.

Tomatoes. Fresh mozzarella from white oxen. Anchovies and

octopus and squid. The kitchen counter covered with squids turned inside out. Your father couldn't stand the sight of raw squid. Or fresh blood. Both made him weak-kneed.

Here's one of Murray with his eyes closed, rolling a cigarette. He could roll a cigarette blind in eight seconds.

Meena and her litter of kittens. They are, count them, they are all there, all four. I don't remember which one Patrick accidentally squashed. Do you?

Now this group includes Lorenzo, our padrone, and his wife. That's Francis Cape again at the end of the table. The others I don't recognize.

This is the mossy statue of Napoleon in the garden at his Palazzina dei Mulini. And here I am with Murray standing on the steps of the Roman villa above Portoferraio.

And here — this is another one of you boys at the top of Volterraio. I remember this day. Murray brought all of us to Volterraio in January to look for diamonds. It's one of our few pictures of the island in winter. The bare vines below look like fishing nets spread across the fields, don't they? That's snow on the peak of Monte Capanne.

Here I am wading back to the beach after a swim. I'm lingering in the water so my legs wouldn't show in the picture.

Here's Nat on the *Roma* with the Statue of Liberty behind him.

Did you know that since Elba, we never successfully paid off a loan without taking out another loan?

Did you consider what we would owe in back taxes, if that deed to the Mezza Luna land was valid?

For you, Ollie, Elba has stood in your memory as the paradise you lost because your father bungled the situation. But I'll tell you, I was relieved to leave that island behind and to have made it home, our family intact, across the ocean and into a house with a washing machine and drier and a fenced yard. I was relieved that Murray found a job and I needed only one course to become certified as a teacher, so I'd be ready to find work when Murray was unemployed again. I was relieved that you children took pleasure in friends and books and the puppy we gave you that spring. I was relieved that though Murray kept on drinking, I knew he would never turn into one of those monsters who, after too much booze, will crash through the door you've locked against him and grab you by the throat. We had many years ahead together, and I was relieved that I had no reason to doubt his word anymore and could keep the old suspicions hidden in the dark stony place in the soul where love mingles with fear.

Now don't I sound grand.

March 1, 2001

To the west, behind the hills, the granite cap of Monte Capanne a shadow in the mist. To the east, the peak of Volterraio crowned by its ruined castle. In the fields, rain soaking the purple tips of lavender. In Portoferraio, the swollen sea lapping at the quay. Straight ahead, an archway leading to a piazza; from the piazza, steps rising, crossing narrow terraces of streets. Water streaming down furrowed stones. Clack of a woman's heels. Wet tires. Someone standing inside an open doorway, whistling for a dog. Yellow paint on stucco. Terra-cotta trim. A pot of red geraniums. A box of white cyclamens. Another set of stairs. A man with a cane. Tap of the cane. Rise of one shoe and then another. A man with thick glasses and a useful cane.

Dopoguerra: "Poi, come per un miracolo, ecco che il successo turistico fa affluire denaro e benessere, grazie a ciò che da sempre queste isole avevano subito: l'invasione dei continentali!" — *Guide d'Italia de Agostini: Isola d'Elba E Arcipelago Toscano*

I am here alone. From my hotel window I can see over the roofs of the bungalows and across the bay to the water. The sea is gray today under a gray sky, though yesterday, seen from the top of Volterraio, the sky was clear and the sea was the blue of blue tourmaline.

I can hear the hum of my computer, the buzz of controlled ventilation, and the television in the room next door. I have my own television on, tuned to CNN, but the volume off.

My brothers and I have always wondered what would have happened if we'd stayed another year or two. What we could have found. What we could have done. If only we'd dug a little deeper, gone a little farther into the hard earth. If we'd been more persistent.

In order to secure the finest optical effect in a cut gem, certain proportions are necessary. I forget the exact formula. The base must be twice as wide as the crown, the table half of the whole stone. Something like that.

The weather: nuvoloso domani, e molto nuvoloso dopodomani. The sun is shining in Tunisia. It is snowing in Milan. The ice cap on Kilimanjaro is shrinking at the rate of 508 feet per year.

Elba was the joke we grew up with. Whenever we wanted to make fun of Murray, we reminded him of Elba. Of Napoleon and Lambrettas. Of black and pink and blue tourmaline. Of uninhabitable acres of rocky earth. Of land that cost more to sell than it did to buy. Once upon a time our father had brought us to Elba, and he was in debt ever since. His last great gamble, from which he never recovered.

What he would call a "nonevent, Ollie, for Christ's sake."

Why bother to write about Elba? Make it up, for Christ's sake. Stick to the imagination.

I've changed the names, haven't I? I can't help but take some liberties. It's in my blood, this inability to tell the simple truth. Though it's true that I'm sitting in a hotel room on the outskirts of Portoferraio on the island of Elba, it's the first of March, 2001, and I was in Siena last week. It's true that I have the television on "mute." It's true that I had a pastry and cappuccino for breakfast.

Untrue is the attribution of Napoleon Bonaparte to the graffito at his palazzo in San Martino: "Ubicunque felix Napoleon." The author is anonymous.

The man with the glasses and cane is eager to talk, if you have time to listen. His brother, a barista in Rio nell'Elba, was in the navy and has been to Montreal, New Orleans, Norfolk, and San Francisco. But this man, standing on a stone landing in Portoferraio, has had poor vision all his life, and the Italian navy didn't want him.

He'll tell you about the difference between the wines of La Chiusa and Acquabona. He'll tell you where to buy olive oil and what to expect from tomorrow's weather. He'll tell you about his cousin, who is selling her house in the village of Marciana. He thinks she's foolish to sell it. Her son will want the house for himself someday. The son has a tumor — tumore, capito? — and goes to Firenze for treatment.

What writer committed to factual representation doesn't miss the freedom of fiction? If I were writing a novel, I'd be writing about coming to Elba in winter of the year 2001 and visiting the Nardi villa. I didn't look for it my first visit, and I couldn't find it when I was here last April. But the other day I found it exactly where my mother told me it was: along the road to Magazzini. I'd describe the villa and its fresh orange stucco, the moss darkening the roof tiles, the terraces of olive groves behind the house — the surrounding land and buildings unchanged for almost fifty years, only the traffic on the street, the automatic gates, and, inside, the satellite channels on the television, to remind the occupants of the modern world.

The gate had been left open. There was a doorbell, but out of timidity I knocked — softly at first, and again with more force.

The truth is, the woman who answered the door was named Elisa Vivaldi, she was the daughter-in-law of the owner of the Vivaldi Hotel in Procchio, she came from La Spezia, and she'd never heard of the Nardi family. Which left me nothing much to do but thank her for her time and excuse myself.

If, instead, Adriana Nardi still lived there —

Buongiorno, sono Oliver Murdoch. My father owned land in the Mezza Luna region.

Sì, prego.

She'd be, what, sixty-six years old, with thin white hair, subtle blue shading around her eyes, deep red lipstick. Her clothes — black slacks and a pink wool sweater cuffed with bunched silk — would be comfortable, bright, unpretentious. Her manner would be relaxed. She'd invite me to come in. She'd offer me something to drink.

The man on the landing will compare the virtues of Portoferraio and Porto Azzurro. He'll tell you about Marciana, if you're interested. Have you been up to Marciana? His cousin is selling the house she grew up in, the house where his whole family hid during the night of violence in June 1944, the night the Allies met the Germans on the island of Elba. The stories this man could tell, you wouldn't believe.

My name is Oliver Murdoch. My father owned land here in the 1950s.

Yes, come in.

Grazie.

Would you care for something to drink?

A glass of water would be fine.

Have a seat. Those pictures, by the way, the ones on the credenza, they are of my two grandchildren, Camilla and Philip. They live in London. My husband and I have a house in Redding. We're only here to prepare our villa for summer tenants.

Her voice comes from the kitchen. For a moment I forget that she is Adriana Nardi and mistake her for her mother, though her mother has been dead for more than thirty years.

She brings me a glass of water. Just water. Secretly, I was expecting a tray piled high with meringues.

Now how can I help you, Signor Murdoch?

What would I say to her? Why was I there?

I am sitting in a hotel room, looking out beyond Punta della Rena at the sea, imagining the story I would write if I were going to start over. The story of Adriana Nardi — a novel based on truth, truth based on hearsay, gossip, rumors, secondhand accounts, and dreams.

Won't you tell me about the guard who worked at the prison on Pianosa? The professor from Bologna? The exact nature of my father's involvement? Your four days in Portovenere? Tell me about Paris. How did you find a willing doctor? Was he really a doctor? How much did he charge? How long did it take? How did you get back to your hotel afterward? Were you alone?

How dare you, Signor Murdoch!

How dare I ask to hear about what this woman endured. My prurience. Her dignity. My disrespect. Life diminished and falsified by the simple act of transcription.

The American Express Travel Guide to Tuscany and Florence

SIGHTS AND PLACES OF INTEREST

PALAZZINA NAPOLEONICA DEI MULINI*

NAPOLEON CREATED HIS RESIDENCE IN EXILE FROM TWO OLD WINDMILLS ABOVE
   THE CITY NEAR FORTE DELLA STELLA. THE FURNISHINGS FOR THIS DELIGHT-
   FUL LITTLE PALACE WERE COMMANDEERED FROM HIS SISTER ELISA'S HOUSE
   AT PIOMBINO; THE PLATE AND LIBRARY WERE BROUGHT FROM FONTAINEBLEAU.

I was just wondering if you remember my father.

He's not easy to forget.

He had liver cancer and passed away in the summer of '92. Actually, he died of pneumonia following surgery.

I study her face, watching for her unspoken reaction, but what I see I can't decipher.

I think, Signora Nardi, that he was very much in love with you.

I know, Signor Murdoch, that he loved his family.

The truth of love being its power to corrupt and divide and destroy.

Your father considered himself a lucky man. Perciò era molto fortunato.

Portoferraio in a soft winter rain. Hiss of steam frothing milk in the café. The man on the landing is wearing a hat and rarely bothers with an umbrella. This man will keep talking, if you don't mind getting wet.

First the Germans. Then the English and French and Senegalese. And then the Americans arrived with their gifts of clothes, shoes, chocolate, peanut butter. What do you do with peanut butter? And meat in a can?

Capsized dinghies clogging the harbor, rubble blocking the streets, and all the Americans wanted to do was play football on the beach at Le Ghiaie.

You want to hear about the war? His own father, a shepherd from San Piero, bringing pecorino and fresh milk to the group of English soldiers camped on Monte Capanne.

Though it is damp and cold today, I'm told that Elba has had a mild winter this year. It is only the beginning of March, and finches and sparrows are singing in the hotel garden, the almond trees have already shed their blossoms, and the vines on the trellis are budding. I've opened my window a crack to let in the fresh air.

Still, the island at bassissima is like a theater before a show opens. Elbans are waiting for their audience, and those of us who are tourists are treated to a gentle bemusement. Why have we come to the island in winter? Don't we know any better? What sort of people are we who at this time of year are able to leave jobs, homes, families, and come to Elba to do nothing? How did we earn such a ridiculous privilege?

Of course I remember you. You had a rock named King George.

A what?

The first time I met you, you took me into your room to show me your rock. You'd named it King George, and you kept it in a shoebox lined with black tissue paper. You'd made a little cardboard throne and filled it with chalk dust. You used a piece of wood for a table, dried leaves for the plates. King George was a piece of rose quartz.

Really? I sip my water. She smiles at me. I think about the murky passage from infancy to childhood, when the experiences we survive become confused with experiences we imagine.

Of course I remember you. Everyone who was on the island at that time would remember you and your brothers. You couldn't have realized it, but we were looking out for the bambini Americani, making sure you didn't get into any harm and didn't cause too much trouble.

In Florence last week, as I crossed the piazza to enter the Baptistery, a young boy — he couldn't have been older than seven or eight — stuck his hand in the back pocket of my jeans, searching for my wallet, which I keep in the inside breast pocket of my jacket. I grabbed his arm, pushed him away, we exchanged a glare, and that was that. He went looking for another stupido Americano, and I went into the Baptistery.

"At lower right, near some open trap doors, a red devil is tormenting some of the damned. He has a robust hairless body, claws instead of feet, and bat's wings; his face is not strongly characterized but it is an animal's one with a few human features. Goat's horns emerge from the nape of his neck." — *Devils in Art,* Lorenzo Lorenzi

During my second visit to Elba, last April, I found a zebra spider in the crumbled stones of the castle at the top of Volterraio. On that same trip I saw specimens of blue and pink and watermelon tourmaline in the mineralogical museum. The day before yesterday, a group of children threw flour at me when I was wandering through Porto Azzurro.

When my brothers and I were growing up in a series of rented houses in various communities in the northeast, we remembered Elba as a place of refuge and magic, and we never stopped longing to return. We had a sense that our father was responsible for giving us the experience of the island, but we also knew that he'd made it necessary for us to leave. We were ashamed of him, even though we didn't know what, exactly, he'd done wrong.

In the years that followed our stay on Elba, up until the time he fell ill, Murray was always struggling either to find a job or to hold on to one. After he quit the job he'd found upon returning from Elba, the Averils would have no financial dealings with him. His mother's death in 1968 ended all vestige of connection with that side of the family. From then on, Murray clung to us, his children and wife, like a man adrift after a shipwreck.

I don't think I'd offend him with these words. He never pretended that he didn't need us. And he was far more forgiving than I will ever be.

Mi scusi, non mi ricordo di lui.

Murdoch. My father owned property on Elba back in the 1950s.

Murdoch . . . Murdoch . . . no, I'm sorry, I don't remember the name.

I imagine a young Elban woman sitting by the window on a train, traveling from Genoa to Marseilles. None of the other passengers tries to speak to her. They can tell that she is deep in thought.

She is thinking about the man, her lover, the guard on Pianosa.

They used to meet in a room in Marina di Campo, a dusty little room overlooking the tin roofs of storage shacks. He was at the window, pulling the shutters closed, when she told him she was pregnant. He gave a nervous laugh and started buttoning his shirt back up. He might as well have smacked her.

Now she is heading toward Marseilles, toward Nice, toward Paris. She feels desperately lonely, wants to weep, would start weeping if there weren't strangers sitting across from her, had cried herself to sleep for three nights in a row back in Portovenere. But loneliness doesn't make her any less determined.

Our house in Le Foci is no longer standing, but I found our Marciana residence on my first visit to Elba. With the help of a map my mother had marked, I made my way from the hotel to Procchio, from Procchio to Marciana Marina, and up from the port into the valley.

The house is below the village of Marciana, situated in the upper slope of Valle Grande. The shutters were closed, the drive empty, the front gate locked, and no one answered when I rang the bell.

The road to the house cuts between terraces of vineyards and olive groves. I parked along the verge and climbed over the wire fence and up through the vineyards until I had a good view of the house. It was smaller than I'd expected, though it looked well-kept, with cyclamens blooming in pots along the windowsills and the soil around the olive trees freshly turned over.

I kept climbing up the eastern slope of Monte Giove, along a footpath that wound through cobwebs of dead pine. Goldfinches and woodchats flitted about, and at one point I heard the scrambling noise of some large animal retreating further into the woods. I was surprised by how far the sounds of the island travel. I heard dogs barking all the way from Marciana Marina. I heard cars on the road leading into Poggio. I heard roosters crowing in the valley.

After an hour or so I reached the ridge connecting Uomo Masso with Monte Giove. This area is part of the park system, and I found myself on a well-marked path leading to Marciana. Just outside of the village I turned off on a cart road and made my way to Madonna del Monte. The doors of the church were locked. I took in the view of the sea sparkling beyond the outcrop of Capo Sant'Andrea and then followed the path that led to the stone table and benches.

I thought I remembered that it was right here where I'd seen my brother Nat float in the air, and this was the reason we'd all been laughing — laughing so hard that Harry fell off the stone bench.

Over the last year I've had to trace and retrace memory through conversations with my brothers and mother. I admit that I'm still not exactly sure what is true.

If you keep listening, the man on the landing in Portoferraio will keep talking. He was telling you about the English soldiers on Monte Capanne. And then the Americans and their laughter, as if nothing had happened. They came to bring gifts of clothes, shoes, food. They were always laughing, having fun, playing football on the beach, bathing in the sea. They stayed for a month. They didn't want to go back to the war.

I can see on the television the American news I am missing. Interest rates are falling. There was an earthquake in Seattle. No one was killed, but damage is extensive.

A woman's voice blurs in echo in the courtyard. Tires squeal when a car brakes on the hotel drive.

"You're going to Elba *again?*" Of all my brothers, it's only Nat who has come right out and called me an idiot for writing about our family. He'd rather remember our time on Elba the way he wants to remember it, without the interference of uncertain history. He tells me that if I have any doubt about what happened, I should keep it to myself.

Murdoch, you say? Mur . . . doch? Ah, yes, of course! Signor Americano. He bought land in the Mezza Luna zone. He should have stayed and built a hotel. That's the way you get rich on this island.

Truthfully, the only person I've met on Elba who remembers my father is a bald little man of ninety who has lived in Sant'Ilario his entire life in the same little house where he was born. I met him last time I was here, after having read about his mineral collection in one of the guidebooks. His living quarters are upstairs. He's given over the downstairs rooms to his collection, which includes more than five thousand specimens of semiprecious stones.

Behind the dusty glass of a display case, there is a white opal with a vibrant rainbow surface. There is a black opal striped like a painted egg with blue and green. The specimen of alexandrite is greenish gray by daylight but turns, as he showed me, a beautiful maroon under a fluorescent light. The man has many specimens of lapis lazuli, cat's eye, and almandine. And though he has no diamonds, his prize is an amethyst geode the size of a basketball.

When I told him about my father, he took me into the back room, where the less valuable minerals are displayed, and showed me a large chunk of schorl dated March 1957. This, he said, came from my father's property, along with quartz crystals and a piece of acquamarine, the rest of which he had to keep in a drawer because, as I could see, he didn't have the space to display everything.

He is a bony, frail man, yet he is surprisingly nimble. When I returned to his house for a second visit a few days ago, I asked him, "Signore, come sta?" and he replied, in English, "I am still here, no?"

Though he remembers that my father was the owner of the land where the piece of black tourmaline was found, he does not remember ever meeting my father. He remembers my mother, though. He remembers her carrying a box of stones weighing ten kilos into his house. He remembers her saying that she thought the stones were worthless but he could have them if he wanted them. He told her that no stones are worthless.

I imagine a girl lying alone on a bed in a boarding house in Paris. She is bleeding heavily and has already gone through three sanitary napkins in the course of two hours. She'd been warned that she would bleed. But how much blood is too much? How can she know?

The phone out in the hallway is ringing. No one answers it. She falls asleep and dreams only of the sound of the ringing phone. When she wakes up half an hour later, the phone is still ringing, and she drags herself out of her room to answer it.

Pronto? She means, Hello. She means, Bonjour.

It is the ragazzo she met the other day at the carousel in the Tuilleries. He wants to take her to dinner. She wants to cry with joy, she is so desperate.

How can you presume to know what I went through, Signor Americano?

How can I presume to know about a twenty-one-year-old Italian woman who in 1956 went to Paris to terminate an unwanted pregnancy?

I dunt know nuttin about nuttin, our father used to say, holding up his newspaper to shield him from us — his strategy for forcing us to complete our homework without his help.

The last mine on Elba closed down in 1982. Rio nell'Elba is one of the island's starkest villages, and the surrounding land, the iron-red earth gouged and abandoned by the mines, has been devastated repeatedly by brushfires.

I walked through gritty, empty Rio nell'Elba the other day. I stopped at a bar for a caffè and had a short conversation with the barista about America. He had been in the navy and traveled to Montreal, Norfolk, New Orleans, and San Francisco. We talked about the winters in upstate New York.

After leaving the bar, I walked out of town up the road toward Volterraio. I picked some lavender as I walked along. I collected colorful pieces of quartz. I saw a white horse grazing on the marshy grass beside a creek.

I imagine a young woman sitting beside my father in a room lit only by moonlight. She has come to ask for help. Signor Americano might know of a doctor. Signor Americano might even loan her money.

She can't find the words she needs to explain her situation. She can hear my father's nervous breathing as he shifts his position on the sofa. He reaches for her, and all at once she perceives his mistake: he thinks she wants to lure him away from his family. She regrets having provoked such misunderstanding. Or else she doesn't regret it at all.

Last night I was woken by a storm. I got up and stood at the window for a long while. Palm fronds blew about like ribbons in the wind. Wisps of fog floated between the sea and the dark bed of clouds. Water spilled from the drainpipe extending out over my terrace. The noise of the wind, a low steady humming, was the sound of memory returning.

In 1944 Elbans gave Americans gifts of amethyst, agate, quartz, hematite, and tourmaline. Blue tourmaline lodged in a block of granite, the spiked blue inside the transparent crystal the exact blue of the Tyrrhenian Sea on a clear afternoon. Take this, keep it so you won't forget. Come back and visit us. We will welcome you. We will share our treasures.

I picture Adriana Nardi on the ferry bound for Piombino. It is a cool, bright autumn day. Fluffy cumulus clouds drift lazily from the open sea toward the mainland. The water is tinted maroon through the lenses of the young woman's dark glasses. It is the same color as her fingernail polish. She is wearing a camel-hair coat and a beret to match. She has wound her red silk scarf twice around her neck, leaving the ends loose to flutter in the wind. Her leather purse is a paler red. Her shoes, made in Florence, rise on two-inch spindly heels. Her net stockings are black. Black cuffs of her lambs-wool gloves, a Christmas present from her mother, peek out from her pockets. Her earrings are simple ruby studs. The rest of her jewelry, packed in her suitcase, she intends to sell.

Surf churning against the headlands of Polveraia. Rain turning the cart ways of the old open-cast mines to mud. Vine stumps sprouting. Cormorants diving in the harbor of Marciana Marina. Smoke puffing from stovepipes. Cars slowing to round the bends of mountain roads. Rain disappearing into the tangle of genista and broom. The rich fragrance of wet moss. Boulders frozen midway in their tumble to the sea.

JOANNA SCOTT is the author of six previous books, including *The Manikin,* which was a finalist for the Pulitzer Prize, *Various Antidotes* and *Arrogance,* which were both finalists for the PEN/Faulkner Award, and the critically acclaimed *Make Believe.* A recipient of a MacArthur Fellowship and a Lannan Award, she lives with her family in upstate New York.